GREEN GROWTH

Ideology, Political Economy and the Alternatives

AF540269

GREEN GROWTH

Ideology, Political Economy and the Alternatives

Edited by

Gareth Dale
Manu V. Mathai
Jose A. Puppim de Oliveira

Green Growth: Ideology, Political Economy and the Alternatives
Edited by Gareth Dale, Manu V. Mathai and Jose A. Puppim de Oliveira

© Editors 2016
© Aakar Books for South Asia 2017

First Aakar Edition 2017
Reprinted 2023

ISBN 978-93-5002-476-8

Published in agreement with Zed Books, London
for South Asia.

All rights reserved. No part of this book may be reproduced or transmitted, in any form or by any means, without prior permission of the publisher.

Published by
AAKAR BOOKS
28 E Pocket IV, Mayur Vihar Phase I
Delhi 110 091, India
www.aakarbooks.com

Printed at
D.K. Fine Art Press, Delhi

CONTENTS

Acknowledgements *vii*

Contributors *ix*

Introduction 1
Gareth Dale, Manu V. Mathai and Jose A. Puppim de Oliveira

Part I: Contradictions of green growth

1 Can green growth really work? A reality check that elaborates on the true (socio-)economics of climate change 22
Ulrich Hoffmann

2 What is the 'green' in 'green growth'? 42
Larry Lohmann

3 The *how* and for *whom* of green governmentality 72
Adrian Parr

4 Degrowth and the roots of neoclassical economics 90
James Meadway

Part II: Case studies

5 Giving green teeth to the Tiger? A critique of 'green growth' in South Korea 114
Bettina Bluemling and Sun-Jin Yun

6 Lessons from the EU: why capitalism cannot be rescued from its own contradictions 131
Birgit Mahnkopf

7 The green growth trap in Brazil 150
Ricardo Abramovay

8 Green jobs to promote sustainable development: creating a value chain of solid waste recycling in Brazil 166
Anne Posthuma and Paulo Sergio Muçouçah

9 Trends of social metabolism and environmental conflict: a comparison between India and Latin America 187
Joan Martinez-Alier, Federico Demaria, Leah Temper and Mariana Walter

Part III: Emerging alternatives?

10 Beyond 'development' and 'growth': the search for alternatives in India towards a sustainable and equitable world 212
Ashish Kothari

11 Reconsidering growth in the greenhouse: the Sustainable Energy Utility (SEU) as a practical strategy for the twenty-first century 233
Job Taminiau and John Byrne

12 Alternatives to green growth? Possibilities and contradictions of self-managed food production 253
Steffen Böhm, Maria Ceci Araujo Misoczky, David Watson and Sanjay Lanka

Notes 271

Index 315

ACKNOWLEDGEMENTS

We would like to express our gratitude to many organizations and individuals that made this book possible. We thank the Asia Pacific Network for Global Change Research (APN) for the support we received from the Scientific Capacity Building/Enhancement for Sustainable Development in Developing Countries ('CAPaBLE') programme through the project 'Training Workshop and Edited Volume on "Green Growth: Political Ideology, Political Economy and Policy Alternatives"' (Reference CBA2014-09NSY-Mathai), particularly Akio Takemoto and Hiroshi Tsujihara, former and current director of APN, as well as Linda Stevenson and Christmas de Guzman.

We are grateful for the support we received from the United Nations University Institute for the Advanced Studies of Sustainability for organizing the Green Growth Symposium in July 2014, especially to Govindan Parayil and Kazuhiko Takemoto, former and current director of UNU-IAS, as well as Takei Chiharu, Nakano Yuki, Fueta Natsuko, Sayo Yoshitake, Yukie Sawada, Shio Terui and the students Xue Ye (Susie), Richard Rastall and Alexis Nakandakari.

We are grateful to the British Academy, which funded Gareth Dale's attendance at the Tokyo symposium (Mid-Career Fellowship, 2013–14), to the Daiwa Anglo-Japanese Foundation for a generous grant that enabled UK-based young researchers to attend, and to the 20 young researchers from around the world who helped make the symposium a success.

Finally, we are appreciative of Kim Walker and her team at Zed Books who have smoothly steered the volume towards completion.

CONTRIBUTORS

Ricardo Abramovay is professor of economics at the University of São Paulo and author of *Beyond the Green Economy* (Routledge, 2016).

Bettina Bluemling lectures at the University of Glasgow, and is research fellow at the Leibniz Institute of Agricultural Development in Transition Economies, Germany.

Steffen Böhm teaches at the Environment and Sustainability Institute at the University of Exeter. His research focuses on political economies and ecologies of the food–energy–water–carbon–environment nexus. His most recent book is *Ecocultures: Blueprints for Sustainable Communities* (Routledge, 2014).

John Byrne is the director and distinguished professor of energy and climate policy at the Center for Energy and Environmental Policy (CEEP), co-founder of the Foundation for Renewable Energy and Environment, and the architect of the Sustainable Energy Utility (SEU) model.

Federico Demaria is a researcher at the Institute of Environmental Science and Technology, Autonomous University of Barcelona (IEST, UAB) with an affiliation at the CSSP JNU (India). His research deals with waste-related environmental conflicts and 'accumulation by contamination'. He co-edited *Degrowth: A Vocabulary for a New Era* (Routledge, 2014).

Ulrich Hoffmann is chief economist, sustainability issues at the Research Institute on Organic Agriculture (FIBL), and former editor-in-chief of the UNCTAD *Trade and Environment Review*, UNCTAD Secretariat.

Ashish Kothari is a founder of the Indian environmental group Kalpavriksh. Active in movements relating to development, conservation, and natural resource rights, he is the author or editor of over 30 books, including (with Aseem Shrivastava) *Churning the Earth: The Making of Global India*.

Sanjay V. Lanka works with coffee cooperatives of indigenous farmers with a focus on fairtrade and biodiversity with regards to the delivery of sustainable livelihoods, using accounts from the margins. He's finalizing his PhD at the University of Essex.

Larry Lohmann works for Corner House.

Birgit Mahnkopf is professor of European politics at the Berlin School of Economics and Law. She received her PhD in sociology and her post-doctoral habilitation at the Freie Universität Berlin. She has published 12 books and over 130 articles and book chapters.

Joan Martinez-Alier is professor emeritus at UAB (Spain) and FLACSO, Quito, Ecuador. He is the author of *Ecological Economics: Energy, Environment and Society* and *The Environmentalism of the Poor: A Study of Ecological Conflicts and Valuation*.

James Meadway is senior economist at the New Economics Foundation.

Maria Ceci Araujo Misoczky is a professor and researcher of Organization Studies at the Federal University of Rio Grande do Sul, Brazil. Her research interests include the organization of social struggles, focusing on socio-environmental conflicts and anti-capitalist movements in Latin America.

Paulo Sérgio Muçouçah is the coordinator of decent work and green jobs programmes at the International Labour Organization (ILO) in Brazil.

Adrian Parr teaches sociology at the University of Cincinnati. She is UNESCO co-chair of water.

Anne Caroline Posthuma is senior specialist in employment policies at the Office of the ILO in Brazil.

Job Taminiau is a post-doctoral fellow at the Center for Energy and Environmental Policy (USA) and a research associate at the Foundation for Renewable Energy and Environment interested in the localization of global climate change policy.

Leah Temper is a post-doctoral researcher in environmental history and ecological economics at UAB and a freelance environmental journalist and video artist. She researches ecological conflicts and social metabolism and she has undertaken fieldwork on conflicts related to land use, mining and energy in Israel, Kenya, Ecuador and India. She coordinates the EJAtlas (www.ejatlas.org).

Mariana Walter is a post-doctoral researcher at IEST (UAB) and at the International Institute of Social Studies, Erasmus University Rotterdam. She researches the political ecology of mining conflicts in Latin America and is developing a framework for sustainable and equitable natural resource use.

Dave Watson is finalizing his PhD at the University of Essex. His research focuses on how participation in community food initiatives impacts on well-being.

Sun-Jin Yun is a professor at Seoul National University. She completed her PhD in environmental and energy policy at CEEP.

INTRODUCTION

Gareth Dale, Manu V. Mathai and Jose A. Puppim de Oliveira

'Green growth', together with the related 'green economy', represents the latest phase in the reconstruction of political discourse in the face of ecological challenges and environmental movements. It encompasses approaches ranging from geo-engineering mega-projects to routine 'efficiency strategies'. By such means, it promises to stem the environmental crisis and mitigate its consequences while simultaneously addressing social challenges of destitution and disempowerment. It is a project with a utopian charge, depicting a path to the future that, thanks to scientific insight, engineering sophistication and managerial smartness, is capable of redressing the accumulated harms of the 'old' industrial paradigm. At the same time, at least in its mainstream variants, it claims to embody a sober realism: the route toward a sustainable future need not stray outside the institutional and normative territory of the current political economic prevalent ideas.

At face value, green growth appears impervious to critique. Yet objections have been levelled against it from several different directions. This volume gives a platform to a variety of its critics. Common to all is a concern that green growth agendas tend to buy into the illusion that techno-economic fixes and improvements in the management of markets will enable the path of endless growth to continue, in harmony with the environment. Some, notably Ulrich Hoffmann in Chapter 1, focus upon the question of climate change. Is global economic growth, however 'green', compatible with capping a rise in the planetary average temperature at two degrees Celsius above the pre-industrial level? If the required reductions in carbon emissions cannot be achieved through a declining carbon intensity of production, then the green growth project, far from being 'realistic', would be a utopia, a mirage that serves only to flatter the ability of existing power structures to tackle ecological challenges. Others focus attention upon those power structures themselves. For Job Taminiau and John Byrne (Chapter 11), the green growth project exemplifies the incorporation of environmental narratives into 'the modernization project', with critical attention devoted solely to the '"end-of-pipe" consequences of current social relations to the environment', i.e. the pollutive excretions of modern industrialism, to the exclusion of the social organism from which they flow, with its corporate energy systems, class differences that generate 'capitalist expansion and community fragmentation', and strikingly inegalitarian patterns of wealth distribution. For James Meadway (Chapter 4), the problematic centres upon the accumulation of capital, which necessarily demotes the relationship between humanity and nature to a subsidiary concern, while Adrian Parr (Chapter 3) puts 'neoliberal governmentality' in the frame, a mode of power that elevates capital accumulation to 'a principle of governance', with green growth understood not as merely 'another instance of the misuse of state or corporate power' but as a strategic initiative to elevate principles of economic competition to the guiding mechanism of humanity's interaction with the natural environment. This, the meaning of the 'green' in green growth, is the subject of Larry Lohmann's chapter (Chapter 2). Green growth stands for a new mode of human engagement with the environment, with nature reconceived as a type of capital, a collection of tradable ecosystem services that are 'mobilized to defend productivity gains, minimize costs of capital expansion, and stave off crises of reproduction'. Just as in earlier eras the commodity of labour-power was 'unbundled from the human activity of commoners (or slaves) and made ownable and transferable', Lohmann argues, so, in the dawning era of the green economy, 'carbon-cycling capacity and other ecosystem services are to be unbundled from the activities of the earth and made circulatable and accumulable'.

Genesis of green growth

Green growth has not come out of the blue but has supervened upon earlier environmental–economic agendas. In the 1970s, environmentalism went mainstream, as soaring oil prices fuelled concern with natural 'limits to growth', accompanied by the advent of 'ecological economics' and a series of moral critiques of industrial civilization such as *Blueprint for Survival*. In 1972 the United Nations (UN) proclaimed its Stockholm Declaration on the Environment. In the same year, the Organisation for Economic Co-operation and Development (OECD) announced the 'Polluter Pays Principle', which proposed that the costs of cleaning up contamination be paid by those who caused it, and is arguably one of the seeds of the green economy idea.[1] Two years later the World Council of Churches conference in Bucharest coined the phrase 'ecologically sustainable society'. There followed, in quick succession, a series of reports by state-sponsored think tanks (notably the Hammarskjöld Foundation and the Brandt Commission) that warned against the conflation of growth and development. 'Sustainable development' became the buzzword of the time; the idea that could make compatible economic development with social goals and environmental protection. It connoted grassroots engagement, equality and social justice, local empowerment and low-impact development. Slowly but surely, however, its radical threads were appropriated by sustainable development's official sponsors: the UN, plus an array of NGOs and think tanks. By 1987 the official hour of sustainable development had arrived: the UN-backed Brundtland Commission defined it as 'development that meets the needs of the present without compromising the ability of future generations to meet their own needs'.[2] Five years later, at the Rio Earth Summit, it assumed a starring role as gospel and mantra of the mainstream environmental movement.

Despite (or because of) the social democratic aspirations embodied in 'sustainable development' it was always under suspicion of applying a green gloss to capitalist expansion in the global South. Its critics, such as Sharachchandra Lélé, dismissed it as 'a fashionable phrase that everyone pays homage to but nobody can define'.[3] Some wondered whether the 'new paradigm' it promised was 'simply a greenwash over business-as-usual'.[4] Others perceived in it a hegemonic 'cover-up operation' designed to reassure a public anxious over the consequences of economic growth that these could be ameliorated without the need for any 'radical challenge' to the prevailing economic system.[5] Little by little, ecological meanings were usurped, such that by the 2000s sustainable development had become all but synonymous with 'sustained economic growth'.[6]

As sustainable development – the discourse and project – lost its way, it gradually, inexorably, found itself folded into a new framework: green economy and 'green growth'. At first sight these could appear simply as a reprise of sustainable development. However, their emergence was significant in that they steered the existing debate in a particular direction. In the green economy discourse three aspects stand out in comparison to its 'sustainable development' predecessor. First, its variants belong for the most part to the tradition known as 'green (neo)liberalism'. They insist much more assertively than the 'sustainable development' school had done that environmental sustainability is not only compatible with but also depends upon the market system. Hope for the world lies with an eco-industrial revolution driven by technological innovation and steered by market signals. 'Going green' is an economic opportunity; its heroes are 'sustainable entrepreneurs', banks and corporations. Second, green growth stands for new methods of intervention in the environment, with nature reframed as 'a specific type of capital, which needs to be measured, conserved, produced and even accumulated'.[7] Green growth strategies were fashioned as tools to enclose commons and to isolate elements of enmeshed relationships, bringing into being purportedly autonomous categories such as 'genes', 'carbon sinks' or 'pollination' and, more generally, 'ecosystem services', which can be externalized, commodified and monetized for exchange. For instance, the response to climate change-induced meteorological unpredictability is to market genetically engineered crops for 'drought resistance' or 'heat tolerance', rather than to develop strategies of reviving and strengthening the astounding diversity of crops and planting methods, and water and soil nutrient management practices, and still less to place constraints upon free trade or speculation in agricultural commodities markets or the spread of highly processed, monocultured food habits. Third, whereas sustainable development tended to foreground questions of social justice, conservation and the active state, these are noticeable by their absence within the green economy framework. As Bluemling and Yun put it (Chapter 5), whereas sustainable development tended to favour 'civil society engagement', green growth, in their case study of South Korea, has been introduced and managed as a top-down presidential project, to be executed by technocrats. If, in its origins, sustainable development tended to go hand in hand with commitments to democratization, wealth redistribution and the political oversight of markets, these found themselves increasingly marginalized in the decades of neoliberal ascendancy that followed the fall of the Berlin Wall.

It was when the neoliberal paradigm appeared to wobble, in the early 2000s and then egregiously in the wake of the global economic crisis of 2008, that the green growth idea arose. In the North, economic growth collapsed, and remained sluggish even after the initial crisis had subsided. Some blue-chip behemoths collapsed while others staggered under mountainous losses – a gargantuan debt burden that was quickly and slickly transferred to taxpayers. Social polarization accelerated, and established parliamentary parties faced sullen or angry electorates. In such circumstances, the mainstream policy regime faced a legitimacy crisis, to which, broadly speaking, three responses were seen as possible. One was to urge it to march on as if nothing had happened – what some refer to as 'zombie neoliberalism'.[8] Another was to seek self-reinvention – a sort of reflexive modernity. It is in this connection, in keeping with Ecological Modernization Theory (EMT), that a good deal of the green growth (and green economy) agenda should be understood. A stand-out example is the case of South Korea under the administration of Lee Myung-bak, discussed by Bluemling and Yun (Chapter 5). Under President Lee, green growth was pushed hard, and not merely as a set of policies but as a means to create, in Lee's words, 'a new civilization'. On the global stage, the green economy and green growth were introduced as a central thematic of 'Rio+20', the UN Conference on Sustainable Development in Rio de Janeiro.[9] A third response was to propose the demise and replacement of the neoliberal order. Here, too, environmental issues played a prominent part, as witnessed in the reports by Britain's 'Green New Deal Group', with its demand for a

Keynesian programme of crisis resolution centred on environmentally oriented fiscal stimuli. Marginally to the mainstream debates, a series of grassroots initiatives also emerged as possible alternatives to green growth, as we will discuss later.

Green growth, in short, can be seen as the most recent 'material-semiotic' reformulation of nature–society relations offered up by a contemporary capitalism, one that found a particularly receptive audience in the wake of the crisis of 2008. It has persuasive power because it 'constitutes a plea for sustainable development without tears'.[10] Relatedly, most of its variants purport to address a range of systemic contradictions but in an explicitly apolitical (or 'post-political') way. It is an approach that is Pollyanna-like in its technological optimism, in its belief that ecological and social crises can be overcome by the same general approaches that underpinned the policy framework in the preceding 'brown' era: innovations in technique (encompassing science and engineering, finance and law) and renewed rounds of enclosures and commodification. In this, the foregrounded aims of environmental improvement, economic growth and rising living standards all appear to be non-contentious and 'apolitical', even as the means by which they are to be achieved are political to the core: the cementing of the neoliberal policy agenda within the field of environmental political economy.[11] To a certain extent, the green growth agenda is reminiscent of the Washington Consensus: a set of loosely connected economic principles and policy initiatives that gained widespread consensus among political and economic elites, found powerful backing in international organizations and particular nation states, and did not suffer much in the way of resistance in the early period of its dissemination. Ultimately, its consequences came to be felt, in the form of widening inequality and social dislocation, and movements of resistance arose. Is green growth headed in a similar direction?

Contradictions of green growth

The social and ideological prominence of economic growth – or the 'growth paradigm': the doctrine that economic growth is good, imperative, essentially limitless, and a matter of pressing concern for society as a whole – flows from fundamental societal transformations associated with the advent of modernity (the linearization of time, the notion of progress, the dissolution of just wage norms, and the quantification of processes of wealth production and distribution), and the rise of industrial capitalism together with its corollary, the commodification of nature and society. In an early effort to characterize and justify the new paradigm, Adam Smith speculated that it is 'in the progressive state', when society 'is advancing to the further acquisition, rather than when it has acquired its full complement of riches, that the condition of the labouring poor, of the great body of the people, seems to be the happiest'.[12] It is in a state of continual economic growth that emancipatory potential is achieved. And, indeed, the subsequent two centuries of industrial capitalism did significantly advance the 'acquisition of riches', as well as raising life expectancy, eroding feudal and patrimonial forms of personal economic dependence, and catalysing advances in individual liberty and democracy that, although crassly uneven in quality and application, were global in scale and momentous in scope.

This narrative of the 'progressive state' of capitalist modernity is now struggling to retain its coherence in three respects. One is internal to the growth paradigm itself. The system's own yardstick of success, global per capita GDP growth, has for several decades followed a downward trajectory. Although global capitalism is systemically 'compelled towards growth', as Meadway puts it (Chapter 4), it appears to be 'decreasingly able to deliver it'. The second is a scepticism vis-à-vis the 'Smithian promise' that growth will emancipate the poor. Against a backdrop of vulgar levels of income inequality, the supposed connection between economic growth and social well-being has been increasingly called into question.[13] Insofar as a perceptible relationship between GDP growth and well-being exists, it tends to decline after a certain point – as a rule of thumb, when per capita GDP exceeds around $15,000 – and today's *average* global per capita GDP, at $6,000 per head, is now greater than that for the Western world in 1950. It is perhaps fortunate, Richard Wilkinson and Kate Pickett have argued, that 'just when the human species discovers that the environment cannot absorb further increases in emissions, we also learn that further economic growth in the developed world no longer improves health, happiness or wellbeing'.[14]

The third is a growth scepticism fuelled by concerns over the diminishing ecological space available to supply non-renewable resources and to absorb the effluents of ongoing growth. Ecological thresholds are being breached, and 'tipping points' appear to be upon us. To this, the dominant response has long been one or other variant of 'green growth': the idea that investment in the production of knowledge, the resulting innovations in technique, environmental awareness that purportedly comes with rising incomes, and a structural shift towards fewer resource and energy-intensive service sector industries will 'save the planet'. In its formalized version, this idea came to be known as the Environmental Kuznets Curve (EKC). The EKC holds that, after a certain point, economic growth correlates strongly with greater efficiency in resource use. At low levels of economic development, a nation's output is too low to generate much pollution. As GDP grows, environmental damage initially grows too, but when a high income level is reached, an inflexion point after which new factors come into play: economic growth becomes increasingly 'dematerialized', and people become 'rich enough to care about pollution and take steps to reduce it'.[15] From then on, environmental degradation tends to fall even as incomes rise further.[16] The ecological economist Herman Daly calls this the 'hair of the dog that bit you' approach.[17]

The hypothesis that there exists a simple, inverse relationship between per capita income and environmental stress has been challenged on a number of counts. Firstly, the idea that concern for the environment is a privilege of rich people is baseless. It ignores the 'environmentalism of the poor' about which Martinez-Alier *et al.* write in Chapter 9 and Ashish Kothari in Chapter 10. And, as Anne Posthuma and Paulo Sergio Muçouçah remind us in Chapter 8, it is invariably the poor among us who clean up and recycle society's waste. Secondly, if the EKC hypothesis has held in particular conditions, then only with respect to pollutants that have short-term costs, such as particulates, and not with respect to accumulating wastes or to pollutants involving long-term costs, such as greenhouse gas emissions (GHGs). Decreases in some pollutants, its critics point out, are often associated with increases in other pollutants within the same country or transfers of pollution to other countries. The EKC hypothesis ignores the fact that reduced pollution in developed countries is often part of the same processes – above all, the outsourcing of manufacturing – that determine the expansion of resource-intensive production elsewhere.[18] Rather than income growth leading to an amelioration of pollution, what seems to be happening is a dynamic, multifactorial and context-dependent interplay between 'scale effect' and 'time effect'. For example, where developing countries take measures to reduce pollution, the higher economic growth rate and resulting increase in pollution – the scale effect – overwhelms their efforts, whereas in slower-growing developed countries the scale effect is subdued.[19] While at face value this might appear to validate the EKC hypothesis, it is undermined by evidence of the environmental performance of economic growth at the macro scale. If macro indicators of environmental stress, such as 'ecological footprint per unit of well-being', are assessed, the findings tend to result in a U-shaped curve when plotted against per capita income.[20] Such results are in keeping with critiques of ecological modernization theory,[21] which find that, regulatory, energy and material intensity improvements notwithstanding, 'modernization leads to supermaterialization rather than dematerialization' at the macro scale.[22] For instance, Wiedmann *et al.* record the divergence between Domestic Material Consumption (often seen to be in decline in developed countries) and these same economies' overall Material Footprint, which in many cases is rising, due to the externalization of material consumption through international trade and the relocation of energy and material intensive mining and manufacturing industries.[23] Martinez-Alier and his co-authors (Chapter 9) find such patterns in international trade to be a trend pointing to the 'structural persistence of ecologically unequal exchange'. They argue that oft-underappreciated 'physical and socio-environmental trade-offs at play' call into question the purported economic growth and development benefits accruing to export-intensive economies of the South.

A major hope of green growth advocates, on which much of their case rests, is that efficiency gains will negate overall increments in attendant energy and material throughput, including a dramatic reduction of GHG emissions. But this, as noted by Bluemling and Yun in Chapter 5, is much too sanguine, not least because it neglects to consider the 'Jevons paradox'. In his book *The Coal Question: An inquiry concerning the progress of the nation, and the probable exhaustion of our coal-mines* (1865), the British neoclassical economist William Jevons expressed an anxiety that the depletion of its coal supplies will lead to Britain's industrial decline and consequent loss of imperial dominance. One seemingly obvious solution would be to effect improvements in the efficiency of steam engines and furnaces; surely that would lead to a reduction in the rate of depletion. In fact, the opposite occurred: it was 'the very economy' of the use of coal that led to its more rapid consumption. 'If the quantity of coal used in a blast-furnace be diminished in comparison with the yield,' he reasoned,

> the profits of the trade will increase, new capital will be attracted, the price of pig-iron will fall, but the demand for it increase; and eventually the greater number of furnaces will more than make up for the diminished consumption of each. And if such is not always the result within a single branch, it must be remembered that the progress of any branch of manufacture excites a new activity in most other branches, and leads indirectly, if not directly, to increased inroads upon our seams of coal.[24]

The improved technological efficiency in the utilization of a natural resource, within a capitalist framework, tends not to decrease but to increase its rate of consumption, because its relative cost is lessened, freeing up capital for alternative uses. This is a key reason why the ability of efficiency strategies to successfully address the crisis in society–nature relations is likely to remain limited.

On one vital issue, that of reductions in GHGs, the EKC hypothesis may yet turn out to be valid – but in a perverse and unconstructive way. That is to say, it is perfectly conceivable that in the coming decades continued global economic growth will coincide with reductions in total emissions, yielding a classic Environmental Kuznets Curve: low emissions and low output in the nineteenth century; high emissions and rising GDP in the twentieth; steady or diminishing emissions alongside rising GDP in the twenty-first. At face value it is a soothing prospect, and it is at the heart of the green growth prospectus. Economic growth, it appears to promise, may continue unabated even as emissions decline, thanks to a decoupling of growth from resource throughput. However, for genuine progress to be achieved on this front, the decoupling of GHG emissions from GDP growth would have to occur rapidly, globally and permanently. Crucially, decoupling would have to be absolute (with an absolute decline in emissions) rather than relative (a decline in the ratio of emissions to GDP). According to Hoffmann (Chapter 1), this is not a feasible programme. The limitation of global warming to the comparatively safe figure of 2°C would require a reduction in the global carbon intensity of production to 36gCO2/$ – a 21-fold improvement on the current global average.[25] If this were attempted while countries of the global South seek a level of per capita GDP comparable with the EU average, a much greater reduction would be required – of nearly 130 times over the next 35 years. To put this in perspective, consider the actual historical instances in which emissions reductions have occurred. Apart from a brief window in post-unification Germany, Russia is the only sizeable economy that has seen a substantial emissions reduction in recent times. Its carbon emissions fell by almost 3 per cent annually in 1990–2005 – and that was thanks to industrial collapse. The world would have to repeat that experience, and without Russia's fall-back on hydrocarbons (and the credit lines based on them), for decades on end and at roughly three times the rate to even achieve medium-term limitation of global warming to the far-from-safe figure of 3°C. To believe that emissions reductions on the scale required is compatible with a growth-oriented world economy is utopian folly.

Green growth in practice

According to the United Nations, green growth first gained shape as a strategic project in 2005; specifically, at the Fifth Ministerial Conference on Environment and Development, at which '52 Governments and other stakeholders from Asia and the Pacific agreed to move beyond the sustainable development rhetoric and pursue a path of "green growth"'.[26] The conference venue was Seoul, and this was no coincidence. South Korea has been instrumental in promoting the concept. In 2008, at the onset of the world economic crisis, the Lee administration adopted green growth as its 'new development vision', and a year later the National Strategy for Green Growth and Five-Year Plan for Green Growth were announced. However, as Bluemling and Yun document in Chapter 5, when the layers of rhetoric were peeled from Lee's Green Growth Plan, its core was revealed to be nuclear energy expansion, land reclamation, canal cutting and dredging, and the construction of a multitude of dams and weirs – all of which would place further strain upon the country's beleaguered natural environment. It was little surprise when Lee's green growth initiative faced a barrage of criticism, or that the following government, under President Geun-hye Park, considered 'ditching' green growth altogether.[27]

A second aspirant to green growth leadership, the European Union, is discussed by Birgit Mahnkopf in Chapter 6. Mahnkopf details a number of the EU's headline initiatives, such as the '20–20–20' programme which sets binding targets for the year 2020: a reduction in GHG emissions of 20 per cent below 1990 levels, a 20 per cent reduction in primary energy use compared with projected levels (via energy efficiency measures), and then a raising to 20 per cent of the proportion of energy supplied from renewable resources (including biofuels). As in the Korean case, however, the initial fanfare has been followed by disappointing results. Green growth, she writes, has been welcomed only insofar as it represents 'a win–win situation' for the corporate sector, with an emphasis upon efficiency strategies and new technological innovations, so long as profits are not harmed. Thanks in part to corporate lobbying, the picture 'is of a counterrevolution in energy policy' before the oft-praised renewables revolution had even occurred.

Our third featured case study, Brazil, has in recent years (until 2013) exhibited a reduced emissions intensity, due principally to lower rates of deforestation but also to efficiency improvements and the energy mix. As detailed by Abramovay (Chapter 7), much of Brazil's electricity is produced from hydropower; it has developed a large biofuel industry and market; and during the 2000s it experienced a spell of rapid economic growth alongside reductions in poverty and inequality. For these reasons, Brazil has frequently been commended as an emerging champion of inclusive green growth. However, while its energy matrix is indeed greener than most, its forests continue to shrink and its fossil-fuel economy is on the rise. Brazil's 'human appropriation of net primary production of biomass' is rising, as

Martinez-Alier *et al.* show, due largely to deforestation. Its hydroelectric plants, as Abramovay points out, are not without serious ecological and social shortcomings. For example, new developments require the eviction of settled communities and deforestation. They are also providing a diminishing proportion of the electricity supply, due in part to rising demand but also to the prolonged drought that has afflicted Brazil's southeast region – a drought that itself is in part caused by rainforest destruction. As regards the biofuel industry, Abramovay argues that insofar as ethanol is considered a straightforward substitute for oil, its use reduces pollution and climate change impacts, yet at the same time it has reinforced a sugar cane monoculture, with attendant social-ecological problems, in rural areas and has failed to reduce vehicle use and urban congestion problems. Meanwhile, little progress has been made in developing more sustainable alternatives in the wind and solar sectors.

What of the 'inclusivity' of green growth? For the most part, it has been framed on 'green market' lines, with little concern for distributional impacts and equity, little concern that green jobs be decently remunerated and unionized, and with the existing structures of inequality and social exclusion left intact.[28] In the Brazilian case, however, under a 'social liberal' government, comparatively strong efforts have been made to connect green growth and poverty reduction programmes, as suggested in the chapters by Abramovay and by Posthuma and Muçouçah. However, as the latter make clear in their discussion of the organization of waste collectors, while in many instances working conditions have improved, the waste pickers remain in a vulnerable position, lacking an independent labour union, and in receipt of a diminutive share of the earnings generated by the sale of their products, a situation which, Posthuma and Muçouçah aver, raises 'important questions regarding the economic and social sustainability of recycling activities' in Brazil.

Another of the facets of green growth is to try to quantify and assess 'environmental betterment' to show that progress has been made. However, though many of those measurements are important, they tend to leave out some other important dimensions of the consequences or impacts of the 'environmental progress'. It is well known now that the typical indicators for planning, such as GDP or number of jobs, do not reflect on all the dimensions of development. Even broader indicators, such as the Human Development Index – HDI, or more direct measurements, such as better water quality, do not capture the more complex social and ecological dimensions of a particular issue.

Although the vision offered by green growth strategies is in many ways attractive – an ecologically balanced affluence engineered through ethical enterprise and smart markets – it is a mirage, an exercise in state-engineered public relations that promises to do little to repair humankind's relationship with 'the environment', as is borne out by the cases of 'actually existing green growth' in countries and regions such as South Korea, the EU and Brazil.

What, then, are the alternatives?

Alternatives

Green growth advocacy is not the last word in environmentalism, even if it is the loudest voice. Other voices point to the potential for non-growth oriented transitions to a sustainable society. Those featured in this volume concur in a critique of the current paradigm, with its faith in technocratic and market solutions (for example that ecological crises can be effectively addressed by internalizing externalities and changing the mix of inputs in the economic process), and in the proposition that a broad societal transformation is essential, operating at different scales from the local to the global. But different emphases and strategies are outlined in the various chapters. One, discussed by Posthuma and Muçouçah (Chapter 8), entails 'the promotion of quality job creation in environmentally sustainable sectors and activities'. A 'green jobs approach', they propose, has the potential to 'bring about a rupture' with the current unsustainable and socially exclusionary economic model, 'by harnessing sustainable practices and social inclusion in ways that are decoupled from a dependency on rising consumption and economic growth'. In the case of any green jobs programme, the degree of transformative rupture will depend upon the social forces that are calling for its implementation, and upon the nature of the jobs created. If green jobs are precarious and informal, they will do the environmental cause a disservice. In addition, many such programmes risk being little but an exercise in creative accounting and greenwash, with jobs designated 'green' merely if they fall within a sector deemed 'environmental' (such as sewage, or waste management) or if they involve ineffectual charades (such as jobs in 'carbon finance') or if they are relatively low-carbon but otherwise environmentally harmful (such as jobs in the nuclear industry). For this reason, some prefer the term 'climate jobs' – as in the trade union-sponsored 'One Million Climate Jobs' campaign in Britain and South Africa.[29]

In a number of chapters, the question of alternatives is unfolded from an analysis of the prevailing socio-economic system. The growth imperative, in their view, is an inherent attribute of the capitalist mode of production, such that 'either we save capitalism or we save ourselves'.[30] As Mahnkopf puts it (Chapter 6), capitalism 'distinguishes itself from all other socio-economic systems in human history by the movement towards the infinite'; its totalizing logic penetrates society in all its facets and converts 'almost the entire world into a field of valorization'. Hoffmann (Chapter 1) and Meadway (Chapter 4) conclude that 'a capitalist steady state economy', as advocated by John Stuart Mill, is a fantasy. For Hoffmann, '... the required transformation goes far beyond innovation and structural changes to include democratization of the economy, better distribution of income and wealth, power over markets, and a culture of sufficiency'. Meadway's focus is 'the process of competitive, blind accumulation that grants to capitalism its distinctive requirement for relentless growth'. He draws attention to the social structures – in particular the labour market – that 'enforce the pattern of accumulation'. In this, unemployment plays a key role: it disciplines the labour force, and when accumulation stalls, the consequent rise in unemployment tends to lower costs and (*ceteris paribus*) to raise profits, enabling accumulation to resume.

Within capitalism, the process of accumulation, the continuous extraction of surplus labour, is not simply a social relation of exploitation but undergirds a nexus of relations of alienation: of workers from the labour process, from their products, from their fellows, and from their selves; and of labour itself from nature, which thereby comes to be conceived as 'external' to society. The system as a whole is administered by political institutions that service the requirements of capital and oversee the management and policing of the population. If viewed in this way, a sustainable society will, ultimately, require the transcendence of, or breaking away from, the systemic, objective logic that dictates capital's ceaseless motions to produce and reproduce itself in ever widening spaces of commodified nature and society. Should strategic agency therefore be envisaged in terms of the massing together of movements that resist different aspects of the broader social system? This is the sense that underlies Lohmann's maxim (Chapter 2) that 'labour struggles are environmental struggles, and vice versa'. However, the convergence of diverse movements around transformative goals is never automatic. All social movements are criss-crossed with contestation and dialogical relations, internal debates and tensions. They find themselves pulled between imperatives to resist structures of capitalist power and to accommodate them. The dilemmas faced by movements seeking sustainable alternatives to technocracy and to the capitalist growth model, and the theoretical questions associated with them, are explored in the final three chapters.

Reporting on progressive social movements from India, Ashish Kothari (Chapter 10) recounts numerous examples of resistance and creativity that demonstrate a radically different logic to that of industrial capitalism and state-led economic development. Among many illustrations, he reports on the 'Dongria Kondh adivasis (indigenous group) in the state of Odisha [who] decided [...] not to allow a multinational mining company to take over their lands', justified in terms of a logic radically different from the externalization and commodification of nature, namely the 'sacredness of the land and forest, and their own notions of well-being'. Similarly, in 'Mendha-Lekha, a Gond adivasi village in the state of Maharashtra, all the farmers voluntarily donated their private agricultural lands to the community, under an old law promoting the "commons" that has almost never been used in the country. This followed a successful move by the village to claim control over forests surrounding it, reversing two centuries of colonial, state-centred control, and to declare "tribal self-rule".'

In an effort to distil the principles that inform these efforts, which he labels Radical Ecological Democracy (RED), Kothari identifies distinctive attributes that intuitively, if not explicitly, counter the totalizing logic of industrial capitalism. These include, but are not limited to, decentralized embedded political governance adhering to the principle of subsidiarity, the decentralization of economic life and economic localization, the recognition of equity and protection of diversity and breaking artificial boundaries and hierarchies of knowledge systems. Illustrations such as these point to a lived reality of alternative logics that fundamentally differ from the externalizing, commodifying, accumulation logic of state-led economic development. However, pondering the role of the state, Kothari ends with a caution: 'peoples' movements will also have to recognize the fine line between policy-based expansion of democratic spaces that aid fundamental transformation, and those [...] that the state uses to soften or even co-opt peoples' movements.'

The community-based energy utility pioneered in the state of Delaware, USA, reported by Job Taminiau and John Byrne (Chapter 11) represents an effort to move the energy sector away from the conventional approach of atomized households served by a distant centralized utility with energy mined from an externalized, commodified nature. Teasing out the operative mechanism that grants the conventional energy–society relationship its daunting momentum, they observe that civil society has become 'reduced to a "consumer democracy"' in which the ability of end-users of energy 'to influence entrepreneurial and capitalistic activity is limited to their daily vote on the means of production through the global marketplace'. Referred to as a Sustainable Energy Utility (SEU), the alternative energy–society model that Taminiau and Byrne report from Delaware envisions steering the energy sector away from 'consumer democracy' to a role where consumers are also producers and, further, are envisioned as 'sustainable citizens' engaged in energy conservation, energy efficiency and renewable energy commons. The SEU seeks to integrate energy (nature) and society in a democratically organized, decentralized and mutually co-producing relationship, representing a marked contrast to the centralized, and undemocratic nature–society model of the standard energy utility and it atomized customers. The SEU reinterprets and reintegrates ideas of 'commonwealth' and 'community trust' into the energy discourse long severed from shared, commons-based practice and sensitivities.

In order to unlock the 'commonwealth – i.e. its energy savings potential', the SEU leverages financial capital from a variety of sources (philanthropic, energy and carbon auction markets, crowdfunding, etc.), and also deploys 'tax-exempt revenue bonds that access the private capital market'. Thus, the SEU marks an innovative practical strategy in redirecting energy–society relations towards commons' resources (energy, commonwealth and community trust) even as it necessarily has to stand within, and emerge from, the all-pervasive system of capitalist social relations.

In seeking to develop non-capitalist alternatives, individuals and movements stand upon terrain that is shaped by it. One of the more illuminating discussions of the possibilities and constraints in this regard is Heather Rogers' *Green Gone Wrong*. It explores, *inter alia*, experiments in the agroecological farming sector, in which contingent successes could be achieved, with the deployment of efficient ecologically sustainable agricultural techniques, and the successful infusion of community engagement. Nonetheless, all enterprises, however mutual, social and ecological, face pressures to cut costs or risk losing customers to rivals. 'The rules of the marketplace support the big guys,' as Rogers puts it. 'Small farmers typically can't make a larger environmental impact because our political and economic system won't let them.' This is the problematic addressed by Böhm and his colleagues (Chapter 12). Their research subject is 'social movements for alternative political economies': groups of people who experiment with 'relations of production and exchange that do not follow the logic of capital accumulation', such as workers' cooperatives, alternative currencies, and community-based agroecological farming. What they found, on the one hand, was the application of creativity, innovation and idealism, combined with principles of mutuality and self-management, to serve goals of community, equality and ecology. On the other hand, in each case compromises were made with major business concerns and with state power: the SAMTFMACS cooperative in India entered into relations of dependence upon giant corporations and the Indian state, leaving its farmers with 'very little, if any, control over the management of the value chain of the coffee' that they produced. Similarly, the MST in Brazil, the world's most powerful land reform movement, has in its capacity as economic agent entered into agreements with a transnational corporation, in a process that led the MST farmers involved to see themselves as 'service providers' responding to market demands more than as the collective producers of 'new socio-economic subjectivities'. Along such pathways, argue Böhm *et al.*, capital tends to assimilate and neutralize ecological projects and social movements.

It would be unfair, caution Böhm *et al.*, to dismiss agroecological cooperatives offhand on the grounds that 'they are simply not revolutionary enough'. Rather, they emphasize the dialectic of resistance and recuperation, as it occurs within movements such as the MST. One path that a movement can take is to accommodate existing power structures, making deals with powerful bodies (such as the corporations discussed by Böhm *et al.*), emphasizing negotiations with government bodies and utilizing the 'proper channels', and remaining strictly local in scope. In short, it internalizes the horizons of the existing order. Alternatively, it can emphasize collective action and self-activity, reach out to wider layers, and seek to connect its interests to those of wider movements against injustice and oppression. Between these two roads no wall exists; what may commence as a modest demand for local reform can develop into a broad, anti-systemic revolt.

Neither in their analysis of 'green growth' nor in their proposed alternatives are the chapters in this volume proposing a common manifesto. Rather, they seek to contribute to a conversation, one that seeks to understand the 'green growth' agenda and to develop alternatives to it. What unites them is a concern that the green growth terrain has been occupied by interests that seek to continue 'business as usual' with only minimal reform, and a conviction that the theoretical and, especially, the practical development of alternatives is imperative.

PART I: CONTRADICTIONS OF GREEN GROWTH

CHAPTER 1

Can green growth really work? A reality check that elaborates on the true (socio-)economics of climate change

Ulrich Hoffmann*

Introduction

In the run-up to the Rio+20 Conference in June 2012 and the UN Climate Summit on 23 September 2014, virtually everyone from multilateral agencies to politicians, to businessmen, and to NGOs has advocated a fundamental shift towards 'green and inclusive growth' as the new, qualitatively different growth paradigm, which would considerably improve the energy efficiency of the economy and lead to drastic changes in its energy and material mix (replacing exhaustible by renewable materials), with corresponding structural changes.[1] 'Green growth' advocates argue that such paradigm change would unleash new wealth creation and employment opportunities; provided that there was sufficient investment and companies had better information and supportive incentives. In other words, the impression occurs that the 'green growth' concept is flawless; just the enabling conditions for it are lacking.[2] 'Green growth', which should be rather seen as a process of structural change, may indeed create some new growth impulses with reduced environmental load, in particular at microeconomic level. But can it also mitigate climate change at the required scale and pace (i.e. significant, absolute and permanent decline of GHG emissions

* The author would like to extend particular thanks to Gunnar Rundgren and Chandran Nair for comments on earlier drafts of the text.

in a historically very short period of time) at macroeconomic and global level?

The reality check below casts a long shadow on the 'green growth' hopes. Our analysis argues that the arithmetic of economic and population growth, energy/resource/material efficiency limits related to the rebound effect and horizontal shifting of problems, governance and market constraints, as well as systemic limits call into question the hopes of decoupling GHG from economic growth. Rather, one should not deceive oneself into believing that such an evolutionary (and often reductionist) approach will be sufficient to cope with the socio-economic complexities related to climate change (and some other global environmental problems, such as loss of biodiversity). 'Green growth' may give much false hope and excuses to do nothing really fundamental that can bring about a U-turn on global GHG emissions. The approach is largely reduced to a technocratic and technology-fetishized one, because changing technologies is much easier than altering societies and their socio-economic drivers.

'Green growth' proponents need to scrutinize the historical macro- (not micro-) economic evidence, in particular the arithmetic of economic and population growth, the colossal reductions required in the GHG-emission intensity of economic growth as well as the significant influence of the rebound effect. Furthermore, they need to realize that the required transformation goes far beyond innovation and structural changes to include better distribution of income and wealth, power over markets, and a culture of sufficiency.[3] Against this very background, an attempt is made below to elaborate on the true economics of climate change. Global warming also calls into question the global equality of opportunity for prosperity (i.e. ecological justice and development space) and is thus a huge developmental challenge for the South and a question of life and death for some developing countries.

Limits set by the arithmetic of economic and population growth

In the last few years, the fossil-fuel-related CO_2-emission trajectory has followed a trend that is worse than the worst-case scenario used in the 4th assessment report of the Intergovernmental Panel on

Climate Change (IPCC) of 2007.[4] If current GHG-emission trends continue unabated, according to the 5th IPCC assessment report of 2014, we are likely on course for temperature increases of 4–6°C and even more,[5] which would undoubtedly have apocalyptic implications. The 4th IPCC assessment report concluded that GHG reductions in the order of 85 per cent for developed countries and some 50 per cent for developing countries would be necessary by 2050 to keep global warming at a range of 2 to 2.4°C.[6]

It is, however, highly questionable whether the required drastic GHG-emissions reductions are really achievable under the prevailing growth paradigm. By way of illustration, global carbon intensity of production fell from around 1kg/$ of economic activity to just 770g/$ (i.e. by 23 per cent) in the 28 years between 1980 and 2008 (a drop of about 0.7 per cent per annum). Even if recent trends of global population (at 0.7 per cent per annum) and income growth (at 1.4 per cent per year) were just extrapolated to 2050, carbon intensity would have to be reduced to 36gCO2/$ – a 21-fold improvement on the current global average to limit global warming to 2 degrees. Allowing developing countries to catch up with the present level of GDP per capita in developed nations would even require a much higher drop in carbon

Figure 1.1 Development of the carbon intensity of GDP, 1980 to 2050

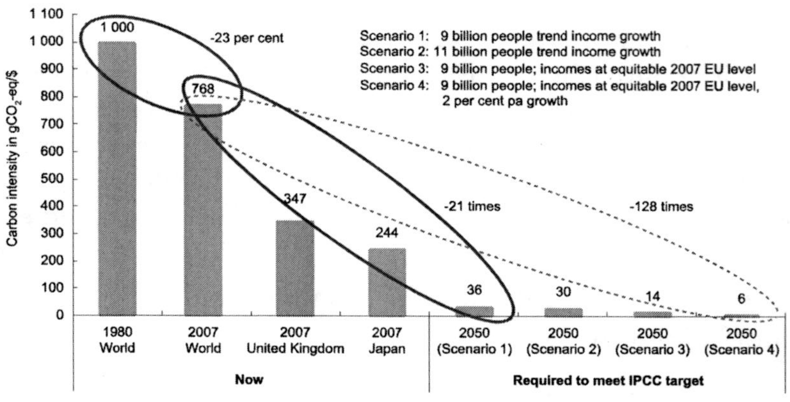

Source: Jackson, T (2009) *Prosperity without Growth: Economics for a Finite Planet*, Earthscan, London, and additions by the author.

intensity of almost 130 times by 2050 (see Figure 1.1). More recent analysis of global carbon intensity dynamics by PricewaterhouseCoopers (PwC) as part of its annual Low Carbon Economy Index supports Jackson's projections.[7] According to the PwC experts, carbon intensity of the global economy would have to be reduced by 6.2 per cent a year between now and 2050. Even a doubling of the current rate of decarbonization (some 1.2 per cent in 2013) would still lead to emissions consistent with 4–6°C of warming by the end of the century.[8]

Not once since World War II has humankind achieved the rate of reduction of carbon intensity of GDP required for limiting global warming to 2°C.[9] In retrospect, apart from Germany just for a short period of two years after reunification in the 1990s, the Russian Federation is the only large economy that has reduced emissions substantially since 1990, mostly caused by a breakdown of its heavy industry (an example of degrowth). The country's carbon emissions fell by almost 3 per cent annually in 1990–2005. The world (not only a handful of technologically very advanced countries) would have to repeat the Russian experience at a roughly three times more drastic extent (and even that would only result in limiting global warming to about 3°C degrees). The closest the world came to the required decarbonization levels was during the recessions of the late 1970s/early 1980s (with almost 5 per cent reduction in 1981) and the late 1990s (with a reduction of 4.2 per cent in 1999).[10] This seems to suggest that, historically, drastic rates of decarbonization have been linked to recessions and thus phases of stagnation or contraction. The highest decarbonization rate ever achieved in a planned fashion was 4.5 per cent per annum in 1980-1985, when France implemented its nuclear energy programme.[11]

The rise of global population by about 30 per cent, from 7.2 billion now to about 9.3 billion by 2050, will drive the scale effect of production and consumption (i.e. their absolute physical expansion). This growth, combined with a three-fold increase in per capita consumption (from about US$6,600 to 19,700) (and even assuming that the rich world grows not much more) would jack up the size of the world economy by four times, requiring 80 per cent more energy.[12] While it is a fact that (with the exception of some oil-producing Arab countries) the countries with the highest population growth have contributed least to GHG emissions thus far, this is only because their populations continue to live in extreme poverty. In other words, population growth does not matter for resource consumption and GHG emissions as long as one accepts that people remain poor, with minimal levels of consumption. But it begins to matter a great deal if the international community has the ambition to reduce poverty amidst rapidly growing populations (if the 1.5 billion people currently without access to basic energy supply obtained that access and had the current average per capita CO_2 emissions, this would increase global carbon emissions by 20 per cent and double those of the developing world).[13]

It is often also overlooked that the drastic reductions in GHG intensity of GDP have to happen in a historically very short period of time, i.e. the next 20–30 years. According to McKinsey researchers, the 'carbon revolution' needs to be three times faster than the industrial labour productivity rise in the industrial revolution. 'During the Industrial Revolution, the United States achieved an increase in labour productivity of ten times between 1830 and 1955. The key difference is the timeframe. The tenfold increase in labour productivity was achieved over 125 years; the carbon revolution needs to happen in only 2–3 decades.'[14]

The asymmetry between carbon intensity, scale and structural effects of economic growth

To really come to grips with ballooning GHG emissions, the global economy needs to decouple GHG emissions in absolute, not relative terms from GDP growth.[15] This absolute decoupling needs to be significant, fast, global and permanent.

The relatively modest progress achieved in reducing GHG intensity of GDP is related to the fact that technological progress in reducing GHG intensity and concomitant structural change has been outpaced by the scale effect of growth. To decouple GHG emission from GDP growth (and thus a qualitatively different economic growth) implies that the technology effect and the composition/structural effect of growth lead to higher GHG-emission reductions – in particular crystallized as higher energy (and related material and resource) efficiency and the more pronounced use of renewable material and energy – than GHG-emission growth fuelled by the scale effect of economic growth. However, there are only very few examples where such decoupling has actually happened, one being the case of refrigerators in some developed countries;[16] another example concerns modern lighting systems.[17] Much more typical, however, has been the case of fuel efficiency of the private car population in the European Union in the last 20 years.[18] Savings through more fuel-efficient cars were outweighed by the strong increase in the car population and the total mileage travelled.[19] Whereas fuel consumption per privately owned car decreased by about 15 per cent in the period 1990–2007, car population and total mileage travelled increased by over 40 per cent. Consequently, total fuel consumption of privately owned cars rose by more than a quarter.[20]

Interestingly, structural changes have also been far less effective in countering the scale-effect-induced GHG-emission dynamics than hoped for. Generally, for restructuring to be effective, GHG-intensive sectors and activities would have to shrink faster than the expansion of GHG-efficient ones, which actually has not happened. 'Ecological' restructuring of the economy is a structural change of gigantic dimension and, as pointed out above, required at break-neck speed, which implies a huge loss in fixed-capital stock. Rather, entrepreneurs tend to gradually replace the fixed capital as a function of amortization cycles (which can be influenced by finance and fiscal policy measures of governments).

Finance capital also plays a key role in ecological restructuring. On the one hand, finance capital provides the loan or share capital for required changes in the fixed-capital stock, which on its own puts pressure on productive capital to generate surplus value (i.e. profit for paying interest or revenues on shares) and thus expands the scale of production. On the other hand, finance capital tends to have a rather short-term interest in the profitability of its invested capital. At the same time, it is risk averse as regards investing in technology for paradigm shifts or revolutionary changes. Hence a preference for supporting investment projects, based on evolutionary or incremental changes as regards energy (and related material and resource) efficiency and changes in the energy mix, which generally fall short of the required quantum-leap changes in a historically short period of time. In essence, scale effects, new technology and structural change all require active use of external finance capital, which on its own requires economic growth to pay interest and revenues on shares.

Also, the structural shift into a service-dominated economy has generated far less GHG-emission reductions than hoped for. This is caused by the fact that quite a number of service sectors, such as transport, health, IT services[21] or tourism, are rather fixed capital and thus energy, material and resource intensive when it comes to setting up their infrastructure or operating base (conversely, operationally, most service sectors are labour-intensive).[22] What is more, emissions from the private consumption of a person are relative to his/her income and not the occupation. So, while shifting jobs into the service sector might reduce emissions in production somewhat, the people working there will drive their car to work, eat meat and go on vacation in the same way as a factory worker. A stockbroker earning a million dollars or more probably uses little resources at work, but she/he will use a lot more resources and energy for private consumption than a worker in manufacturing.[23]

Increasing the use of renewable energy – easier said than done

Much hope was put on the contribution of changes in the energy mix to reducing GHG emissions. However, evidence suggests that a complete or significant replacement of fossil fuel by renewable energy (RE) is very challenging on a number of fronts:

- There is the need for compacting RE.
- One needs a significantly modified, renewed or new transmission infrastructure.
- There is a reduced energy return on energy input (EROI).
- Certain REs have to face up to material scarcities.
- There is not yet a really sustainable alternative for conventional transport fuel.

Wind and solar, the two most promising RE sources, are variable and intermittent, and therefore cannot serve as 'base-load' electricity, requiring substantial conventional electricity capacity as backup. They also require significant material input into the production of solar panels and wind turbines and a major upgrading of storage capacity, transmission lines and the creation of intelligent grids, all set to drive up material consumption (and related costs), in some cases completely exhausting the supply of strategic materials.[24] Furthermore, two-thirds of fossil fuel is used as transport fuel, for which there is no real substitute within sight (biofuels cannot meet more than a small fraction of the world's transport fuel demand).[25]

Hänggi cautions that a change in the energy mix does often not lead to a straightforward replacement of fossil by renewable fuel.[26] Rather, the new energy is likely to be used in parallel with the old one for quite some time (a phenomenon that applies to many social innovations), both for technical reasons, but also linked to the rebound effect (see below). For instance, the present global consumption of coal is higher than that before the oil age; so is the current consumption of fuel wood compared to what was used before the coal age. Also, to assure reliable electricity supply, gas-reliant power stations are likely to play an important role in backing up wind and solar power facilities.[27]

It should also not be overlooked that, unlike conventional fuel, renewable energy is usually only available in non-concentrated form; it has to be 'compacted' to generate sufficient power. This 'compaction' or, in technical terms, the reduction of entropy of a system, can only be achieved by increasing the entropy in other parts. In practical terms of renewable energy, this means that one can only compact wind, solar, bio or hydro energy by increasing the use of conventional fuel or raw materials.[28]

As a result, EROI is low and sometimes even negative (in fact, even for conventional fuels the EROI has dramatically declined in recent decades).[29] According to Hall *et al.*, it is not important to have renewable energy alternatives per se, but that they have:

- a sufficient energy density;
- an appropriate transportability;
- a relatively low environmental impact per net unit delivered to society;
- a relatively high EROI; and
- that REs are obtainable on a scale that society demands.

Hall *et al.* stress that 'we must remember that usually what we want is energy services, not energy itself, which usually has little intrinsic economic utility'.[30] MacKay adds that 'for a sustainable energy plan to add up, we need both the forms and amounts of energy consumption and production to match up. Converting energy from one form to another ... usually involves substantial losses of useful energy ... Conversion losses (in the United Kingdom, for example – added by the author) account for about 22 per cent of total national energy consumption.'[31]

In sum it should be noted that low EROI, losses in storage, transmission and conversion, and less efficiency at the point of use for renewable energy can mean that the need for energy supply can increase considerably compared to the current fossil-fuel-dominated energy mix – just to keep energy utility at the point of use the same.

The efficiency illusion: the rebound effect

Enhanced energy (and related material and resource) efficiency and ample availability of cheap renewable energy will encourage a 'rebound effect', i.e. physical consumption is likely to increase as a result of productivity increases, which leads to lower costs and prices and the shifting of thus saved consumer money or investment funds.[32]

The rebound effect was first described by the English economist William Stanley Jevons in his book *The Coal Question*, published in 1865. Jevons observed that England's consumption of coal soared after James Watt introduced his coal-fired steam engine, which greatly improved the efficiency of Thomas Newcomen's earlier design. Watt's innovations made coal a more cost-effective power source, leading to the increased use of the steam engine in a wide range of industries. This in turn increased total coal consumption, even as the amount of coal required for any particular application fell. Jevons argued that improvements in fuel efficiency tend to increase, rather than decrease, fuel use: 'It is a confusion of ideas to suppose that the economical use of fuel is equivalent to diminished consumption. The very contrary is the truth ... no one must suppose that coal thus saved is spared – it is only saved from one use to be employed in others.'[33]

The rebound effect reflects the causality between efficiency increases and additional demand. The definition not only includes the energy/

material/resource (EMR) efficiency, but also the additional demand impact of increased labour and capital productivity.

Besides the financial rebound effect (denoting that part or all of the EMR-efficiency-induced cost savings are used for reinvestment or additional consumption) there is also a material rebound effect. In addition, there are psychological and cross-factor rebound effects. Material rebound effects are caused by higher EMR consumption resulting from the need to change fixed capital and infrastructure for increasing EMR efficiency. The psychological rebound effect provokes higher EMR consumption, because the user of more efficient technologies is under the impression that he/she has economized on EMR use and that there is thus no harm in using the concerned device a bit more (e.g. the user of a more fuel efficient or electrical vehicle increases the mileage). The cross-factor rebound effect, in turn, is triggered by enhanced labour productivity, which replaces labour by mechanization and motorization, driving material and resource consumption, but in particular energy use. In other words, labour productivity increases are bought by reduced energy efficiency. Technological developments that besides EMR efficiency also increase the capital efficiency and labour productivity are likely to cause 'backfire effects', i.e. ultimately increasing EMR demand.[34]

There is yet another, more complicated aspect of Jevons' paradox.[35] Even if higher labour productivity can make workers redundant, it also increases the remaining workers' salaries. This creates new demands and new employment opportunities. Those that are made redundant, in turn, are mostly productive in some other trade. Even if we see a lot of unemployment globally, one must admit that the enormous gains in productivity have not resulted in widespread or mass unemployment. To some extent, workers have reduced their work hours, but certainly not at all in parity with the increase in labour productivity. Therefore, despite all efficiency improvements, our society has significantly reduced neither the number of hours worked nor the resources used, not in total and not per capita. Rather, efficiency gains have fuelled increased consumption. Against this background, Foster, Clark and York point out that 'An economic system devoted to profits, accumulation, and economic expansion without end will tend to use any efficiency gains or cost reductions to expand the overall scale of production ... Conservation in the aggregate is impossible for capitalism, however much the output/input ratio may be increased in the engineering of a given product. This is because all savings tend to spur further capital formation ...'[36]

Rebound effects have been poorly analysed so far, with some estimates limited to the financial rebound effects. The latter alone are estimated to neutralize up to half of the total EMR efficiency gains.[37] Empirical information on material and cross-factor rebound effects is not yet available. Against this background, it will be simplistic to assume that EMR efficiency gains can play the main role in reducing GHG intensity. The key dilemma is that efficiency and productivity gains tend to boost economic growth, thus ushering in more physical consumption. This is one of the key reasons that call into question the effectiveness of the 'efficiency revolution' as a key element in the decoupling strategy at macroeconomic and global level.

Theoretically, some rebound effects could be neutralized by eco-taxes. However, such taxes (being increased in line with higher EMR efficiency) would have to be designed in a way that does not remove the incentive for efficiency innovation and would also have to be coordinated internationally. Setting absolute EMR consumption limits would be more promising, for instance in the context of caps for emission/pollution trading schemes. However, almost all of such trading schemes on carbon-emission reductions have not been very successful so far – the virtual collapse of the EU Emissions Trading Scheme in recent years is a case in point.[38] One should also not overlook the equality challenges of emission trading schemes and the fact that there is no link between the value of the service in a free market and the total cost for society. What is more, even the smartest-designed carbon offset trading scheme cannot overcome the constraints set by the above-mentioned limits of the maths of decarbonization – as stressed by Pielke, carbon 'markets cannot make the impossible possible'.[39]

Linear thinking and horizontal shifting

There is also a tendency for too much linear thinking and approaches to enhancing EMR efficiency, often resulting in an outcome that only shifts the problem. Some of the technical advances in EMR efficiency gains, for instance, rely on material that is either scarce or very energy intensive to produce or difficult to re-use, recycle or safely dispose of. According to Bleischwitz *et al.*, 'the upswing for eco-industries in the North may have a dark side in the South: resource-rich countries being moved into rapid extraction paths exceeding the eco-systems and socio-economic institutions of those regions and fuelling civil wars with resource rents'.[40] To use a concrete example, according to Schmidt-Bleek, 'the damages in nature caused by electrical vehicles are far bigger than the ecological savings obtained by lower emissions'.[41]

A considerable proportion of GHG intensity drops in developed countries has been achieved not by 'real physical savings', but by 'outsourcing' very EMR-intensive production to developing countries (almost a quarter of GHG emissions related to goods consumed in developed countries has been outsourced). A team of scientists at Oxford University, for instance, estimated that under a correct account, allowing for imports and exports, Britain's carbon footprint is nearly twice as high as the official figure (i.e. 21 t CO_2eq/person/year instead of 11). The share of CO_2 net imports to total carbon emissions of individual developed countries has recently ranged from about 15 per cent for Greece to almost 60 per cent for Switzerland.[42] Against this background, EMR and carbon-efficiency gains in developed countries need to be scrutinized with care and are often far less impressive than they appear at first sight.

Governance and market constraints

No doubt, the drastic and quick changes required for achieving the unprecedented absolute, permanent and global GHG emission reductions necessitate a clear political vision, a sound strategy and consistent implementation. Yet, in practice we remain far away from that. The climate is changing much faster than the international efforts to address it and the political rhetoric does not match the scale and the seriousness of the problem.[43] The international climate regime, though without alternative, is not providing a coherent and sufficiently effective approach yet.[44] According to Fatih Birol, the chief economist of IEA, 'potentially, we are already with our feet in water, reaching the level of our knees. Yet we make decisions and keep promising that our toes will remain dry.'[45]

Moreover, the current public debt and financial crisis in numerous Western countries is likely to complicate the much required structural and technological change that underpins 'green growth'. Governments in the crisis-stricken developed countries find themselves in a budgetary straightjacket, being obliged to drastically cut back public expenses and investment in the next few years, increasing deflationary and recessionary tendencies in the concerned economies. Most of these countries will be unable to launch big economic stimulus or restructuring packages as was done in the wake of the 2008–2009 crisis.[46]

Existing market structures are also complicating the 'green' transformation of economies. For instance, from a systemic point of view, a considerable part of renewable energy can (and should) be deployed in a local, decentralized way, avoiding much of the required investment in new grids, avoiding transmission losses and matching supply with demand. Yet, the market domination of a few energy companies leads to a preference being given to central, grid-based approaches that retain their market power (offshore wind parks, nuclear energy and project proposals for huge solar power generation facilities, for instance, in the Sahara are cases in point).

The externalization of environmental costs and massive subsidization of fossil-fuel-dependent industries and industrialization approaches have become a fundamental part of the capitalist market economy. More generally, there is a systemic problem of free riding by 'conventional producers' that take advantage of all kinds of 'perverse' subsidies and misguided incentives. Conversely, sustainable producers, who want to distinguish themselves, have to provide (and pay for) the evidence/certification that they are indeed meeting specific sustainability criteria (usually partly reflected in public or private sustainability standards).

Internalization is a cost-shifting process. As correctly emphasized by Giorgos Kallis, it is naïve to think that internalization is just a matter of policy and can be done without significant political and social change. Powerful interests will not sit back quietly, accept environmental caps and taxes and adapt to economic restructuring. On the contrary, they will use their political muscle. Valuation is subjective and thus also subject to power manipulations. Many activities that form the core of the current economy would have never come to be if they had had to pay for their externalities. Properly priced, civil aviation would have come to a halt, and there would probably not be many cars on the streets.[47]

Changing consumption patterns: a very hard nut to crack

The colossal decarbonization of the economy and human life required will only be achievable if current consumption patterns, methods and lifestyles are also subject to profound change. Yet, far-going and lasting changes will be very difficult to bring about. The globalization of unsustainable Western life styles and consumption trends, including the tendency towards higher animal protein content of food and the high mobility obtained through modern, but carbon-intensive transport systems, will be very hard nuts to crack on the consumption front. What is often underestimated by the advocates of 'green growth' is the fact that changing consumption and concomitant lifestyles need to be understood as a social issue, factoring in equity, not just as an environmental issue. Consumption patterns are unlikely to significantly change unless income distribution changes as well. No matter whether it concerns the purchase of goods with a certain longevity, organic food or the renting of well-insulated flats, consumers will only switch to them if they dispose of a proper income.

Only when employment, standards of living and social security are assured and the social rifts in society are kept in check will there be sufficient willingness among a majority of the population to support changes in lifestyle and an ecological policy that abandons the economic growth fetishism and the concomitant increase in income to drastically cut GHG emissions.

Systemic limits: economic growth fetishism

If the technological, governance and market constraints were not already enough, some systemic issues are also calling into question the 'green growth' hopes. Their essence is that the capitalist economic system cannot operate without growth, with the exception of short cyclical crises. 'Expand or perish' is an inexorable force and the constant accumulation of capital has inherent expansionist features, i.e. all economic agents are under competitive pressure to either undercut the costs of their competitors or conquer markets by creating new products. Increases in labour productivity and the permanent creation of new consumer needs generally lead to more, not less, physical production and consumption (i.e. the principal of capitalist accumulation).

This increase in growth can bring, but does not necessarily mean, additional benefits to society. Capitalist actors are not interested per se in growth of societal benefits, but in sales increases so that profits rise. As correctly put by Lockwood, 'growth is inherent in capitalism, which means you can't have capitalism without growth, and you can't have a capitalist steady state economy', as advocated by Herman Daly and others.[48] Rather, under capitalism, as nicely described by Green, 'growth is like a bicycle – if it stops, you fall off'.[49]

This is why virtually all policy makers and analysts fetishize economic growth, positing the means as the ultimate end, simply to ensure that there is sufficient ongoing income generation to plaster the social and ecological cracks of the capitalist system.[50]

'Green growth' naïvely postulates that technological progress and structural change would be sufficient to uncouple economic from GHG and resources/material/energy consumption growth, without questioning the existing asymmetrical market structures, related supply-chain governance, and economic driving forces. Dematerialized growth remains an illusion under the prevailing capitalist accumulation imperative. Without democratization of economies and changes in income distribution and culture related to consumption behaviour, the required fundamental transformation will remain illusory. Furthermore, it should not be overlooked that there are natural science and technical limits to growth, which cannot be circumvented by green technology alone. According to Tienhaara, 'an overemphasis on technology ... tends to displace solutions to problems that are simple, yet effective, and reinforces the belief that changes in lifestyle (or in ways of doing business) are not necessary in order to reduce humanity's impact on the planet'.[51]

The mammoth challenge: how can we extricate ourselves from the economic growth predicament?

What the above-developed analysis on the true (socio-) economics of climate change has brought to light is that a paradigm shift, rather than a green turn is required.

However, the, ongoing and collective ballooning of GHG emissions has squandered the opportunities for 'evolutionary change' afforded by the earlier 2°C carbon budget. Furthermore, let's face it, a spate of positive practical examples on GHG reduction opportunities and a large body of knowledge on the catastrophic consequences of likely temperature increases of 4–6°C and more will not be sufficient to alter the current GHG-intensive, GDP-growth-fetishizing development paradigm. As emphasized by Chandran Nair, it is also pointless to hope that the world's countries will find a universal notion of responsibility and then act on it. The rich nations will not opt to halt or reverse growth while the poor catch up, and, conversely, the developing world will not forgo growth while the rich countries try to figure out if they can maintain their current lifestyles in a sustainable way.[52]

The growth paradigm ignores the fact that in a bio-physically finite system, beyond a certain point, marginal growth makes mankind poorer, not richer, because the incremental income generated is overtaken by the incremental damage, thus reducing global wealth (if properly calculated). As put by Randers, once in overshoot, the sustainable carrying capacity of the planet can only be re-established in one way: down – 'either through managed decline, or through collapse – leaving it to the market or to nature to reduce human activity'.[53] It thus seems likely that recurrent crises in nature and the economy, which are sufficiently large, will be required to bring about the required change. The question is not whether the world economy – in particular the economy of rich Northern countries – has to shrink, but how this process will happen: in a chaotic or organized way and how it will end.[54] This is the very background against which Tim Jackson pointed out that 'the climate may just turn out to be the mother of all limits'.[55]

Admittedly, this is scary prophetism, to which there are alternative transformative measures under what was above termed 'managed decline of the current overshoot'. The question to be posed, however, is: how likely will they be harnessed under prevailing power relationships and do such transformations not imply very far-going system change?

Three elements seem to be imperative for the required transformation:

- Assurance of consistency so that the development of production and consumption methods and related technologies is in harmony with nature (in particular its reproductive capacity).
- Taming the growth paradigm by practising sufficiency, the collective use, rather than individual ownership, of products (through the so-called sharing economy),[56] a more local and social, rather than global, focus of the economy, and the realignment of the financial sector with the real (material) economy.
- A better distribution of income both within and between countries.[57] Essentially, ecological sustainability needs to go hand in hand with social justice and in this regard the question arises as to what (parts of the economy and social system) shall grow for that objective and what parts should rather shrink.[58]

To get there, a number of analysts favour an alternative regulation of capitalism (capitalism 3.0) that overcomes its neoliberal phase. An accumulation regime with a strong social-ecological thrust should lead to a boost of eco-technological solutions, reduce rates of profit, overcome the alienation of finance capital from the real economy and pay greater attention to a regional focus of supply chains.[59] For this objective, the following directions (or rather aspirations) for development are proposed:

- Giving up the extreme fixation on GDP as central indicator of welfare by differently valuing productive and reproductive performance, including at family level, voluntary activities and in the informal sector.[60]
- Checking the all-too-embracing trends of commercialization of human activities and nature services.

- Development of new work and living models that reduce the growth of labour productivity and cut the working time.
- Reorientation of companies on quality- and less on price-focused competition. Companies should find ways of extracting value from longer-lived goods, from services built around the performance of their goods rather than their sale, and from reselling and recycling their materials and components.[61]
- Development of a taxing regime that discourages striving towards higher physical production and profit and that improves income distribution.
- Stimulation of social and ecological innovation.
- Providing incentives to develop and maintain public goods and services.
- Regionalization of supply chains. Re-adaptation of economic activities to local and regional resources.
- Increasing the room for public and common property, including sharing property/economy elements.
- Reform of the monetary system so that money is only created and put into circulation by central banks, which would avoid the detachment of the monetary system from the real economy.
- Reform of the rules governing international trade and foreign direct investment so that regionalization of economic activity is not jeopardized and a race to the bottom for ecological and social standards is avoided.

The key question related to the proposed directions in the bullets above is: how can they really be translated into practice? Their implementation would challenge many well-established and vested power interests and positions, which are unlikely to give up their influence without resistance. Some issues are bordering on systemic changes, for which sufficient societal or political support needs to be created. Furthermore, some new 'post-growth' elements, such as the sharing economy, might run the risk of being undermined by vested interests of large companies.[62] In sum, under prevailing circumstances and the current political system, some of the flagged directions are only likely to be conceivable as a result of severe or frequently reoccurring crises and catastrophic situations[63] as well as related public pressure for change.

On a somewhat less pessimistic note, as emphasized by Randers, some recent projections on population and consumption growth might suggest a less dynamic development of the world economy and a resulting less dramatic global warming trend.[64] Randers, for instance, projects that world population might peak at roughly 8 billion people in 2040 and be in decline by 2050. Furthermore, the workforce in developed countries will decrease and rich countries will hardly grow on a per capita basis over the next 40 years. As a result, the world economy might not be four times as big in 2050 as it is today, but only two times. Moreover, although global GDP will double, global society may be forced to spend so much labour and capital on repair and adaptation that global consumption would level off before the middle of the century.[65] As a consequence, Randers projects CO_2 emissions that might limit temperature increase to 3–4 degrees by the end of the century.[66]

Some scientists pin a lot of hope on new technologies for directly removing CO_2 from the air. Most of these technologies are producing methane, methanol, plastic and foam material. Yet all these technologies are very energy-intensive and would require a considerable part of the globally generated renewable energy. What is more, the produced fuel through these technologies would be eventually consumed and regenerate a considerable part of the carbon emissions removed from the atmosphere before. Estimates suggest that about 2 billion tons of CO_2 could thus be removed from the atmosphere annually, i.e. equivalent to some 6 per cent of annual global CO_2 emissions. In other words, these new technologies will remain far from playing a pivotal role in mitigating climate change.[67]

To wind up, a strategy of quantitative sufficiency is in blatant contradiction with the rules of prevailing capitalism that are based on cut-throat competition. Only if capitalism succeeds in (i) creating value while reducing the quantitative throughput (i.e. making profit from dematerialized activities and regeneration of resources) below planetary boundaries (and the reproductive capacity of our environment), and (ii) improving the socio-economic conditions for the majority of mankind will it have a chance of survival in the future.

From a more practical point of view, in the light of the above analysis and existing time constraints for mitigation, it seems logical that the pendulum of international attention should swing more towards effective adaptation and enhancing resilience to climate change in the next few decades. Many of the adaptation measures can be combined with mitigation. One should, however, not lose sight of the fact that a not unimportant part of the much-required adaption measures, such as the protection of coastal zones, river banks or adaptation in the building sector, is boosting economic activity and thus also GHG emissions. Yet, successful adaptation and enhanced resilience can effectively prevent and/or reduce damage, but it can most importantly protect and save human life. One needs to remember that the seriousness and scale of the forthcoming climate change challenge is new to humankind, but not to our planet and its wildlife; the species that have survived climate extremes are those that have proved to be the best adapted and the most resilient.

CHAPTER 2

What is the 'green' in 'green growth'?

Larry Lohmann

The term 'green growth', like the phrase 'sustainable development', always sounds a bit defensive. It's as if its users were saying, 'Sure, most people expect growth *not* to be green – but in fact it can be!' Yet mingled with that defensiveness is grandiosity: 'We now have the power to break altogether the links between capital accumulation and degradation of the conditions of human existence that have marked the last half millennium.'

Proposals for green growth ambitiously seek to engage at least three crises at once. First, they promise to respond to economic crisis by developing new environmental assets, rentable properties and repair projects that, it is asserted, will someday be objects for profitable investment. This investment, it is suggested, will address ecological crises ranging from climate change and water shortages to biodiversity depletion and deforestation in depoliticized ways that help free business from constraints that would otherwise be imposed on it by environmental movements, planners or state regulators. Finally, green growth proposals claim to be able to relieve the state of much of the increasing expense of environmental protection.

Can this pompous, implausible triple promise be fulfilled? There are reasons for scepticism on all three fronts, but this chapter will focus largely on the claim that green growth can address ecological crises. It will argue that, in practice, green growth is not about solving ecological crises but rather reinterpreting them, creating new opportunities to take business advantage of them, and diffusing responsibility for them. It is not about forging a benign kind of growth, but about creating a new type of 'green' – new types of 'nature'. These new natures, while distinctive, turn out to feature much the same sort of contradictions and unsustainabilities as do older natures that have historically grown up with and helped to constitute capital. Various aspects of their construction are being and will continue to be resisted by those whose lives and livelihoods involve defending commons.

The chapter unfolds in five parts. The first section introduces the idea that there are distinct historical natures associated with various eras of capital accumulation. A second section elaborates how these constantly contested natures came to be constituted as 'external' to a society that represents, exploits and conserves them. A third suggests that placing the 'green' of 'green growth' in this tradition can help to explain both its special features and its continuity with previous capitalist natures. A fourth part sketches how the new 'green' might be seen as responding to capitalist crises. A final part reiterates the inevitability of the contradictions of and resistances to the new 'green' in the course of drawing together a few conclusions.

Some prehistory

For over two centuries, poets, memorialists, historians, sociologists, technologists and political theorists have stressed that to create new kinds of human being – wage workers – is also to create new kinds of nonhuman 'nature', and that attempts to convert commons into anti-commons always involve drives to convert commoners into anti-commoners. When commons are enclosed, relationships among humans and nonhumans that involve, say, subsistence cropping, gathering practices, seasonal and solar rhythms, feudal obligations, communal constraints and collaboration practices, or human identification with water sources tend to come under pressure from meshes of other relationships including the wage relation, dependence on food markets for subsistence, private property relations, discipline of workers via industrial machines linked to networks of extraction of coal and oil, and so forth.[1] Like most relationships, the new connections and processes involved in enclosure and the exploitation of wage labour are beset by instabilities and contradictions. In Karl Marx's view, they worked only by 'simultaneously undermining the original sources of all wealth – the soil and the worker'.[2]

Recently, Jason W. Moore, following in the footsteps of feminist theorists, has expanded and refined Marx's picture. Moore argues that every increase in the productivity of paid labour – which, together with growth in the mass of working consumers, has been especially central to the expansion of capital since the Industrial Revolution – is made possible only by a proportionately greater appropriation of the unpaid work of both nonhumans and humans, extracted from 'frontiers of uncapitalized natures' which lie 'outside the circuit of capital but within reach of capitalist power'.[3] Every small step in productivity improvement, Moore argues, requires a great leap in the appropriability of what he calls the 'Four Cheaps' (labour power, food, energy, raw materials). For example, impressive increases in the productivity of pulp and paper workers culminating in the operations of today's giant, hugely capital-intensive pulp mills and their adjoining capital-intensive tree plantations have become possible only through the progressive theft or enslavement of vast areas of (often originally forested) land and soil fertility, the low-cost extraction of ores and fossil fuels from ever-wider territories to make and run the machines, and the 'free gift' of the supportive work of workers' families, especially women.

Such appropriations – and subsequent capitalizations – are not achieved by a single, historically invariant form of violence. They become possible only through changes in human and nonhuman relationships. These relationships appear partly in the emergence of contested 'natures' that become more detachable, more measurable, readable, standardizable, combinable and mobile, as befits their partial or intermittent transformation, via new entanglements and processes, into bearers of value that can circulate in capitalist exchange. Although the new connections are often referred to with shorthands such as 'quantification', 'abstraction', 'fragmentation', 'monetization' or 'alienation', such labels are clumsy synechdoches that foreshorten much of the conflict-ridden politics involved by telescoping changes in large complexes of relationships into a few, often highly-mystified, 'intellectual' zones of the process. In reality, the quantifiable 'unit' so critical to capital accumulation, as George Henderson emphasizes, 'is neither unit nor thing as such, but a highly volatile set of social relations and processes'.[4] It is those processes in their entirety that must be appreciated if the contradictions inherent in the restricted types of quantification and abstraction specific to capital's natures are to be grasped. A 'critique of quantification' gets no closer to the deeper contradictions involved in capital's appropriations than a 'critique of violence' would. If, as Moore suggests, today's class struggles increasingly revolve around reproduction – the 'hidden abodes' on which production relies – then they are less about the 'monetization of nature' or the 'quantification of nature' than about the constitution of nature.[5]

For example, the early European wood-pulp industry (like some frontier wood-pulp industries today) used surveying techniques as well as developments in navigation, roadbuilding and so forth not as applications of academic theory to an invariant nature, but as an integral part of a complicated process of wresting raw materials from forests that, still earlier, had been co-created through relationships linking trees, soils, microorganisms, various nonindustrial agrarian, trading or hunting and gathering communities and so on. By the same token, most of today's advanced pulp mills feed on 'fibre resources' that are harvested from regimented tree plantations of a type that could only have been fashioned through modern forestry techniques, agrochemicals based on oil extraction, contemporary property law, the use of state power to apply that law to the benefit of capital, internal combustion engines, cloning techniques, harvesting machinery, pulping devices, and the appropriation and accumulation of the intellectual commons of forest scientists – that is, again through a set of complex relationships among human beings, trees, territories and soils, as well as the undermining of other relationships. Neither of these 'natures' – the exploitable forests, the high-tech plantations – was a passive substrate related to a distinct 'social' entity called 'capital' merely through a primitive relationship of 'violence' or 'extraction'. Nor were they pre-existing objects whose appropriation came about only at the point at which they happened to be measured or exchanged for money. Nor were they imaginary objects created by a reductionist 'politics of knowledge' involving numbers and calculations, nor a sort of 'superstructure' built on a separate base of purely 'economic' relations. Rather, they helped constitute those relations. Both the exploitable forests and the high-tech plantations formed part of capital itself, insofar as the innovations entwined with the existence of each were integral both to the development of wage labour and to increases in its productivity.

On Moore's view, it is by finding revolutionary ways to 'appropriate new streams of unpaid energy/work' and deliver them cheaply into the 'circuit of capital as a whole' that capital overcomes periodic productivity crises.[6] '[N]ot only does capitalism *have* frontiers; it *is* a frontier civilization.'[7] These frontiers – where 'a small amount of capital [can] appropriate a very large basket of nature's gifts: cheap forests, fertile soil, workers unable to offer effective resistance, and so forth'[8] – are not pre-existing givens, but are continuously constructed just as labour power is constructed. Thus, in early phases of capital accumulation, colonial-zone 'cheap natures' were identified, codified, rationalized and organized with the help of new shipbuilding technologies and cartographic techniques propelled in part by – for example – the Renaissance reinvention of linear perspective as well as other representationalist technologies that in certain ways make territories quickly legible from afar to imperialistic communities. In this way, capital could collect windfalls from, for example, the rich *massapé* soils of seventeenth-century Brazil's sugar cane lands, or the work of the families of millions of forced labourers at the Potosi silver mines, or of the African families whose children were impressed into American plantation labour. Later windfalls, in the form of cheap food for manufacturing labour, arrived, via a world market, from the fertile prairies and grasslands of settler frontiers such as those of North America, and, still later, from new 'petro-farmed' lands of the Green Revolution made possible by state subsidies for violence in the oil-bearing territories of the Middle East.[9]

In the nineteenth century, the steam engine and the science of thermodynamics became frontier techniques for turning coal from a rock into a 'fossil fuel' and freely appropriating the 'work' of past ages of plant life, vastly boosting the productivity of factory labour and agriculture alike. Indeed, energy itself presents another good example of the seemingly more 'abstract', 'external' natures whose construction has always formed part of the evolution of capital. The frontiers supplying the cheap energy so crucial to economic growth have never just been 'out there', but have always been actively 'made'. Before nineteenth-century thermodynamics – which came out of the development of fossil-fuelled steam engines and electric motors and batteries – nobody talked about energy at all in its current sense. People talked about horses, fire, trade winds, lightning, the ripening of wheat and so forth. Each was connected less with a common 'energy' than with ploughing, cooking, sailing, eating and so on, with all the limits to interchangeability and accumulation that the existence of such disparate meshes of relationships imply. In some contexts, the actions and beings involved were even seen as having individual personalities, dignities or rights. By about 1870, however, 'energy' had become part of the currency of 'nature'. The commensurability of heat, kinetic energy, electricity, magnetism and chemical energy had been cemented not just in the discourse of physicists, but also in the materiality of everyday life, in the conversion engines, factory floors, wires, pipes, travels and relationships linking goods, metals, and peoples and their territories, routines and governments across the world. And it was only through the new relationships constituting the 'nature' of energy – combined with the appropriation of slave or cheap plantation and mining labour across the globe – that such phenomena as the enormous nineteenth-century profitability increases in Britain's textile industry became possible.

The rise of the new 'nature' of thermodynamic energy represented not just a transformation of the landscapes of workshops, cities, coal-bearing hills and human habits of movement and interaction, but also a metamorphosis of fields and forests at great distances from extraction or industrial sites. As historian Stephen J. Pyne has documented in a series of books, European elites had long opposed open-air, vernacular fire – such as that used in specific regimes by swidden farmers to restore their fields and pastures or by forest dwellers to encourage preferred tree species and the growth of forest mosaics attractive to game animals – as threatening to fixed property as well as 'unproductive' or 'unimproving' in a capitalist sense.[10] The thermodynamic energy/fossil-fuel complex gave this prejudice new muscle by shunting more fire out of fields and forests and into the combustion chamber. As wood fuel became less significant for urban dwellers and 'scientific' nature conservation programmes gained ground, uniform strictures on wildfire turned territories hitherto packed with species dependent on place-specific rhythms of anthropogenic burns for their germination or growth into different sorts of 'nature' entirely. At the same time, 'high-productivity' agricultural regimes – such as the Peruvian guano- or Chilean saltpetre-dependent European farms of the nineteenth century or the Green Revolution fields of the twentieth – replaced the nutrient pulses provided by periodic burning with potent, exotic inputs imported from the past and over great distances. One outcome was an unsustainable compulsion toward a global Euclidification and externalization of agricultural space, an attempt to 'rise above, as it were, local soils, local landscape, local labor, local implements, and local weather'.[11] This shift reinforced, from an oblique angle, the earlier Mercatorian attempt to reformat the world as a geometric, uniform space friendly to centralized surveillance, long-distance trade, large-scale extraction and huge transfers of labour, money and other 'units' from one place to another – materialized, as always, in the steel, concrete, fibre, ports, charts and international treaties of global 'infrastructure'. Again, all such changes inhered in relationships linking humans and nonhumans alike – as, for example, when humans working together to practise careful, periodic agricultural or forest burns changed into humans working together to dig firebreaks or struggle against the explosive, massively destructive fires that came with the new, unprecedented build-ups of tinder on the forest floor.

'Externalizing' nature

One aspect of the new relationships was that they made it easier to lump nonhumans (and some sets of humans) together as an omnibus set of beings 'external' to society. This becomes most obvious in dualistic colonial and industrial practices of instituting a nature that is, roughly speaking, divided between resource or commodity on the one hand and 'wild' on the other – that is, between (1) titled raw material to be carried over the border of 'society' to be processed or 'improved' and (2) 'protected area' supposedly quarantined from human beings (with the exception of scientific and technical specialists and caretakers professionally licensed to interpret communications from across the new nature/society boundary). Such dualisms often wound up articulated in property law and other writings of intellectuals. T. R. Malthus, for example, worked to depoliticize the struggles of his own day over the constitution of nature by refining a picture of scarcity as a fixed, eternal condition of existence, positing a theoretical land eternally menaced by equally theoretical, uncontrollably breeding poor humans. Such so-called 'discursive' moves could in fact never be easily separated from material acts. The enclosure of commons broke subsistence relationships linking millions of human beings with their land, crops and animals, replacing them with longer-distance connections involving food markets. To a considerable extent, agriculture was depopulated and given over to the mechanized provisioning of distant, urban-centred labour forces with food made 'cheap' partly by successive seizures of underground carbon reserves. Forest reserves and national parks partially excluding indigenous peoples from land and forests became what Benedict Anderson calls a 'quotidian universal' with which every reputable 'nation' had to be equipped.[12] Such 'externalized' natures, moreover, were not new to the eighteenth or nineteenth centuries, but had been appearing in some fundamental (and always conflict-afflicted) forms at least since the time of the emergence of what Marx called abstract labour three or four centuries earlier.

One example is space treated as a neutral backdrop for far-flung sets of human activities detachable from it. Renaissance perspective's lone centralized observer stationed 'outside' a scene rubs up against not only the roving medieval artist who, mingling with the crowds, paints buildings or tables from several intimate vantage points[13] or the medieval king who 'surveys' his realm only through a pair of horse's ears[14] but also the contemporary Palikur of the Brazilian Amazon who take into account the perspectives of objects seen as well as that of their human viewers.[15] Sixteenth-century surveys of English landed estates, as well as the seventeenth-century land and population survey of Ireland carried out by William Petty (with people appearing as detachable units in a homogeneous, quantifiable space), controversially privileged the emerging point of view of landowners, conquerors, the state and investors trying to stand above and outside meshes of relationships constituting spaces that were being profitably redefined by hedges and fences,[16] land titling, new policing and military routines, and maps on the walls of manor houses or colonial administration buildings.[17] Authors of maps measured land not by how much ground a pair of oxen could plough in a day but by chains and triangulation, in a process that is better described as the supplementation of one set of political relationships with another than simply as 'abstraction'. Many of the colonized, thanks to the work of printing presses, were soon themselves pitching in to co-produce the new space as part of a dynamic that was both supplanting dynastic realms in favour of nation states and, as Neil Smith notes, playing a key role in the 'evolution and survival of capital'.[18] Throughout, the new space was all about power. It did not rise to relative prominence because a few isolated geniuses decided to throw off encrusted bias and face the physical world as it 'really is', but through intensive alliance-building involving what Bruno Latour calls theatres of persuasion, in which far-flung inscriptions and visualizations of all kinds were assembled in a single framework and technologies built for comparing and manipulating them.[19] Today, making 'external' space continues to be hard work and intensive struggle, a matter of forcefully articulating or clashing together new relationships with old.[20]

The same is true of the new time that historians would later misleadingly characterize as having become '"isolated" as a pure form, exterior to life'.[21] Just as Renaissance perspective contributed to the construction of a space whose shape was not determined by the buildings, human figures or interactions that it contained, so polyphonic music helped to construct, between 900 and 1200, a quantifiable, graphable time that existed outside the contour of any particular religious chant.[22] The emergence of church and city clocks and then – centuries later – railway station clocks synchronized into showing the 'same time' across entire nations helped develop further a temporality partly disentangled from coordination routines specific to particular places.[23] It was through parallel processes that, in the nineteenth century, energy came to seem external to the embodied work of, say, family cooks or dynamo engineers,[24] and in the twenty-first, a generalized, exchangeable risk became increasingly disentangled from the specific antics of, say, traders, currencies or tectonic plates.[25]

Each new 'external' nature, moreover, helped externalize others. The struggle of apologists of land surveying was also a struggle towards a conception of property as an 'absolute right' unconditional on the 'owner's performance of any social function',[26] contributing towards efforts to make real an emerging ruling class ideal according to which a Cartesian 'mind' could do anything it wanted with a passive, externalized, predictable and controllable 'body'. In similar ways, the scientific work that today makes possible the 'alienation, individuation and abstraction involved in constructing the discrete "thingness" of genes and organisms' functions not only to help render these 'bits' mutually equivalent and exchangeable, but also, as Scott Prudham shows, to make it seem that they have been 'invented' by individual experts and investors.[27] The accurate clocks and Mercator projections that facilitated trans-oceanic trading voyages indirectly made possible imperial botanical collections that in turn helped enact a divorce of germ 'raw material' – which could now more easily travel the world in an 'immutable' form – from established human and nonhuman contexts. The thermodynamic energy that arrived with fossil fuels, meanwhile, helped engender not only national or regional time – as Aldous Huxley noted long ago, 'in inventing the locomotive, Watt and Stevenson were part inventors of time'[28] – but also the idea of a progression linking shoulder harnesses, sailing ships and nuclear power plants in a single master timeline of 'energy use',[29] as well as the synergy apparent today between a 'background' consisting of fixed, large-scale infrastructure and masses of rapidly circulating 'foreground' units of labour, commodities, machines, tools and so forth.[30] As Peter Galison shows, the tricky problems of defining simultaneity (time A = time B) at a distance in the expansive technopolitical contexts of late nineteenth-century capitalism stimulated the development of the still newer temporality described in Einstein's 1905 Special Theory of Relativity. Relativity was in turn instantiated in, for example, today's Global Positioning Systems, which have further 'externalized' space to the point where drivers can no longer necessarily answer the question 'how did you get here?' in terms of narratives involving vernacular landmarks.[31] And when, over the twentieth century, economics assumed the role of delineating the 'nature' of human societies and of being a 'container' for area studies and other social sciences, a fresh impetus was given to the old, constantly contested tendency towards treating land as what Joel Wainwright and Trevor Barnes call 'economic space' – geometrically mapped plots of land under single owners.[32]

Resistance-tempered attempts to 'externalize' a discrete nature (including human nature) form a pair with the conflict-ridden processes, analysed by Marxists, through which the products of labour come to seem 'external' to the worker. Both are closely linked to the crafting of exchange- and accumulation-friendly equivalences, which in turn are regularly tied to violence.[33] Just as the equivalences implied by the wage relation are, in a sense, devices expressing the 'freeing' of labour as well as the elision of resistance to appropriation and to damage to human organisms and relationships, contributing to a framework making it possible for bosses and workers to 'call it quits' with each month's paycheck,[34] so too the equivalences embodied in the successive new natures of the era of capital are devices that express the exclusion of certain entanglements and responsibilities in favour of others. For example, the equivalences between points or areas in coordinate space (when the proper variables have been entered) are expressions of relationships that help make it possible for partners in great numbers of commercial land transactions to 'call it quits' and move on quickly to the next transactions and their obligations, while other shapers of the land find certain of their relationships with and obligations to it symbolically excluded from its future. The equivalences formatted by turbines and internal combustion engines and expressed in the First Law of Thermodynamics facilitate new global motions and disciplines (for example, as coal and oil are exchanged with each other and transformed into heat, heat transformed into mechanical energy, and mechanical energy transformed into electricity in an externalized 'energy economy') while tending to interfere with other motions and disciplines that many peoples worldwide maintain between distinct 'little energies' and their ways of life. The convenient word-to-word, phrase-to-phrase or belief-to-belief equivalences solidified through colonial practice and professional interpretation and dictionaries meanwhile facilitate a class of rapid interactions that can be quickly 'closed off' at the expense of the embrace of what the logician W. v. O. Quine called the indeterminacy of translation,[35] or what the anthropologist Eduardo Viveiros de Castro terms the 'controlled equivocation' that characterizes longer, differently entangled, more democratic linguistic and inter-linguistic interactions,[36] encouraging a conception of meaning, belief and language itself as 'external'.[37] The new equivalences associated with an aggregatable 'uncertainty' made it possible, during the era of accelerated securitization beginning in the last decades of the twentieth century, for banks to sever relationships with borrowers that they had had to pursue under a previous 'originate and hold' model of lending, and, increasingly, regard risk as 'external' to such relationships. In short, the so-called 'abstract labour' that represents a business's ability to transform, appropriate and store up human subsistence and flourishing activity as an income stream or asset develops to its maximum extent in concert with the evolution of so-called 'abstract natures' that can be symbolized or 'notated' partly by panoplies of new equivalences.

Today's all-encompassing 'environment' – a pre-existing 'container' to be filled by various societies[38] – acquires political force where it becomes common sense to see mapping techniques and clocks as measuring objects and durations in units of a pre-existing 'background' space and time; thermometers and voltmeters as registering units of an eternal, 'external', homogeneous energy; and dictionaries as recording equivalences that were already present among the 'meanings' that made up one or more languages, conceived as infrastructural 'conceptual schemes' standing above their speakers and their traffic of beliefs and desires. When time becomes a container for history and space a container for place, nature becomes a container for cultures, civilization a layer placed on top of a primeval bestiality, and humanity an organism that leaves 'ecological footprints', tries to hog the earth's 'net photosynthetic product' all for itself, and needs to pay more attention to 'energy return on investment'. Intellectuals start to feel impatient with resistant souls who object to the idea that modern European maps' geometric space constitutes a neutral matrix equally compatible with all human practices. If a container is distinct from the things it contains, how could it possibly disrupt, conflict with, or take anything away from any of them? As long ago as the mid-sixteenth century, apologists for land surveying such as Robert Recorde were protesting, against sceptical 'Tennauntes' of landed estates, that geometry 'hath no man opprest' since it 'measure[s] all truely,/ And yelde[s] the full right to everye man justely'.[39] Today, well-meaning geographers may find themselves adopting a similar attitude toward indigenous peoples who are wary of using European mapping to defend their territories. By the same token, intellectuals accustomed to the world of policy planning and physics classrooms are likely to find irritatingly paradoxical the idea that the energy of thermodynamics, which seems a neutral way of conceptualizing and 'containing' or subsuming all of the vernacular 'energies' of subsistence, might actually be in conflict with them. They may not appreciate, for example, that the 'little energy' of kitchen firewood in a village in Southeast Asia – which may be entangled with the forest commons from which it is gathered and the civil custom of not using more wood to boil rice than is strictly necessary – cannot be maintained when that commons is treated as an obstacle to extracting the 'big energy' of thermodynamics from dams, coal mines or biomass pellets to feed an economic growth conceived of as unlimited.

Intellectuals seeking a critical understanding of the prehistory of green growth need to resist the invisibilization of the everyday struggles by which the 'externality' and quantifiability of nature are achieved. Effective alliance-building requires reminders of the practical and everyday ways in which commoners constantly ignore or contest this externality[40] – as well as the ways in which capital itself depends, in a contradictory and conflicted way, on the less-externalized natures of commons. Centuries-long struggles refusing capitalist work have always relied on the defence and development of subsistence commons, as have movements resisting dispossession by infrastructure or resource-development projects. Various contemporary Andean and Amazonian conceptions often decline to countenance a notion of nature as a nonhuman foundation over which society is draped. And while the ideal-type capitalist logic explored by Marx involves perpetual, competition-driven attempts to dynamite material 'roadblocks' along capital's magical route from investment to payoff, an inevitable 'revenge of the finite'[41] highlights capital's own ultimate dependencies on natures that cannot be conceived of as 'external'. The vision of unending production based on the machine always comes up against what Marx called the 'weak bodies and strong wills of its human assistants'.[42] Via ecological crises, attempts to disentangle land, water and work from commons relationships in order to re-entangle them in commodity circuits are always brought up short at a certain point, necessitating moments of re-re-entanglement. Via financial crashes, even interest-bearing money periodically 'discovers its intimate ties to the finite world of use-values'.[43] Many fundamental ties can never be broken at all. Where would capital be unless people on their way to work disregarded the geometric space that is so conducive to transoceanic trade and speedy DHL deliveries and obviated calculation by simply following their fleshly noses past a succession of familiar landmarks and vernacular obligations?[44] How could labourers be induced to surrender a surplus at all unless they operated largely in a homely, often ludic workspace of 'making out', 'baseline communism', pattern recognition, procedural rationality, foot-dragging, and the commons of jokes and daily lampoons of their bosses' quality-assessment schemes?[45] What would capital do on the coast of China or Viet Nam in the twenty-first century if there did not exist commons regimes in the interior from which workers could be cheaply drawn and which provided continuing partial backup for a reserve labour army? How could the Black-Scholes-Merton formula for option pricing ever have been effective without traders' craft knowledge of markets?[46] How could translation go forward without the possibility of indeterminacy? How could the economic subject even be constituted in the absence of commons relationships?[47] If capital has an architecture, such divergent and *ad hoc* materials will always form its precariously-constituted bricks and mortar.

The new natures of green growth

How the history of natures is divided up depends on what the end in view is. If the end is to pin down more precisely what is distinctive about the nature named by the word 'green' in 'green growth', it may be useful to speak in a rough-and-ready way of successive natures of capital, each built on top of, or using materials from, previous natures. Imagine an old building constantly being added to, partly demolished, restored, rebuilt and modernized, featuring a never-final collection of new wings, storeys, turrets, odd gargoyles and high-tech fittings. Such a construction project could symbolize the stages, branchings and transformations in the co-construction of non-commons natures, with the substance of the whole dependent in innumerable ways on (as well as thwarted by) the encompassing, also ever-changing, natures of commons in which it is set, and out of whose materials it is built.

Preserved in the foundations and building material of the structure as it exists today is the nature that includes the time and space of the Renaissance and the early colonial era, exemplified by the emergence of wage labour, the printing press, and new accounting procedures; enclosure or appropriation of the work of the commons; increasing transmission of land and labour through capitalist circuits; and the tapping of ever more distant mines and plantations – all of which helped open new vistas for accumulation. Built on this base are new storeys consisting of the eighteenth- and nineteenth-century nature of 'resources' – of thermodynamics, scientific forestry, steamships and industrial factories, which vastly boosted wage labour's productivity, the numbers of worker-consumers to absorb its products, and the scale and speed of extraction, inaugurating the expansive universe of ownable, globally circulatable containers of value of the type traded today as Ford cars, Lenovo computers, barrels of West Texas Intermediate Crude Oil or tonnes of Bleached Eucalyptus Kraft Pulp. Developing in tandem with this 'resource' and 'commodity' nature are counterpart natures consisting of scientific conservation zones and ecosystems. Thus, early colonial efforts including botanical collections expand into more fully fledged movements promoting forest reserves, national parks and so forth, together with constructions of peasants and indigenous peoples as threats to nature. Ecological or ecosystem relations emerge partly as imperial projects or cybernetic accompaniments of technocratic rule.[48] And environmental regulation eventually becomes a commonplace of industrialized societies threatened by their own poisons. Indeed, so fully blended are these natures that a better name for the later versions of 'resource' nature would perhaps be 'resource/conservation zone/ecosystem' nature: a nature which, whatever its 'green' tinges, is not opposed to but rather an integral part of the expanding appropriation of the 'free gifts of nature'. Manifestations of this nature include the continuing 'bloody and fiery' evolution of protected or reserved areas as counterparts to production forests and industrial agriculture zones, the invention of recreation, and the emergence of explicitly environmental legislation.

Classical conservation zones and reserves tend to be defined more as areas where exploitation is partly or wholly absent than as areas where commons are present. Under colonialism, they were first and foremost the other side of the coin of extraction and plantation agriculture; under industrialism, a reversed mirror image of industrial resources and production. Similarly, the regulated nature enjoyed by the residents of a city in which lead levels in air are restricted to less than 0.15 $\mu g/m^3$ is defined in terms of external state controls on the excesses of an industrial system which is treated as a background and, not, say, in the terms indigenous peoples might use. This is also the way climate is treated today by the United Nations – as a nature to be regulated negatively, by making absent a certain proportion of industrial-era gas emissions. All this is merely to reiterate that the externalizing webs of relations defining protected areas or regulated natures – including labour relations – are different from those defining, say, commons, *pachamama* or indigenous territories. Now, new natures – the late twentieth- and early twenty-first-century natures of ecosystem services and green growth – are being bricolaged onto these older natures, facilitating the appropriation of the 'free gifts' of commons in novel ways. Like its predecessors, these new natures are defined in terms of absences rather than presences, of control rather than respect, maintaining the old industrial, anti-commons bias. Their innovations are twofold. First, yet more absences are created in order to help remediate the excesses of a pattern of accumulation that continues to be regarded as normal. Global pollution that does *not* happen; oil that is *not* exploited; degradation that *would* have taken place but did not, thanks to the intervention of experts and green capital: all these are fresh aspects of today's industrial natures. Second, even more crucially, all such absences, venerable and novel alike, are made tradable. Natural resource management, conservation reserves, ecosystems and conventionally regulated spaces of 'environmental quality' are mobilized for circulation. Nature as a disparate set of bounded spaces from which conventional capitalist extraction or production has been partly excluded is retooled as a 'producer' of tokens representing a conservation whose exact place of origin is generally no more relevant to traders than is, say, that of No. 2 Yellow Corn and no more relevant to consumers than that of Apple computers or Rolex watches. In principle indifferent to the ultimate sources of the standardized permits and credits that they deal in, ecosystem service traders and bankers instead pay heed to the certification provided by newly constructed state or private technocracies (as it were, the 'credit rating agencies' of nature trading). Nature becomes 'liquid', to use Bram Büscher useful phrase,[49] and its value becomes *de dicto* rather than *de re*.[50]

Unlike the conservation component of nineteenth- and twentieth-century industrial nature, which can be read crudely as mixed baskets of relatively uncommensurated ends (for example, individual forests here and there declared off limits to logging, hunting or gathering; Red Lists of endangered species; particular 'airsheds' relatively uncontaminated by lead; or unique landscapes unblighted by windmills), the new natures are zones of 'no net loss'[51] or 'net zero carbon'[52] in which such items are commensurated as means to a new end of an 'averaged', 'flexible' nature.[53] One example of such natures is the tokens of 'functional lift' traded in US water quality markets. These represent increases in 'environmental quality or function' generated by a piece of landscape, measured against what experts say it 'would have contributed without the abatement activities'.[54] Another example is the pollution allowances that circulate in the European Union Emissions Trading Scheme (EU ETS). These are fungible units of the aggregate carbon-cycling capacities of oceans, mountains, forests and anthills worldwide, and have been made exchangeable under certain circumstances with units of reduction of non-CO2 greenhouse gases such as CH4.

These units would not be possible if states had not first agreed to (and claimed the ability to measure) scarcity-creating 'caps' on emissions – an arrangement in which nature is construed as something belatedly walled off from capital for future use or for reproduction. Thus, the UN Framework Convention on Climate Change at first envisaged the earth's atmosphere as a potential zone of regulated, externalized molecules somewhat in the style of the environmental laws of the 1970s: atmospheric concentrations of greenhouse gases, it was proposed, were ultimately not to exceed such-and-such a level; those nations not doing their fair share would be punished; and so forth. The 1997 Kyoto Protocol's flexible mechanisms were then able to convert this agreement to reduce pollutants to a certain level into entitlements to emit them up to that level, and to make those entitlements tradable. Disparate activities that could be calculated to result in achievement of the relevant molecule levels were made interchangeable, transforming them into units of an abstract, aggregate 'mitigation' process without any single location, pedigree, time frame, technology or set of historical entailments. Title over this new abstract nature (in the sense of the right to charge rent on it) could then be awarded to the states of the industrialized global North.

This distinctive way of appropriating the 'free gifts' of commons can also be seen as a way of appropriating the generations of work embodied in them. Just as human subsistence and flourishing has been partially and problematically transformed into an asset stream for the past 500 years and more, so, too, in the prospective era of green growth, the diversely entangled activities of other denizens of earth are to be partially and problematically alienated into what Morgan Robertson calls 'an immense collection of services'. To take just one example, the 'hybrid' human–nonhuman concrete labours that, in innumerable constellations bringing together the efforts of local plant and animal species with those of human caretakers, specialists or police, had generated conventional bits of capitalist nature conservation in specific places are now, in effect, made to circulate in abstract form.[55] Of course, rejiggering and appropriating the activity of nonhuman life has always been a part of the 'resource' organization of nature that accompanies wage labour. When capital constitutes and extracts oil as a fossil fuel, the work of prehistoric organisms is seized and their relationships with contemporary territories and the people who dwell in them broken apart and reassembled in different forms in order to boost the productivity of paid human work and multiply outlets for manufactured goods. With the green economy, however, oil can also be constituted and appropriated by being set aside *in situ* as a quantifiable commodity-that-*would*-have-been-extracted-were-it-not-for-environmental-service-payments-and-the-initiatives-of-consultants-bureaucrats-and-industrial-firms. The old oil is part of a nature of fluid dynamics and pipelines, internal combustion engines, concession contracts, seismology and chain-link fencing, as well as of an older Newtonian space and time. This is a nature of pathways that channel finance into extraction; wage goods, state education and police into subsistence communities; and toxins into children's bodies – and a nature that blocks pathways linking soil nutrients with plant roots; marital discord with community mediation; subsistence activities with forest genesis; and shamans with the 'blood of the earth'. The new oil is part of a nature that consists of all this and more – of ecosystem relationships; biotic monitoring; channels through which three units of water pollution from nonpoint sources can be traded for one unit from a point source; emissions factor negotiations; and equations through which biological uncertainty and ignorance can be converted into measurable risk. This is a nature performed partly by carbon registry transactions, environmental economics, and financial transfers to the accounts of environmental consultants, brokers, and 'deception marketers' for their work in packaging and attesting to the value of ecosystem service contracts. Dissociating subsistence activities and nature genesis, it takes human activity and further bifurcates it into production and reproduction while parsing nonhuman activity into ecosystem services and unindividuated background. This is not, of course, the narrative that appears in environmental economics. Just as modern apologists for industrial capital saw value as created mainly through the initiative, sacrifice or organizing ability of owners and managers, not through the work of society, today's market environmentalists tend to view green value as shepherded into being by economists and other experts, not derived from the historical work of commoners and commons. Although apologists for ecosystem service markets often recognize the entitlement of indigenous peoples to wages for acting as caretakers of the new natures, they tend to be silent on the ways that the appropriation of and collection of rent from these natures amounts to the appropriation of the surplus work of generations of humans in interaction with their nonhuman surroundings.

The new natures are natures not only of CO_2, but also of 'CO_2 equivalents'; not only of species, but also of 'species equivalents'. Thus, according to the United Nations, climatic stability can be defended in the face of rising carbon dioxide emissions as long as a sufficient amount of other gases certified to have an equal 'Global Warming Potential' are claimed to have been reduced.[56] According to the UK government, forests can now be kept in a steady state of preservation when 10,000 ancient-forest trees are cut, as long as a million monoculture trees are planted in compensation.[57] In the US, a tradable unit of 'functional lift' refers not to improvements in the overall relationships a particular community enjoys with a patch of floodplain common pasture, nor even just to improvements in the biophysical properties of the soils in that pasture from the perspective of optimal local commercial production of milk, but only to such improvements insofar as they are made capable of being equated with various commodities in regional or national exchange. The nature of pollution changes as well. Fenceline communities whose children fall ill from the poisons discharged by a factory adjoining a schoolyard can today be told that the factory is, in effect, 'not polluting', because it has offset its pollution by buying emissions credits from elsewhere. While the nature that many such communities continue to try to defend is locatable in their own daily interactions, the nature associated with the new trade in ecosystem services, like risk in an age of derivatives, is located in a space less accessible to them – and often even to national states. In an analogue of what Marx called the drive to maximize relative surplus value, this nature is 'capitalized' or 'mechanized' as much as possible through computer-friendly quantitative formulas and techniques of segmentation into 'stacks' of ecosystem functions, for whose inevitable, multiplying shortcomings human and nonhuman workers in the environmental services industry are then compelled to compensate. In short, just as military protection costs were internalized by the Dutch business/state class of the seventeenth and eighteenth centuries, production costs brought within an economizing logic by the nineteenth-century British business class, and transaction costs internalized by the vertically integrating US business class during the twentieth century,[58] so too is the 'environmental governance' exemplified by nineteenth-century conservation or 1970s-era regulation now being economically rationalized, with environmental problems reframed as internalizable externalities, market failures or negative value.[59]

The technical, legal and scientific apparatuses through which the 'green' of green growth is being fashioned today are built on, and in some senses advance the complexity of, the cadastral surveys, Mercator projections, and thermodynamics that helped build the natures of earlier eras. Sprawling committees of scientists are needed to work hard to compromise on methods of calculating the relative

Global Warming Potentials of various greenhouse gases. Supercomputer-powered Global Circulation Models taking account of Himalayan weathering processes and the nitrogen fixation of bacteria in Norfolk are needed to help states decide how many entitlements to world carbon-cycling capacity are available to appropriate and hand out to private industries. Mass-produced real-time smokestack monitoring instruments developed first in the 1970s, together with the latest electronic networks of intercapitalist coordination, are indispensable to help keep track of how much of their rights to the new natures industries are actually making use of. Similarly, satellite imagery interpretation (an enormous advance over the aerial mapping and note-taking that, in the 1920s and 1930s, shaped the emerging colonial nature studied and managed by ecology),[60] while not consciously developed for the purpose,[61] now helps assemble 'environmental asset' portfolios reflecting the 'potential and realized economic values' of ecosystems and ecosystem services.[62] Troops of scientists are needed, too, to create and negotiate the units of an external nature which biodiversity is diversity *of*, and then to simplify them into quantifiable tokens that can circulate as freely as possible in the constrained, flat space and time of policy-making and markets 'without containing too much historical baggage'.[63] Hardly less challenging are the continual technical efforts needed to build the probabilistic modelling of 'natural' catastrophes – pioneered by engineers and planners starting in the 1960s – into a foundation for the disaster risk markets now promoted by Wall Street and the World Bank.[64]

The new natures and capitalist crisis

It is through the creation of the new, 'liquid' natures of green growth that hitherto uneconomic activities presented as ecological protection are to become worthy of capital investment and susceptible to mass production and the attentions of financial-sector 'quants'; and the state to be relieved of much the costs of reproducing a liveable environment. But what aspects of crisis, if any, might in fact be relieved by this innovation? How? And for how long?

These are vexed questions that will be debated for years to come, but some promising directions of inquiry can be suggested immediately. First, the new natures are clearly sources of innovative colonial rents benefiting both Northern states and Northern industry. Under the Kyoto Protocol, for example, industrialized countries are 'grandfathered' rights to collect rents on the earth's carbon-cycling capacity roughly in proportion to their prior use of it; Southern countries are allowed to continue using the capacity, but are not granted rights to it that they can trade. Under the EU ETS, European states in turn redistribute this new form of property *gratis* to their high-emitting industrial sectors, again approximately depending on the extent of their past greenhouse gas pollution.[65] The equivalent of hundreds of billions of dollars in rent income has subsequently quietly accrued to Europeans. Private owners of European fossil-fuelled power plants, for instance, have been permitted to charge electricity customers for the nominal value of their rights in the new global nature that their governments have given them for free, in spite of the fact that the nature in question is instantiated in Bangladesh as well as Belgium, Brazil as well as Britain. Assuming that rent is the capture of a share of the total surplus value extracted in the production process, the ultimate providers of the benefits generated by the creation and seizure of the new nature have been workers in general and the human and nonhuman inhabitants of the global South in particular.

Colonialist-style annexation is also exemplified by the process of constructing and trading offsets. Markets in ecosystem credits require vast imaginary tracts of service-providing counterfactual biota to be 'discovered', described and quantified by certified experts in order to provide the 'business as usual' baseline against which to calculate the service improvements brought about now or in the future by offset project investors, and thus to determine the value of the nature credits they own. Buyers and sellers of wetland or biodiversity offsets, for example, must be able to measure the degree to which service provider interventions (will) constitute an improvement over 'what would have happened otherwise'. But because there can be only one baseline, activities of non-investors (forest peoples, farmers, bureaucrats, mycorrhizae, muskrats and so forth) that affect the land must be treated as a deterministic background to the free initiatives of capital and its technocracy, which are allowed to be multiple and a matter of choice. This is essentially a rerun of the Lockean programme by which colonizers gain property rights by 'improving' land that, despite its ever-changing relationships with its indigenous inhabitants, is, like those unworthy inhabitants themselves, regarded as a static 'natural' background. A political stance historically bound up with colonialism, classism and racism is thus logically necessary to the operation of the offset markets central to the project of green growth. This politics has nonhuman as well as human embodiments. The view that nature is external to human beings and predictable in the progressive degradation it suffers at the hands of commoners tends to become a self-fulfilling prophecy insofar as it is deployed to privatize commons and denigrate common rights. Just as natural resource policy 'performs' people as potential 'overusers of nature' through resource seizures that unbalance the power relations that had formerly kept overuse in check, 'no net loss' policy, methodologically forced to conceptualize ordinary people as a deterministic force that would have destroyed a precisely calculable modicum of nature were it not for green market interventions, helps undermine commons norms in concrete ways.

Second, the new natures provide raw materials for the mass production of permits that cut costs to industry of complying with environmental regulation, thus indirectly defending even if not directly augmenting productivity. Conventionally-regulated natures emblematize a mixed regime in which states and even citizens have some power to restrict the freedom of investors to decide what and how much is produced, by whom and for whom, and can undercut profits in a way that is especially irksome during productivity crises. Figures such as the economist Ronald Coase helped devise a successor nature whose value would reappear in the form of price: the objective of ecosystem service markets, in the words of Pedro Moura-Costa, founder of the Bolsa Verde of Rio de Janeiro, is 'to transform environmental legislation into tradeable instruments'.[66] In no way does that imply a reduced role for the state, which is crucial in creating and maintaining the new tradable units of nature and in pushing through the transformation of law into price; it is merely that the state's own practices obey more closely a commodity logic. Just as, in industrialized countries, 'public services' such as health care and education had first to be won through labour struggles before they could be privatized and converted, in the neoliberal era, into standardized, deliverable, appropriable 'units' in an ongoing process that Ursula Huws terms 'secondary primitive accumulation',[67] so too the 'nature' associated with post-1970 environmental regulation – based on disciplines such as 'pollution control' and 'natural resource management' – had first to be co-created through popular pressure before it could be metamorphosed into marketable 'ecosystem services'. Today's neoliberal forms of 'capital levered on the state'[68] are thus not confined to railway or post office privatizations, public–private partnerships, lavish corporate subsidization programmes, and the privatization of national and international law,[69] but also include 'green growth'.

The regulatory relief that the new trade provided is related on the one hand to a renewed insistence on the externality of nature and on the other to a movement of capillary deresponsibilization of political actors throughout society, as pollution fines are converted into fees, offences become entitlements, and environmental violators are converted into environmental heroes through their sponsorship of the new natures. Participants in carbon markets, for example, track, manage and price greenhouse gases only as the purified molecules of chemistry, not as 'hybrid' social/natural categories divided between 'survival' and 'luxury' emissions, or commons and industrial emissions, or permissible and impermissible emissions. A further step in externalizing nature is taken when the fossil-fuelled history of anthropogenic climate change is erased by equating biotic and fossil origin CO_2, implying that, per molecule emitted, forest dwellers and industrial users of fossil fuels are equally responsible for global warming. As tens of thousands of scientists, experts, traders, bankers, lawyers, accountants, consultants and bureaucrats go to work setting fuel emission proxy factors, commenting on carbon project design documents, making submissions to the Clean Development Mechanism Executive Board, hedging investments, buying land, tallying molecules, balancing accounts, formulating schedules and criteria for payments for forest conservation certificates, establishing ownership and discovering prices, they each day produce a bit more political deresponsibilization in each of the offices and purportedly 'apolitical' bureaucracies in which they work, often insouciantly pre-empting any formal mandate for market extension handed down from the parties of the UN Framework Convention on Climate Change or the state.

The more that environmental concerns and skills are refigured into the terms of participation in markets for units of new environmental goods (whether as producer or consumer), the greater the extent to which environmental movements are diverted, hollowed out and replaced with newly-constituted and -certified expertise, and manoeuvred into alignment with investor interests.

Third, while units of the new natures may not yet be successful commodities in their own right, they are often attractive as a part of risk-sensitive investment packages that include more conventional assets such as oil, timber, water rights, hunting rights, or the infrastructure used in national, continental or intercontinental extraction and trade corridors. A carbon credit-generating REDD+ project, for instance, might, with the help of NGOs, be bundled into a mineral investment in order to sweeten it for the markets, or even directly facilitate its owner's access to mineral lands; wind farms set up by fossil-fuelled conglomerates partly to produce carbon credits can also serve the purpose of depriving potential renewable-energy competitors of control over land, subsidies and prices. Ecosystem service units can also pull their weight in a diversified portfolio by tapping subsidies from state nature conservation coffers. In the US, the private equity firms known as timber investment management organizations attempt to derive returns on the high conservation value forests they buy by fragmenting them into a wide range of assets derived from both new and old natures, including not only timber but also recreational leases, holiday home lots, carbon-cycling capacity and wetland damage mitigation. Other assets exploited include claims on public subsidies through tax reductions and conservation easements.[70] Indeed, one place where the continuity between historical and current capitalist natures becomes most evident is in the close synergy between extractivism and ecosystem service trading that has often been noted by grassroots environmental movements. An infrastructural 'nature space' transformed and expanded by the addition of ecosystem services fits well with the efforts of an increasingly powerful financial sector and the states with which it is allied to redefine virtually everything as a guaranteed asset stream.

In addition to their role in a redistributive or extractive politics of rent and finance, are the new natures also a source of system-wide surplus? That is, do markets in ecosystem services add to total value in circulation or merely siphon already-existing value off in the general direction of the owners of the new natures? Is there anything new about the 'growth' in 'green growth', or is it just the same old growth supplemented by more extensive green grabbing? It is true that little if any capital accumulation seems to be taking place in the new ecosystem services economy[71] despite considerable state investment in the infrastructure of commodity creation and the enthusiasm of theorists who nevertheless generally seem hard put to specify what the commodities are that they claim to be trading in.[72] However (and this is to suggest a fourth avenue for future inquiry), it should not simply be assumed that no new forms of surplus can be extracted from nonhuman/human activity once it has acquired the aspect of a new abstract nature in the way human subsistence and flourishing has in the past acquired the aspect of abstract labour. There is no space to pursue this difficult question in this chapter, but the anti-Cartesian perspective it adopts suggests the potential importance of troubling the hard and fast distinctions that Marxists usually make between rent and profit and between land and labour.

Endless resistance

The story of the green growth project, this chapter has suggested, is not a story of capital inexorably encroaching on an external, invariant nature until it either is overthrown or heroically 'greens' itself. Despite the geographic metaphor, the 'internalization of externalities' that defines green growth is not an action performed on an eternal, exogenous entity that persists intact through a completable operation, but rather constitutes a change in that object derived from the changes in the relationships that constitute it. This is why it is fatuous to enter into debates about whether new markets for nature conservation – or, for that matter, for health care, risk control or transport – can deliver the goods more 'efficiently' than the state or other agencies: it will not be the same nature conservation – or health care, risk control, or transport – that is delivered. Because the 'green growth' project of transforming environmental protection into mass-produced units circulating freely in a market is not accomplished by sticking price tags on unchanged objects, still less on unchanged objects that are somehow separate from labour and other human activity, its deeper contradictions cannot be traced to the action of sticking on those price tags – to the 'incorrectness' of the amounts shown on the tags, to the tags' inability to recognize the 'unmeasurability' of what they are attached to, to the tags' use of money as a 'yardstick', nor to the tags' 'reductionism'. Nor can the contradictions be resolved through new metrics, better experts, or a 'more holistic approach to valuation'. The processes through which capitalist natures are organized have always been contradictory, contested, thwarted and forever incompletable, and none more so than those associated with the project of green growth. Yet the forms of resistance that reflect the contradictions through which each nature evolves and in turn engenders new natures are specific to particular circumstances. Understanding the green growth programme means learning to recognize the opposition that is distinctive to it while not losing track of the continuity of that opposition with the longer history of battles against exploitation generally. It involves recognizing, for example, that, as in the English countryside of the sixteenth century, measurement itself is being contested: that like the unit of commodified labour, the units associated with the new nature (CO_2-equivalents, 'functional lift') are even in some sense the '*source* of the political'.[73]

Resistance to ecosystem services is often most powerful where the prior nature of 'natural resources' on which ecosystem services are based is also contested. Movements such as La Via Campesina, for example, are quick to grasp that the defence of commons against conversion into ecosystem services is continuous with the battle against older capitalist natures:

> [P]easant agriculture ... is not compatible with ... 'ecosystem services' or the notion of 'natural capital' ... This economic view of nature does not serve peasant acro-ecological practices but ... on the contrary undermine[s] the foundations ... [It] is a continuation of a project first begun with the Green Revolution in the early 1940's and continued through the 70's and 80's by the World Bank's poverty reduction projects and the corporate interests involved.[74]

If treating a forest as a stack of ecosystem services entails relationships that are at odds with those involved with treating it as a commons, that has a lot to do with the history from which ecosystem services has emerged. As ecosystem services, a forest can only be a 'forest-which-otherwise-would-have-been-destroyed' according to scientific and economic projections based on the assumption that it is a piece of 'external' nature in the vein of nineteenth- and twentieth-century industrialism.[75] Small wonder that production of ecosystem-service 'offsets' so often involves eviction and land-grabbing reminiscent of the era of forced establishment of protected areas in the nineteenth and twentieth centuries.[76] Small wonder, too, that many Latin American indigenous groups see as perfectly obvious the continuity between the scientific nature organized during early colonial times 500 years ago and the new nature beginning to feed today's green markets. Such groups are well placed to point out that it is a serious error to identify the development of purported nonextraction commodities with the defence of commons or indigenous territories: to assume, for instance, that movements to keep oil in the soil in the Ecuadorian Amazon are about 'caps' and 'biospheric limits'; that indigenous practices of *sumak kawsay* or *buen vivir* amount to green developmentalism or 'natural resource management'; that indigenous territories are instances of the abstract spaces invented by sixteenth-century European mapmakers; that *pachamama* is the externalized 'nature' of capitalism, whose rights, it is implied, can only be defended by humans considered to be outside of it; or that a rejuvenation of 1970s-style environmental regulation will provide the solution to ecological crisis.

The continuity of contradictions, of course, is visible in a great deal more than just the history of human protest. If it has always been a question of how human survival and flourishing can be transformed into an asset stream without being undermined, so too is it today a question of how ecosystem services can continue to be mobilized once they are no longer integrated with previous contexts of nonhuman and human interactions. Can a woodland retrofitted as a producer of carbon and a stack of other environmental services persist any better than a forest retooled as a producer of industrial fibre, a worker subjected to the extremes of pre-Fordist Taylorian time-and-motion discipline, or seeds frozen in a seed bank without the possibility of being outgrown? The increased alienation and appropriation that is the flip side of internalizing economic externalities (or making them 'visible' in an economic calculus) always throws up further economic externalities, which themselves have to be internalized, and so on *ad infinitum*. Economic internalization does not relieve, but rather accentuates, the contradictions involved in making nature external: internalization *is* externalization.[77]

Where nineteenth- and twentieth-century resource management has taken firmer hold, human resistance may in some ways be more difficult. In Norwegian fisheries, as Petter Holm points out, the struggle against the new trade in individual transferrable quotas (ITQs) has been handicapped by prior entrenchment of the 'cyborg fish' co-created by modern fisheries resource management – fish predictable in their behaviour, divisible into discrete units, private property-ready, and so forth:

> When the cyborg fish is already in place, the most violent acts of dispossession against coastal communities have already been undertaken [and] most of the organizational and institutional apparatus that could have served as power-basis for those who wanted to resist ITQs has already been squashed.[78]

The new kinds of abstraction associated with ecosystem services often blunt resistance by masking the very fact that appropriation is taking place. For example, it was partly because the global greenhouse gas-cycling capacity represented by the Kyoto Protocol's tradable tokens could not be identified with any specific parcel of land, ocean, forest or rock outcrops, nor any particular set of flowering plants, microorganisms or subduction processes, that relatively little outcry was raised when a form of ownership over them was handed out exclusively to wealthy countries. The fact that such annexations are generally accomplished not by military operations but through law – and in a way that prevents future countervailing actions by the state – can make opposition even more challenging. Yet even in the heartlands of the older capitalist natures, resistance is inevitable and obvious to anyone paying close attention. In 2014, for instance, a study done for the European Commission mooted equations that redefined pollution (e.g., one molecule of SO_2 = 4.45 molecules of NOx) in ways that, provided environmental laws were amended, would enable EU Member States to exceed ceilings for one pollutant in proportion to the reductions they made in the emissions of others below their ceilings;[79] the study had to be suppressed. Meanwhile, at many middle-class locations where experts are assisting in the construction of ecosystem services, a more genteel form of strife simmers among 'capitalists, scientists and regulators concerning value', the 'functional interdependence of ecosystems', and so forth.[80] As Morgan Robertson observes, 'in calling on ecosystem sciences to provide answers' to questions about how to unitize ecosystems, 'economists are sometimes met with information, sometimes with cacophony and sometimes with silence'.[81]

Although these various conflicts tend to be depicted as being about privatization, marketization, commercialization, monetization or reductionism, they are equally well described as being about the 'green' of 'green growth'. As Moore remarks, class conflict today is 'over value itself'; what Nancy Fraser calls the further 'hidden abodes' behind Marx's 'hidden abode' of production have become a, if not the, primary battlefield.[82] It is perhaps clearer now than it has been at any time since the early nineteenth century that labour struggles *are* environmental struggles, and vice versa. Strategic alliances contesting the 'green' of 'green growth' that bring together what may still seem divergent leftist, indigenous and peasant movements against neoliberalism and mainstream environmentalism will be among the important political forces based on and feeding that understanding.[83]

CHAPTER 3

The *how* and for *whom* of green governmentality

Adrian Parr

> [G]overning people is not a way to force people to do what the governor wants; it is always a versatile equilibrium, with complementarity and conflicts between techniques which assure coercion and processes through which the self is constructed or modified by himself.[1]

> Today, on the occasion of the 60th anniversary of the founding of the Republic of Korea, I want to put forward 'Low Carbon, Green Growth' as the core of the Republic's new vision ... Green technology will create numerous decent jobs to tackle the problem of growth without job creation. The renewable energy industry will create several times more jobs than existing industries. In the information age, the gap between the haves and have-nots has widened. On the contrary, the gap will narrow down in the age of green growth.[2]

This is a time when the outlook for environmental health and well-being is troubling and the culprit for many lies squarely with the economy.[3] For many the conundrum is how to introduce an environmentalist agenda into the machinations of a global capitalist economy without slowing growth. This is also a time of deep inequities in wealth, income, education, health and opportunity. When these two factors – social inequity and environmental harms – concomitantly become political issues, they present a seemingly untenable political reality especially for those on the Left who aspire to strengthen and increase social welfare programmes. Social services, so the party line goes, depend upon solid economic growth for funding and yet growth also causes the climate to change and environmental harms to proliferate.

The political problem becomes ostensibly more insurmountable with the realization that environmental and social injustices intersect.[4] That is, poor environmental health disproportionately affects marginalized sections of the population. The literature on environmental justice presents three political axes for analysis and critique.[5] First, representative politics has failed to fully represent the civic realm. Second, there are some serious policy omissions that need to be rectified in order to better protect the rights of all citizens and fairly distribute the costs and benefits of environmental goods and harms. Third, the law has not kept up with the times and needs to be modified and better implemented so as to prevent environmental injustices from occurring.

Organized in this way, the scaffolding of some environmental justice advocates falls into a liberal trap. 1) The institution of representative democracy needs to better integrate the interests of individual political actors. 2) Economic policy needs to use the tools of the free market and create a new market in environmental goods and services all the while incorporating environmental externalities into the price structure. 3) The legal apparatus needs to make offenders legally accountable by punishing irresponsible behaviour (remembering a corporation now enjoys the legal standing of personhood). Inclusive green growth neatly ties together all three strands of these solutions.

Using the principles of economic rationality to respond to environmental concerns, inclusive green growth advocates assume economic growth is politically neutral. In this chapter I will argue that the tripartite framework of inclusive green growth, which reconciles the struggle between the environment, social inequity and the economic sphere, masks the social contradictions this struggle once exposed. First, I will lean upon Thomas Piketty to show that economic growth is not necessarily redistributive in the way that inclusive green growth proponents assume.[6] Indeed, by leaving the premise and rate of economic growth unchallenged, theories and practices of inclusive green growth do not adequately confront the complex political landscape of inequity, the accumulation of private wealth/property, and the logic of competition upon which capitalist market mechanisms rest. Second, I will explore how inclusive green growth reproduces neoliberal governmentality, paying close attention to the constitutive effects of neoliberalism. In this regard, the ideational problem of how social relations and environmental politics become the means with which to acquire a competitive edge in a global marketplace and to produce resilient subjects is central to the machinations of what I call green governmentality.

Whom does government speak for?

Inclusive green growth refers to a low carbon model of efficient economic growth that uses a combination of economic and policy instruments to lower carbon emissions, foster investment in clean energy technologies, produce environmentally friendly commodities, grow the green job market, develop and institute green infrastructure, adopt integrated natural resource management, and invest in climate change mitigation strategies. All this while aspiring to improve human well-being and social equity.[7] The problem of environmental degradation is approached as an opportunity to transform the economy and unjust social relations. The theories and practices of inclusive green growth clearly attempt to bring the principle of economic growth into better balance with social and environmental justice concerns.[8] In this respect, the model has a great deal of potential in so far as it does not artificially separate economic, social and environmental variables. Rather it addresses all three in tandem.[9]

In 2012 the United Nations Economic and Social Commission for Asia and the Pacific (ESCAP), the Asian Development Bank (ADB), and the United Nations Development Program (UNDP) issued a report on *Green Growth, Resources, and Resilience*. The report advocates for adopting a model of economic growth that both minimizes the negative costs to the environment and maximizes social inclusiveness by working toward a 'future where all people have an opportunity for a better life'. It states that the 'global market for green goods and services is vast and growing fast', correlating competitive economic advantage with inclusive green growth.[10] The primary argument put forth in the report is: if a country is committed to instituting policies and strategies that can ease the environmental costs associated with meeting the demands for food, housing, transportation, water and energy, then that country would enjoy the economic opportunities that come from transforming a dirty energy-intensive resource-use economy to a low carbon-efficient one. Explicitly the authors argue this will result in more jobs, economic growth, and prosperity. More importantly, the report stresses the importance of aligning economic growth with the inclusive and accessible objectives of sustainable development.

Inclusive green growth presumes economic *growth* is an a priori social good. The assumption rests with the argument that each and every day the economy serves more and more people.[11] Namely, economic growth can be neatly aligned with a rise in living standards and a fall in poverty rates. In the words of World Bank Group President Jim Yong Kim:

> We live in a time of great contrasts, when fewer than 100 people control as much of the world's wealth as the poorest 3.5 billion combined. But we also live in a time when many developing countries have the strongest growth rates in the word, which each year helps millions of people lift themselves out of extreme poverty.[12]

The primary policy tools used to achieve economic growth in the service of an inclusive green agenda include: eco-tax reform, subsidies, green stimulus investments, investments in green infrastructure, eco-tourism schemes, improved natural resource management, socially inclusive development, and research and development that will address knowledge gaps. The suggested approach is integrative and systemic, using the principles of efficiency and maximizing market solutions. Unsurprisingly, proponents of inclusive green growth view one of the challenges to realizing significant efficiency gains as 'a lack of instruments to "monetize" the benefits of conservation and efficiency and to reward sustainable consumption'.[13] The solution to this is to introduce more innovative financing tools and to substantially increase investments in economic activities that improve natural capital. Emphasis is placed on the importance of public–private sector partnerships, whereby the private sector is viewed as an 'active partner of governments', in addition to the institutionalization of local knowledge and politics which has triggered a gamut of new political actors such as non-profit and non-governmental organizations, communities and religious groups entering the political frame of economic policy making.[14]

Despite ambitiously setting out to bring social, economic and environmental concerns into balance by adopting a multi-scalar approach to governance that institutionalizes local political actors, the inclusive green growth model continues to push the neoliberal idea that the role of government is to encourage economic efficiency and privatization.[15] Unsurprisingly, one of the primary strategies of green growth is the privatization of the commons. By putting a price on what are otherwise common pool resources such as water, forests and ecosystem services, the model puts its faith in market mechanisms to solve social and environmental issues without defusing the circuitry of structural violence driving social inequity and environmental degradation.

Environmental degradation and climate change are problems we share in common with people in different parts of the world, with other species, and future generations. These are therefore potentially solidarity-building issues. Although proponents of inclusive green growth acknowledge the common at the core of environmental issues, by analysing the situation from the vantage point of economic efficiency and by using criteria such as surplus value, private property, and price, the commoning condition of the problem is appropriated and privatized. In the name of saving the commons, inclusive green growth takes the self-sufficient character of a commons and inscribes it with the law of the market, hereby denying the commons its distinctly autonomous condition. Accordingly, the commons is rendered non-common. In the process the violence capital inflicts on all life forms, a violence environmental degradation and climate change forces out into the open, becomes invisible and inaudible once more. It is at this juncture where the political significance of prioritizing economic growth and efficiency comes into the light of day. Predictably, the assumption driving inclusive green growth is that economic growth is value neutral. Namely, that it is an unquestionable good in and of itself. However, as Piketty demonstrates, economic growth is not a reliable predictor of justice and equality and the reason is not just economic; it is political.

In what is nothing short of a tour de force analysis of rising global inequality, Piketty's study of global economic history reaches as far back as the late eighteenth century. The three pillars of his account of economic history are capital accumulation, population growth and technological advances. In particular, he shows how individual capital accumulation has superseded national capital accumulation. As a few individuals enjoy the majority of wealth and income, it is fair to say that today the world is experiencing a return to the patrimonial capitalism of America's Gilded Age or Europe's Belle Époque. During the late nineteenth century, Europe had a high level of private wealth with the 'total amount of private wealth hovering around six or seven years of national income'.[16] After two world wars the capital/income ratio fell to 2 or 3. However, from 1950 onwards the figure rose such that 'private fortunes in the early twenty-first century seem to be on the verge of returning to five or six years of national income in both Britain and France'.[17] In the United States the 'top decile claimed as much as 45–50 percent of national income in the 1910s–1920s before dropping to 30–35 percent by the end of the 1940s ... We subsequently see a rapid rise in inequality in the 1980s, until by 2000 we have returned to a level on the order of 45–50 percent of national income.'[18]

The interesting point Piketty makes is that inequality doesn't just grow because of wage disparities but, more importantly, when the rate of return on capital exceeds the rate of economic growth. What this means is that inherited wealth steadily rises more than output and income. He clarifies:

> People with inherited wealth need save only a portion of their income from capital to see that capital grow more quickly than the economy as a whole. Under such conditions, it is almost inevitable that inherited wealth will dominate wealth amassed from a lifetime's labor by a wide margin, and the concentration of capital will attain extremely high levels.[19]

On this issue Piketty offers an important take-home lesson – serving the interests of elites, government policies have skewed the socio-economic landscape in a manner that favours the most financially privileged members of society.

Piketty is especially critical of the failure of economic policies to adequately redress and redistribute income. Wealth is no longer tied to the innovations of an entrepreneurial and creative class; rather the income of the extremely rich is increasingly generated from capital more than earnings. What this means is that there is less investment back into the economy. This negatively impacts job growth. When we add the realities of a growing global population into the mix, the picture becomes bleak indeed. He describes a situation of growing economic disparity and an economy dominated by those with inherited wealth. He warns that without government taking a proactive role in rectifying the imbalance through progressive taxation, inequality will worsen with the rate of capital return on capital being greater than the rate of economic growth, which he summarizes with the following equation: $r > g$.[20] The reason for this massive shift in economic power lies with government. He warns that in a world where economic growth 'generates arbitrary and unsustainable inequalities that radically undermine the meritocratic values on which democratic societies are based' it is a tough call to assume those self-same weakened political institutions will have enough muscle and clout to put the needs and interests of disenfranchised people ahead of the special interests who exert undue influence over governments across the world.[21]

The economic portrait Piketty paints links to David Harvey's analysis of neoliberal ideology and the process of neoliberalization, which as Harvey insists

> has celebrated the role of the rentier, cut taxes on the rich, privileged dividends and speculative gains over wages and salaries, and unleashed untold though geographically contained financial crises, with devastating effects on employment and life chances in country after country.[22]

Generally speaking, neoliberal economic theory aspired to disembed the market economy from the regulatory structure of the state. Notable examples include the two icons of neoliberal governance, UK Prime Minister Margaret Thatcher and US President Ronald Reagan, whose modus operandi was to roll back on big government and restructure the economy.

Yet, we would be digging our heads in the sand if we ignored the many governmental ghosts that continue to lurk in the shadows of neoliberal capitalism: governments the world over have privatized public assets, deregulated exchange rates, lowered taxes on businesses and investors, cut back on social welfare programmes and turned these into services and products to be exchanged on the free market, and instituted international policies that promote global economic integration by opening up borders to the movement of capital, goods and services (concomitantly stiffening controls against people migrating). When taken together all of these examples attest to the widespread 'shock treatment', to borrow from Naomi Klein, governments inflict upon society, restructuring it into a launch pad for the advancement of private interests.[23] This means the problem of neoliberal governance is not simply a matter of rolling back on big government; rather the problem is what Jamie Peck has aptly described as 'market-oriented governance' and the manner in which neoliberalism has become an 'adaptive form of regulatory practice' as Philip Mirowski insists.[24] It is important to ask: Whom does government speak for? Who benefits from governmental regulation – the powerful interest groups or the common interest?

Citing Karl Polanyi, Harvey states the 'neoliberal debasement of the concept of freedom "into a mere advocacy of free enterprise" can only mean "the fullness of freedom for those whose income, leisure and security need no enhancing, and a mere pittance of liberty for the people, who may in vain attempt to make use of their democratic rights to gain shelter from the power of the owners of property"'.[25] We can get a sense of how this plays out in practical terms if we follow the money trail of campaign contributions, kickbacks, lobbying, bribery and corruption, all of which have compromised the emancipatory pulse of democratic political life in the late twentieth and early twenty-first centuries. Or to borrow from Mirowski, a critical assessment of neoliberalism requires that analysis move into the 'weeds of everyday market governance, routine regulatory failure, and unprincipled political accommodation'.[26]

The lobbying power of private industries directly undermines the representative power of Western democracies. The figures compiled by the Center for Responsive Politics neatly summarizes the situation in the US: From 1998 to 2013 the total amount spent by companies, labour unions, and other organizations on lobbying elected officials and political candidates grew by US$1.77 billion.[27] In the European Union after the 2008 financial crisis, the financial industry spent over £120 million a year lobbying against regulation of the financial industry.[28] In the United Kingdom, from 2010 to 2013 government ministers reportedly met with representatives of the big six energy giants 128 times and only 26 times with representatives of energy consumers.[29]

On the international stage of geopolitics the 'sole effect' and 'police powers' doctrines of international law regularly collide. For instance, when environmental concerns were raised over a Mexican waste treatment plant, the Mexican government did not renew Tecmed Corporation's operating permit for the landfill. In 2003 Tecmed responded by suing the Mexican government for US$5.5 million in compensation for damages (International Centre for Settlement of Investment Disputes, 2003). Then there is the case of US fracking company Lone Pine Resources who under Article 1117 of the North American Trade Agreement (NAFTA) sued Quebec for $250 million when the government introduced a moratorium on hydraulic fracturing to study the environmental effects of fracking. Article 1117 of NAFTA states an investor can sue on the basis of damage to a 'valuable right ... without due process, without compensation and with no cognizable public purpose'.[30] The company claimed it had invested millions in acquiring the permits for natural gas exploration under the St Lawrence River and that those permits were abruptly revoked without consultation.

A bridging country (bridge between developed and developing), such as South Korea, also suffers from the same political challenges posed by the financial interests of the private sector. Heavy criticism has been levelled against green growth exponent and visionary of the Global Green Growth Institute, former South Korean President Lee Myung-bak, for his star green growth project: the Four Rivers Project. In their detailed evaluation of the project in this volume, Bettina Bluemling and Sun-Jin Yun describe the underhanded politics of Korea's Four Rivers Project and the definition of Korea as a 'water stressed country' by government agencies to justify the project, despite the Eco-Hydrological Institute in the UK ranking South Korea's water resources forty-third among 147 countries. The project went ahead regardless of widespread public opposition to it, including over 10,000 law suites against the government for violating the Rivers Act, the Cultural Heritage Protection Act, and the National Finance Act to name a few.[31] The Korean Board of Audit and Inspection report accused the former president of corruption during the bidding process, explaining this had inflated the cost of the project. More significantly, the project suffers from poor water quality management with the new weirs causing algae blooms and the destruction of ecological corridors around the waterways. The problem is so acute that Park Chang-geun, professor of civil engineering at Kwandong University recommended 'dismantling the weirs and restoring the rivers to their natural state'.[32] The problematic political landscape of green growth policy in South Korea that Bluemling and Yun describe comes from the assumption that the primary objective of environmental policy is economic growth at all costs, even if it comes at the expense of socially repressive outcomes and, ironically, even despite negative ecological outcomes.

Basically, the issue at stake is the discursive operation of environmental policy geared to the realization of growth and the abuse of power whether by governments or the private sector to facilitate this. Here it is helpful to briefly recall Piketty and his historical analysis of the data, which shows that economic growth has not produced a level playing field. The reason is that we are caught in a vicious cycle of the most economically privileged members of society enjoying undue influence over governments, which in turn concentrates wealth in the hands of a few. This would lead us to the conclusion that the primary political problem inclusive green growth presents is the dominance of neoliberal political and economic practices and institutions.

Drawing this conclusion, however, misses the other half of the neoliberal story. For instance, what Piketty doesn't address, as he laments the demise of a creative class and all the investment in job growth and a growing middle-class that this supposedly brings, is that the term 'creative class' is not politically neutral. Mirowski elucidates how governments use creativity to facilitate neoliberal agendas, such as the 'new urban imperative' that cities become more hip (lingo for gentrified) and attractive to function as a draw-card for the mobile and creative class, so as to give cities a competitive edge alongside the global cities of the world and the dominant economic position they enjoy in a global and rapidly urbanizing economy.[33] It all comes back to the logic of competition at the core of capital accumulation.

Inclusive green growth is seen to provide a competitive advantage in what is otherwise a weak global economy. In the words of President Lee Myung-bak: 'If we make up our minds before others and take action we will be able to lead green growth and take the initiative in creating a new civilization', which he envisions will use 'low-emission and climate-resilient development pathways'.[34] In this scenario, good governance creates the conditions for a resilient and competitive economy. Similarly, inclusive green growth policies are being employed as a means of promoting competition between individuals and facilitating competitive social relations, which are believed to be the most efficient and effective way to motivate socio-economic change and competitively position a state in the global economy. Indeed the World Bank reports that 'the cost of environmental degradation, estimated at 9 percent of gross domestic product (GDP), is threatening both economic competitiveness and welfare'.[35]

If inclusive green growth places the subject in capitalist relations of production and the realization of surplus value (growth and competition) and neoliberal ideological relations of signification (independent, responsible, motivated economic actors), what kind of political project does inclusive green growth support? What kind of political subjectivity does inclusive green growth produce? By asking these questions I am especially interested in examining inclusive green growth as a mode of neoliberal governance. The issue these questions share is one of political knowledge and the kind of rationality employed in governance. Moreover, I am interested in how forms of neoliberal rationality inscribe themselves in green governance practices, and what role they play within them.[36] In other words, following Foucault, inclusive green growth policy is not just another instance of the misuse of state or corporate power; it is a relational mechanism of power that is strategically exercised to inject a principle of competition into the core of social relations. This prompts me to return to the representative question concerning *whom* governments speak for. The question now leaves the domain of representational politics and transforms into a machinic problem of *how* governments speak. The answer: governments speak using a neoliberal rationality whereby the logic of competition driving capital accumulation is adapted as a principle of governance. This is an ideational matter.

How does government speak?

Government, in the way Foucault intends, not only denotes 'political structures or ... the management of states'; it also refers to how government designates, namely 'the way in which the conduct of individuals or of groups might be directed'.[37] Foucault posits three types of government that align with different ways in which power has been historically exercised. First, sovereign power exercises control over land and wealth, with people obeying the law. Second, disciplinary power marks the rise of the administrative state where individual bodies and behaviours are regulated and disciplined as they are situated in a variety of institutional arrangements (school, asylum, hospital, prison, barracks). Third, governmentality marks the advent of biopower and the management of populations through the use of statistical knowledge.

Governmentality, Foucault tells us, entails the governance of conduct, 'the way in which one conducts the conduct' of people.[38] Namely, government is not just the political practice of sovereign states governing a population; it also operates as a system of management in other domains such the self, family or religious guidance. Muddying the distinction between freedom and constraint, Foucault maintains that the state is both configured by and in turn configures individuals. In this reflexive schema of mutual determination, Foucault breaks from the centralized understanding of power offered by liberal and Marxist theories. For the former, power is a juridico-political concept legitimating sovereign state governments, whereas Marxists argue the bourgeoisie uses the state as a means to advance its economic interests. Foucauldian power, however, is a strategic operation involving political governance, economic management and individual self-rule. The state is not a fixed or universal entity. It is a practice involving a variety of activities and institutional configurations that come together to produce a system of governmental rationality that Foucault terms 'neoliberal governmentality', one of the primary effects of which is the reconfiguration of social relations around a principle of competition, a clear example of government ensuring capital function as capital.

In his contribution to this anthology, James Meadway points out that by erasing the difference between wealth and capital, Piketty's analysis has the unfortunate result of occluding different forms of capital. If capital 'is required for production over time, and if it (in practice) takes different forms – buildings, machinery, office equipment, and so on, then it cannot', he says, 'be collapsed into a single measure of "wealth"'.[39] More worrying for Meadway is the manner in which the single measure of wealth conceals the important role competition plays in ensuring capital functions as capital. The situation of endless economic growth is the result of the owners of capital competing with one another. Like Marx, Meadway does not assume growth entails a choice. Furthermore, he perceptively draws attention to the hidden neoliberal assumption of choice that lies at the heart of market-based solutions to the environmental problem and governmental regulations aimed at curbing environmental degradation. The artificial separation of the conditions needed to create economic growth, such as the accumulation process and a falling rate of profit that leads to greater exploitation of labour and the environment, from the conditions driving growth, namely competition, detracts from the larger issue of how best to reorganize the economy in such a way that the competitive relationships underpinning growth are removed.

Foucault observed that under liberalism market activity was premised upon equivalences established through the process of exchange between two individuals. Unlike the system of exchange, the shift to the logic of the free market meant the principle of exchange was replaced with that of competition. Competition establishes price, making price the organizing principle for choice. Inclusive green growth, as a series of policy initiatives governments institute to promote competition and to internalize negative environmental externalities using the price mechanism, reinforces Foucault's point that neoliberalism does not entail rolling back on government in the way that Hayek viewed it.[40] Instead of pushing the public sector under the hammer of the private sector, neoliberal governmentality turns the inequities produced by the free market into an economic rather than a political issue. The effect of this is to disguise the exploitation and violence produced by the slippery terrain of neoliberal institutions, practices and reasoning which morph to fit the times and stay afloat one financial meltdown at a time. As Mirowski astutely announces: 'By its nature, as an oxymoronic form of "market rule", neoliberalism is contradictory and polymorphic. It will not be fixed', going on to concede that '(n)eoliberalism, in its various guises, has always been about the capture and reuse of the state, in the interests of shaping a pro-corporate, freer trading "market order", even though this has never been a process of cookie cutter replication of an unproblematic strategy'.[41] Inclusive green growth is just another chapter in a long but contested history of neoliberal promiscuity as it carves out new ways for governments and the corporate sector to collaborate, this time on the back of socio-environmental politics.

Aspiring to bring the poor into the fold of the global economy, in the way that inclusive green growth advocates, detracts from the deeper issue of how, in the first instance, the poor are unequally incorporated into the free market economy as casualties of the principle of competition driving economic relations. Add into the mix the aims of the inclusive green growth paradigm (developing new green technologies or a free market in carbon offsets) to solve environmental harms by commercializing or putting a price on them and we are left with a potent, albeit misplaced gesture of inclusive governance that sets out to solve the twofold problems of poverty and environmental injustice in one fell swoop whereby the source of the problem is used as the solution. Inclusive green growth extends the power and reach of the free market (competition, privatization, commodification) that establishes the unequal location of people and the exploitative situation of the environment in the global economy, hereby reproducing the self-same political rationality and system of power relations. Capital accumulation and the logic of competition driving social and environmental injustices are no longer viewed through a political lens as the cause of these injustices; rather, using an economic frame that views capital and competition as the solution to injustice simply depoliticizes the economic practice of accumulation and competition.

When the principle of competition reappears as part of another discourse around resiliency the biopolitical character of inclusive green growth is exposed. On the one hand, inclusive green growth policies and actions are endorsed as promoting more resilient economies. On the other hand, resilience 'has emerged as an important reference point when discussing appropriate responses to the increasing levels of risk faced by societies and economies'.[42] In this way, the model of inclusive green growth neatly aligns with the growing popularity around producing resilient subjects who are better positioned to fend off the catastrophic effects of climate change, environmental degradation, and impoverishment.[43] A resilient subject is flexible and better equipped to adapt to the variegated landscape of threats, crises and emergencies. Brad Evans and Julian Reid uncover the political implications of resilience theory, skilfully describing how it places the responsibility for security squarely back in the court of the world's most vulnerable subjects, who it should be noted are unequally impacted by environmental harms and the cycle of economic boom and bust.[44]

Joining resilience to inclusive green growth morphs the political subjectivity of resistance into one of adaptation. Instead of a politics that demands more of our politicians and political institutions and which imagines alternatives to what currently exists, we are left with a fragmented social field of individual agents responsible for their own future in the face of a hostile reality, absorbing the multiplicity of threats that come their way. Resigned to a 'catastrophic imaginary' that accepts the definition of life as one big endless disaster zone, succumbing social life to the limited political horizon that insists the only road through the rubble is to try to render subjects more secure in an increasingly precarious world, only creates a deeply depoliticized subject. For it means we surrender ourselves to the prospect of living dangerously and along with it we strip transformative politics of its affirmative and creative pulse.[45] In this way, the model of inclusive green growth constitutes a system of green governmentality.

Green governmentality, in the way I am using the term, refers to a neoliberal rationality that treats the environmental crisis as a new politics of truth, one that then legitimizes the expansion of governance into new areas of mediation, legalization, management and supervision. One such example would be the wave of new political protagonists entering the realm of governance, such as community groups, non-governmental organizations, non-profits and religious institutions. These politically informal strategies of government have gone on to reshape social relations by obscuring the difference between economic and political power. Indeed, in the World Bank's working paper on green growth the authors clearly state: 'growth does not cause inequality – policies do.'[46] This conclusion not only protects the economic sphere from criticism by clearly pointing the finger of blame in the direction of government; it also rests upon a false distinction between the economic and political spheres, one that is arguably an effect of neoliberal governmentality.

Green governmentality uses a variety of policy instruments ranging from price-based mechanisms along with 'norms and regulation, public production and direct investment, information creation and dissemination, education and moral suasion'.[47] The easy conflation of an economically rational view of the individual with a morally responsible one is telling indeed. The focus on priming individuals to accept green growth policies through educational outreach and moral suasion transfers responsibility for the risks arising from living in polluted environments and the economic hardships non-elite members of society incur as the economy slows. Although neoliberal governmentality has comfortably adapted to the once challenging demands of environmental and social justice concerns, it is nevertheless important to reflect upon how this runs along a very different current to that of the more activist strains of the environmental and social justice movements. The leitmotif of *governance* in inclusive green growth theory and practices recognizes the significant role government activities, rationalities and practices play in reconfiguring subjects away from a collectivist political subjectivity in solidarity with others, into a competitively resilient subject whose independence is achieved at the expense of another's autonomy. Green governmentality aspires to produce a competitive social configuration made up of a potpourri of resilient subjects. This simply reinstates neoliberalism as the horizon of socio-environmental politics, rejecting alternative political agendas and experiments that form solidarities across different political lines in an effort to institute emancipatory political agendas.

For these reasons, green governmentality fails to tackle the deeper political struggles ensuing between the public and private sectors. At the heart of that struggle is the problem of neoliberal governance whereby vested interests and relations of power orient how society is organized, complemented by a logic of competition governments employ to ensure capital functions as capital. In addition to economic factors, environmental harms are aggravated by deeply compromised political process. The neoliberal demand for less government intervention is indeed a demand for more government manipulation of the market so as to skew the market mechanism in favour of powerful interest groups. In this regard the ideological work of neoliberal rhetoric comes from the way in which it effectively conceals this contradiction. In the same vein, inclusive green growth embraces government involvement in greening national economies, all the while ignoring how power shapes governance the world over. Predictably, under these circumstances green growth will never become inclusive. This is because the dominant political modality is depoliticizing.

At its core, inclusive green growth is an economic outlook that presents an important alternative to high carbon emitting and polluting practices associated with business as usual, offering forth an environmentally friendly economy powered by renewable energy, clean and efficient technologies, natural resource conservation, and green goods and services. However, the focus on using market mechanisms and the principle of economic efficiency to solve the problem of rising global greenhouse gas emissions, environmental degradation and inequitable social relations overlooks the myriad ways in which power, privilege and influence intersect across a variety of socio-political scales.

The prevailing obedience to a logic of competition and a political modality of neoliberal governance that demands nothing but endless servitude to capital accumulation is intensifying global inequity and environmental degradation. Rather than gently poking the bear of Capital with an economic stick, choosing to engage with its competitive logic by using neoliberal governance as the primary strategy to overcome social and environmental problems, we need to poke the bear harder and with a bigger political stick. Namely, we need to acknowledge Capital as its own animal with its own internal logic of competition that allows capital to function as capital. So while we need to continue engaging with the bear in order to diffuse the growing power and influence of elites over *whom* governments speak for, two effects of which are environmental degradation and growing inequity, we cannot afford to underestimate the political depth of the problem as one involving *how* governments speak to the beat of a neoliberal drum. At the risk of sounding prophetic, social and environmental movements certainly have their work cut out for them. They need to speak both more loudly and more strategically, re-imagining how politics works, creating and testing alternative political paradigms that are both practical and utopian, and inventing unusual political trajectories that move in ways that are as equally supple as neoliberal governance so as to successfully fend off appropriation by the very forces they are trying to surmount.

CHAPTER 4

Degrowth and the roots of neoclassical economics

James Meadway

This chapter explores the problems presented by the twin alternatives of green growth and steady-state growth to carbon-intensive capitalist development. In particular, it examines the claims made by the protagonists of steady-state economies as a radical alternative to conventional, growth-led capitalism. It argues that because these critiques accept too much of conventional economics, failing themselves to present a systemic critique of capitalism, they fail to critically address the underlying drive in capitalism towards crisis. To do this, we examine the development of accounts of steady-state economies, initially from the work of John Stuart Mill, often cited as an originator of the concept. We show how the development of the conventional techniques of national accounting and valuation themselves embodied a particular conception of the economy, and that alternative means of presenting the behaviour of economic aggregates can provide a deeper insight into the functioning of capitalism. It is the conception of the economy as a circular system, implicit in the concept of GDP but essentially overlooked in the conventional treatment of growth, that allows us to develop a more consistent account of capitalism as a system that is both compelled towards growth but decreasingly able to deliver it.

Perhaps the clearest single account of the case for anti-growth can be found in Tim Jackson's (2009) *Prosperity Without Growth*.[1] This is exemplary in its approach to the question in focusing on a very clear and pressing version of the broader anti-growth claim and, in detailing the impossibility of securing a 'decoupling' of environmental impacts from increases in GDP, provides a case that is difficult to argue against, at least in the first instance. Jackson suggests that *relative* decoupling – a steady reduction in the environmental harm done for each extra unit of GDP produced – has certainly taken place. Newer technologies have tended to be more energy-efficient and less harmful than old. This constitutes the core of the neoclassical argument: that innovation, by providing the capacity to indefinitely substitute newer, cleaner technology for older, dirtier technology over time will provide the means by which environmental degradation and collapse can be avoided. Embodied in this is a very strong claim about technology, consistent with the general neoclassical vision of substitutability among inputs into a production process, on one side, and then the endless capacity to substitute among outputs on the other. Between them, these two strong assumptions help reinforce a case in which, left to its own devices, free markets will not just select the most efficient available distribution of the output, and the most efficient use of the input in a static setting. A free market economy, subject to technological change, will even select the most efficient path for growth into the future. At most, intervention may be desirable solely to deal with preferences over the desired distribution, through taxation and transfer, and to patch up 'market failures': those spaces in society where, for whatever reason, the market cannot function, typically education.

To a significant extent, this is what has occurred. Taking CO_2 as an example, Jackson's figures suggest that 'The global carbon intensity declined by almost a quarter from just over 1 kilogram of carbon dioxide per US dollar ($kgCO_2/\$$) in 1980 to 770 grams of carbon dioxide per US dollar ($gCO_2/\$$) in 2006.'[2] However, as he further demonstrates, given binding physical limits on the environment, the improvement in harm reduction per unit of GDP produced has to be improbably large, if GDP also carries on rising. With world population, on central UN estimates, expected to peak at 9 billion in 2050, and allowing (in the interests of social justice) that we would wish for these people to all have a similar standard of living to that currently enjoyed in the developed world, the strong implication is that the total size of the economy needed would be exceptionally large. With GDP per capita at the equivalent to the 2007 EU level, globally, and 9 billion people on the planet, the world economy would need to be six times larger than it is now.

Assuming, however, following the standard IPCC assumptions, that we would wish to stabilize the world's climate at around 2 degrees Celsius over the next century – an ambition that now, admittedly, seems hopelessly optimistic – we are required to hit a 450ppm target for atmospheric carbon dioxide, therefore stabilizing world CO_2 output to around 4 billion tonnes annually by 2050.[3] Taking this as our limit, however, we find that a global economy six times larger than it is now would need an extraordinary reduction in its carbon impact. At present, each $1 of GDP globally produces 770g of carbon, on average. To meet the IPCC target with a 9 billion population and a reasonably equitable distribution of resources means reducing this figure to a mere 14g per dollar GDP, globally. Theoretically, this is possible; in practice, as Jackson forcefully suggests, we cannot plausibly envisage any future technology or set of technologies providing this exceptional reduction in emissions. Growth, at least in the richer countries, cannot be sustained.

This, then, is the argument against 'green growth': that growth, under any circumstances, is a problem. It looks watertight, on its own terms; that instead of chasing 'material wealth' we should look to immaterial qualities. Jackson thinks a reduction in working hours would allow both a fairer distribution of work, and reduce the environmental damage implied by continual pursuit of material wealth at any cost. It is an argument attracting some support, most recently from the slightly implausible direction of Carlos Slim, currently one of the richest men in the world, and some effort has been made to build out and develop alternative, low-hours models of economic development.[4] Moreover, if we argue for a broadly meliorist position, in which the proceeds of growth (perhaps through suitable government policy) are directed towards research on low-emissions and emissions-reduction technology, thus allowing rapid technological advance, the strong implication of Jackson's simple calculations is that the rate of growth must be implausibly high to deliver significant R&D increases.

The challenge of the steady state is, however, taken by its exponents to be far broader than addressing what might be considered the social and moral implication of a growth-driven society. The weaker part of Jackson's argument is when he offers solutions, based on this moral vision, to the problem of growth. His vision of a society of small-scale and low-emissions service producers owes something to the arguments of E.F. Schumacher,[5] but, as we suggest below, it is in the implicit relationship to a much older tradition in economics that we think the most critical problems emerge. In a similar vein, Serge Latouche's *Farewell to Growth* can stand as something of a manifesto for the 'degrowth' movement precisely because it presents, with some brio, a radical vision of a society no longer impelled by its materialistic values towards its own destruction.[6] Degrowth, a developing movement, can stand as a more politically radical and engaged variant of the older, steady-state literature.

The steady-state vision

The moral vision that lies in the centre of Jackson's work, and other growth sceptics,[7] has a long history. It can be traced back to the work of John Stuart Mill, writing at the very birth of modern economic thinking. Mill notes, in his *Principles of Political Economy*:

> It must always have been seen, more or less distinctly, by political economists, that the increase of wealth is not boundless: that at the end of what they term the progressive state lies the stationary state, that all progress in wealth is but a postponement of this, and that each step in advance is an approach to it. We have now been led to recognise that this ultimate goal is at all times near enough to be fully in view; that we are always on the verge of it, and that if we have not reached it long ago, it is because the goal itself flies before us. The richest and most prosperous countries would very soon attain the stationary state, if no further improvements were made in the productive arts, and if there were a suspension of the overflow of capital from those countries into the uncultivated or ill-cultivated regions of the earth ...
>
> It is scarcely necessary to remark that a stationary condition of capital and population implies no stationary state of human improvement. There would be as much scope as ever for all kinds of mental culture, and moral and social progress; as much room for improving the Art of Living, and much more likelihood of its being improved, when minds ceased to be engrossed by the

> art of getting on. Even the industrial arts might be as earnestly and as successfully cultivated, with this sole difference, that instead of serving no purpose but the increase of wealth, industrial improvements would produce their legitimate effect, that of abridging labour.[8]

Mill, like Jackson and others, envisages a world in which the productivity of labour, rather than being used to increase the material distribution of goods (and therefore material impacts) is instead used to deliver 'mental culture' and a broader conception of prosperity, away from the 'the trampling, crushing, elbowing, and treading on each other's heels, which form the existing type of social life'.[9]

The remainder of this chapter explores two related issues that follow directly from this. The first concerns the definition of wealth, and the ways in which wealth can be mobilized and used by society. The second concerns the production of that stock of wealth, and how it is organized. By examining both, a critique of the Millian conception of the stationary state is brought forward.

Productivity and labour

At the centre of the critique is the problem of productivity. Conventionally defined, this is the capacity of a set of inputs to transform into outputs. It is, in the conventional presentation, read directly from the national accounts, with valuations of inputs and outputs provided at market prices. Each 'factor' input, typically capital and labour, supplies a certain volume of input and each production process, as modelled, in the conventional setting, through a 'production function', provides a specific, marketed output. As has been appreciated at least since the work of Robert Solow on growth models in the 1950s, the size of the inputs provided does not always account for the size of the output generated: there will, generally, be a 'Solow residual' left unaccounted for. Typically, this is attributed to technological progress – to the (as yet unexamined) benefits of the advance of technology. For an entire economy, Gross Domestic Product (GDP) can be taken as the value of output – the 'value added' through production.

This is a view of the world that can, broadly, be described as *neoclassical*: as reflecting the epistemological and methodological preferences of the economics mainstream, as it has developed since the 'marginal revolution' of the 1870s, on which more later. But these accounting tools, notably including GDP, are not themselves either value-neutral, as is well understood; nor are they necessarily the best tools available for capturing the sort of issues the steady-state literature wishes to address. Specifically, the neoclassical framework, based around the treatment of market valuations as indicators of value, and the treatment of production as determined by a stable 'function' over time, does not adequately address the problem of wealth in society: who holds it, what qualifies as it, and what we do with it.

Neoclassical economics, at least in its macroeconomic variant, has come under increasing criticism in recent years. The Great Financial Crash of 2007–8 saw the legions of extraordinarily sophisticated models, and their mathematically adept builders, found wanting: unable to account for the crash, or its aftermath, or its build-up. Indeed, a comprehensive assessment of their performance for the US Federal Reserve Board has noted their 'very poor' results in forecasting,[10] for all the technical sophistication. Nonetheless, neoclassical economics continues to dominate the mainstream of the economic thinking about the macroeconomy: that is, about the economy considered as a distinct system, driven towards the maximization of GDP.

Our concern here, however, is not the well-known criticism of neoclassical macroeconomics' weaknesses in explaining short-term issues, like financial crises. Rather, we are concerned here with how some of the same biases and methodological issues that appear in the short-run manifest themselves when considering long-run processes of development, and how, in turn, they can leave a steady-state critique wanting. Taking the typical distinction, as presented by the neoclassicists themselves, of positive (technical and value-free) and normative (opinion-led and value-laden) economics as the starting point, it is because steady-state focuses on the failures of neoclassical economics' normative outcomes, centred on the weaknesses of GDP, that it does not fully address the failures of its 'positive', technical tools, weakening its proposed solutions as a result. Instead of breaking the neoclassical paradigm, 'degrowth' too often remains trapped inside it, precisely as a result of its assessment of 'growth' as the critical issue to be addressed.

Wealth vs capital

At the centre of the neoclassical problem is its failed conception of the productive process, with the problems that follow from this. For the neoclassical school, production is a 'black box', its workings unknown and the sole task of the economist is to examine only the observed relationship between input and output. Adding additional factors – for example, as is popular in the environmental literature, energy inputs – or changing the (presumed) shape of the production function – for example, to one of constant elasticity of substitution – does not fundamentally shift this. Factors are simply added to the process, and their presumed contribution to the process measured by their 'marginal product': the increment to output, valued at market prices, that single additional input units will provide. To find what is happening to the whole economy, then, we can simply add up all the inputs to production, and all the outputs. This will give us our aggregate production function – if we can find the correct price for the inputs.

However, as an extensive debate eventually settled, the neoclassical theory could offer no reliable guide to the pricing of the critical input of *capital.* Since the neoclassical system was dependent on the belief that the value of the output of a 'factor of production' was related to its marginal contribution to total output, and since capital goods and outputs from them are heterogeneous – how, then, are we to value the outputs produced, relative to the inputs? If inputs are priced relative to the value of the output they produced (as in the marginal productivity theory), we need an independent measure of the value of the outputs. But this is precisely what the neoclassical theory in general denies can exist.

This dilemma gave rise to the so-called 'Cambridge capital controversy', pitting the neoclassicals of Cambridge, MA, like Paul Samuelson, against the post-Keynesians of Cambridge, England, like Joan Robinson. By the end of the 1960s, the neoclassicals had all but conceded the point: neoclassical theory could not properly price capital.[11] This did not, however, prevent the complete domination of the neoclassical school within economics research.

More recently, the controversy has re-emerged following the publication of Thomas Piketty's bestselling *Capital in the Twenty-First Century* (2014). James Galbraith, reviewing the book, noted that Piketty's reliance on the neoclassical 'production function' relating inputs to outputs opened his claims up to the Cambridge critique.[12] Fundamentally, Piketty's isolation of a single rate of return, 'averaged' across capital, in fact disguises the conceptual problems the Cambridge critique highlighted: in particular, the difficulties of isolating returns to the different factors of production where outputs and inputs were heterogeneous. Piketty avoided this difficulty by essentially eliding the difference between 'wealth' and 'capital', treating them (as in the national accounts) as purely interchangeable. But if the latter is required for production over time, and if it (in practice) takes different forms – buildings, machinery, office equipment, and so on – then it cannot, as the Cambridge controversy showed, be collapsed into a single measure of 'wealth'. The real, underlying rate of return on capital could differ from the observed rate of return on wealth, as derived through a national accounting technique, with obvious consequences for Piketty's bold claims about the relationship between this rate of return and accumulation over time.

At a very high level of abstraction, this occlusion of different forms of capital in the general conception of wealth involves also the hiding of competitive relationships among the different owners of capital. It is precisely the presence of these competitive relationships that guarantees the functioning of capital as capital – that is, it structures the process of competitive, blind accumulation that grants to capitalism its distinctive requirement for relentless growth. By treating the problems of wealth, and of capital, as interchangeable, however, the *objective* requirement for growth at the level of individual capital disappears behind the apparently *subjective* requirement for the system as a whole to expand.

The problems with GDP

For all its wide use, GDP has recently come in for sustained criticism, most notably from the 2009 Stiglitz-Sen-Fitoussi commission.[13] Like other critiques, they strongly suggest that the measurement of GDP, as

Kuznets himself said, had little to do with the improvement of human welfare, and should, instead, be replaced by a measure that more comprehensively captures the desirable features of any economy: the promotion of subjective well-being, say, or health outcomes, or falling inequality. We could, for shorthand, call this a *moral* critique, since it is claimed GDP does not capture what truly matters to us. Here, we will be looking at the other side of GDP – at the methodology used to construct it.

Specifically, there is a danger in treating GDP as a simple variable of 'scale' within the economy, akin to the scale of physical processes that is captured by the claim of limits to growth. Clearly, economic activity occupies (and must occupy) some physical space; clearly, too, there are limits to the extent of this space. But the ability of one to map onto the other, and, in particular, for those physical limits to appear as a barrier to actual accumulation is not obvious: since GDP is valued in monetary terms, and since the index of scale it represents is also, in this sense, nominal, there is (in theory) no reason why monetary valuations cannot be forever substituted for physical inputs – if, that is, we hold to the neoclassical view that the aggregate is no more than the sum of its parts. This substitution is what John Bellamy Foster, Brett Clark and Richard York have elsewhere labelled the 'Midas Effect': a belief, in neoclassical economics, in the infinite substitutability of all economically relevant commodities for any other, via the miracle of the market.[14] It therefore provides the neoclassical school with the means to argue that physical limits are no such thing.

The response of steady state is to assert, instead, that output must have physical consequences. It is these physical consequences, within finite resource constraints, that prevent the substitution of economically relevant commodities, since any action taken to reorganize production, if the scale of production remains the same, will still hold a physical consequence. The speed with which those consequences become apparent will vary, depending on the magnitude of their impact per unit of output. The consequences will remain. However, while it is possible to concede, in theory, that *perfect* substitution cannot occur, in practice substitution can be less than perfect and impacts kept within presumed safe limits, over time. And certainly the neoclassicals have argued, in the past, that the economy *has* been able to substitute inputs, given price incentives: witness the rising fuel efficiency of US cars in response to the oil price shocks of the 1970s.

But the problem here is deeper than the empirical claims made about the possibility of sufficiently rapid substitution, using perhaps new technologies, to enable growth to continue. Jackson presents his case as empirical. Because new technologies are unlikely to allow a sufficiently rapid reduction in environmental impacts to mitigate growth, we cannot rely on technological change alone to meet environmental goals. But there is a deeper issue involved here.

The focus on pure aggregate 'output', considered (as in the formulation of GDP) indifferently between its appearance as production and its consumption, blurs a necessary distinction. The use, in degrowth literature, of Ehrlich and Holdren's IPAT (Impact=PopulationxAffluencexTechnology) function,[15] in particular, is problematic: the central variable A, 'affluence', is intended to capture the wealth of a given society. Yet it is not wealth as such that is the problem here: it is the *accumulation* of wealth, that is, its *production* that is the critical issue. Production and consumption are not the same thing, even if the standard formulation of GDP suggests that they can be treated as such. Consumption possibilities are constrained by production, and, while consumption today can help determine the priorities of later production, this only appears as a second-order effect. A meaningful distinction can be imposed if we view the whole economic cycle as a system of interlinked flows of productive output and use in consumption, held together by the money system. But this requires looking closely at the role of production and consumption as a separate processes. 'Affluence' alone does not enable us to do that. What IPAT and similar formulations do is blur a necessary distinction, as we will argue in the following section. In doing so, they reproduce an underlying Millian conception of growth as fundamentally a *moral* problem, in which growth is a choice made by society.

Production and consumption

It is this production/consumption distinction that the Millian accounts of the problems of growth do not fully address. The blurring is reproduced in the standard national accounting framework, in which it can be assumed that both production and consumption come to the same thing. The logic here seems initially sound, and follows Keynes' insights: since everything sold in the economy must *also* be bought, we should, therefore, be able to say that, for the economy as a whole, production and sale of goods *must* equal purchase and consumption of goods; or, mathematically: Y=C.

The decision to invest then becomes merely a decision to *not consume*: that is, in the aggregate, to save. It follows that the calculation of GDP can be developed on either basis of consumption or production; it is a matter of indifference which one we use and, indeed, conventional national income accounts are presented in precisely this manner, with goods and services sold simply equating to incomes earned.

This equation can be treated, after production and consumption decisions have been taken as tautologically true. But this *ex post* (after the fact) relationship holds for the flows of *money* between the two processes only; the actual processes of production and consumption that underlie the flows of money can imply quite different sets of relationships. We can see this more precisely if we think not of production and consumption, but in more direct monetary terms as purchase and sale: while ex post, it must be the case that all that was bought must have been sold, and vice versa, ex ante it need not apply that all that is *offered* for sale is necessarily purchased, at least in a monetary economy. Goods can easily remain unsold. This insight, of money as a barrier to equating sales and purchase, was key to Keynes' (and Marx's) critique of Say's Law, which held the sale-and-purchase equality would hold both ex post and ex ante. Moving from the flows of money to the flows of commodities they engender, the relationship is very clear: production must, of necessity, come before consumption with commodities produced and offered for consumption prior to their actual consumption.

This has a direct bearing on the notion of scale, as treated in the Millian literature. The 'size' of the economy is a function of its productivity, as presented by Jackson and others: relying on the IPAT formulation effectively makes this the case. Yet the relationships that IPAT treats as linearly multiplicative are, if the question of ends and uses is addressed, clearly something more complex, as we argued in the previous section. The physical world itself imposes the need to create the possibility of consumption, through production, prior to the actuality of consumption. You can have a cake, and then eat it. But you can't eat a cake, and then have it.

Once the GDP measure of output is used to measure productivity the problem worsens still further. Productivity is conventionally measured by GDP divided by the number of workers, or the number of hours worked. But either top or bottom of this function can change, and both are related to each other. Unpacking the (implied) production function to incorporate energy use, as Armon Rezai *et al.* suggest,[16] moves us part of the way forward, since the introduction of a physical quantity provides a non-market point of stability to analyse the system from; but even here we cannot assume that the factor inputs are themselves stable, at least in the aggregate. As a later section aims to show, the presence of unemployed labour – the volume of which is itself dependent on the rate of growth – renders the whole operation uncertain, since the availability of labour for use in production will depend on prior decisions to produce to establish the current volume of unemployment, while decisions to invest in the future will depend (through its effects on the wage rate) on that stock of unemployment.

More concretely, we cannot under these conditions presume that a redistribution of work as means to reduce the impact of economic growth – using, in effect, the rise in productivity to maintain the same level of output for decreasing labour inputs – will lead to the desired impact on emissions. Since the relationship between energy use and labour inputs is, in fact, mediated by the presence of a *labour market* (that is, by the presence of a reserve army of labour and a hierarchy within the labour process), there is no easy correspondence between the reduction of labour hours applied to work, and the reduction of energy used. It is as possible, under these circumstances, to see rising productivity associated with rising employment (greater output creating more demand), or falling (better machines replacing workers). Equally, falling productivity could produce rising employment (as is currently happening in the UK), or falling. Attempts to restrict the labour input (for instance through limiting hours worked) on the basis of measured productivity may lead to falling or rising growth, if decisions over the desired rate of aggregate output (and therefore the desired rate of input) are left to disaggregated and unplanned market mechanisms. Moreover, the possibility of *local* substitution of inputs – swapping labour for energy, say, or vice versa, on a smaller scale than across the entire economy – also opens the possibility of unstable relationship between measured productivity, attempts to restrain growth, and reductions in environmental damage.

Instead, we need a dynamic understanding of the economy that recognizes the presence of a hierarchy inside capitalism. Owners of capital determine priorities for production and, thanks to the reserve army of labour, have a permanent, flexible bias built in to the system; the priorities for production are both substantially unplanned and superior to the needs of consumption.

The circular 'underground'

There are non-neoclassical methods of analysis available that emphasize this dynamism and hierarchy. Augusto Graziani has described the 'underground' tradition of the circular flow in macroeconomics,[17] tracing a lineal descendancy that stretches from François Quesnay's *Tableaux Economique* (1758), through Karl Marx, himself strongly influenced by Quesnay's presentation, taking in Joseph Schumpeter, Rosa Luxemburg and John Maynard Keynes. Central to these 'circuitist' conceptions of the economy is the importance of money as the mobile element that brings the separate parts of the economy together, stressing the dynamic relationships between (in the aggregate) consumption and investment. It stands in stark contrast to the dominant presentation in modern economic thought, that of neoclassical economics, with its emphasis on static, equilibrium analysis, its stress on real (rather than monetary) factors, and its general belief in the 'neutrality of money' – that is, the (somewhat surprising) irrelevance of money to the fundamentals of economic decision-making.

However, while national accounting and its primary variable, GDP, have their roots in the earlier circuitist work, they represent a decisive break with it. As is well known, the calculation of GDP presents serious conceptual difficulties: leaving aside its relevance to subjective welfare, highlighted as early as 1934 by Kuznets himself in his evidence to the US Congress, the decisions about what to include and what to exclude from GDP are not economically neutral. Work performed outside of the market, but still essential to the economy, is entirely ignored; since, in the case of housework and care-work, this is still overwhelmingly performed by women, a significant feminist critique of national income accounting has developed.[18] In a similar vein, the ecological criticisms of GDP as both ignoring environmental depletion and rewarding environmentally damaging activities are well known. However, we want here to focus on the way in which the conceptualization of GDP as such represents a break with circuitism and with conceptions of the macroeconomy as sets of joined processes.

The national accounting matrix expressed its output solely in terms of aggregate prices – as value sold for final market. Equivalently, since the underlying logic of national income implied that every sale must also be a receipt of income for someone, the same number could be arrived at by summating the value of all incomes received by all participants in the national economy. This removed a qualitative distinction, otherwise present in circuitist accounts, between the end-uses of products, reducing all considerations to a purely exchange-based calculation of value, here conceived as observed price. This created certain anomalies: most obviously, the payment of interest, in general treated as a non-productive pure transfer of monies (and therefore ignored in calculating GDP), becomes 'productive' if the interest paid is received within the financial sector. There was no necessary reason for this distinction to exist; it is a matter of accounting convenience that, as it happens, is rather to the benefit of financial institutions. The divide between 'productive' output, forming inputs elsewhere in the economy, and 'unproductive' output, being treated as pure consumption, was wholly lost.

The conception of circularity within the economy tends to undermine the treatment of GDP as a scale variable. The equality, implied in its formulation, between consumption and production tends to break down, precisely because, if the economy is truly dynamic in the sense intended here, with inputs forming outputs of fresh processes, it is not possible, at any given point in time, to assess the size of the economy without some conception of how those processes relate to each other. To analyse this fully requires a conception of the processes of production.

The labour theory of value

That would require opening up the 'black box' of production and factoring into the analysis an account of its organization. Neoclassical economics explicitly does not do this; production is treated, as we have seen, as the outcome of a 'production function' whose inner workings are not made explicit. Inputs are applied on one side, and outputs appear on the other.

The classical school resolved the difficulty through the 'labour theory of value', insisting on the primacy of labour as the key to all economic activity. Derived from Adam Smith, but developed most fully in the work of David Ricardo, the labour theory of value attempted to resolve two knotty analytical difficulties in studying economics: the first was to provide the means by which the dynamic relationships between the different elements of the economy could be kept in balance; since clearly the economy reproduced itself, it was necessary to describe the mechanism by which this reproduction, over time, could occur. This was, and is, primarily a problem of *flows*: of movements of value and wealth between different parts of the economy over time, in such a way that the economy can sustain itself. In the classical (non-Marxist) labour theory of value, these flows would appear with a money value, but would be based on the movement of claims to labour-time.

The second problem, and the one that caused far greater difficulty, was the need to understand not just the flows of value, but how value could accumulate over time. Wealth, and especially wealth in the form of capital, presented a particular form of the problem: how to capture the value of accumulations of capital, held as a stock, over time? Wealth in the form of capital, producing a return, was a particular challenge, since this was wealth (as a stock) that engendered particular flows. These are two clearly analytically distinct categories.

The Ricardian solution was simple: since all existing capital, and any value it contained, was the product of accumulated labour, any existing *stock* of capital could be considered solely the result of a *flow* of past labour. Pricing capital, then, becomes fairly simple: its current value is the sum of the labour applied to create it, dating back to some point in the past, and expressed in terms of the current price of labour. That, in turn, helps establish the comparatively simple conditions under which different goods will exchange: according to Ricardo, '[t]he aggregate sum of these various kinds of labour determines the quantity of other things for which these stockings will exchange, while the same consideration of the various quantities of labour which have bestowed on those other things will equally govern the portion of them which will exchange for stockings.'[19] There was a simple correspondence between the sum of accumulated wealth, current labour, and the exchange value of commodities.

However, there is a distinctive problem here. We have lost the sense of *physical* production processes, since any physical process can be substituted by its labour-time equivalent, including accumulations of prior wealth. In Ricardo's hands, this helped lead him back towards a variant Malthusianism, in which declining rates of return would be directly tied to the presumed declining rate of return in agriculture, mitigated somewhat by improvements in technique over time. As agricultural productivity declined (Ricardo assumed), wages would have to be increased continually to secure food for workers, squeezing profits over time. The problem was not so much that capitalism *should* not carry on growing; rather, on this basis, it may appear that capitalism *could* not carry on growing. It would simply grind to a halt.

Labour, nature and wealth

This rather blunt conclusion, certainly unsatisfactory given the immense improvements in agricultural productivity since Ricardo was writing, can be mitigated by an extension of the Ricardian conception. Karl Marx, notably, offered a development of the Ricardian labour theory of value that explicitly drew on the presence of the natural environment as a distinct feature in human society. 'Critique of the Gotha Programme', written as a series of marginal notes on the proposed programme of the newly founded German United Workers Party in 1875, makes his attitude forcefully clear. 'Labour is the source of all wealth and all culture,' in the original is replied to immediately: 'Labour is *not the source* of all wealth. *Nature* is just as much the source of use values (and it is surely of such that material wealth consists!) as labour, which itself is only the manifestation of a force of nature, human labour power.'[20] This 'bourgeois' phrasing should not have appeared in a socialist programme: as Marx notes, the idea that labour is the sole source of wealth is perfectly acceptable to those who employ labour, since if wealth is dependent on labour it must follow that a society in which some depend solely on labour will be the 'slave of other men'.

This reconceptualization of labour as a process uniting both the exertion of effort by people, and its work upon the natural world, opens the route to overcome the problem of Ricardian regress – the belief that all wealth in existence can be traced, ultimately, back to its origins as the product of labour. Instead of all capital being simply a sum of past labour, capitalism requires, at its starting point, a non-capitalist space from which an initial stock of wealth is drawn. Marx's example of the 'primitive accumulation' of capital, through slavery and colonialism is one infamous example of this; but we can consider, following Bellamy Foster, the depredations inflicted on the non-capitalist environment (a space always beyond the market, into which the market advances) as another variant.

The Ricardian problem has been turned on its head: rather than the natural world acting as a barrier to accumulation over time, once it is seen that the natural world can act as a means to overcome barriers to accumulation, it can be used to *overcome* problems in production. In Marx's conception of the economy, it was the differences in power within the market that provided the basis for accumulation of capital over time. For those lacking access to capital on any significant scale, which means the great majority, capitalism throws up structures designed to discipline and enforce the pattern of accumulation. The 'reserve army of labour', or the unemployed, are an essential part of the functioning of the labour market precisely because it is the means by which the labour market, with its demands for work performed, to order, for money, can be sustained. The relationships in the end are here not determined by free choices, but by the 'dull compulsion' of unemployment.

The reserve army of labour must be a *permanent* feature of life under capitalism or else, as Michal Kalecki suggested, the discipline necessary to sustain capitalist production would break down.[21] It could be argued that, during the post-war boom, something like this in fact occurred, trade unions in the developed world enjoying a power and autonomy they have never had before or since. Mass unemployment and later neoliberalism emerge as disciplinary instruments for labour.

It is this *disciplinary* character of unemployment and the absence of work that is missing from the steady-state literature. It means that the relationship of labour to nature that lies at the heart of the productive process is further mediated by the structures of the labour market. *Less* work (including a reduction in hours worked) does not necessarily mean less consumption of nature: it can equally mean greater destruction of nature, since the absence of work for some is used to compel work by others. Enormous environmental destruction can sit alongside mass unemployment. Of course, all sides would argue that there is a need to distribute work more evenly, and therefore (through programmes like the restriction of hours) reduce environmental damage. But this implies a far more substantive challenge to the structures of the labour market than is sometimes given credit for in the steady-state literature. It is not enough to argue piecemeal for a reduction in hours; rather, the use of unemployment as a disciplinary instrument would need to be reduced or removed, which implies a profound shift in the relationships that emerge in the centre of the production process: a shift in control and ownership away from capital and towards labour and its allies. Experience under capitalism with attempts to mandate shorter working weeks (for instance, the French 35-hour week) have run into difficulties precisely on this point. To the extent that the requirement of any individual to work at all is reduced, as is implied by Universal Basic Income (UBI), this can be partially effected. But this leaves the social capacity to control and organize labour unaffected. The complete programme would involve UBI, reduced working hours *and* the democratization of accumulation by both workers and consumers.

Among the more contentious of Marx's proposals was the suggestion, contained in the (unfinished) third volume of *Capital*, that capitalism, over time, was subject to a declining rate of profit. That is, as the size of investment in capital, relative to labour, expanded, the rate of profit available to be made from that increase in investment would itself fall. There is a logic to this: if surplus value is produced from the exploitation of labour, then it follows that a diminishing use of labour relative to capital should, over time, produce a decline in the rate of profit. Since the accumulation of profit was the fundamental driver of the system, a decline in its rate would imply a steady worsening of the conditions for accumulation over time. In this, Marx was drawing heavily on the work of the classical school, Ricardo most especially, but abandoning their natural law version of the tendency – in which agricultural land gradually becomes less productive over time – in favour of a claim that it was the accumulation of capital as capital that generated this self-defeating tendency. And with profits as the driver of accumulation, it therefore followed that accumulation (that is, growth) would slow in turn.

Disputes since have centred on the theoretical assumptions underlying this, and a search for the empirical evidence. Theoretical objections largely descend from Böhm-Bawerk, who, writing in the 1900s, noted that the law did not apply over time, reasoning that since the additional investment in capital would reduce the costs of output (other things being equal) and with these outputs becoming inputs at the next round of production, lead therefore to falling input costs.[22] On a similar basis, the 'neo-Ricardians' used Piero Sraffa's striking results to derive the same result, by a similar analytical method: that outputs from one production period form inputs into another.[23] Marx himself never finished the sections on the falling rate of profit, and fairly substantially hedged his own conception of the problem. It is certainly possible, too, to observe a declining rate of growth over time, and the problem of 'secular stagnation', at least in the developed world, has begun to attract mainstream attention.[24]

The critical insight here is that changes in the rate of accumulation over time are determined not *directly* by the physical limits, but *indirectly* by the process of accumulation itself. To this extent Marx's reconfiguration of the problem of growth is a break with the classical tradition, but it does not (therefore) assume either that growth is a choice, in the style of Millians, or that growth is unproblematic, in the style of the neoclassical school. Rather, growth is determined by relationships established among capital-holders themselves; and barriers to growth, given the need for accumulation to proceed on the basis of labour *and* nature, will be overcome through one or other (or both) of these factors: cutting real wages, for example, is a simple means to boost profits; upping the rate of environmental depletion, perhaps through the exploitation of otherwise untouched land, could be another. The relationship between all three, however, will not be determined beforehand, except insofar as the falling rate of profit may act to compel a search for greater exploitation. And it will certainly not be, in any sense, a choice.

Mill and the problem of accumulation

This brings us back to Mill. Mill stands between two traditions: the classical school, on one hand, and the emergent neoclassicals on the other. As such, he appeals to an objective theory of value, while rejecting the (Ricardian) labour theory of value. He argues that use-value can be safely discarded as irrelevant to the study of economics. He rejected the Ricardian search for an *absolute* standard of value, instead claiming that only a *relative* form of value was necessary for the understanding of the economy, with the task of economics being to explain the ratio of exchange between different commodities. Although all commodities exchanged would, of necessity, have some use-value, this would only in exceptional circumstances determine the price of the commodity – Mill suggests unique objects, such as works of art, might be subject to this. More generally, commodities' prices would be determined by their conditions of production, with the 'natural price' being dependent on the long-run costs of producing the commodity. Mill imposes a dualism on the economy: between production, where a presumed 'natural law' still operates, and distribution, which is determined in the Millian scheme by social institutions.

It is here that Mill's theoretical frame encounters difficulties. His definition of the long run, excluding the day-to-day volatility of prices, is dependent on the weak observation that prices tend, over time, to gravitate around the natural price.[25] This natural price sets a floor below which observed prices, whatever short-run conditions of demand and supply exist, may not fall over the long run.[26] The natural price, formed on the basis of costs of production, consists of a part paid to labour, expressed as a wage paid relative to other labour. The second, smaller part of the cost of production in general circumstances would be profit – the return paid to the owner of capital, which Mill baldly defines as the 'return on abstinence'. Those owning capital are paid for their patience, holding back from the consumption opportunities that are otherwise available to them.

This, rather vague, definition of the rate of return should alert us to the underlying problem here: at the heart of Mill's theory of *production* is, in fact, a theory of *consumption*. With the labour process left as a 'natural' condition of the economy, but the distribution of its proceeds left to social choice, Mill redefines the object of the economy as a concern over how best to organize consumption. Even the decision to accumulate, intended for further production, is at its heart a decision over consumption: in this case, what would become the early neoclassical justification for the payment of profits and interest as *abstinence* from consumption.

The weakness here is that Mill reduces the structures of power within capitalism, which work against both humans and nature, to something like a choice. We may make *bad* choices, given bad circumstances. But the choice still exists. Far from a world in which the natural environment is systematically destroyed by a blind process of accumulation, it is now, ultimately, an act of choice that leaves the process in place. This, of course, makes the environmental crisis both harder, and easier, to resolve. The structures of power need not alter, since they are there only to passively facilitate what amount to choice-led decisions over the form of consumption. On the other hand, without a theory of power built in to the economic analysis, it becomes very hard to see why or how anyone would want to shift from one mode of consumption to another. We are left with the hope that an autonomous shift in morality, freely taken by free individuals, would lead us to change consumption patterns and move into the steady state.

Conclusion

What lurks beneath Mill's conception of the steady state, and of later, Millian versions of the same, is the assumption that growth remains, to some extent, a *choice*. Given the political will, it should be possible to introduce reforms to the system that remove its drive to endless, environmentally destructive growth, and replace that drive with a different bias: towards, in Jackson's phrase, 'prosperity without growth'. It should be noted, too, that this implies, as it does for the neoclassical school, a theoretical separation between the consideration of the conditions necessary for growth over time, and the conditions that drive the more ordinary business cycle of recessions and booms.

We have argued here, instead, for a conception of the economy that breaks with the techniques of neoclassicism in favour of a labour–nature reconceptualization of economic processes, drawing on the work of Ricardo, the 'circuitist' school in general, and Marx in particular. The distinction, somewhat buried by Marxist scholarship, but stressed by recent work by ecologists, between labour and natural wealth allows us to see how environmental crisis can, rather than forming a barrier to growth, act as a spur to further accumulation. It therefore directly poses the question not just of ending growth, as such, but of the need to address the problems of economic organization directly: both in removing the competitive relationships that structure organizations, and in paving the way for an ecologically motivated planning of the economy. That, in turn, as ecosocialist Joel Kovel has noted, requires political contest: 'No administrative path leads to the society we need.'[27]

That economic restructuring would draw on critical insights from the degrowth literature, expanding the extent of non-work time, providing a basic income, and stressing the weakness of 'growth' as a target – however 'inclusive' or 'green'. But it would lean, too, on the more traditional concerns of the left in democratizing the production process, both at the point of production and as part of a wider planning effort.

PART II: CASE STUDIES

CHAPTER 5

Giving green teeth to the Tiger? A critique of 'green growth' in South Korea

Bettina Bluemling and Sun-Jin Yun

Introduction

Since climate change has come to the core of policy-making, as well as since the 2008 financial crisis, 'low-carbon development', 'green economy' and the 'global green new deal' have emerged as discursive formations, with 'low-carbon green growth', or simply 'green growth', as a more recent discourse.[1] Green growth has become the focus of a variety of reports by international organizations, and, while definitions slightly differ,[2] there is agreement that green growth shall combine economic growth with higher resource-use efficiency and fewer emissions,[3] to the end of sustaining society's resource stock,[4] and by the means of a process that catalyses investment and innovation, in the course of which new economic opportunities are created.[5] Furthermore, there is agreement that green growth has to be seen as a sub-set of sustainable development,[6] as it 'is narrower in scope, entailing an operational policy agenda that can help achieve concrete, measurable progress at the interface of the economy and the environment'.[7]

In this chapter, we shall argue that green growth, as it has been put forward by South Korea's Lee administration, has considerable constraints in serving as a discourse in complex times of dynamic changes in the environment, economy and society. First of all, these constraints stem from its genealogy. Green growth is a policy discourse, and as such it is important to understand the political context out of which this discursive process has emerged and in which it is situated. Second, we argue that green growth is built on out-dated grounds. Particularly after the 2008 economic crisis, criticism of growth ethics has become more widespread, and counter-discourses of 'degrowth' and 'a-growth' have been set forth that move beyond 'greening growth'.[8] Third, green growth assumes that technological progress can support a decoupling of growth from the 'sustenance base'. While this is to some extent true, South Korea, a forerunner country of green growth, failed to achieve such a decoupling despite making green growth its national development strategy. And fourth, green growth is a performance-oriented concept. While, with sustainable development, the focus has first and foremost been on the process of development, green growth all of a sudden is 'there', presented in indicators and shiny brochures. This focus on performance without the involvement of civil society – as sustainable development allowed – is likely to make it an empty concept.

We will in the following elaborate on each of these claims by contrasting green growth with sustainable development, to which green growth is generally expected to contribute.[9] Green growth builds upon sustainable development, and thereby strengthens certain of its elements while belittling others. For example, sustainable development did certainly not neglect economic growth;[10] however, the primacy of growth over social and ecological concerns appears to be distinct to green growth. Green growth hence can be understood as a contemporary reinterpretation of sustainable development. By a comparison, we will be able to understand the shift that is happening if green growth indeed becomes a more prominent policy discourse. We situate this discussion using the case of the Republic of Korea. The Lee Myung-bak administration (2008–2013) played a pivotal role in propagating green growth worldwide.[11] According to UNEP, the Republic of Korea is 'a model green-growth nation'.[12] Similarly, the Asian Development Bank sees the Republic of Korea, together with Japan and Singapore, as a forerunner of experiences in coupling emission reduction and growth, from which developing Asia could learn.[13] However, the international endorsement of the Republic of Korea's green growth efforts was tightly knit with the endorsement of then President Lee. Angel Gurria, the OECD secretary-general, called him the 'Father of Green Growth'.[14] In 2010, Lee was awarded the 'Zayed International Prize for the Environment', i.e. 'the most prestigious and valuable international environmental award worldwide'.[15] The laudation praises his 'vision and leadership ... [as] a central driver in transforming the Republic of Korea's development path into a low carbon, resource efficient, and Green Economy. ... President Lee Myung-bak has signaled that Green Growth is a strategy well beyond current economic recovery efforts and is intended to fashion a green economic future. This has the potential of starting a domino effect on the major Asian economies'.[16] It is the intention of this chapter to also enquire how President Lee's influence played out in the Republic of Korea's green growth policy.

Green growth is a discourse that was initiated by Asia-Pacific leaders as an alternative to 'sustainable development', which was deemed to be losing its suitability for the Asia-Pacific context. It therefore can be assumed to take into consideration the particularities of the region. This is why, at the end of this chapter, we will ask whether, given South Korea's experiences, the green growth discourse bears a greater promise for other countries in the region than sustainable development.

Green growth: an autocratic environmental discourse

In the beginning of 'sustainable development', there was a commission of environmental experts and former UN high functionaries, the Brundtland Commission, which had the mandate to bridge the gap between developing countries seeking economic development, and developed countries increasingly concerned about the deterioration of the environment. The Commission consulted widely for four years, asking advice from expert bodies, meeting representatives from political movements, and holding public sessions in several countries.[17] The result was the 1987 published final report *Our Common Future*, which became the basis for the United Nations Conference on Environment and Development (UNCED) in 1992. In parallel with the conference, nearly 20,000 civil society representatives met at the 'Global Forum'.[18] The two events were 'obviously co-ordinated',[19] and NGOs tried to influence negotiation outcomes throughout the UNCED process. They lobbied at preparation committee meetings and participated in national delegations, as well as trying to raise awareness and appealing to national governments participating in

UNCED.[20] Together, these two conferences provided momentum for societal debates and policy programmes still ongoing today. Consider, for example, declarations like the Local Agenda 21 where, throughout its 40 chapters, sustainable development is described as requiring partnership with a wide range of actors, including citizens, NGOs, businesses and government agencies of different levels.[21] Accordingly, this multitude of actors took the Rio debates further and initiated (local) environmental initiatives.[22] While sustainable development has been criticized for being ill-defined and vague,[23] its vagueness has also been considered its strength.[24] The prerequisite that it shall be defined further within the respective societal contexts enabled civil society[25] engagement and debates on the character of their respective local 'common futures'. As Papadakis[26] puts it: 'It is through participatory governance procedures that the vague and ill-defined notion of sustainable development is expected to be eventually clarified and consolidated.' While there are mixed results as to the participatory character of these procedures[27] at least, sustainable development enabled the involvement of civil society.

In contrast to sustainable development, 'green growth' was never debated, at the outset, within civil society such that civil society could have shaped it and supported its implementation. The earliest mention of green growth in policy-making dates back to 2005, when it was proposed in Seoul, the Republic of Korea, at the Fifth Ministerial Conference on Environment and Development in Asia and the Pacific. One of the outcomes of this conference was the establishment of the Seoul Initiative Network on Green Growth,[28] and the publication 'Green Growth at a Glance'.[29]

From this publication, the idea behind green growth can be better understood. While Asia-Pacific governments acknowledge that ecosystems show signs of stress, they posit that the need for further economic growth still remains pressing in the region because there are still many poor countries where poverty is the most urgent problem to be solved. Green growth is proposed to reconcile continued growth and a reduction in environmental damage. In a sense, by initiating a growth-oriented discourse, Asia-Pacific leaders make their claims to the 'right to development' that was debated in Rio, and is captured in Principle 3 of the Rio Declaration.

Green growth is supposed to 'give teeth', clarity and direction to sustainable development.[30] The economic system is put at the centre of sustainable development, as it 'to a significant degree underpin[s] the structure and functioning of all countries'.[31] While the economy stands at the centre, public policy is considered central for its regulation:

> The key argument to be made here is that the rapid economic growth which several countries in the regions are currently enjoying – and which serves as a key driver for poverty reduction – is in essence a reflection of these countries' deliberate public policy initiatives. ... Just as rapid economic growth is not a chance of occurrence, so is environmental sustainability achievable only through deliberate integrated policies. Green Growth proposes to harness the power of economic growth while guiding it in a way that will enhance the immense possibilities provided by innovative technologies and industries, so that progress can be registered in more than gross domestic product increases alone.[32]

The positioning of green growth within society can be directly understood from this citation: just as economic growth is seen as a result of public policy, policy is understood to be able to invent a new understanding of economic growth, i.e. green growth, and steer the economy towards the realization of such kind of growth. Civil society hereby receives only limited attention. On one page of the 50-page document it is assigned the role of 'setting agendas', 'providing scientific knowledge', 'conferring legitimacy' to policies and 'implementing solutions'.[33]

'Green Growth at a Glance' ends with a question that is addressed to the Asia-Pacific governments, i.e. 'Do we have the collective will to take on the challenge?'[34] In 2008, the newly elected South Korean government indicated its will by presenting 'green growth' as its new national development strategy.

The centrality of 'green growth' in Korea's new government can be attributed to Mr Rae Kwon Chung, then director of UNESCAP and head of the Fifth Ministerial Conference. In Korea, he was a government official for international affairs. He had initiated the writing of the report 'Green Growth at a Glance', and was familiar with Paul Ekins' publication 'Economic Growth and Environmental Sustainability – The Prospects for Green Growth'.[35] Ekins was also involved in 'Green Growth at a Glance', as a reviewer as well as by providing materials. By allying with the academic who had published first on green growth, by establishing the Seoul Initiative Network on Green Growth, and by devising green growth as a national development strategy, Korea's government staked its claims as a green growth pioneer. This was well understood and utilized by President Lee. In a speech in 2008, he proclaimed: 'If we make up our minds before others and take action, we will be able to lead green growth and take the initiative in a new civilization.'[36] He foresaw the country being 'reborn as a green power'.[37]

Unlike the genealogy of sustainable development, 'green growth' was devised by national policy-makers. In January 2009, the Korean government announced the 'National Strategy for Green Growth and Its Five-Year Plan', in which its green growth strategy was combined with a job creation policy.[38] While this national strategy was formulated in cooperation with 12 joint working groups from the public and private sector, and opinions were also collected from NGOs and local governments, the approach of the national strategy was criticized as being strongly government-centred. According to Lee and Yun,[39] it 'heavily depends on government authority and regards citizens as passive agents'.

Green growth, however, became central for domestic policy. Every ministry developed projects related to green growth, 'with the label "green" being used to describe numerous initiatives and policies'.[40] The central 'Green New Job Creation Plan' was organized in four themes and nine core projects were allocated across these themes.[41] For the theme environmental protection, the 'Four Major Rivers' project, together with 'securing water resources', was the core project. It formed 'the backbone of the Lee administration's plan for green growth'[42] and was praised by the UNEP as a 'key to green growth'.[43]

The general goal of the 'Four Major Rivers' project was to 'restore the Han, Nakdong, Geum and Yeongsan Rivers and to provide water security, flood control and ecosystem vitality'. The project would also 'prevent natural disasters such as floods and droughts, protect the environment and promote historical and cultural tourism'.

Furthermore, the project would 'result in the creation of many new jobs, furthering economic growth that also broadens the horizon of Korea's green growth initiative'.[44]

What sounds like a perfect combination of several interests turned out to be a disaster from the perspective of civil society. 'Four Major Rivers' was a large engineering project with two specific objectives: 1.) to build, on the four major rivers, 16 new dams, rebuild 87 old dams, reinforce 209 miles of riverbanks and to dredge 570 million cubic meters of sediment to deepen nearly 700 kilometres of riverbed; additionally, bike trails and parks were to be constructed for public use; 2.) to build, on 14 tributaries, five new dams, rebuild nine dams, and buttress 243 kilometres of riverbanks with concrete.[45] These massive engineering projects were aimed at reducing the costs that had occurred due to flood damage, river restoration and flood prevention. While projects were mainly located at the main streams of the four rivers, only 3.6 per cent of flood-incurred costs had arisen at these streams during the period from 1999 to 2003. At the same time, local and small tributaries were neglected by the project, where, however, the great majority of damage costs had occurred.[46]

The engineering works were also intended to provide water security; to this end, massive dam projects were realized under the name of 'Korea, the water-stressed country'. However, past national water-related plans, including long-term water resource plans, had never defined South Korea as a water-stressed country. The concept of water stress utilized (total water capacity divided by the number of population) is very simple as it does not consider how efficiently water is used based on technologies and water management. The concept of a 'water-stressed country' had been invented by a private institute, the 'International Population Impact Institute'. The title of the institute already signifies that its focus is not on water-related issues. Therefore, it can be questioned whether it was able to provide sufficient expertise for a large-scale water engineering project as the Four Major Rivers project. However, the Korean government tried to persuade the public to accept 'Korea, the water-stressed country' by claiming that it stems from the UN. According to the Water Poverty Index, which was invented by the UK Eco-Hydrological Institute of Keele University, South Korea ranks 58 among 147 countries in terms of water poverty. Its Index is 59.5, slightly less than Germany (61.3) and New Zealand (60.8).[47] This suggests that it does not suffer from water shortage problems. The Index takes the water resource, distribution rates of tap water, water resource management technologies, social infrastructure, income levels, the amount of water use, and the degree of environmental protection into consideration.

A budget of US$18 billion was assigned to the project for the period 2009 to 2012.[48] This was 'the biggest investment of government money over the shortest time period in modern Korean history'.[49] From the nearly 200,000 jobs that were to be created, all would be within the construction sector, with limited potential of, to quote the government, 'broadening the horizon' of Korea's economic growth. As of August 2010, only 1,222 jobs had been created, and, while the project had been intended to support the local economy, local company participation was limited.[50]

All these shortcomings in conception and implementation led to widespread opposition from civil society.[51] A large variety of civil society groups jointly took action against the project, ranging from religious groups initiating pilgrimages to scientists providing simulations and calculations on its impacts on the ecosystem, researchers conducting open lectures on the project or initiating field trips to the construction sites and lawyers supporting more than 10,000 citizens' suing of the government as it 'had violated the Rivers Act, the National Finance Act, the Framework Act on Environmental Policy, the Environmental Impact Assessment Act, and the Cultural Heritage Protection Act'.[52] Opposition to the project also led to the foundation of POMAC, the 'Professors' Organization for Movement Against Grand Korean Canal', in March 2008, right after President Lee took office. It was composed of 2,544 professors from different disciplines and from 115 universities nation-wide. This kind of action on such a scale was so unique in South Korea since the democratization movement in 1987 that it drew the attention of the internationally renowned journal *Science*. According to Normile,[53] the formation of POMAC is unprecedented in Korean history, and maybe even internationally. While this opposition could not stop the Four Major Rivers project, it was able to mitigate some of its effects. Findings by scientists in several instances contributed to a modification of original plans, such as adjusting the height of dams.

After the project was carried out, the national Board of Audit and Inspection, which under the Lee administration had not seen any 'particular problems with the project', published its last report in 2013. In this report, it states that the project was realized because of 'President Lee's determination'. The board, however, concludes that the project 'should never have happened'.[54]

A further, controversial point in regard to the national green growth policy was the role that the government assigned to nuclear power as a 'clean energy'. Also in other Asian countries, nuclear power has undergone a revival due to its diminished carbon footprint.[55] The Republic of Korea already had, as of 2011, the highest density of nuclear power reactors in the world, and the fifth highest installed capacity.[56] While 23 reactors are in operation, the government planned to increase their number to 41. The long-term goal was to increase the share of nuclear power in total power generation capacity to 29 per cent by 2035.[57]

The plans of the Korean government under the umbrella of 'green growth' show the autocratic nature of the green growth discourse, and therewith make it distinct from 'sustainable development'. The Four Major Rivers project exemplifies green growth's autocratic nature 'in the field'. Civil society involvement in shaping 'green growth' was impeded, e.g. by not approving the registration of an NGO who would critically deal with river restoration; or by only inviting a selected 'public' to consultation meetings or local briefing sessions.[58] The discourse had been initiated at a high-level Ministerial Meeting, and its 'key project' was implemented in opposition to widespread civil society concerns. Green growth was used to legitimate a project that lacked legitimation by civil society.

As mentioned before, the Republic of Korea has been made a 'model' for green growth internationally. The autocratic implementation of this major project under the umbrella of green growth by the Lee administration, against the protests of civil society, has not found much resonance in international records. However, this conflict between civil society and policy-makers finds parallels in the Rio +20 summit, where civil society denounced 'green growth'.[59]

Green growth is built on outdated premises

Already within debates on sustainable development, growth was attributed 'almost religious connotations of ultimate goodness',[60] and still today the ethics of growth can be found 'in most of the documents of economic organisations' where it 'often appears as an unquestioned fundamental condition for acting on climate change'.[61]

At the beginning of the 1990s, growth did not yet play a major role. First, the Rio Declaration mentions 'growth' only once, i.e. when it proclaims that the international economic system should lead to economic growth, interestingly, in parallel to sustainable development.[62] The focus in the Rio Declaration is given upon 'development', i.e. the 'right to development' (Principle 3[63]), with 'development' including the consideration of environmental protection as an integral part (Principle 4). At Rio, the conflict was between developing countries who wanted to have the right to develop, and developed countries being concerned about the deterioration of environmental conditions.

The focus on development at that time is also evident in the rejection of the combination of 'growth' and 'sustainable', with 'sustainable growth' being called an 'impossibility theorem'.[64] Development is fundamentally different from growth. It is 'a process which results in the increased welfare of the group under consideration, perhaps with special reference to the least well-off members of the group'.[65] It does not, unlike growth, imply only more output, but 'different kinds of output than were previously produced, as well as changes in the technical and institutional arrangements by which output is produced and distributed'.[66] These changes would include alterations in 'organization, government policy, patterns of ownership, human skills and tasks, and consumer tastes and preferences'.[67]

However, in contrast, 'growth' is essentially taken to mean 'economic growth', i.e. GDP growth.[68] Some economists consider that GDP growth is inadequate to measure progress. Among the most frequent criticisms is that GDP mainly measures market production, expressed in monetary units, and does not include the great majority of non-monetary economic production. Particularly in Asian countries, the non-monetary economy, e.g. the subsistence economy of smallholders, forms a crucial part of the domestic economy.

Research has shown that a functioning non-monetary economy reduces the vulnerability of the poor, and that it therefore should be understood as a part of the economy.[69] 'Green growth' was to some extent devised because there are still countries in the Asia-Pacific region where poverty alleviation is of utmost importance. By referring to conventional measures of growth, green growth does not incorporate and represent the particularities of the region from which it emerges and for which it was devised. It misses the chance to capture and set the stage for a different kind of development in the Asia-Pacific region.

A second common criticism of GDP, which is also important for the Asia-Pacific region, is that it does not mirror the economic situation of households. Real household income has grown quite differently from real GDP per capita, and generally at a lower rate.[70] The Asia-Pacific has shown the second largest increase in income inequality worldwide, with inequality increasing by 13 per cent from the early 1990s to the late 2000s.[71] Again, the concept of 'growth' cannot capture these trends.

Even among conservatives, the value of GDP as an indicator is questioned. In 2009, the conservative president of France, Nicolas Sarkozy, assembled a commission with leading economists, social scientists and Joseph Stiglitz as the president in order to 'identify the limits of GDP as an indicator of economic performance and social progress' and to assess the feasibility of alternative measurement tools.[72] The committee concluded that the measurement of economic activity should 'better reflect the structural changes which have characterized the evolution of modern economies'.[73] Measurement should 'shift emphasis' from 'economic production' to 'people's well-being' within a context of sustainability.[74] The reason for this change would be that 'there appears to be an increasing gap between the information contained in aggregate GDP data and what counts for common people's well-being'.[75] This is also why they recommended looking at income and consumption per capita, rather than production, as well as wealth accumulation of households, and the distribution of income, consumption and wealth.

The promise of decoupling

Green growth hence still foregrounds economic growth as the main objective for economic policy. The idea is to decouple economic growth from its sustenance base. Physical limits to growth are accepted, and GDP can 'free itself from these limits only to the extent that it "decouples" itself from growth in physical production'.[76] Decoupling is understood to happen by increasing the productivity and use efficiency of resources per unit of benefit generated by the economy,[77] and by reducing waste through the reuse of resources. In order to realize such decoupling, technical measures are required, and technical innovation again is assumed to lead to growth in the respective economic sector. For example, in the energy sector, as an important sector for realizing low-carbon development, decoupling of energy use and economic growth shall be achieved by efficiency increases as well as a reduction of the reliance on non-renewable resources. The exploitation of renewable energy and respective technological innovation again would lead to growth in the energy sector.

Taking the Republic of Korea as an example, the question arises as to what extent decoupling has been achieved, six years after the green growth paradigm was implemented. According to statistics from the Korea Energy Economics Institute,[78] final energy consumption and CO_2 emissions increased after 2008. Furthermore, since 2009 the economic growth rate has been lower than the energy consumption growth rate – decoupling in this respect has not taken place. Also in international comparisons, the Republic is hardly a forerunner in terms of a decoupling of energy use and growth. Korea ranks twelfth in terms of its GDP and purchasing power, but among this list of 12, only the US and Australia have higher energy consumption per capita.[79] Korea's government, furthermore, increased the share of nuclear power in overall energy production. Not to mention the tremendous risks associated with nuclear energy, the deposition of nuclear waste still is a major problem, particularly for a peninsula such as Korea. Promoting nuclear power could hardly be said to be in line with an avoidance of waste in the process of economic growth. We can conclude that this 'model' did not achieve a decoupling of growth and energy.

Green growth focuses on performance and indicators

In its beginnings, the 'sustainable development' discourse incorporated a wealth of issues. Exemplary for this is 'Agenda 21', whose 40 chapters cover a variety of environment and development issues, ranging from children and youth to the management of toxic chemicals. While this did contribute to conceptual ambiguity, it also made possible the involvement of a diversity of actors concerned with the dichotomy of development and the environment. However, while sustainable development focused on the process and involved a variety of stakeholders, green growth seems to be an outcome-oriented concept with a focus on performance with little concern for civil society's involvement. Furthermore, as outlined above, it does not consider social equity, beyond balance between economic growth and environmental protection.

In 2012, green growth is still considered a concept 'in the making';[80] however, the OECD already in 2011 published a report on indicators to measure green growth, and in early 2012 'Statistics Korea' published its report 'Korea's Green Growth – based on OECD Green Growth Indicators'. The publication happened without any involvement of civil society in defining what green growth may be in South Korea, and how it should accordingly be measured. While the introduction to the report states, 'Hopefully, green growth indicators are further developed for environmentally-friendly and sustainable economic growth in the midst of attention and participation of the government, businesses, and citizens',[81] hardly any actions were undertaken by the government to stimulate such a debate. Rather, the government did not participate in debates on controversial green growth projects. The concept of green growth remained in a technocratic sphere, while sustainable development – to which it hopes to contribute – saw the participation of civil society as crucial, so that the latter can shape the 'common future'.

A brief review of the Statistics Korea report supports this claim. The large majority of indicators of environmental and resource productivity are based on GDP as a reference unit. Greenhouse gas emissions productivity uses annual GHG emissions productivity divided by real GDP. It is argued that a higher productivity indicates a decoupling of economic growth and GHG emissions. Data is only provided from 2000 to 2009. From 2007 on, productivity increases stop, and the effects of the green growth policy of the government are not shown further. Also consumption-based CO2 emissions productivity is only shown before the green growth policy could have taken effect (until 2009), and while energy efficiency (real GDP/primary energy consumption) is shown until 2010, again from 2008 on energy efficiency shows a downward trend.

Both indicators of efficiency and GDP-based productivity have been widely criticized. The criticism of GDP has been outlined above. Efficiency indicators show changes in the ratio of inputs and outputs, which is to be improved through the optimization of the underlying process.[82] Efficiency cannot show if, by improving a process, the total use of inputs decreased as it does not include a limit to these inputs. This is why 'sufficiency' has been proposed as a concept that includes limitations,[83, 84] i.e. the total scale of the economy and its carrying capacity. Indicators based on sufficiency would allow civil societies to understand the status quo of their society's withdrawal from the sustenance base. This is important information for a society deciding which development direction to take and whether development is to be based on 'growth'.

Conclusion

In this chapter, we outlined that green growth has weaknesses in four regards, which we illustrated in the case of South Korea, a country that was praised as a 'model green-growth nation'. First, green growth has been, from the outset, a discourse in which citizen involvement appears peripheral at best. In South Korea, the National Strategy for Green Growth was implemented in opposition to widespread civil society concerns. Green growth was used by the government to legitimate a project that lacked legitimation by civil society. The Lee administration partly could do so as it received full support from international organizations,[85] which provided an uncritical form of external legitimacy.[86] A second weakness is that 'growth' has not only faced renewed criticism due to the 2008 economic crisis; it also fails to capture some Asia-Pacific economic particularities, e.g. the importance of the non-monetary economy to a society's development, as well as a worrying trend of increasing income inequalities, which also influences a country's quality of development. While with green growth, Asia-Pacific leaders can be understood as having made their claim to the 'right to development' (as declared in Rio 1992) and as having brought forward green growth to give shape to this claim, the concept itself inherently fails to respond to certain Asia-Pacific particularities of development. The idea of decoupling economic growth from the sustenance base, and here we get to the third weakness of green growth, is an important one as many Asian economies are in a phase of modernization. By bringing in new, less resource dependent and more efficient technologies in the earlier stages of their modernization process, economies will not be trapped in a resource-dependent development pathway as many more developed countries are. However, the projects that were realized under the umbrella of green growth in South Korea do not indicate any change in technological paradigms. The Four Main Rivers project is a very resource-intensive engineering project with little potential for technological innovation. National-level indicators furthermore showed that energy intensity has increased since the inauguration of the Green Growth National Development Strategy – a decoupling of energy use and growth has hardly taken place. Finally, it is questionable if the indicators of GDP and efficiency really respond to the problem of the 'limits to growth'. If, after a certain transition process, changes were to be measured, other indicators, notably 'sufficiency', may be better suited as they include the limitations of the sustenance base.

When the Lee administration's term ended, it left the new president, Park Geun-hye, with a dilemma. On the one hand, given the opposition to domestic green growth policies as implemented by the Lee administration, the new government distanced itself from the green growth paradigm. It demoted 'green growth' offices or abolished them and removed 'green' from the names of government departments.[87] An audit of the Four Major Rivers project revealed corruption among officials of the former government, in which even President Lee was found to be involved, and revealed major construction defects and irresponsible spending.[88] However, on the other hand, criticism arose that the new administration would not advance a progressive climate and environmental policy. Furthermore, South Korea had internationally been acknowledged as a pioneering country for green growth.[89] The 'Global Green Growth Institute' established under the Lee administration was the first Korea-led international organization.[90] Furthermore, since 2011 Korea has hosted the 'Green Climate Fund', and has run the 'Korea Green Growth Partnership' together with the World Bank.

In October 2013, the government issued what it called 'Green Growth 2.0' and re-launched a commission on green growth.[91] This commission, however, is not a presidential committee; it belongs to the prime minister's office. Furthermore, 'Green Growth 2.0' is intended to contribute to a new discourse, that of the 'creative economy', and does not have a major place in the government's policy agenda. While the 'Green Growth 2.0' commission is said to follow a 'bottom-up approach',[92] this can be questioned on the basis of this commission's composition: 17 members are officials from ministries, and 21 are from the private sector, of which only one member is from a civil society organization, a consumer organization. How far 'Green Growth 2.0' will be more participatory remains to be seen. The autocratic character of green growth is also evident in other countries. In India, green growth seems to be realized in a 'primarily techno-bureaucratic policy framework'.[93] With Japan's and China's climate change governance based on exclusive state intervention,[94] we cannot expect green growth to be very different from the Lee administration's 'green growth'.

Countries in the Asia-Pacific have been diversifying in their economic structures. However, the autocratic way in which the Green Growth National Strategy was implemented in South Korea; the GDP as a measure of growth; or simple productivity and efficiency indicators will not be able to capture and respond to the complex dynamic changes that countries undergo.

Even if ill-defined and vague, sustainable development at least allowed for a locally specific definition of what development should be about, and a discussion of the tensions and consequences of maintaining the 'sustenance base'. Under sustainable development, social justice and non-monetary development play a role. This is why we argue here that as long as new discourses do not manage to capture and support current complex dynamics within societies, sustainable

Development will do well enough, as it allows local stakeholders to define and deal with the complexities of 'the double crises' and to reflect on modernization's 'own excesses and vicious spiral of destructive subjugation'.[95] In more developed countries, discussion may focus on how to realize 'sustainable degrowth';[96] in less developed countries, the focus may be on equitable, inclusive and sustainable development. A variety of questions need societal consensus. Which kind of development does society want and at what costs? What is 'the environment' to a certain society? Can it be subject to biotechnology or shall it be exposed to the risks of nuclear power? These questions still require debate. At least, sustainable development provides the room for discussion.

CHAPTER 6

Lessons from the EU: why capitalism cannot be rescued from its own contradictions

Birgit Mahnkopf

The question of how to foster economic growth and social equity while minimizing the negative consequences of climate change, energy shortages, and rising prices of raw materials and food is no longer discussed under the rubric of sustainable development. Recent decades have seen that concept lose its meaning. In place of an agenda of specific interventions to reduce the consumption of natural resources has come one of a low carbon, resource-efficient green economy, particularly in the European Union. At first glance, the green economy may be seen as a modernized variant of the sustainable development approach that had been institutionalized in the EU's environmental and energy policy since the late 1990s. However, since the outbreak of the financial and economic crisis in 2008 it has become a mainstream approach, advocated not only by European Green parties, NGOs and civil society organizations, but also by social democrats, sections of the conservative parties, business lobby groups and academics. This distinguishes the European debate from other cases such as the South Korean, where the green growth approach can be seen as an autocratically defined and implemented concept that drew its legitimacy from international organizations (see Bettina Bluemling and Sun-Jin Yun in this volume).

While the earlier sustainable development discourse referred to the impossible, namely an environmentally sustainable relationship between human and nonhuman nature based on the dynamic of capitalist accumulation and private property, the new green economy approach promises to find a way out of the structural crisis of capitalist accumulation, by stimulating green investment opportunities. Within the European context, the green growth narrative is synonymous with *green capitalism*, characterized by a low carbon, resource-efficient and highly competitive economy. Keynesian-influenced social scientists too, although dissenting from other aspects of the green-economy mainstream (such as social and industrial policy within a 'Green New Deal'), aspire above all to expand the limits of growth. The core message of the 'green narrative' is that intelligent macroeconomic policies and technological advances in the form of new products, processes and services can create 'sustainable' or 'qualitative' growth that is largely uncoupled from environmental damage and resource consumption. Such optimism relies on the assumption that capitalism is capable of yet another turnaround, this time of a social and ecological nature, and that it is still able, on the basis of the profit motive and the market, to become a 'decent capitalism' through targeted government intervention and improved institutions. Green capitalism is presumed to constitute a win–win situation in which investment in the energy sector, public infrastructures and environmental protection can generate additional jobs in the short term in environmental industries and, at the same time, create low-carbon infrastructures. In the medium term, this would increase national energy security by reducing reliance on energy imports and would also create competitive advantages through technological leadership. Thus, everybody would be better off and no one would lose out. New investment opportunities would create new profits for businesses. Workers could look forward to new, possibly even high-quality jobs that would boost their incomes and consumption chances, while governments could hope to reduce their debt levels, fostering economic and political stability. The environment would be protected and future generations could look forward to a life worth living. In short: higher efficiency would reduce the costs for energy and materials and would thus allow private households to spend more on consumption and businesses to invest more in fixed capital. The crisis of over-accumulation, from which the global economy has suffered for several decades and which keeps producing new bubbles and busts, would be solved through a new regime of investment and accumulation.

Obviously, this scenario of green growth, to which many European countries subscribe, is composed of a strange mix of, firstly, a naïve confidence in the dynamics of technical progress, ignoring most of its unintended side effects and unprecedented risks, and the limited possibilities of decoupling economic growth, resource consumption and pollutant emissions (as referred to by Ulrich Hoffmann in Chapter 1). Secondly, it includes a moralizing critique of consumer society that rarely admits its class-based sociological assumptions. Thirdly, the green growth approach as adopted within the EU, despite fears of crisis, places a high degree of confidence in the self-healing power and capacity of competitive markets.

However, given the biophysical depletion of natural resources clearly apparent today, the decisive question is whether it is possible to extend the boundaries of accumulation still further. At present, as in the past, only two strategies are available: first, spatial expansion, i.e. the further expansion of markets and integration of subsistence agriculture into a global, capitalized agricultural industry, as well as the appropriation of mineral and non-mineral raw materials, and, second, temporal acceleration, i.e., further increasing labour productivity, which has to be secured through the capital intensive combination of human labour (or the human knowledge and expertise embodied in technologies) with increasingly expensive raw materials and energies.

The EU as an advocate of green growth

In the past, the EU has often been portrayed as the bearer of hope for a new global ecological awareness. It could claim responsibility for the First World treaties on legally binding emission targets for greenhouse gas emissions and for the Cartagena Protocol on biodiversity. The goal of sustainability is firmly anchored in Article 3 of the consolidated version of the Treaty on European Union. The EU has agreed a far-reaching and integrative strategy according to which environmental, social and economic interests are to be aligned at every level and it has broadly acknowledged the transition to a renewable energy regime as a necessity.

However, the crux lies in the role of the 'precautionary principle', which is supposed to guide the EU's environmental policy. This principle, which is written into EU law, introduced the reversed burden of proof with regard to environmentally hazardous activities and requires industries to demonstrate the safety of their products to regulators, rather than regulators having to prove harm. But following the re-launch of the so-called 'Lisbon Strategy' in 2005, when the EU Council agreed to reform priorities on 'growth and jobs', the 'regulatory pendulum' in the EU has begun to shift towards an approach associated with a strict cost–benefit analysis. Recent years have witnessed a decreasing consensus within the Union as to application of the precautionary principle in its strict form, with the argument being that 'costs on those regulated (e.g. industry) may simply be too high'.[1]

The EU's environmental policy is encapsulated in the dominant ideological discourse of neoliberalism, which assumes that the private sector and market mechanisms will find the optimal solutions for so-called 'environmental problems', that competition is the most effective method of innovative discovery, and that government interference in social and economic processes inevitably leads to inefficient and suboptimal solutions of environmental problems. Therefore, the centrepiece of the EU's combined environmental and energy policy is to exploit win–win opportunities – by promoting eco-efficient innovations, increasing energy efficiency, greening public procurement and establishing an appropriate regulatory framework. In addition to *market instruments* such as ecological tax reforms, pollution charges, policies to reduce environmentally harmful subsidies (in agriculture, mining, air and road transport), and emissions trading, *voluntary commitments* by economic actors is the second basic principle which is applied.

This is a view widely shared by many Green parties, who are the most outspoken advocates of a Green New Deal, with a major focus on the promotion of renewable energy sources and other low-carbon technologies. Some even assume that economic growth could become largely independent of the consumption of non-renewable energy sources. Other proponents such as the European Trade Union Congress, heterodox economists and some public sector trade unions place more emphasis on the problem of private markets failing to drive green growth as strongly and quickly as required. Thus, they want governments to play a more active and leading role.

However, Green party members, trade union representatives, business lobbyists and economists in the EU share some common assumptions: firstly, that even though human civilizations do have to reduce their impact on the planet, the socio-economic system of capitalism does not need to be fundamentally restructured. Secondly, that low carbon production, based on appropriate technologies, can substantially 'dematerialize' economic activity, thus 'environmentally friendly growth' is technically possible. Thirdly, that if unavoidable 'externalities' like carbon dioxide and other pollutants were to be priced, markets would work their magic and the economy could keep growing indefinitely. Fourthly, government intervention is needed to compensate for market failures, but government is important only as an enabler of the green economic activity that has to originate from the private sector. Fifthly, that the development of a new investment and accumulation regime will solve the over-accumulation crisis that harmed the world economy for decades and has caused continuous financial bubbles and busts. Of course, the necessity to increase profits and therefore consumption would remain because the crucial credit mechanism, which requires that profits be made, would stay in place. The 'green stimulus' aims to lead the economy back onto the path of continuous consumption and rising profits – in one word: growth. There is no intention of breaking the unholy alliance of profit maximization and rising consumption.

At the same time, the EU serves as a 'best case' example for addressing the climate and energy crises by implementing innovative policies which aim to harmonize climate and energy legislation across the EU to ambitious levels that are thus far unmatched by other nation states or regional groups. Following the green growth debate in Europe, one might get the impression that incremental adjustment to economic incentives linked to long-term end-point targets – such as an 80 per cent goal in electricity production from renewable energy sources for 2050 – will help to mitigate future adverse climate impacts. Since the end of the 1990s, the EU has been working towards an increase of renewables in overall energy consumption and in particular in electricity consumption. However, it was only after a scenario of rising oil and gas prices, and warnings in the 'Stern Report'[2] that inaction on greenhouse gas emissions would impose losses in global GDP, that a combined package of climate and energy polices was initiated by the European Commission (EC) in 2008. It proposed by the midpoint of this century a near phase-out of greenhouse gases produced by the power sector, assuming that by then renewable energy sources would range between 64 per cent and 97 per cent of total electricity production.[3] However, the aims of the *EU Energy Directive* adopted in 2009, the *Lisbon Strategy* of 2000, and even more explicitly the objectives of the *EU 2020 Strategy* and the *EU's Energy Roadmap 2050*, all focus foremost on the 'security of energy supply' and on environmental policy as a source of 'competitive advantage for Europe', while 'sustainability' ranks as only one of three policy objectives, and obviously not as the most important one.

The EU works on the assumption that, firstly, investments in low-carbon technologies could be seen as a positive driver for the development of future market leaders. The *Renewable Energy Directive* of 2009 already emphasized the *competiveness* of a low-carbon economy; it encouraged any sort of technological change and the prospect of first-mover advantage for European firms in global markets. Later the *Energy Roadmap 2050* specified how the energy sector (particularly the power sector) should contribute to meeting the reduction target of an overall 80 per cent decrease in greenhouse gas emissions by 2050. Secondly, it was assumed that the EU, being the biggest importer of natural resources worldwide, could benefit economically through lower vulnerability to energy and raw material price fluctuations.

However, instead of eagerly promoting renewable energy as the future of its energy production, the EU, under the influence of strong corporate lobby groups, in the past has set only moderate, albeit binding, targets for the year 2020: to reduce the consumption of energy (compared to 1990 levels) in the EU as a whole by 20 per cent, to increase energy efficiency by 20 per cent, and to increase the share of renewable energy in the energy mix to 20 per cent. Furthermore, EU climate and energy policy was also, and still is, 'designed to be technology neutral, cost effective and fully compatible with the internal energy market'.[4] Obviously, the EU continues to hold reservations about a power sector completely based on renewables. Instead of eagerly promoting renewable energy as the future of its energy production, EU Member States and EU institutions not only overwhelmingly put their trust in competition policies and liberalization, and new supply routes for gas and oil, but also in nuclear energy and coal. A rapid conversion towards 100 per cent renewable energy sources (at least) for electricity production, which would be both desirable and necessary if fossil-fuel sources are to be left unexploited, was and is far from view. Thus, the concept of 'technological neutrality' considers all 'low carbon technologies', including nuclear, coal and gas with carbon capture and storage, as well as the 'cap and trade system', abstaining from a preference for any particular technology. It is inherent in the competitive principles of the *EU 2020 Strategy* that ultimately markets, i.e. big corporations, and not politics, will determine which technologies can deliver at the cheapest price.

Despite the neoliberal emphasis on market forces, the energy-intensive industry in Europe has not been left to these forces. In order to ensure that the competitiveness of selected industrial branches and industrial processes is not jeopardized by high energy costs, support for energy-intensive industries has increased over the years (including exemptions from energy taxes and special compensation rules). Both the modest targets for the EU as a whole and the idea of 'technology neutrality' reflect the deep-rooted contradictions of a 'green' policy that focuses primarily on economic growth and thus on the cost of energy production. Modest short-term targets regarding CO_2 emissions have the effect of enhancing the use of technologies which might deliver modest reductions in the near future – such as new coal power plants, carbon capture and storage technologies, and nuclear energy. Yet, at the same time, the use of these technologies falls well short of reaching climate stability goals by the middle of the century. In addition, renewable energy production requires the highest investment in infrastructure, at least for the part of it which cannot be deployed in a local, decentralized way. All the other technologies can profit from existing infrastructure – although to different degrees. Not surprisingly, if the *green* option of renewable energy sources has to be organized within the existing market structures and under the domination of big energy companies which prefer a central and grid-based approach, then it still can be outcompeted by *brown* alternatives (see Hoffmann, Chapter 1).

Furthermore, the EU's focus on pollutant emissions from the power generation system and the increase in renewable energy – accounting for the majority of new electricity generating capacity in the EU in 2013[5] – tends to neglect that energy production with photovoltaic systems or wind turbines, even with the newest technology, is actually not that 'green'. At first glance, for the renewable energy chains, not only emissions of greenhouse gases but also the impact of finite energy resources is extremely low compared with non-renewable systems. But if an integrated life-cycle assessment is conducted, it turns out that the material requirements per unit generation of renewable technologies are still higher than for conventional fossil generation.[6] This is due to the energy-intensive technology which is used for the construction and maintenance of renewable energy production as for storage systems and energy back-ups for electricity production from renewable sources. 'Thus it would appear that a shift from non-renewable to renewable energy sources would result in declines in both quantity and EROI values of the principal energies used for economic activities.'[7] Certainly, over time also the EROI[8] of fossil fuel has decreased considerably and new technologies (such as 'fracking' shale gas, tar sands extraction and deep sea drilling of oil) can improve the low EROI of oil and gas only temporarily. But if the close relationship between energy and the metal sector is taken into account, the EROI of renewable technologies is gravely altered. The production of one unit of renewables simply requires large amounts of matter, along with common and rare metals; and the extraction and refining of these metals represent a significant share of total energy consumption. Therefore, a transition towards renewable technologies could easily result in a potential vicious circle between the energy and metal sectors.[9]

Under these circumstances, the transition to a renewable energy system also contributes to strong and increasingly aggressive competition between producer and consumer countries over a variety of materials which are limited not only for narrow technological and economic reasons, but also due to social and environmental conflicts connected to the mining of these metals and the governance of resources.[10] Consistently, through its well-propagated *Raw Materials Initiative*,[11] the EU is on the path to exacerbating the worldwide competition for raw materials and resource conflicts.

European Member States have shown some progress towards their three climate and energy targets set for 2020: greenhouse gas emission reduction, the contribution of renewable energy sources in final energy consumption, and increases in energy efficiency. The planned share of renewable energy sources in overall final energy consumption will be reached by 2020 thanks to the systems of feed-in tariffs. However, after years of economic stagnation, with only weak signs of recovery from the financial and economic crisis, concerns over high energy costs in Europe are increasingly undermining support for a progressive energy policy. Recent developments demonstrate that even a modest change of technological systems is difficult to effect if it impacts on the powerful and broad political coalitions of the incumbent industries for which current arrangements have been optimized.

Under pressure from intense lobbying, support for the modest binding goals for 2030 is heralded. BusinessEurope, the voice of EU corporations in Brussels, argues that climate action is not compatible with cost competitiveness and secure access to natural resources; nor should efficient use of energy or the recycling of materials be enforced by strict approaches such as numerical targets. But without binding targets for renewables investment in some sectors (such as large offshore wind power projects in the UK), investment would not have happened in the past and in the future such projects will be less likely, as investors may no longer believe in the promise of rapid market growth. Thus, it comes as no surprise that the new set of energy and climate targets for Europe to be reached by 2030, which was adopted by the European Council in October 2014, is far from ambitious. Even though for 2050 the EU has endorsed the objective of reducing greenhouse gas emissions by 80–90 per cent, only the target of getting the EU's emissions down to at least 40 per cent on the 1990 level until 2030 is binding at the national level, while this is not the case for the targets on at least 27 per cent energy efficiency increases and equal share of energy from renewable sources by 2030. Poland and other Eastern European countries were reluctant to sign even this deal, which could slow down progress on energy savings after 2020 compared to current trends. They backed the targets only after concessions were offered, including more free allowances in the EU Emissions Trading Scheme and access to a fund which will be used to 'modernize' coal plants in Eastern Europe. Even a backdoor for the expansion of shale gas development and fracking technology might be opened in the near future.

Furthermore, in early September 2014, a new structure of the EU was proposed by its new president, Jean-Claude Juncker. It will shrink the environmental component and reads like a wish-list of private sector interest groups: The newly elected president of the EU wants to put a 'competition filter' on all initiatives and has given instructions to his proposed team requesting that the new Commissioner for the Environment review all recently launched and urgently needed legislative proposals and questioning the effectiveness of some outstanding pieces of environmental legislation in the light of the 'jobs and growth' agenda. The climate and energy portfolios and posts will be merged, meaning that climate action is considered subordinate to energy market considerations and the mandate will be put under a Vice President for Energy Union with close links to the fossil-fuel industry. Environmental policy will be merged with maritime affairs and fisheries, and seems to be entirely centred on deregulation. Furthermore, some crucial responsibilities that currently rest with the environment directorate – such as protection from harmful chemicals – will be shifted to others, meaning, for instance, that competences over chemicals will go to the directorate responsible for enterprise and industry.

The newest shift in the EU's energy and climate policy favours a *business as usual* scenario;[12] it cannot reasonably be seen even as a green growth strategy. The justification given for the recent recalibration of the EU's energy strategies emphasizes a widening EU–US energy price gap, caused by the ramped-up production of shale gas and oil in the US, which in the future may affect the competitiveness of energy-intensive industries in Europe compared with the US but also with other EU trading partners such as Russia or China. Subsidies supporting renewable energy production are blamed for driving up energy costs for European industry and undermining its competitiveness. Even though the price of oil is nearly the same across the world and in most EU Member States, electricity prices for large industrial users are at about the same level as in the US. But, undoubtedly, comparable cheaper shale gas from the environmentally devastating technology of fracking gives US companies a competitive advantage. As witnessed in the negotiations for a Transatlantic Investment and Free Trade deal, European corporations certainly would like to be released from the strictures of EU climate and energy policy. Under these new constellations there seems to be less need for the EU to pursue 'green leadership' internationally. Instead, the interests of Corporate Europe have become more relevant. The picture is of a counterrevolution in energy policy before the oft-praised revolution in renewables has taken place.

Not surprisingly, despite the unwanted degrowth in most EU Member States, which resulted from the financial and economic crisis since 2008, and the share of power from renewable energy sources in the EU energy mix already reaching almost 25 per cent, the EU's import dependence on fossil fuels has not decreased – quite the contrary. This indicates that as long as energy-intensive production is not scaled down (further), energy from renewable sources is simply added to fossil-fuel extraction – without replacing it.

With regard to this development, a closer look at the paradoxes of the German 'energy transition', which is remarkable for its scope and it widespread support among citizens, cooperatives and communities owning more than half of Germany's renewable capacity, is particularly telling: On the one hand, solar power in Germany has already reached grid parity, meaning that the price of commercial solar power is now equal to retail electricity rates; on a Sunday in May 2014 renewable energy generation surged to a record share of nearly 75 per cent of the country's overall electricity demand, indicating that policies that incentivize clean energy could succeed in a radical 'turnaround' at least by mid-century. On the other hand, new CO_2 polluting brown coal plants came onstream in 2012, with the result that coal power output in 2013 reached its highest level since German unification 20 years ago, resulting in record German electricity exports. This shift was justified firstly by the need to compensate for the loss of nuclear energy caused by the decision taken after the Fukushima disaster to completely phase out nuclear power and, secondly, to meet the country's baseload power demands, with coal imports being cheaper than gas imports.

Since a reduction in energy demand is not at the centre of policy, the price is crucial – and here we are faced with another paradox of the German 'energy transition': The country's feed-in tariff policy granting renewable energy producers a set amount for the electricity they produce under long-term contracts has driven rapid growth in installed solar power capacity (but only until 2013) and has driven wholesale electricity prices down. However, since the system is financed by a surcharge paid by utility customers while industry is largely exempted, only the giant German firms enjoy the benefits of renewable's near-zero operating costs while retail electricity rates are high and rising, raising the household price of electricity by 7 per cent while at the same time lowering big industries' wholesale price by around 18 per cent. Obviously, it would be perfectly possible to rescind industry's exemption, in order to reduce rising energy prices for lower-income households. But due to powerful lobbying, in August 2014 a reform of the German law on renewable energy came into force, which will only restrict small players and not the big power providers.[13] Against this background, the 'energy transition' threatens to stall before it has even begun to become an alternative mode of energy supply and consumption.

In this scenario, both Germany and the EU not only illustrate a type of ecological modernization focusing on green innovations in so-called *lead markets* and the advantages accruing from an early reduction of CO_2 emissions. Both the German and the EU case also highlight competing interests and the challenges of overcoming well-established power structures. Any kind of socio-technical transition towards a 'greener' (if not a 'sustainable') path of development which attempts to fully mobilize all available options might face comparable obstacles – since the most promising options may conflict with short-term economic growth objectives.

In a nutshell: The green growth approach is welcomed in the EU, as long as it represents a win–win situation for industries. Basically, it should be seen as part of the EU's growth strategy, which seeks to maintain the status quo, including the competitive advantages of EU-based transnational corporations in resource-intensive industries through spontaneous decarbonization, backed up by market-creating and market-driven processes and financial incentives. In international competition on innovation, the main purpose behind the EU's green mission – transferred via its influence in the OECD, the World

Bank and the UNEP, to countries in the global South – is to convince governments across the world to invest in research and development, stimulate existing markets and create new ones.

In this context, European policies to stimulate green growth set a rather poor example. The clearer it becomes that greenhouse gas emission mitigation cannot be achieved only through investment in the efficient use of resources and profitable new technological innovations but also requires a substantial reduction in production and consumption, entailing major sacrifices in profits, the more those who stand to lose a lot (particularly shareholders of energy- and resource-intensive industries, alongside the big energy companies) can be seen using their political power to maintain a fossil-fuel and growth-based economy

With this in mind, two conclusions can be drawn: Firstly, in the EU the green growth approach is predominantly a growth and business issue, and if the most promising options towards a 'greening of the economy' conflict with short-term economic interests of well-established powers, the 'green path' will face growing resistance. Secondly, the case of EU environmental and energy policy brings us to a broader issue: the question of whether 'green growth' could help rescue capitalism from its own contradictions, that is, whether it could help the socio-economic system grow out of its structural crisis, as illustrated by the EU's latest round of economic woes.

Behind the green discourse: a structural crisis of the world-ecological system of capitalism

Capitalism does not distinguish itself from other systems of dealing with human nature and the nonhuman natural world by its profit-making or through the exploitation of labour. It distinguishes itself from all other socio-economic systems in human history by the movement towards the infinite, which is inherent in that system.[14] Since only continuous new investment can generate new surplus value, markets have to keep expanding beyond all needs. In this way, Marx (and J.M. Keynes similarly) explains this compulsion for growth, which, as an 'automatic subject', is an inherent element in capital.[15] Capitalism's in-built growth imperative constantly expands the 'metabolic rift' between human social systems and nonhuman natural systems.[16] The logic of profit indicates an unlimited spiral process. In capitalism profits are the 'return on capital', i.e. they have to revert to their origin, which is the capital advanced, whereas in nature physical and energetic transformations are irreversible.[17] At the same time, all types of limited productive potentials at the disposal of capital usually translate into a declining 'return on capital invested' – and when return flows on capital are decreasing radically, financial crisis breaks out.[18]

An important precondition for the valorization of nature is transformation of the 'free gifts of nature' (forests, fertile soil, silver mines, oil fields etc.) into economic prosperity. If mineral, energy and agricultural resources are *not* part of the capital advance, therefore not a product of previous labour,[19] they will increase the wealth of private owners very easily, who will firstly appropriate and secondly transform the natural riches into 'enclosures' and then will exploit these. This process of 'primitive accumulation', which Marx described as the starting point of historical capitalism as a system of accumulation and production, is still ongoing today. But even though the modern paradigm of 'plunder' shows some aspects of continuity with earlier European colonization, it also includes aspects of change. Usually the rule of law is used to justify policies that reinforce inequality and threaten human well-being – through means such as grabbing land and resources. However, today such processes are further facilitated through multi- and bilateral trade and investment agreements.

Infinite accumulation of capital requires that new rich frontiers can always be found and exploited on the 'input' side of the process, that sinks are not yet overflowing on the 'output' side, and that the 'tipping points' of bio-physical systems are not transgressed. While in capitalism 'limits to growth' resulting from current pollution levels are constantly ignored, limits to growth resulting from resource constraints can turn into serious constraints for capitalist accumulation – even before other prospects come into view: of capitalism as an ecological world system collapsing, and of a 'world without us' becoming a reality. This is particularly applicable to the issue of peak oil (and other resource peaks), referring to a constellation where producing oil (gas or minerals) is not as convenient as it was before and we are left with the more expensive resources to extract. As long as market prices are high enough to produce energy from resources with even an extremely low net energy return (such as shale oils, biofuels, tar sands, and others) production will continue. But if prices suddenly plummet, as was recently the case for crude oil, huge amounts of the world's production lose profitability, resulting in lower production.

From this, some conclusions can be drawn: Firstly, it is not realistic to assume that a 'green revolution' will save the day. Such a revolution would demand that most of the fossil-fuel reserves held as assets will not be drilled and burned. This would turn assets held by financial investors into 'toxic' assets – in a double sense. But financial investors who currently spend large sums on finding new reserves[20] are not prepared to be directed away from high-carbon options; the structure of a fossil-fuel economy creates an inertial situation that cannot easily be changed. Therefore, financial investors in 'toxic assets' trust in their own capability to blackmail governments across the world with the financial and economic consequences of a 'carbon bubble' bursting; they do not have to expect a possible absolute loss of value in the near future – even if this means the likelihood of greenhouse gas emissions actually increasing by 2050 by nearly 100 per cent against 1990 levels. Secondly, energy is not the only limit to capitalist accumulation today. Other natural riches, which are essential for industrialized economies and a modern way of life, are depleting very quickly. Not only oil and gas but also lead, silver, copper, nickel, uranium and other major minerals at an acceptable price will become exhausted between 2030 and 2050.[21] This is due to the fact that discovery rates of major mineral deposits are decreasing while exploration costs are rising; lower grade ores need exponentially more energy for extraction; and mining businesses' harmful environmental practices are facing growing resistance in many areas of the world. Therefore a 'scarcity' of natural resources and its impact on system stability is under discussion not only among concerned natural and social scientists but also by military forces and the International Energy Agency, by national agencies in the EU dealing with international relations and new geopolitics, by management consultancies such as PricewaterhouseCoopers and think tanks across the world. Only 'the fraternity of conventional economists appears to be highly resistant to these sorts of challenging ideas'.[22]

Thirdly, financialization of capitalism during the neoliberal era has accelerated the tendency of the system to constantly enlarge the 'metabolic rift'[23] between human social systems and the nonhuman natural system. Today, financial markets are a driving force for increases in commodity prices, the price of fossil fuels and their substitutes, as well as the price of water, fertile land and thus also of food. As an attempt to reduce complex ecosystems into tradable commodities, new 'fictitious commodities'[24] from nature and its so-called 'services' are also created. In addition to carbon markets and the commodification of natural products such as coal into credits, there are other mechanisms which transform nature into so-called 'natural capital' (including the Clean Development Mechanism, payments for ecosystem services, REDD+, conservation marketing and conservation financing mechanisms such as biodiversity derivatives and species banking.[25]

Uncertainty concerning climate change impacts can be turned into an opportunity for profits – through the creation of markets for weather risk management, including 'catastrophe bonds, securities that manage the risk of improbable but catastrophic natural events and environmental derivatives' all designed to 'respond to unpredictable fluctuation in the weather'.[26] Originating and exchanging pieces of derivative nature or seeking trademarks on human, animal or plant genes can easily be seen as a way of 'converting nature' into a form of 'capital'. However, through its submission to capital and its subsequent revaluation in capital terms, neither can nature be 'saved' nor will the ecological limits be overcome.

Fourthly, although it is the case that neoliberal environmental and conservation markets can result in accumulation avenues and profits for some people over a period of time, whether this will result in opening up a sufficiently large new frontier for capitalist accumulation is highly debatable. In the neoliberal era of capitalism, which has been characterized by David Harvey as 'accumulation by dispossession', it became increasingly difficult to revive the real basis of accumulation, which is labour productivity growth, and thus compensate for the higher capital intensity of production. However, increases in labour productivity resemble a double-edge sword if they go hand in hand with an increase in capital intensity per labour unit – caused by growing expenditure on advanced technology (including patent fees), raw materials (including energy) and capital costs.

During the last few decades profit shares have been on the rise at the expense of the wage share, as has been documented in recent studies.[27] At the global level, the share of wages seems to have contracted, while this development has not been associated with investment acceleration. Capital intensity is increasing nearly everywhere, and when it is not compensated for by an increase in labour productivity the effect on the profit rate is negative. If prices for fossil energy and many other resources also increase, huge-scale investment will become even more risky, and likely to be postponed.

In such a constellation, when 'free gifts' of nature are not abundant anymore, nor easy and cheap to access, a new 'long wave' of accumulation is unlikely to be triggered. As Jason Moore argues,[28] at the present juncture we are confronted with socio-ecological limits of capitalism that translate into the erosion of the 'four cheaps', which are indispensable for establishing conditions for 'great waves of accumulation' – cheap energy, raw materials, food and labour. Under these conditions, the prospects for compensating rising capital costs through a decline in input and labour costs are not very promising.

Moving beyond green capitalism?

If the term *green* was equated with environmental sustainability the argument would hold that something like sustainable capitalism is an inherent contradiction. Notwithstanding this, green growth can be seen as a business activity, a chance to invest and make money. There are growing markets for any product that can reduce emissions or at least their effect on human health. Furthermore, the green growth agenda is indispensable for channelling public money into the so-called green sectors of the economy, bearing at least some part of the private sector's risks in investments to increase 'resource productivity' or guaranteeing a certain rate of return on capital invested, thus leveraging private investment. But, most importantly, in order to create new markets and exclude those who are not entitled to have access to natural resources, state authority is needed to protect property rights. The promise of green growth, therefore, builds upon the neoliberal project of a free market discourse together with stressing the authority of the state. Western hegemony should be strengthened in a multipolar and crisis-driven world. This is the reason why financial institutions have been rescued and social resistance marginalized – because it did not challenge the power structure. As can be studied in the case of EU environmental and energy policy, incremental change based on market- and technology-oriented ecological modernization is insufficient, as it remains committed to the concept of infinite growth. It prevents regime change towards an alternative policy of sustainable development – even though the window of opportunity to organize society and the economy on the basis of energy sources other than fossil fuels and on a much smaller mineral base than in 'capitalism as we know it' is closing very quickly.

However, as we come closer to the tipping points of ecological systems and to 'peak everything', it is no longer possible to gamble on the self-healing powers of capitalism and its presumed ability to transform itself and absorb all criticism. But neither can we expect a voluntary shrinking of the economy. A radical critique would have to face up to the conclusion that what would be required – in the EU as in other highly industrialized countries – is not green growth but a drastic retrenchment or even a shutdown of many industries. This, however, would place the question of power relations at the core; it would demand, *inter alia*, a confrontation with the fossil-fuel industries as the most important (but not the only) obstacle preventing a 'just transition' towards a sustainable development paradigm. Finally, the economy could not be left to competition between people who own capital operating in free markets.

Consequently, the green growth discourse in all its facets cannot hide that we are confronted with a structural crisis of the system as such – and not simply with these sorts of destructive crises which throughout the history of capitalism have contributed to renewing the reproduction of the capital relation. All of the crises within capitalism were based on the opening of biophysically rich frontiers in addition to sufficiently mobile capital and socio-technical innovations in production; together these have generated revolutions in labour productivity and have enabled a high rate of profit. From socio-ecological metabolism and the insights of bioeconomics an important insight can be gained, which concerns a dilemma. On the one hand, the accumulation dynamic of modern capitalism relies on 'free gifts' from biotic systems, continuous plunder of finite mineral and agricultural resources and the availably of sinks for pollutants. On the other hand, modern capitalism turns almost the entire world into a field of valorization, which undermines the same conditions. As a consequence, what in earlier phases of capitalism constituted the 'revolutionary force' of (Schumpeterian) 'creative destruction', namely the 'Promethean' capacity to go constantly beyond and to ignore natural boundaries, has now become a limit to capitalist accumulation.

As long as the greening of the economy is organized under the 'iron fist of capital' and the social, political and democratic dimensions of economic activity are excluded, the green road cannot end up in a 'win–win' constellation. But a green road that would guide us beyond capitalism would create new contradictions and conflicts. The green discourse neither delivers on the turnaround necessary to stay within the planetary boundaries, nor contributes to facing the structural violence connected to regional, transnational and domestic inequalities. Nevertheless, only if the limits to growth are considered to be an issue worthy of addressing will discussion of environmental justice become a pressing concern. This is because the apportionment of growth will become a political issue if future growth potential is limited due to the fact that scarcities, something capitalism is familiar with, are becoming shortages.[29] In order to facilitate a green transformation, approaches such as 'energy democracy' and environmental justice are of utmost importance, particularly in the field of energy policies, where the failure of regulatory and market-based approaches – as has been illustrated with regard to EU policies – no longer can be ignored. It is an open question whether there is a historic opportunity for a 'great transformation' beyond capitalism or whether reactionary forces will take advantage when the socio-ecological crisis starts to turn into political instability.

CHAPTER 7

The green growth trap in Brazil

Ricardo Abramovay

The idea of green growth has the virtue of stimulating a reduction in the negative effects the supply of goods and services has on the environment. However, it suffers from two fundamental flaws. First, it is entirely compatible with 'business as usual' and with the gradualism that typifies the undeniable socio-environmental changes that the great global corporations are undergoing.[1] Very positive goals have been set for the reduction of water use and greenhouse gas emissions and for socio-environmental certification. Nevertheless, in spite of those goals, the global economy continues to expand its use of materials, the erosion of biodiversity and the emission of greenhouse gases.[2] The Green Business Report 2015 is clear in this sense: 'business is becoming more efficient, but not quickly enough to counter growth, leading to an overall rise in resource use and emissions.'[3] One of the reasons behind the paradox is that the reduction goals rarely offset the actual increase in consumption; a kind of generalized rebound effect.[4] The second problem is that if the overall goal is growth, then it is perfectly feasible to carry on supplying goods and services that jeopardize the development process, even when they have been obtained in a way that reduces the environmental damage usually associated to their provision.

The Brazilian case is exemplary in that regard. Any definition of a green economy, according to UNEP,[5] must involve not only strictly environment-related objectives but also poverty and inequality reduction goals. Over the last ten years Brazil has managed to achieve economic growth while at the same time significantly reducing not only poverty and absolute destitution but also, in an unprecedented way, income inequality, as shown by the document the country presented at the Rio+20 Conference.[6]

Furthermore, three other factors have contributed towards placing Brazil on the list of countries heading in the direction of a green economy. First, the country has the cleanest energy matrix among the countries with an economy of a comparable size. In addition, Brazil has played a pioneer role in the mass production of a type of fuel for automobiles that, from the greenhouse gas emissions angle, is low. Lastly, the deforestation rate in the Brazilian Amazon fell by 80 per cent between 2004 and 2013. In spite of its recent increase, this reduction is largely recognized as a success thanks to a set of successful public policies targeting it.[7]

The main goal of this chapter is to show the evidences according to which these undeniable successes do not represent a path towards sustainable development.

The gap between income and well-being

In June 2013, riots broke out in the streets of São Paulo, triggered by an apparently prosaic motive: an increase of less than 7 per cent in the standard bus fares. At the outset the movement appeared to be limited to a group of youngsters clamouring for a 'free pass', [8] that is, urban public transport completely free of charge, based on the idea that it is a duty of the State and a right of the citizenry. It so happened, however, that the movement immediately caught on and expanded, especially in the light of the violent reactions of the State of São Paulo police force, whose rubber bullets seriously wounded various demonstrators, some journalists among them. The images of the repression and the rubber bullets being fired into the crowd circulated in the social networks, setting off a reaction that soon involved the entire city, and the violent repression and use of rubber bullets were severely criticized. In a few days, the wave of protest had swept over the entire country, embracing over 350 cities and millions of people in a completely spontaneous manner. It was not possible to identify any of the well-known social movements, labour unions or political parties that could be held responsible for calling people onto the streets. In fact it was quite the opposite. There was a widespread feeling of mistrust in regard to those consecrated forms of political representation.

Singer[9] has shown the social composition of the protests on the basis of a survey of newspaper reports at the time of the demonstrations. In spite of the important presence of people with university education, there was strong participation by groups from the lowest echelons of the social pyramid, which, in itself, represents a fundamental paradox and calls for a reflection on the relation between wealth and development. After all, since the turn of the millennium, poverty in Brazil has been steadily and demonstrably reduced. In the period from 2003 to 2013 no fewer than 20 million people saw their income increase to an extent that enabled them to rise above the poverty line. The contingent of poor people fell by half over the same period. Over a longer period, the percentage of the population living in poverty in Brazil fell from 68.3 per cent in 1970 to 10.1 per cent in 2011. The reduction in recent years has not been tied to income transfer alone but also to the increase in formal employment opportunities, to the enhanced value of the official minimum salary and to improved access to an important set of public services, particularly in the fields of health and education.[10]

The drop in poverty levels has been accompanied by a historically unprecedented transformation in Brazil: since the beginning of the new millennium, the income of the poorest stratum of the population has grown at a faster rate than the income of the richest. Since 2003, household income in Brazil has grown at a rate inversely proportional to the degree of poverty of the families. From 2003 to 2009, the poorest 20 per cent of the population experienced an 8 per cent yearly increase in their incomes whereas for the richest 20 per cent the increase was just 4 per cent.[11] That corresponds to a 10 per cent drop in the Gini index for the period 2001 to 2011.[12]

So if all that is true, and the country has gone through a vigorous process of reduction in poverty and income inequality, how can the massive protest demonstrations of June 2013 be explained? The main hypothesis that has been put forward so far is identified in a recent World Bank paper which concentrated its attention on the process of social ascension so evident, not only in Brazil but also in other Latin American countries, since the turn of the millennium. On the one hand the paper shows that 'at least 40 percent of the region's households are estimated to have moved upward in "socio-economic class" between 1995 and 2010'.[13] Nevertheless, the same report described that group as still a 'vulnerable class'. One of the underlying reasons for its vulnerability goes far beyond the question of the income of its members. It concerns, first and foremost, the supply of those goods and services (such as education, health, mobility, security, access to justice) that are indispensable to the development process. According to the World Bank report, the social contract that underpins the current wave of poverty reduction in Latin America is fragmentary and reduces the opportunities offered to the majority of the population, in spite of their income gains. Comparisons with other regions of the world are highly revealing in this aspect. 'Whether in postwar Western Europe or post-revolutionary China, whether in the post-land-reform Republic of Korea or in the United States under the New Deal, socioeconomic progress has often required a combination of economic freedom and a sound foundation of public education, health, and infrastructure.'[14]

A highly significant part of the complaints and demands expressed in the streets in June 2013 was directed precisely at those public goods and services. One of the slogans of the street protests was 'it's not just for 20 cents' (the increase in bus fares authorized by the municipal government of São Paulo and overthrown by the riots). Another factor was the proximity of the FIFA World Cup event, which led the crowd to demand 'FIFA quality' education, health and urban mobility.

It is true that the right to health in Brazil is universal and that today basic education reaches practically the whole population. However, there could hardly be a greater contrast than that which exists between the quality of education offered in private schools attended by the children of better-off families and that under the responsibility of the public authorities, where, more often than not, teacher shortages, overcrowded classes, unmotivated students and violence prevail. According to research conducted by the Union of Government School Teachers in the State of São Paulo, 32 per cent of teachers, 37 per cent of parents and 25 per cent of the students identified violence as the main problem in São Paulo's schools. Furthermore, in spite of the level of government spending on education, Brazilian students' performances in widely recognized international tests are among the worst in the world, reflecting the crucial difference between government school education and that offered by good-quality private schools.[15]

The average grade achieved by government-run schools in the Basic Education Development Index for lower secondary education is 3.9 compared to 6.0 for the private education network. The result reveals a paradoxical situation. Instead of increased income levels among the poorer strata of the population being accompanied by an improvement in the quality of what is a decisive public asset, namely, education, what has happened is that millions of families at the base of the social pyramid have abandoned the education being offered by government in favour of private schools. From the crèches to higher secondary education, 3.8 million Brazilian students throughout the country abandoned government schools in the period from 2008 to 2013. Over the same period, private schools matriculated 1.5 million new students.[16]

However, more often than not, the private schools that poorer families have access to are precarious and far from able to prepare their students for professional activities supported by a good knowledge base or for competing for a place at a public university.[17] Thus, in the light of that absence of a good-quality public education, part of the enhanced income of poor families is spent on an education that falls far short of their expectations of preparing their children to achieve a better social position.

The same situation applies in the field of health, where, once more, there is a glaring contrast between the universal right to access and the precarious conditions of the public services. Campino[18] shows that 7 per cent of those situated in the poorest fifth of the population spend more than 20 per cent of their income on health. Poor people have less access to the public health systems than people who are not poor. The situation is made worse by the insufficiency of basic sanitation systems, one of the most important public assets for ensuring improved health levels for the population at large. The national average figure for households connected to a sewage collecting system is 48.29 per cent. Even in Brazil's one hundred largest municipalities the service is not universalized and 37 per cent of the population is not benefited by it. Worse still, not all the sewage collected is treated. While 63 per cent of municipalities have sewage collection systems installed, only 41 per cent have treatment systems.[19] More recently these basic sanitation problems have been seriously aggravated by water shortages caused by prolonged droughts in the southeast of Brazil and severely affecting the poorest families living in the outlying neighbourhoods of the big cities. They have no water storage tanks of their own and supply to their homes is increasingly irregular.

This paucity of public goods and services is repeated in the area of mobility. A study undertaken by the National Confederation of Industry provides an excellent diagnosis of the situation. The CNI stresses the connection between transport and housing location and illustrates the process whereby, in the big metropolitan regions, most people's workplaces have become concentrated in the central regions of the cities while their housing has become dispersed to the outlying areas. In those peripheral areas, population densities may be lower but so is the presence of public goods and services. As a result, even when they manage to get some form of housing, poor families do not have the infrastructure available to them that would be consistent with social emancipation. As the CNI document put it, 'the family produces the household but only the collectivity can produce the infrastructure. Lack of investments in high yield public transport and the option for road transport, especially the stimulus to the use of automobiles, have brought urban transit almost to a standstill.'[20] As a consequence there is a lack of 'equality of access to the right to enjoy the benefits of the city'. It is highly significant that Brazilian industry's most important corporate organization recognizes that reality.

The intention in dwelling on this item is not to constitute an in-depth analysis of what led to the June 2013 demonstrations. What it brings to the discussion of the idea of green growth is the contrast between the increased income of the poorer segment of society and the lack of those public goods and services without which the capabilities that such additional income should enable will never be fulfilled. The Brazilian case corroborates the central idea of the capabilities school.[21] The emphasis must be not simply on income, but on what individuals will be capable of doing when they obtain it. The poor quality of education, health and infrastructure all jeopardize any possibility of individuals using their income to effectively enhance their well-being. Obviously that does not mean that increases in income are irrelevant. What it does mean is that one of the decisive purposes of economic growth must be the expansion of those public goods and collective services without which the expansion of substantive human freedoms that define development itself can never take place.

However, the trap set by Brazil's supposedly green growth (as claimed in the already quoted Brazilian document to Rio+20, particularly in its chapter II) is not revealed solely by the glaring contrast between enhanced family income and the precarious public goods and services provision, but for the questionable quality of some environmental outcomes, as the following three sections will show.

Hydroelectricity: extent and limitations

Hydroelectric plants seem to be, in principle, one of the most concrete expressions of what could be called green growth. They are among the energy sources with the lowest levels of greenhouse gas emissions and they are supposed to guarantee permanent access to a reliable electricity supply. In Brazil they provide 69 per cent of the electricity supply. That proportion was once much higher: 81 per cent in 2011 and 75 per cent in 2012.[22]

There are four reasons, however, that keep them far removed from sustainable development.

a) First of all, in Brazil and Latin America as a whole, the construction of hydroelectric dams and plants represents an ever-growing threat to both natural ecosystems with high biological value and traditional communities that are victimized by the works associated with the projects, such as the Belo Monte hydro plant in Para State.[23] Those features are not restricted to Brazil alone. Mathieson[24] undertook a review of various recent studies and identified a correlation between the fragmentation of rivers brought about by the 50,000 dams that now exist around the world and water quality deterioration and biodiversity losses. The great frontier for hydroelectric development in Latin America today is the Amazon. The Brazilian government is planning to build 30 hydroelectric plants in the Amazon region until 2023. Six of them will produce more than 50 per cent of the energy that Brazil plans to add to its energy matrix over the period. There are huge social costs attached to these enterprises: 90,000 people are expected to migrate to Altamira before the construction of the Belo Monte dam is finalized. The risk of deforestation stemming from that migration is also immense whereas the benefits the installations will bring to the people of the Amazon themselves are pitifully small: 98.5 per cent of the Amazonian municipalities have social indicators[25] lower than the Brazilian national average. The municipalities where the hydroelectric plants are constructed will not even enjoy the eventual revenues from them because taxation on the energy produced is levied at the consumer end (far from the Amazon) and not where it is produced.[26]

b) Obviously hydroelectric plants depend on an abundant water supply. The prolonged drought that has been afflicting the Brazilian southeast macro-region since the end of 2013 is threatening its hydroelectric system and, with that, threatening what has always been its strongest trump, a reliable permanent supply. Furthermore, today's hydroelectric plants can no longer count on forming huge reservoirs of water because the latter destroy natural systems of great biological value. Instead they have to function at water level using the natural flows. That means the amount of energy they produce varies in the course of the year and the plants only operate at full capacity in the high water season. As a result, doubts are now beginning to be voiced about the economic viability of such vast hydroelectric dam projects. Thayer Scudder, one of the world's most respected experts in this field, after 58 years of working on the issues involved has issued a public warning that the socio-environmental costs of the great dams outweigh their benefits.[27] Scudder's conclusions are not based on his own experience alone; they are strongly supported by a far-reaching survey conducted by a University of Oxford team.[28] They studied 245 large-scale hydroelectric projects constructed in various parts of the world between 1937 and 2007. They found that the real costs of executing the works are almost always double the estimated costs even when the costs associated with displacing local populations and damage to the environment are excluded from the calculations. Furthermore, such projects systematically take much longer than planned to become operational. The construction of the Belo Monte dam in the Amazon is emblematic. When finished, it will be the third biggest in the world. It was originally budgeted at US$16 billion, but by the time it is finished it will have cost around US$30 billion. Also, corroborating the findings of the University of Oxford team, Belo Monte was scheduled to go operational in December 2014 but that has not happened.[29]

c) Unlike what has happened in the fields of solar and wind energy, hydroelectric plants have not been noted for any permanent, dynamic innovation processes. That contrasts strongly with the impressive increase in energy efficiency that has been achieved with the more modern renewable energy sources where the increases in efficiency and reduction of costs of solar and wind energy have been exponential.[30]

d) The process of decarbonizing the global economy involves, and will increasingly involve, not only the so-called modern renewable energy sources (basically wind, solar and biomass) but also revolutionary transformations in energy production and distribution processes, which contrasts with the large centralized generation brought by the hydroelectricity plants. The most important one is decentralization and the possibility that a significant part of the supply could be produced by the consumers themselves. The data on the reduction in the prices of solar panels in Europe and the United States are clear. The electricity sector, historically characterized by a tremendous concentration of power and economic resources, is now finding a decisive source of change in self-production and connection in networks.[31] While China and India are among the main protagonists of this revolutionary progress in the field of energy, Brazil and Latin America are condemning themselves to be the eventual consumers of their products. India and China have global companies that are among the leaders in renewable and decentralized renewable energy.[32]

Supporting economic growth on the basis of hydroelectric power means being relegated to the rearguard of those advanced processes that are going to command the global economy. Even worse: constructing hydroelectric plants (and the same reasoning is applicable to pre-salt oil exploitation) means creating a path of dependence in regard to technology basically typical of the twentieth century; and, furthermore, it will take decades for the respective investments to be amortized. Thus, insisting on big hydroelectric dam construction to meet Brazil's energy needs is a course that could be considered green from the greenhouse gas emissions angle but it will most certainly take the country further away from achieving sustainable development.

Green fuel and mobility

The vast majority of criticisms made of biofuels by their severest detractors do not apply to sugar cane. It cannot be denied that Brazilian sugar cane production depends on the availability of vast tracts of land, especially in areas of Cerrado savannah, or that it has destructive impacts on ecosystem services.[33] However, its recent expansion has not been based on a massive process of replacing food crops and it has a positive energy balance, especially in comparison with other liquid fuels for internal combustion engines.[34] Even its supposed secondary effect of displacing cattle-raising activities towards the Amazon region has been almost entirely disproved by scientific research.[35] The crop is capable of producing far more calories per unit area than any other cereal, oil-bearing plant or palm species that can be grown in tropical regions. Furthermore, sugar cane factories in Brazil not only produce their own electricity by burning the residual bagasse but also have the potential for producing electricity that is almost carbon-neutral to feed the power grid.[36] All those factors led the US's Environment Protection Agency to recognize Brazilian ethanol as being an advanced biofuel, in 2010,[37] and they are just some of the reasons that have made Brazilian ethanol a global pioneer in solutions for decarbonizing the energy matrix in the transport sector. Given the short period of time it took for the Flex technology for vehicle engines to be made generally available (five years during the 2000s), the Brazilian automobile industry has come to be considered as part of the green economy and its expansion as part of the expansion of green growth in the country.

That may well be the most emblematic example of the conceptual trap that is embedded in the notion of green growth. Even if the automobile sector significantly reduces its emissions thanks to ethanol, the growth of the industry dramatically removes Brazil from any proximity to sustainable development, for two fundamental reasons.

a) The internal combustion engine happens to be one of the most inefficient ways of producing what physicists refer to as work.[38] The latest important innovations in the global automobile sector are in the conjunction of electric motors and digital devices.[39] A report published by global consultants KPMG[40] shows, however, that in the minds of industry executives in the BRIC countries the internal combustion engine still has a long way to go. In the Brazilian case this is absolutely clear. Car production capacity now stands at 4.6 million vehicles a year even though in 2013 the number of cars actually leaving the manufacturing plants was considerably lower: 3.8 million units. By 2017 that production capacity is expected to hit 6.8 million vehicles a year. That may well lead to an idle capacity of as much as 35 per cent, according to the forecasts of global consultant Roland Berger.[41] What is more important than idle capacity, however, is the patent lack of any innovative traits in the Brazilian automobile industry as a whole. The country is actually investing in technology and forms of mobility that are taking it away from the frontiers of technology in the twenty-first century. The Brazilian automobile sector invests a mere 1.4 per cent of its turnover in innovation as compared to the 5.6 per cent invested by Germany, and the 4.3 per cent average figure for the OECD countries. Nevertheless, this sector, with extremely low levels of innovation, actually leads the pack in the overall set of Brazilian industries. According to the calculations of a large Brazilian consultancy organization, automobiles were responsible for 69.1 per cent of the increase in industrial production in 2013. In 2008 their participation was just 18.4 per cent. Government subsidies in the form of tax exemptions are at the root of the industry's growth. Government refrained from levying R$12.3 billion (US$5.1 billion) in taxes on the automobile industry in the period from 2008 to 2013.[42] Even so, there has been no counterpart effort on the part of the industry to increase the efficiency of automobile engines. From the macroeconomic angle, the Brazilian economy is highly dependent on the automobile and on the whole set of parts and devices that go with it; the spare parts industry, the automobile retailers and outlets, as well as the thousands of repair workshops all over the country. However, the problems delineated here are not applicable to the sector alone but actually reveal the way society is making use of some of its most important material and energy resources: it is using them simply to reproduce that which is already being done. The fact of adopting a fuel that does not emit net greenhouse gases in no way diminishes the inefficiency and the paucity of innovation that typifies the automobile sector and eventually affects economic life as a whole. It must also be noted that not even the objective of reducing emissions by adopting ethanol as a fuel has been achieved. Over the last five years, Brazil, in spite of its pioneering action with ethanol, has been implementing its decision to subsidize gasoline as a way of reducing inflation. The result has been a crisis in the ethanol sector and there are no signs of a recovery as yet.

b) The paucity of innovation and the energy inefficiency of the automobile sector are further exacerbated in the light of a question that contemporary macroeconomics does not have the conceptual instruments to construe. It concerns the distance separating the finality of the goods that are offered to society (the automobile) and the service that it is supposed to provide (mobility). In the contemporary world, and especially in the big cities of the developing countries, the automobile has become exactly the opposite of what, in principle, it was supposed to be and which indeed it was in the developed countries during part of the twentieth century. The hidden costs are exorbitant. The Technische Universität of Dresden has estimated that the external costs associated with the automobile (that is the costs the user of the means of transport does not pay but which are paid for by society as a whole) as being 373 billion euros a year in the 27-country European bloc, corresponding to no less than 3 per cent of their GDPs.[43] In the case of the city of São Paulo, a study conducted by the Getulio Vargas Foundation (FGV/SP) has calculated that those costs go beyond

> 50 billion dollars a year; US$10 billion more than the municipality's total budget figure.[44] Such costs are not only due to the pollution stemming from the use of fossil fuels, but also due to the gigantic traffic jams which, as the above-mentioned Brazilian industry organization has declared, are strangling the cities; the biggest traffic jam registered for the city of São Paulo in 1992 at 7 pm was 28 kilometres long whereas in 2012 it was up to 292 kilometres and, on 23 May 2014, the city's Traffic Engineering Company registered the biggest traffic jam in the history of São Paulo: an unbelievable 344 kilometres long.

The report conducted by KPMG[45] shows that the global automobile sector is typified by a production capacity that already shows signs of excess and over-production. That contrast will tend to worsen as technologies destined to delineate the automobile of the future assert themselves. Adopting green sources of energy will do nothing towards solving the very serious problems portrayed here. That means that, in this sector, social well-being will only be reflected in the production of a lesser, not greater quantity of automobiles and that is a decisive conclusion for the discussion of green growth. The industry is working with a catastrophic horizon of two billion automobiles by 2030.[46] The world's largest credit insurance group, Euler Hermes, has forecast global automobiles for 2017 at 100 million vehicles produced yearly.[47] Not even a fuel with no net greenhouse gas emissions can make that quantity of vehicles compatible with the territorial integrity of the big cities. If the automobile industry were to offer society mobility instead of cars, it might perhaps grow, but that growth would have to be supported on bases entirely different from those of today. Perhaps a grain of hope can be found in the fact that some of the automobile industry's own protagonists, like Bill Ford, have begun to recognize the evidence and admit that global automobile production needs to be reduced.[48]

The Amazon and the ecosystems

The significant drop in deforestation of the Brazilian Amazon was a historic conquest underscored by its rhythm, intensity and for its being the result of a public policy that involved an interesting blend of the power of the State and the mobilization of private and civil society actors.[49] Nevertheless, in recent years, Brazilian Amazon's growth (and of that of the other eight countries that have part of their territory in the Amazon region) has been marked by an accelerated process of what the UNEP[50] refers to as reprimarization. That shows itself in the expansion of mining,[51] in the great efforts to exploit oil in biologically precious regions like the Yasuni Reserve, in Ecuador,[52] and in the investments undertaken in large-scale hydroelectric projects in several Amazonian countries.

Chinese capital plays a crucial role in all of this. Of the total amount of Chinese investments in the countries with part of their territories in the Amazon basin, 80.7 per cent are in sectors notorious for their impacts on the environment.[53] Notwithstanding the drop in the deforestation rate in Brazil, the Latin American Amazon can be characterized overall as a part of an economy of destruction of nature. In 1970, only 1 per cent of the Brazilian Amazon territory had been deforested in spite of the tremendous reduction in deforestation that has been achieved beginning in 2004, by 2013, 19 per cent of the Brazilian Amazon forest had been destroyed. It is also important to note that in 2013, after five successive years of reduction, deforestation increased again.[54]

An important document was presented to candidates disputing the second round of the 2014 presidential elections elaborated by prestigious non-governmental organizations active in the Amazon region. The document proposed that deforestation in the Amazon should be brought down to zero by 2020.[55] The measures necessary to make that goal achievable are fundamental to the green economy discussion. The first consists of suspending the construction of any new large-scale hydroelectric installations in the region given the already mentioned power of attraction such project works have on the population in search of jobs and the associated threat generated to the neighbouring forest by their arrival in the areas.

In addition, the study demonstrated the urgency of investing not in producing energy for the rest of the country, but instead, and as a top priority, in providing the 25 million inhabitants of the Amazon with access to basic sanitation, good-quality education and, above all, opportunities for the sustainable valuation of biodiversity, making it possible to generate income while preserving the forest.

The challenge set out in United Nations documents and above all by The Economics of Ecosystems & Biodiversity (TEEB[56]) has so far not been confronted. No corporate skills are being developed to make the sustainable valuation of biodiversity the base of any minimally significant economic initiatives. Instead of expanding activities capable of valuing Amazonian ecosystem services and biodiversity products, economic activities in the region are essentially predatory. Even considering the reduction achieved in deforestation, the situation in the region is still a far cry from anything that could be construed as green growth.

Conclusions

Developing countries need to amplify their infrastructure and expand those services that will enable them to meet the basic needs of populations currently living in poverty. To that end, the provision of goods and services has to be expanded.

However, the criterion for judging that expansion cannot be economic growth, even when it incorporates policies/strategies that attempt to avoid the worst forms of damage to the environment. This chapter shows that although raising the income of poorer segments of the population is necessary, it is on its own far from sufficient to accelerate the expansion of substantive freedoms of human beings. In the absence of public and collective goods inherent to the process of development, more income will not necessarily lead to any increase in well-being. Furthermore, reducing impacts on the environment stemming from certain activities (such as energy production, mobility and the use of ecosystems) cannot guarantee that the use of resources will be compatible with the maintenance of those ecosystem services on which social life itself depends. The reprimarization of the Brazilian and Latin American economies is not a sector-based problem. It actually condemns the countries to relinquishing the innovations that are going to mark the course of sustainable development in the twenty-first century.

The main lesson that can be learned from the Brazilian case is that even with the cleanest energy matrix of all the countries of a comparable size, even with a biofuel that has low net greenhouse gas emissions and in spite of the significant reduction of Amazonian deforestation, Brazil is not drawing any closer to sustainable development. The Brazilian economy has grown less than those of most of its Latin American neighbours since 2011. In spite of this stagnation emissions increased 7.8 per cent in 2013, compared to 2012. The response to the energy crisis resulting from the effects of the drought on the hydroelectric system was the enlargement of coal and gas participation in the Brazilian energy supply, as shown by the Observatório do Clima.[57]

This recarbonization shows that in the current conditions, when growth does get underway again, it will be marked by extremely serious socio-environmental impacts. The investments in infrastructure for the pre-salt deposits and in large-scale hydroelectric projects have set Brazil on a path dependence which is leading it farther and farther away from the frontiers of technological innovation in the field of energy. That withdrawal represents a serious threat to a country with 200 million people and the seventh largest economy in the world. Furthermore, the continuous expansion of the automobile industry is now threatening the integrity of the social fabric of the urban and metropolitan territories. The lack of innovation that has become the country's hallmark is even more evident in relation to the Amazon, where the conventional forms of entrepreneurism have actually become a menace to the ecosystem services provided by the forests, instead of valuing them highly.

The greatest difficulty besetting attempts to contain economic growth within the limits of ecosystems is not in finding other techniques that might make it possible to achieve other forms of urban mobility, modern, renewable sources of energy and sustainable forms of entrepreneurism. The greatest difficulty lies in facing the consolidated vested interests that dress their 'business as usual' in robes of green. Supposedly 'green' economic growth, if not properly scrutinized, can be an example of this masquerade.

CHAPTER 8

Green jobs to promote sustainable development: creating a value chain of solid waste recycling in Brazil

Anne Posthuma and Paulo Sergio Muçouçah*

Introduction

The concept of 'green growth' involves a strong belief that scientific research, technological innovation and engineering solutions are capable of controlling the pace of environmental degradation, raising efficiency of natural resource usage and ensuring well-being while also raising productivity and economic growth.[1] Yet, a key criticism of the green growth concept is that it is an insufficient policy guideline for achieving a sustainable future given the harsh realities of finite and unequally distributed resources, poverty and socio-economic exclusion that characterize so much of our current development paradigm.[2] Green growth proponents include leaders of corporations, investors and policy-makers, but often the social dimensions of a more sustainable society receive inadequate attention, including how to ensure employment and income opportunities and paths for socio-economic inclusion, particularly for the poorest sections of society. In this way, the green growth concept risks leaving in place the existing structures of inequality and socio-economic exclusion that underpin and perpetuate the current unsustainable paradigm of production, consumption and distribution.[3] In contrast, the 'sustainable development' framework seeks a more integrated approach, being founded upon three interlocking economic, environmental and social dimensions.[4]

---

* The views expressed in this chapter are those of the authors and do not necessarily reflect the views of the International Labour Organization.

Hence, when considering the economic and environmental components of sustainable development, it is equally important to take into account the role of social well-being that is attained through the promotion of stable and decent opportunities for employment and income generation. Within this perspective, the concept of green jobs[5] emerged, which reinforces the promotion of quality job creation in environmentally sustainable sectors and activities, and contributes to the greening of existing enterprises and economies through the use of renewable energies, new technologies and materials, skills development and ensuring markets for sustainable products and services.[6] It is important to highlight this recognition that the creation of decent work and incomes is not an automatic outcome of market mechanisms in the shift to a green economy.[7] For this reason, a key task involves identification of good practices and their respective drivers, or policy instruments and institutions, which play a crucial role in ensuring the creation, remuneration, safety and other relative quality aspects of green jobs.[8]

The growth of recycling industries exemplifies how shifting economic perspectives and societal values can lead to the creation and growth of jobs linked to environmentally sustainable practices. The growth of recycling itself is based upon a recognition that waste has an economic value (i.e. it is less expensive to recycle, reprocess and reuse materials), an environmental value (i.e. the growth of waste recycling can result in less mining and deforestation, processing and consumption of raw resources), as well as a social value (i.e. waste recycling can generate green jobs and income-generating activities). Governments, particularly at the local level, have realized that recycling provides important public benefits, in addition to substantial cost savings.

In this context, the present chapter uses a value chain framework to examine the Brazilian experience in promoting solid waste recycling through a 'bottom-up' approach of generating green jobs among solid waste collectors at the base of the solid waste recycling value chain. This experience describes how an integrated and multifaceted approach can be put in place, whereby policies, legislation, institutions and enforcement mechanisms work together to create a set of incentives and regulations to promote scale and efficiency in a recycling sector. A key dimension of this case study is the successful integration of precarious and informal work in the lower tiers of the recycling value chain into the broader market economy, and thereby enabling waste gathering to become a recognized occupation, with adequate wages, safe working conditions, forms of organization and voice and social protection and with the labour entitlements of formal employment, thereby making it possible to be categorized as 'green jobs'. Furthermore regulations have also supported the supply, demand and disposal of solid waste (e.g. by stimulating recycling practices among consumers and workplaces, restricting the amount of packaging waste generated by producers and limiting the use of landfills) and sustainable behaviour is enforced in economic sectors and the government (thereby creating markets for recycled inputs, recycled products and recycling services).

The value chain framework is an effective analytical tool with which to examine the various interventions and their impacts in this Brazilian case study and to place these in a wider context. Productive activities worldwide are increasingly organized along value chains. In a value chain framework, the lead firm, or key buyer of goods and services, is linked to multiple suppliers down the value chain, which thereby strengthens the bargaining power and potential profit margins of the buyer.[9] A value chain framework can not only shed light upon the structure of production and markets, but also can reveal the unequal distribution of rents within the value chain.[10] Where profits tend to accrue to the higher echelons of different producers, this raises the need to target interventions on those firms and workers embedded in the lower tiers of the value chain to ensure that these work opportunities do not involve precarious and unsafe work at survival levels of remuneration, but instead, can be upgraded and considered green jobs, with decent work conditions. Through governance structures of policies and legislation as well as strategies and collective organizations of waste pickers themselves, this case study from Brazil aims to show it is possible to counterbalance the tendencies toward socio-economic exclusion and instead promote safer, more productive and formal jobs among these workers at the lower tiers of the recycling value chain.

This case study raises the possibility – while maintaining a realistic recognition of the challenges to be addressed – that the green jobs approach can bring about a rupture with the current unsustainable and exclusionary paradigm of production and consumption, by harnessing sustainable practices in ways that increase productivity in the use of the natural resources, thus reducing the need for their primary extraction, and also supporting socio-economic inclusion through the promotion of green jobs in the recycling value chain.

The first section below provides a definition and contextualization of the concept of green jobs, its potential and challenges. In the second section, the discussion introduces the case study of the Brazilian experience in promoting socio-economic inclusion of waste pickers into green jobs and strengthening the recycling value chain. In subsequent sub-sections, various dimensions of the experience are explored as related to the promotion of green jobs among recyclable waste collectors, the strengthening of cooperatives and representative associations and income generation among recyclable waste gatherers.

Origin and definition of the green jobs approach

In 2007, the Green Jobs Initiative was launched jointly by the United Nations Environment Programme (UNEP), the International Labour Organization (ILO) and the International Trade Union Confederation (ITUC). The International Organization of Employers (IOE) joined the initiative in the following year, 2008. This new concept of 'green jobs' was broadly defined as any decent job[11] that contributes to preserving or restoring the quality of the environment in agriculture, industry, services or administration. Such green jobs were identified as having several key characteristics, including their contribution towards:

(i) reducing consumption of energy and raw materials;
(ii) limiting GHG emissions;
(iii) minimizing waste and pollution;
(iv) protecting and restoring ecosystems; and
(v) enabling enterprises and communities to adapt to climate change.

As a corollary, green occupations were defined as being responsible for monitoring and limiting negative environmental impacts, and green sectors or industries as those which are environmentally sustainable or contribute towards environmental sustainability.

The conceptual and operational link between environmental and labour issues has evolved over more than two decades. As such, the emergence of the concept of green jobs constitutes an important contribution towards enhanced coherence between sustainable development and decent work.

Looking back at how these links have evolved, it is useful to recall that Agenda 21 and the Outcome Document of the Earth Summit held in Rio de Janeiro in 1992 emphasized the need for balance between economic, social and environmental dimensions of sustainable development. Mention was also made of the role of employers' and workers' associations as stakeholders in promoting sustainable development at national and workplace levels. Ten years later, at the World Social Summit for Development in Johannesburg in 2002, the final Declaration and Plan of Implementation briefly mentioned labour issues.

Over time, the role of decent work in promoting sustainable development received more consistent attention. At the World Summit on Social Development, in 2005, full employment and decent work were adopted as global goals. The convergence between these areas ultimately led to the launch of the Green Jobs Initiative in 2007. In 2010, the parties to the United Nations Framework Convention on Climate Change included a specific reference to decent work in the 'shared vision' for a future global climate agreement. These various agreements culminated in the Outcome Document of the United Nations Conference on Sustainable Development (popularly known as Rio+20) that established the role of decent work for achieving sustainable development in a dedicated chapter, and also in other cross-references.

While the contribution of green jobs to sustainable development has been increasingly understood and strengthened, the operationalization of its measurement is still unfolding. In 2013, the International Conference of Labour Statisticians (ICLS) established guidelines concerning the statistical definition of green jobs. The discussion agreed that 'employment in the environmental sector' includes both (i) employment in the production of environmental outputs and (ii) employment in environmental processes. Crucially, green jobs only involve employment in the environmental sector that is decent. In other words, green jobs involve a subset of employment in the environmental sector that meets the requirements of decent work – employment that includes adequate wages, occupational safety and health, workers' rights, social dialogue and social protection.[12]

Moving forward, the ICLS has set a future agenda around ILO activities in collaboration with host countries and organizations to test the green jobs concepts and definitions as specified in the ICLS guidelines, to refine the concepts and to test an estimation methodology of data collection. Green jobs include new forms of work in environmental sectors, but also the greening of existing jobs through a socially just transition (ibid.). By placing decent employment and income as the dynamic at the centre of the transition to sustainability, the green jobs approach breaks with the concept of green growth that rests on technological innovation and economic growth as its key drivers.

The green jobs approach has a strong sectoral dimension. Eight sectors stand out due to their close relationship to environmental sustainability, namely: agriculture; forestry; fisheries; energy; resource-intensive manufacturing; recycling; construction; and transport. These eight sectors have been estimated to account for roughly half of global direct employment, with approximately two-thirds of these jobs in agriculture. In particular, three sectors – agriculture, building/construction and waste management/recycling – have been identified as having the greatest potential to impact positively upon sustainable development, as well as job creation, if correct interventions are provided to boost growth and job creation potential.[13]

In particular, waste management and recycling has great potential for job growth. Well-designed policies, incentives, technical support and laws can work together to support the upgrading of productive practices, access to new markets and improvements in job quality, leading to the creation, expansion and strengthening of green jobs in this sector. However, important policy implications and challenges exist in the goal of promoting green jobs, as seen in the following sub-section.

Challenges in the promotion of green jobs

Policy-oriented studies have shown that green jobs outcomes can be mixed. Therefore, impact evaluations must take into consideration sectoral and country specificities. For example, the impact of green jobs in the renewable wind power sector was compared with the conventional power sector in China using four main dimensions: (i) working hours; (ii) wages and benefits; (iii) social security; and (iv) working environment.[14] In this Chinese case study, jobs in the renewable energy sector generally involved longer working hours than the conventional energy sector (although this was largely explained by a dearth of workers with the required skills in the renewable energy sector at the time of the research). Wages varied depending upon the technological sophistication of the firm involved; meanwhile, benefits were better overall in the conventional energy sector (largely due to the strong presence of public sector firms). Participation of workers in social security and insurance schemes was higher among energy sector employees as a whole – including both renewable and conventional energy sectors – than workers in other sectors on average. Finally, working conditions were found to be better and cleaner in the renewable sector than conventional energy plants.

Policy choices play a strong role in shaping the green job outcomes in a sustainable economy. This crucial point was highlighted in a recent ILO report that stated: '... outcomes for employment and incomes are largely determined by the policy instruments used and the institutions which implement them, rather than being an inherent part of the shift to a greener economy.'[15] Furthermore, as this transition involves complex and cross-cutting issues, it is important to maintain policy coherence, consistency and coordination.[16]

Another challenge involves the concern that transitioning to a sustainable economy may lead to a reduction in overall employment, as well as unemployment for workers without the appropriate skill sets. In this regard, studies have shown that net job gains are possible in the shift to a more sustainable economy, but a successful transition with green jobs requires an appropriate framework of policies and investments.[17] More specifically, both active and passive labour market policies and services (such as unemployment insurance, retraining, job guidance counselling, financial assistance and other social supports) can play a crucial role in helping affected workers adjust successfully.[18] The active support of workers and their representative associations also plays an important role in achieving this goal.[19]

Levels of technological sophistication, skill-intensity and job quality vary widely in the recycling sector. It was estimated that four million workers were employed in 2010 in the formal recycling sector in the United States, Europe and China.[20] Furthermore, an estimated 1.8 million direct jobs could be created over the next 10 to 20 years in the European Union and the United States, if recycling rates were increased by 70 to 75 per cent. These figures would be much higher if one includes the estimated 15 to 20 million informal waste pickers in developing countries that rely on this activity to sustain themselves and often other family members. In this light, the growth of recycling offers a promising dual-response that could address the unsustainable levels of waste together with the creation of green jobs. At present, the recycling sector (which includes a large number of informal work by individuals, families or small-scale, low technology units) poses a significant challenge to transform informal and precarious waste picking into viable economic activities and green jobs. Waste pickers are generally vulnerable individuals and social groups that are economically and socially marginalized, and work in precarious conditions without a regular source of income, often in the informal economy, yet they provide a social and environmental service by collecting waste that also can generate economic value.[21] Hence, in this context, policies and incentives within an integrated perspective have a crucial social, environmental and economic role to play. In addition, investment, labour market, education and skills policies have been shown to play a central role in promoting this transition.[22]

Gender challenges in the transition to a sustainable economy have been rarely addressed.[23] This is in part because women are under-represented in the sectors in which green jobs tend to be concentrated[24] and in part because of a perspective in economic investments and government strategies to promote a sustainable economy that rarely takes into account the situation of women. Policy attention will be required in order to avoid a replication of gender-based job segregation and under-representation of women in more highly technical and specialized careers. A good example in this regard has been the effort by the European Parliament that called upon the European Union and its Member States to give higher priority to green jobs for women.[25] Relevant issues concerning the promotion of equal opportunities (such as fair treatment, recruitment practices, equal access to employment, the gender pay gap, and the development of technical career paths for women) are fundamental concerns to be addressed in the shift to green jobs and a sustainable economy.[26]

In Brazil, a major challenge involves the promotion of quality jobs in the transition toward green jobs. Brazilian studies show that policy support has been decisive in transforming the existing economic paradigm toward environmental sustainability and quality job creation.[27] Furthermore, policy coherence has been crucial in ensuring coordination across different policy domains such as environment, infrastructure, housing, energy, agriculture and rural development, social protection and employment.

As a good example, recent Brazilian legislation has required mechanization of the heavy manual labour in cutting sugar cane, used in the production of sugar cane-based ethanol, which the ICLS classification considers as employment in the production of an environmental output. Each machine substitutes 80 sugar cane cutters (thereby eliminating dangerous, labour-intensive work) and creates 16 jobs that are safer and less strenuous to feed the machine. Employers have promoted professional training courses in tasks related to the operation and maintenance of machinery for workers released from manual sugar-cane cutting, through programmes such as the Programa Renovação.

The sectoral dimension can pose additional challenges in linking decent work with sustainable development in the value chains of green sectors, where some firms in the supply chain may have decent work deficits in their labour practices and difficulties for individual workers and small producers to increase value-added and their profit share. Studies of the dynamics of outsourcing in GVCs have already identified the tendency to transfer risk and costs from larger lead firms to micro, small and medium sized enterprises at lower tiers of the value chain, with consequent negative impacts upon employment, working conditions[28] and ability to capture greater rents in the value chain.

A similar dynamic could be involved in recycling chains and thereby would pose challenges to the goal of creating green jobs under conditions of decent work as well as increased earnings of workers, small producers and associations of waste pickers. This challenge would need to be addressed by explicit policies towards upgrading of production practices and job quality among micro, small and medium enterprises. Smaller production units have financial and human resource limitations to undertake the necessary investments, changes in production, organization and market strategies to achieve both economic and social upgrading in green sectors. Therefore, there is a crucial role of policies (while also maintaining policy coherence) and institutions to promote upgrading of economic activities, jobs and environmental practices in an integrated way and at the different levels of the value chain of green industries. Nevertheless, one should bear in mind that the particular nature of the recycling sector, based upon waste and end-of-lifecycle products, may have forms of governance that differ from those of more conventional consumer goods,[29] possibly requiring some adaptation of governance strategies together with incentives and awareness-raising such as among companies (to create markets for purchase of recycled goods) and consumers (to increase their separation of recyclable waste).

We now turn to the Brazilian experience in promoting green jobs in the value chain of the recycling sector.

The Brazilian experience in promoting green jobs within the recycling value chain

In Brazil, where urban poor engage in waste picking as an income source, the opportunity to join economic and environmental concerns with socio-economic inclusion and job creation has laid the foundation for an integrated approach towards the promotion of green jobs in this sector. Policies and legislation have provided crucial incentives, regulation and enforcement in this regard.

The National Solid Waste Policy (NSWP) adopted in 2010 was a landmark piece of legislation that established a shared responsibility for the destination of more than 150,000 tonnes of waste produced daily in Brazil. The NSWP set a four-year timetable to implement adequate solid waste management among Brazilian municipalities by reducing the quantity of waste sent to rubbish dumpsites and raising the recycling and composting of organic waste. When the NSWP was adopted, the Brazilian National Statistical Office estimated that a mere 2.2 per cent of waste was recycled in Brazil.[30] By the end of the deadline of 2 August 2014, 40 per cent of Brazilian municipalities had complied with the elimination of open-air rubbish dumpsites.[31] Only between 2012 and 2013, 133 municipalities introduced selective waste collection programmes, raising to 62 per cent the percentage of municipalities participating in some part of the recycling chain.[32]

In 2012, the collection, separation and processing of recyclable materials by businesses in Brazil generated an estimated R$10 billion of earnings.[33] Considering the estimate that 27 per cent of all recyclable material found in urban waste that year was recycled, this indicates there is strong economic potential to raise earnings through increased recycling. Using an input–output matrix for the state Rio de Janeiro, a study estimated that potential savings, if all solid urban waste in the state were recycled, would be roughly equivalent to 25 per cent of state GDP.[34]

Another recent study has identified materials most commonly found in urban waste (such as steel, aluminium, paper, plastic and glass) and estimated their environmental impact in terms of energy consumption, greenhouse gas emissions, water consumption and biodiversity impacts.[35] Both economic and environmental advantages of recycling in Brazil were considered in Table 8.1 by calculating

Table 8.1: Estimated economic and environmental benefits from recycling in Brazil

Materials	Benefits related to the production process (in Brazilian reais per tonne)		Benefits related to solid waste management (in Brazilian reais per tonne)		Total Benefits (in Brazilian reais per tonne)
	Economic Benefits	Environmental Benefits	Collection	Final Depositing	
Steel	127	74	(136)	23	88
Aluminium	2,715	339	(136)	23	2,941
Cellulose	330	24	(136)	23	241
Plastic	1,164	56	(136)	23	1,107
Glass	120	11	(136)	23	18

Source: IPEA (2010).

the benefits that arise from reduced use of raw materials and their growing substitution by recycled materials, plus additional savings generated from the declining cost of waste management through diminished use of dumpsites.

Promotion of green jobs and income generation among waste recyclers

The solid waste recycling value chain can be visualized in Figure 8.1, which presents a flow chart illustrating the multiplicity of economic actors involved in the recycling sector. Waste pickers are located at the lowest value-added tier on the recycling value chain. Nevertheless, these initial stages of collecting and separating recyclable materials create the greatest number of jobs and are a source of jobs and income for many low-income urban inhabitants who otherwise have limited opportunities to find gainful sources of income.

In Brazil, waste pickers have long played a crucial role in the process of transforming solid urban waste into raw materials and inputs to manufacturing industry. An important legislative reform in 2001 formally recognized this role as the occupation of 'Recyclable Material Gatherer', which was included in the Brazilian Occupational Classification (CBO – Classificação Brasileira de Ocupações) of the Ministry of Labour and Employment.[36] Despite this formal recognition, waste pickers continue to suffer social stigma and remain a marginalized group, although the creation of collective associations helps to combat this type of socio-economic exclusion.[37]

In order to estimate the number of solid waste recyclers in Brazil, the Demographic Census in 2010 identified 387,910 self-declared waste pickers or recyclable waste gatherers.[38] However, the genuine number of waste pickers is surely much greater, if one considers that many prefer to hide their activity due to the stigma surrounding this occupation. Furthermore, many waste pickers are homeless street dwellers who derive their primary source of survival from this activity, but are difficult for Census officials to locate and interview. In addition, there remains a large contingent of workers in various categories who dedicate themselves to the gathering of recyclable materials as a secondary activity, to complement their main source of income, or for whom this serves as a temporary activity while they seek another job.

Figure 8.1 Flow chart of the solid waste recycling value chain

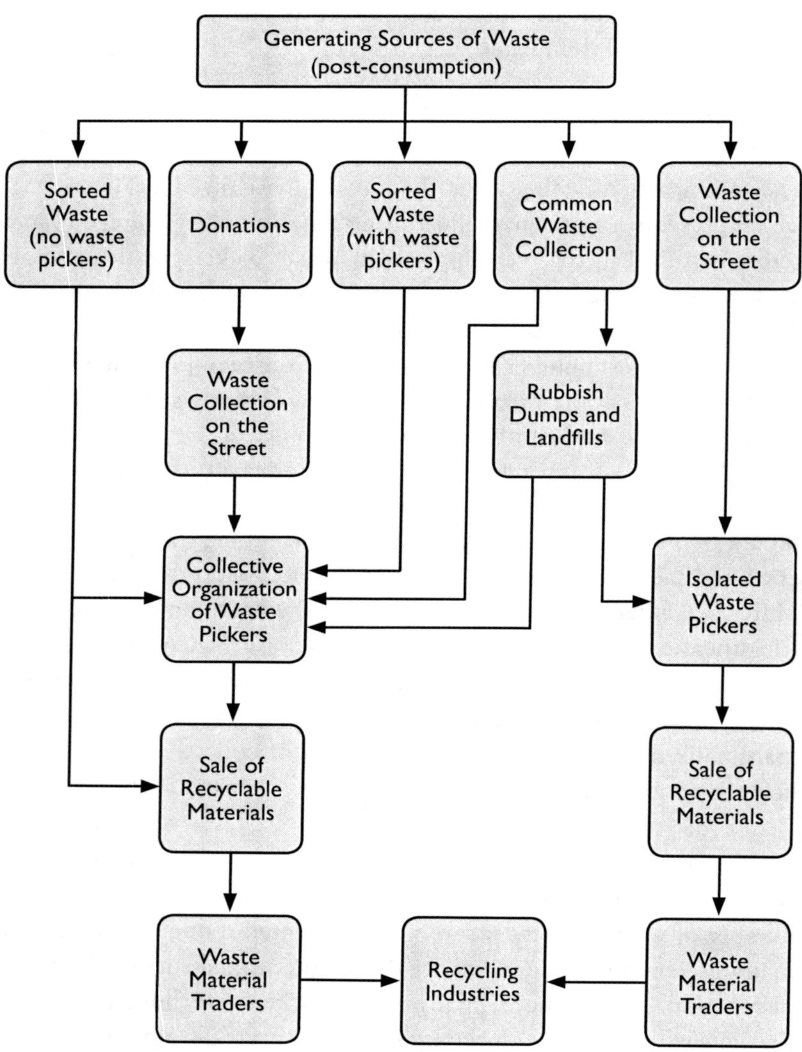

Source: IPEA (2013).

It is striking that a relatively high percentage (38.6 per cent) of waste pickers declared in the 2010 Census that they have a formal work contract, whether through the Signed Work Card (*Carteira de Trabalho por Tempo de Serviço*) or through the Unified Regime for Public Employees (*Regime Único do Funcionalismo Público*). Although this percentage is far below the average rate of formality in the Brazilian labour market[39] (ILO, 2012b), there are grounds to believe that these figures have been overestimated. For example, the ILO cites data from the National Household Survey Data (*PNAD – Pesquisa Nacional de Amostra por Domicílio*) that an estimated 15.4 per cent of own-account waste gatherers make the necessary social security contributions. Efforts to increase formal employment among waste pickers are important, as this will provide them with access to labour rights, social security and a pension.

Formation of cooperatives and workers' associations

Another issue is the ability for the waste pickers to organize themselves into cooperatives. The creation of associative organizations can play an important role in enabling recyclable waste pickers to capture greater rents in the value chain, as collective organizations have greater capacity to access credit, make new investments, as well as upgrade and increase installed capacity, all of which contribute to generating economies of scale, raising productivity, reduce workplace injuries, eliminating some of the intermediaries (i.e. middlemen) and increasing new market opportunities for their products and services.[40] Organizations of workers can help to represent their collective interests, and ensure they have formal work contracts including access to social protection, health and holidays as well as other labour rights guaranteed in Brazilian law through the Signed Work Card (*carteira assinada*). Research indicates that the creation of cooperatives of recyclers tends to improve their working conditions and income.[41]

Incentives have been put in place to encourage recycling waste pickers at the local level to form collective organizations and cooperatives to become commercially viable enterprises that can capture scale economies, improve their negotiating power with purchasers of recyclable waste material and access credit, more stable incomes and market opportunities. Consequent investments in improved equipment and processes could, in turn, lead these collective organizations and cooperatives to raise productivity, value-added, health and safety in the workplace and wages. It is necessary to recognize the crucial role played by the Interministerial Committee for Socio-Economic Inclusion of Waste Pickers, created in 2003 to support in various ways the self-organization of these workers, as an antecedent to the evolution of the current multifaceted and inter-sectoral approach towards promoting quality jobs and sustainable entrepreneurism among waste pickers at the base of the value chain.

Despite incentives for the creation of representative associations, the cooperatives and associations of waste pickers still do not account for more than 10 per cent of all waste pickers in the country, according to even the most optimistic estimates.[42] The National Basic Sanitation Survey conducted by the National Statistical Office identified the existence of 1,175 cooperatives and associations of recyclable waste pickers in Brazil, distributed in 684 municipalities.[43] In 653 of these municipalities, the waste pickers already had established some type of participation in public services for the gathering and separating of solid waste. However, the members of these organizations numbered not more than 30,390 workers, representing merely 8 per cent of those who self-identified as waste pickers in the 2010 Census. Other waste recyclers identified in the Census could possibly be linked to firms or government activities. Meanwhile, the *Yearbook of Social Indicators* (RAIS, 2010) of the Ministry of Labour and Employment, which is the most complete survey of formal jobs in the country, registered a total of 71,807 workers involved in various stages of recycling activities in 2010.

This formality rate includes waste pickers with an individual work contract as well as those associated with a legal cooperative that provides services of collection, separation and processing of recyclable materials for private firms and municipal authorities. This latter group of legal cooperatives enjoys various legislative advantages that include a reduced rate of social security contribution (of 12 per cent) for their members, while own-account workers are subject to a contribution of 20 per cent of their earnings.

In addition to promoting formal work among recyclable material gatherers and ensuring more dignified income, the cooperatives formed by these workers have also been responsible for substantial improvements in the conditions of work. For example, collective organizations tend to be recognized by public authorities, which greatly facilitates the development of their activities and attributes higher social status to affiliates than own-account waste pickers. In Europe, affiliation with trade unions has provided waste pickers with representation and improved bargaining power that have enhanced their ability to obtain improved health and safety in the workplace, higher wages and access to social protection among other advantages.[44]

A large majority of these cooperatives have working space, generally granted by municipal authorities, for storing, separating and bundling the collected materials, thereby avoiding the risks associated with more improvised working spaces. Furthermore, many of these organizations have basic equipment that makes work more efficient, less difficult and safer, such as light wheelbarrows, benches, scales, mills, pressing machines and individual protective equipment. Many have escalators, forklifts and motorized vehicles. Some have purchased more sophisticated equipment for in-house processing of collected material for final consumption (thereby raising their rents by increasing their value-added activities and eliminating intermediaries).

Although waste picker cooperatives, in general, provide better conditions of work to their affiliates than own-account gatherers, there exists great heterogeneity between cooperatives in terms of equipment used, technical know-how, skills training, level of organization and, consequently, their productivity and efficiency. A typology was developed, comparing efficiency with organization type, based upon a study of 83 cooperatives, associations and groups of recyclable waste pickers from different regions of Brazil. Only 14 per cent of these organizations were considered highly efficient and 27 per cent were considered of average efficiency. Meanwhile, 59 per cent of these organizations were evaluated as either low or very low in efficiency. Organization size was not necessarily an advantage.[45]

The recognition that nearly 60 per cent of waste picker organizations were operating at low or very low levels of efficiency led the federal government to implement a series of policies destined to reverse this situation. The National Policy for Solid Waste, approved by the Brazilian Congress in 2010, reserves a privileged role for cooperatives of recyclable waste pickers in municipal services of solid waste management as well as in the systems of reverse logistics that are to be installed by companies in various sectors for the collection of their products and packaging after use.[46]

Additional public policies to promote cooperatives and representative associations among waste pickers in the recycling value chain

Strengthening of operations and commercial viability of representative associations of waste collectors was further advanced with the Waste Collectors' Programme ('Programa Pró-Catador') launched in December 2010 with the aim of integrating and linking the activities of the federal government that work with recyclable waste pickers to promote the creation of productive organizations, improve their working conditions, expand waste collection, reuse and recycling, and increase opportunities for socio-economic inclusion of workers and their families.[47] Areas of technical support to cooperatives of waste pickers under the Waste Collectors' Programme include training and technical assistance, incubation of cooperatives, support for acquisition of equipment, machinery and vehicles, development of technologies geared towards increasing value-added and opening special lines of credit.

These activities were introduced through a project entitled *Cataforte*, the fruit of an agreement between the National Secretary of the Solidarity Economy of the Ministry of Labour and Employment and Bank of Brazil Foundation (which uses the Bank's financial resources to promote social initiatives). Between 2010 and 2012, the *Cataforte* Project developed social, professional, political and cultural training of recyclable material collectors in 21 states, involving 10,600 participants. The primary result of this initiative has been the organization of nearly 400 enterprises of waste recyclers, which include 26 solidarity cooperative networks having the objective of exchanging technical assistance, promoting the collective use of equipment and jointly commercializing collected waste materials.

Additional measures have been adopted in recent years to strengthen the cooperatives of waste recyclers and to boost the development of recycling activities in Brazil. Government procurement of goods and services from recycling cooperatives has been particularly significant, as have tax incentives provided to products made from recycled materials that were acquired from these cooperatives.

Working hours and working environment

The vast majority of waste pickers (70 per cent) work no more than 44 hours a week, in line with the limit established by the Brazilian Constitution. A relatively small percentage (13 per cent) work between 45 and 48 hours a week and another group including mainly own-account waste pickers (17 per cent) works more than 49 hours a week.[48]

Cooperative members tend to experience much better working conditions and more effective safety protection than autonomous waste pickers. For example, a comparison between two different studies on health and safety of waste pickers showed that a group of 32 self-managed cooperatives of waste pickers in the Metropolitan Region of São Paulo had a much lower rate and frequency of health and safety problems than was the case among independent scavengers who sold their collected materials to traders and recyclable materials institutions in Curitiba.[49]

Income generation

The average earnings of recyclable waste pickers, according to the 2010 Census, was BRL 571.56, around 12 per cent above the official minimum wage of BRL 510 at that time,[50] although this varies across the country.

The organization of waste pickers also impacts upon their earnings. The structure of the local market for recycled material is another significant variable. In some cases, formalized waste recyclers received higher income than informal waste recyclers.[51] An average increase of 50 per cent in the earnings of individual waste recyclers was reported after they had associated with a cooperative, as well as evidence of an increased quality of life after being associated with a cooperative.[52]

Despite these improvements, there remain challenges to help waste pickers' cooperatives to continue raising value-added and gaining greater bargaining power in the solid waste recycling value chain. The distribution of income within the recycling chain is still unfavourable for the recyclable waste pickers, even those affiliated with cooperatives and associations with all the requisite benefits and support that have been provided to them. This low share of rents for waste pickers in the solid waste recycling value chain raises important questions regarding the economic and social sustainability of recycling activities. If recycling is a high priority, looking towards the need to attain a more environmentally sustainable society in the future, then appropriate incentives and support are required not only for companies at the top of the chain, but also to encourage and ensure sustainable livelihoods for those responsible for gathering and sorting recyclable waste at the bottom of the value chain.

Conclusions

This chapter has used the green jobs approach of the ILO and the global value chains analytical framework with which to examine the approach of the Brazilian government in promoting the socio-economic inclusion of waste pickers, through a multifaceted policy mix that has contributed towards strengthening the solid waste recycling value chain, encouraging associative organizations, increasing the potential earnings of waste pickers and creating green jobs. If the 'green growth' approach aims to contribute towards sustainable development, then it must also translate into social well-being, through the generation of jobs and income, especially for the poorest sectors of society.

The interventions in Brazil have included policies and legislative reform that have recognized recyclable waste picking as an occupation, thereby opening the way for these workers to be registered formally and access their labour rights, as well as incentives to strengthen the associative capacities of these workers through forming cooperatives and associations of recyclable waste pickers.[53] Initiatives to strengthen the productive capacities of these cooperatives and associations have included access to credit and technical assistance, as well as creation of more stable market access by guaranteeing a share of public purchases to be made with recycling cooperatives and associations. Social benefits have included a reduction of the payment rate made to social security for those members of cooperatives and associations.

Wages and efficiency of members of cooperatives and associations have been found to rise and well-being enhanced. These improvements in physical and human capital have paved the way towards expanded operations and aggregation of more processing operations, which are intended to lead towards attaining scale economies and higher value-added of the final product(s) and improved access to more stable market opportunities for the sale of recycled materials. Studies also indicate other subjective benefits can be attained, including pride in their cooperative or association, transfer of improved health and hygiene practices from the workplace into their personal lives, as well as removing children of poor waste picking families from these activities and encouraging their school attendance. In this way, the low-income, unprotected and unsafe work of informal waste pickers has been supported with the policies and conditions that aid transformation into green jobs.

Increased solid waste recycling has the potential to grow as an important sector in the Brazilian economy. These interventions described in this chapter to support green jobs among informal solid waste pickers can contribute to the strengthening and integration of all three pillars of sustainable development, showing that policy support can attain more environmentally responsible and sustainable management of scarce resources, and the growth of economic activities, while also providing a source of green jobs and income for waste pickers.

The achievements examined in this chapter make it possible to consider this Brazilian case study as an example of successful promotion of green jobs in the solid waste recycling value chain.[54] This is not to deny that difficulties exist. For example, the formalization of jobs within cooperatives did not always lead to new job creation; in fact, sometimes jobs were lost. Furthermore, some people returned to informal waste picking if they felt that they had more freedom and were able to earn more in the informal sector. It was also reported in a study that growing competition in the market for recycled waste could result in cooperatives losing market opportunities to other groups.[55] Earnings and conditions of work of recyclable material collectors still leave much to be desired, and the current numbers of workers could be considered unsustainable, despite the valuable contribution they make to society. While gatherers overall express their preference for cleaner and safer conditions in recycling cooperatives, in some cases they claim that earnings are lower than when they worked in the open-air rubbish dumps.[56]

Furthermore, the approach taken by the Brazilian government in the promotion of the recycling value chain does not break totally with current patterns of production and consumption. Wasteful practices persist, despite the National Solid Residues Policy of Brazil established in 2010. This indicates that the path towards sustainable development in this case is currently following an evolutionary trajectory that involves incremental improvements together with other persistent challenges.

While the Brazilian recycling experience can provide valuable lessons learned and inform policy formulation, there remains scope for continuous improvement. Many rubbish dumps remain around the country and recycling is still conducted in informal and unsanitary ways, even in large cities such as Rio de Janeiro. Paradoxes exist in the promotion of green jobs among waste pickers. The framework of a value chain analysis has contributed to visualizing the various economic, social and environmental links within the solid waste value chain, the relationships of power and unequal opportunities for rent capture among waste pickers at the bottom of the value chain, as well as the challenges for transforming work into green jobs and opportunities to access greater value-added in the value chain. The waste pickers still remain the weakest link in the recycling value chain, but the evolutionary trajectory that has been initiated through the multi-faceted policy mix has created a solid basis on which to build future improvements in the promotion of green jobs in this sector.

CHAPTER 9

Trends of social metabolism and environmental conflict: a comparison between India and Latin America

Joan Martinez-Alier, Federico Demaria, Leah Temper and Mariana Walter

In this chapter, we consider comparative data on India and Latin America (and also some variables on Africa and Europe) to explore the links between changes in the social metabolism (i.e. the flows of energy and materials in the economy) and the appearance of ecological distribution conflicts.

We show that Latin America and India are at different moments in the race (concomitant with increased GDP per person) and in the use of material flows. Latin America has reached a level of extraction of about 15 tonnes per person/year of all materials (comparable to the European Union). It is unlikely that this will increase much. A substantial part goes for export, much larger than the imports (and this is the obverse of the situation in the EU, where the tonnage of imports is much larger). In contrast, India is at a level of only 5 tonnes of material use per capita/year. If the economy grows, as is likely, this will increase more or less in proportion to economic growth. Biomass will increase much less than building materials and fossil fuels. This follows the regular patterns of economic growth.

This chapter traces the origins of ecological distribution conflicts in the changes in flows of energy and materials (and also in waste disposal), and makes some comparisons in this respect between Latin America and India. Other factors also play a role, such as population density.

'Green growthers' could argue that ecological modernization will reduce conflicts as it will make more efficient use of resources. However, the impetus of growing social metabolism is stronger than the increases in eco-efficiency. Moreover, improvements in efficiency cause to some extent increased energy and material flows because of the operation of Jevons' paradox or the rebound effect.

Regarding conflicts, one must remember that there is no 'green growth' in the sense that the industrial economy is based on the use of fossil fuels. Therefore there is a need for 'fresh' supplies of energy all the time. Materials can be recycled to some extent. When the economy grows, inputs of fossil fuels, biomass (food and feedstuffs, paper pulp, wood, agrofuels), building materials and mineral ores keep increasing. As we demonstrate, there is not even relative dematerialization in Latin America and India. So, economic growth is not 'green' because it implies more material flows.

We focus on the trends in the material flows of the economies of India and Latin America since 1970, comparing them, and tracing links to ecological distribution conflicts, and therefore to resistance movements. In India, the per capita level of extraction is low but there are many conflicts in such a high-population density context. Extraction will grow *pari passu* with economic growth and population growth. Imports (in tonnes) will also grow somewhat, probably more than exports. In South America, the level of extraction is per capita about three times higher than in India, and exports have grown fourfold in 40 years. However, there is a clear trend for the rate of growth of material flows to stop. The terms of trade are moving against primary exports after 2013.

Many of the findings in this chapter come from the EJOLT (Environmental Justice Organisations, Liabilities and Trade) project (2011–15), a global research project bringing science and society together to confront environmental injustice. EJOLT assembled and analysed information on resource extraction conflicts and waste disposal conflicts in many countries (georeferenced in the Environmental Justice Atlas, EJAtlas, www.ejatlas.org), connecting them to general trends in social metabolism and also to their immediate local causes.

Questions that we aimed to answer in EJOLT include the following. What is the rate of 'success' of environmental justice in such conflicts? Does population density help to explain the incidence of socio-environmental conflicts? Is local scarcity of water a relevant factor? How does the presence of indigenous populations affect the rate of successful outcomes? At the end of this chapter, we present a few results from the EJAtlas focusing on some of the research questions of a new 'statistical political ecology'. If 'green growth' would be a reality, if there had been much increased productivity from the same amount of material resources, such conflicts would presumably not be so widespread.

From ecological economics to environmental justice and political ecology

Ecological economics studies the social metabolism, using methods (presented below) developed over the last 20 years. In turn, political ecology studies socio-environmental conflicts (or, equivalently, ecological distribution conflicts). In such conflicts we realize that different valuation languages are used by the social actors, from monetary compensation of damages to ecological values or to the sacredness of mountains or rivers, including also the unalienable rights of indigenous people to their territories.

When did the global environmental justice movement appear? This was earlier than Seattle in 1999 and the World Social Forums of the 2000s, which certainly pushed forward the globalization of environmental justice.

United States academics and activists such as Robert Bullard[1] belonging to the EJ movement travelled and became influential in Brazil and South Africa. Academic work, from the mid-1990s if not before, made explicit connections between the EJ movement in the United States (born in the early 1980s) and other manifestations of EJ in Latin America, Africa and Asia. This connection was obvious after the deaths of Chico Mendes in Brazil in 1988 fighting deforestation and of Ken Saro-Wiwa and his Ogoni comrades in Nigeria in 1995 complaining against Shell. By the mid-1990s classic books analysing environmental justice movements against dams[2] and against tree plantations[3] had been published.[4]

The alternative 'treaties' signed at Rio de Janeiro in 1992 had demonstrated the many links among environmental groups. Friends of the Earth (born in California) went international, spreading also to Southern countries or rather bringing in organizations which had already existed since the 1980s, like CENSAT in Colombia or Acción Ecológica in Ecuador. Nnimmo Bassey of ERA, Nigeria, was president of Friends of the Earth International in the 2010s. But also outside Friends of the Earth one could find important local organizations in many countries linking the 'environmentalism of the poor' with wider notions of environmental justice and climate justice as the Centre for Science and Environment in Delhi did in 1991.

Focusing on case studies, the field of political ecology[5] studied since the 1980s many environmental conflicts in Southern countries. Going beyond case studies, some researchers started to generate statistics of conflicts over resource extraction and waste disposal. For instance, Gerber[6] researched conflicts over industrial tree plantations for wood, palm oil and rubber production, which are among the fastest growing monocultures and are currently being promoted as carbon sinks and energy producers. Such plantations cause a large number of conflicts between companies and local populations. Gerber investigated the impacts of the plantations, the social traits of the protesters involved, and the modalities of the conflicts – which included conflicts over/around/concerning rubber trees, eucalyptus, oil palm, gmelina, and acacia trees. In EJOLT we followed in Gerber's steps, when preparing an Atlas of environmental conflicts, which drew to a large extent on 'activist knowledge', not forgetting however that while conflict often signals injustice, many injustices do not immediately produce open conflicts.

Methods for the study of social metabolism

'Social metabolism' refers to the manner in which human societies organize their exchanges of energy and materials with the environment.[7]

A socio-metabolic approach acknowledges that inputs into the economy ultimately become outputs in the form of waste (except for the part that accumulates as a stock, as in buildings). The main output in volume from rich economies (apart from wastewater) is carbon dioxide from the burning of fossil fuels, the excessive production of which is a major source of climate change. Solid wastes produced by the economy are disposed of locally (in landfills or incinerators), or sometimes exported to distant regions or countries. All goods circulate through 'commodity chains',[8] i.e. from cradle to grave or from point of extraction to waste disposal. Ecological distribution conflicts occur at different stages in the commodity chains (from extraction to waste disposal) as different social actors (peasant or tribal groups, national or multinational companies, national governments, local or international NGOs, consumer groups, urban dwellers) have different stakes.

The economy may be described in terms of economic indicators such as GDP growth, the savings ratio, budget deficit as percentage of GDP, current account balance in the external sector, and so on. Social factors may be taken into account, as in the Human Development Index, which nevertheless correlates closely with GDP per capita, and leaves aside environmental and cultural losses.

The economy may also be described in terms of physical indicators. Economic, social, and physical indicators are non-equivalent descriptions.

This complexity cannot possibly be reduced to a single unit of measure. Instead one can do a multicriteria analysis to assess a variety of incommensurable indicators of performance. As physical indicators, we present three methods: MFA (material flows accounting), EFA (energy flows accounting) and HANPP (human appropriation of net primary production).

Such accounts (including carbon or energy 'rucksacks', 'virtual' water and 'embodied HANPP') are relevant to understanding current ecological distribution conflicts and also for historical and current debates on ecologically unequal exchange and the ecological debt.

Materials flows accounting (MFA)

The MEFA (a combination of MFA and EFA) is a set of methods for describing and analysing socio-economic metabolism. They examine economies as systems that reproduce themselves not only socially and culturally, but also physically through a continuous exchange of energy and matter with their natural environments and with other socio-economic systems. Here we focus on material flows accounts (MFA) drawing on methodologies established by the research group led by Marina Fischer-Kowalski[9] in Vienna and other groups over the last 30 years.

MFA aims to complement the system of national accounts, with a compatible system of biophysical national accounts using *tonnes* per year as the key unit of measurement. Such methodology provides a picture of the physical dimension of the economy, where the total turnover of materials of the socio-economic system can be analysed historically or by cross-section through the accounts of input flows (tonnes of biomass, fossil fuels, construction minerals, etc.) or output flows (tonnes of materials exported, waste or pollutant generated). We focus on the input side by taking into account all materials that enter into the national economy and acknowledging also the physical dimension of foreign trade.[10]

In material flows accounting we calculate first the domestic extraction (in tonnes per year) divided into biomass, minerals for building materials, mineral ores for metals, and fossil fuels. They show different levels and trends in different countries. Domestic extraction is denoted DE. The DMC (domestic material consumption) is equal to DE plus imports minus exports. Physical imports and physical exports measure all imported or exported commodities in tonnes. Physical trade balance (PTB) equals physical imports minus physical exports. So countries like Brazil or Russia (among the BRICs) have large PTBs, but India does not.

Energy flows accounting (EFA)

Energy flows accounting (EFA) is an integral part of the analysis of social metabolism. Primary and final energy delivered are usually classified in the statistics according to source. Such energy flows (including hydro-electricity) are also unequally distributed, and in India they are creating not only coal mining conflicts and new nuclear conflicts but also many conflicts in the Himalayas and in the North East over hydroelectricity. Notice that energy accounts are separate from the material flows. They are not computed in the present chapter. The most interesting EFA indicator is that of Energy Return on Energy Input (EROI). EROI is a useful coefficient for assessing the increasing costs of obtaining energy in developing tar sands or heavy oil in Alberta in Canada or the Orinoco Delta, Venezuela, or when taking oil from the bottom of the sea (as in Brazil's *pre-sal*) or in gas fracking, or for agrofuels such as those derived from sugar cane or *Jatropha curcas* (with low EROI).

Human appropriation of net primary production (HANPP)

The HANPP (human appropriation of net primary production) of biomass is an index of pressure on biodiversity (because the higher the HANPP, the less biomass is available for 'wild' species). It is calculated in three steps. First, the potential net primary production (in the natural ecosystems of a given region or country), NPP, is calculated. Then, the actual NPP (normally less than potential NPP, because of agricultural simplification and soil sealing) is calculated. The part of actual NPP used by humans and associate beings (cattle, etc.) relative to potential NPP is the HANPP.[11]

In India, due to high population density and land conversion, and due also to a relatively high use of biomass per capita (which would be higher still if the population ate more meat and used more paper), the HANPP is very high. Simron Singh *et al.*[12] put it at 73 per cent compared to about 40 per cent in the EU (with comparable population densities), and only 24 per cent in Japan (which imports much biomass). The HANPP in Latin America is low but it is increasing because of deforestation for cattle raising and for domestic or export crops in Brazil, Argentina and elsewhere. One could also explore the distributional aspect, in the sense of which humans get the HANPP.

Social metabolism of Latin America

MFAs have been conducted in most OECD countries and also in Latin America. For instance, MFA for Argentina was studied by Pérez Manrique *et al.*,[13] and by other authors for Colombia,[14] Mexico,[15] Ecuador and Latin America[16] as a whole.[17] For Argentina, we show that the recent increase in some forms of metal ore and biomass extraction (soybeans, in 20 million ha.) has led to new types of conflicts.

Figure 9.1 shows the trends in extraction of materials in Latin America over the last 40 years and until 2008. By 2008 extraction reached more than 14 tonnes per capita, of which over 10 per cent was exported. Exports exceeded imports by a large amount (Figure 9.2).

Figure 9.1 Domestic extraction in Latin America by major category of material for the years 1970–2008, in million tonnes

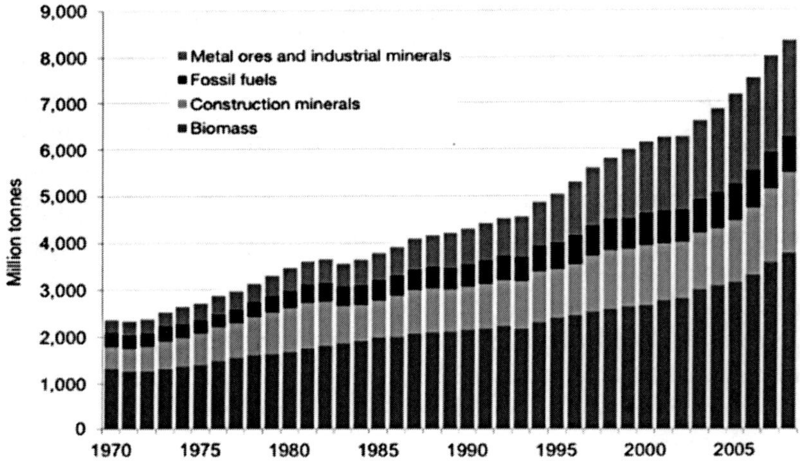

Source: West and Schandl, 'Material', 19.

Overall there was a fourfold increase in material flows between 1970 and 2008 for domestic consumption and also for exports. The Latin American economy has certainly not become 'dematerialized' – one could compare such trends with other continents, such as Europe where the rate of increase in material extraction has been much lower, or with India which still has a much lower rate of per capita material extraction than Latin America and which is not at all a net exporter in physical terms (see next section). Such physical indicators are useful to characterize the economic structure of countries or regions.

As remarked above, the physical trade balance (PTB) is the difference between the number of tonnes of materials that are imported from an economy and the number of tonnes that are exported. If exports exceed imports in physical terms we call it a physical trade deficit: the country is losing 'substance'. The monetary trade balance (MTB) is the difference between how much is paid for the imports and how much is earned by exports in monetary terms. Latin American economies and particularly South American economies have a persistent and increasing physical trade deficit.[18] Exports in tonnes are larger than

Figure 9.2 Latin America, physical trade deficits (imports–exports) in million tons, 1970–2008

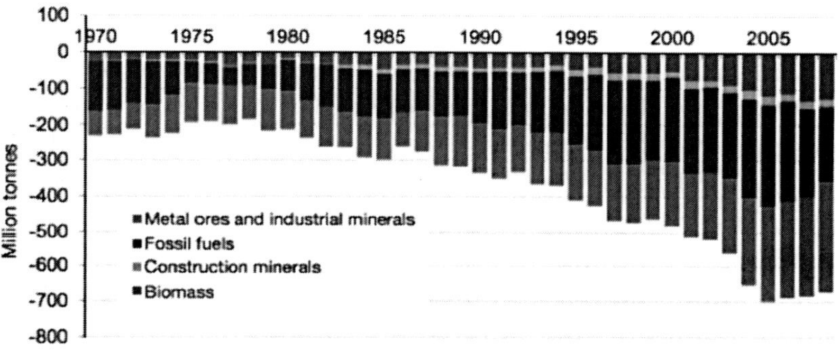

Source: West and Schandl, 'Material', 19.

imports in tonnes, resulting in a 'deficit' in the same sense that would be applied to a tree plantation that grows less than the harvest rate. Figure 9.2 presents a yearly PTB of Latin America (including Mexico) by type of material from 1970 and 2008. Notice in Figure 9.2 the increased physical trade deficit for metal ores and industrial minerals, which reflects the growing pressure to extract and export these materials. Latin America as a whole has about 600 million people, so the physical trade deficit is over one ton per capita/yr. It is unlikely that this will grow much in the next decades – just maintaining this level implies very heavy pressure at the commodity extraction frontiers.

We admit that one ton of uranium is environmentally extremely different from one ton of sand and gravel, or one ton of cellulose from one ton of shrimp. However, we are showing here trends within broad material categories rather than focusing on specific commodities. There are internal and external pressures to increase the extraction of materials, for domestic use and for export. Such increasing pressures to extract materials displace the commodity frontiers to new territories often inhabited by peasant and indigenous groups who complain accordingly.

As regards external trade, trends point to a structural persistence of ecologically unequal exchange.[19] This concept challenges the argument that exports from developing nations (or regions inside a country) foster economic growth and development and points to the physical and socio-environmental trade-offs at play.[20] Studies in this field highlight how poor countries are exporting goods at prices which do not take into account local externalities or depletion of natural resources, in exchange for the purchase of expensive goods and services from richer regions. One can measure ecologically unequal trade in terms of the inequality of various dimensions, such as hours of labour, hectares of land, joules or calories, tonnes of materials, or water footprints. When all or most indicators point in a similar direction we can state that there has been an unequal exchange.[21] Ecologically unequal exchange arises from the structural fact that the metropolitan regions or countries require for their metabolism increasing amounts of energy and materials at cheap prices.

The terms of trade are persistently negative for South America as a whole and most countries individually (one ton of imports is always more expensive than one ton of exports, from two to five times), in the very long term. Clearly, not all continents can behave in the same way. Thus, in the EU and in Japan, exports are more expensive than imports per ton. This is another way of saying that flows of energy and materials at relatively cheap prices must flow from the peripheries to the industrial metropolis.[22] However, the terms of trade in Latin America improved somewhat in the first decade of the twenty-first century, fuelling a wave of optimism regarding economic growth, but later they deteriorated again.[23] Currently, the large physical exports can scarcely pay for the imports in most South American countries. A large physical trade deficit does not imply a positive commercial balance, and on the contrary recent Latin America trends point to simultaneous physical and monetary deficits. Either in 2013 or 2014, or in both years, there were commercial deficits in Brazil, Colombia, Ecuador, Peru and other countries, while Argentina's commercial surplus has been much reduced.[24]

Social metabolism of India

Following the example of Japan over the 20 years until 2013 (if not beyond), economic growth has faltered in many rich countries since 2008 (less by design than due to the economic crisis), while in the

BRICs but also Peru, Indonesia, Colombia, Turkey and many other countries there has been sustained growth. Poverty in terms of income per capita has declined in all such countries, including India.

This growth is achieved at great environmental and social cost, so that it is neither 'green' nor 'inclusive'. Peasants are squeezed out of the land, tribal groups in India and elsewhere are being displaced because they happen to live at the commodity extraction frontiers. Biodiversity is being rapidly lost, and the concentration of carbon dioxide in the atmosphere is still increasing at 2 ppm per year.

This is the background to the study of India's material flows from 1961 to 2008 carried out by Singh *et al.* and published in *Ecological Economics* in 2012. Per capita, India consumes less fossil fuel, less building materials and less mineral ore than most other countries. To reach a physical dimension per capita similar to Latin America (which has half the population), the total material flows of India (whether locally extracted as at present, or to a relatively small extent imported as coal is from Australia) would have to multiply by almost a factor of four. One potential advantage for India could be to proceed directly to rural electrification through solar energy. Another small advantage is India's high density of population, which diminishes internal transport flows (although on the other hand extractive industries and infrastructures impact on densely populated areas).

The trends in total and per capita material domestic consumption in India (extraction plus imports minus exports) and in physical trade are summarized in Figure 9.3. Notice that in Figure 9.1 we gave rates of extraction for Latin America. For India we give rates of domestic consumption (extraction + imports – exports), which for India are very similar to rates of extraction because of the physical irrelevance (in tonnes) of external trade for the economy of India as a whole. We give totals (Figure 9.3) and per capita results (Figure 9.4).

Table 9.1 overleaf shows the domestic material consumption (domestic extraction + imports – exports) per capita from 1961 to 2008, excluding biomass, compared with growth of GDP and population.

In the 1960s, about three quarters of India's total material consumption consisted of biomass while construction materials were second in importance. In India, biomass is for human and domestic animal subsistence. The domestic animals provide milk and dung.

Figure 9.3 Material flows accounts of India 1961–2008, domestic consumption in gigatons per year (thousand million)

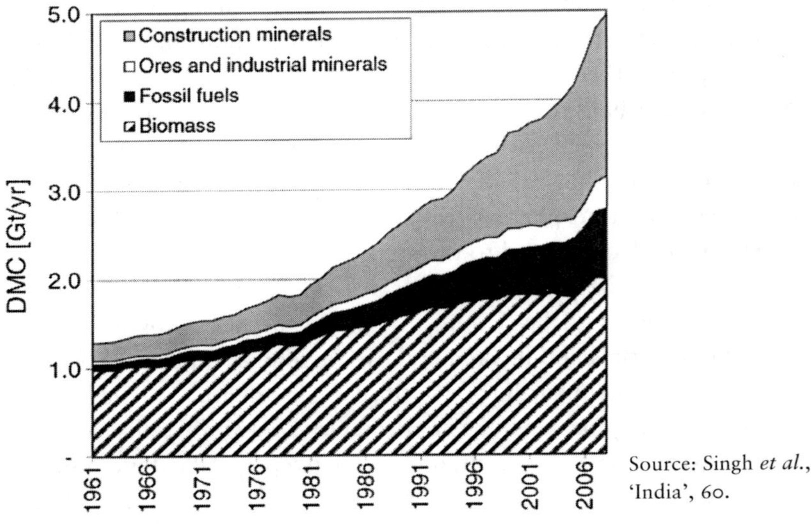

Source: Singh *et al.*, 'India', 60.

Figure 9.4 Domestic material consumption in India, tons per capita/year

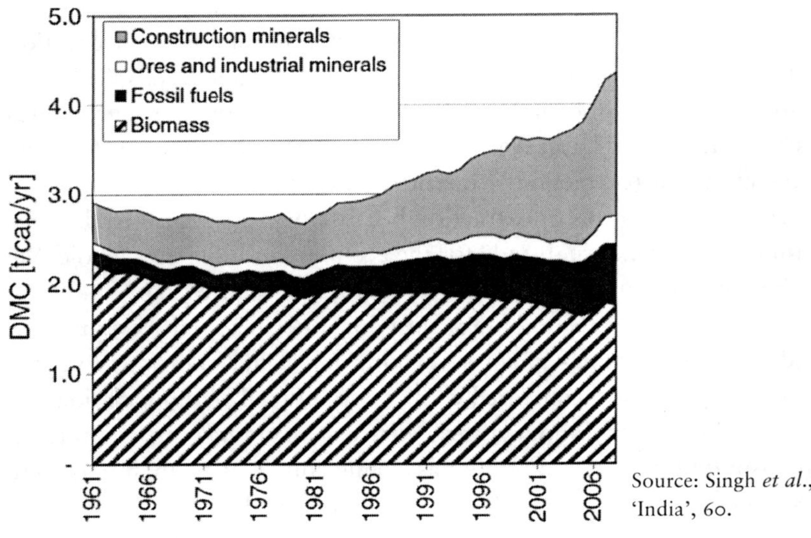

Source: Singh *et al.*, 'India', 60.

Table 9.1 Domestic material consumption (DMC t/cap/yr) of India for the three main groups of mineral and fossil materials and their average annual growth rates (%) in comparison to population and GDP

	1961	1980	2008	1961-80	1980-2008
GDP (billion USD at const. 2000)	66	156	812	3.5%	6.0%
Population (million)	444	687	1140	2.3%	1.8%
Fossil energy carriers (DMC t/cap/yr)	0.1	0.2	0.6	4.7%	6.0%
Ores and industrial minerals (DMC t/cap/yr)	0.1	0.1	0.3	3.4%	5.6%
Construction minerals (DMC t/cap/yr)	0.4	0.5	1.6	2.0%	6.2%

Source: Singh *et al.*, 'India', 60.

In South America a lot of the biomass is for meat consumption or for exports. Fossil fuels and industrial minerals and ores were insignificant in relation to the total flows. In the course of the almost 50 years under study, this changed in quantity and composition. The use of biomass only doubled. Fossil-fuel consumption multiplied by a factor of 12.2, industrial minerals and ores by a factor of 8.6, and construction materials by a factor of 9.1.

Until the 1980s the population grew at a slightly faster pace than material throughput. Throughout the 1960s and 1970s, material use remained at a low and slowly declining level of less than 3 t/cap/yr. Only in the early 1980s (ten years before Dr Manmohan Singh became finance minister in 1991 launching neoliberal reforms) did sustained growth in per capita material consumption set in, growing to 4.3 t/cap/yr and accelerating after 2004. Taking into account further growth from 2008 to 2013, India is at a level of 5 t/cap/yr. In comparison, per capita material consumption in EU countries is about 15 tonnes per person/year.

Notice, moreover, that in the EU imports are very significant, and they exceed exports in tonnes by a factor of 3 or 4. Conversely, in South America exports exceed imports (in tonnes) by a factor of 3 or 4 (Mexico has a different pattern because of maize import and its *maquila* industry). In contrast, India's external trade is more or less in balance in physical terms, and it is a small part of its physical economy.

However, some states in India show a considerable physical trade deficit, and these are states (Odisha, Jarkhand, also Goa because of iron ore exports) that have seen significant ecological distribution conflicts. These states are subject to an ecologically unequal exchange, signalling internal colonization. India as a whole has no physical trade deficit.

In Singh *et al.* we wrote that, in general, construction minerals are abundant, and scarcity and conflicts are usually only regional phenomena. But in fact almost all regions of India suffer from the phenomenon of 'sand mafias',[25] as we shall see in the next section.

Ecological distribution conflicts

Ecological distribution conflicts are struggles over the burdens of pollution or over the sacrifices made to extract resources, and they arise from inequalities of income and power.[26] The concept of ecological distribution conflicts is born in the intersection between the fields of ecological economics and political ecology that links the emergence of environmental conflicts in the global South with the growth and reconfiguration of the metabolism of societies in the global North (which includes parts of China). Political ecology focuses on the exercise of power in environmental conflicts; in other words, the question is, who has the power to impose decisions on resource extraction, river dams, land use, pollution levels and biodiversity loss? And, more importantly, who has the power to determine the procedures to impose such decisions, allowing or excluding some valuation languages and therefore bypassing complexity?[27] Actors engage in a struggle over reality construction, in the sense that they become signifying agents engaged in the production of alternative and contentious meanings,[28] e.g. livelihood, development or sacredness.

Ecological distribution conflicts (which, for simplicity, we also call 'environmental conflicts' or 'socio-environmental conflicts') emerge from the structural asymmetries in the burdens of pollution and in the access to natural resources that are grounded in unequal distributions of power and income, in social inequalities of ethnicity, caste, social class and gender.[29] Sometimes the local actors claim redistributions, leading to conflicts, which are often part of, or lead to larger gender, class, caste and ethnic struggles.[30] In this line, the concept of 'environmental justice' is important. It has gained growing acceptance all over the world in relation to extractive industries, water use and waste disposal conflicts.

Not all conflicts are born from immediate metabolic needs. Demand for certain commodities such as gold arises in part from the search for investment outlets that allow further speculation. Other metals such as copper can also be stored and used as guarantees for speculative loans. Speculators are suffering losses in the downturn of prices in 2014–15, caused by excessive world supply (and declining demand in China). The fact remains that energy carriers (coal, gas, oil, biomass) and construction and most metallic minerals are essential inputs for the industrial economy, and their use, in total, grows more or less in proportion to the growth of the economy.

Economic change generally occurs for the benefit of some groups and at the expense of other existing or future groups. Externalities can be positive (like the free environmental services provided by a forest) or negative. Negative externalities are not seen here as market failures but rather as (provisional) cost-shifting successes[31] that often give rise to complaints from environmental justice movements or from the 'environmentalism of the poor and the indigenous'. Optimistic views regarding ecological modernization and 'dematerialization' of the economy are confronted with the reality of increased inputs of energy and materials into the world economy, increasing production of waste and ecological distribution conflicts such as those we are mapping in the EJOLT project.

The environmentalism of the poor and the indigenous

Activists in many countries understand and use the concept of the 'environmentalism of the poor'. Thus, in India (which is its cradle), Sunita Narain wrote on the 'environmentalism of the poor' on 10 January 2011 in an article in *Business Standard* from which we quote:

> The year 2010 was a loud year for the environment. High profile projects – from Vedanta to Posco and Navi Mumbai airport and now Lavasa – hit the headlines for non-compliance with environmental regulations. While 2009 was the 25th anniversary

> of the Bhopal gas tragedy, it was only last year that we were all outraged by the disaster. The realisation of how every institution – the judiciary, Parliament and government – had miserably failed to provide justice to the victims shocked us deeply. [...]
>
> It would not be wrong to say that virtually all infrastructure and industrial projects – from mining to thermal and [hydro] and nuclear power to cement or steel – are under attack today from local communities who fear loss of livelihoods. These communities today are at the forefront of India's environmental movement. They are its warriors. But for them environment is not a matter of luxury – fixing the problems of growth, but of survival – fixing growth itself. They know that when the land is mined and trees are cut, their water source dries up or they lose grazing and agricultural fields. They know they are poor. But they are saying, loudly and as clearly as they can, what we call development will only make them poorer. This is what I have called the environmentalism of the poor ...

This kind of environmentalism is very different from 'the cult of wilderness'. The 'cult of wilderness' is only one of the varieties of environmentalism. From the late 1980s onwards, a different kind of environmentalism was identified as 'the environmentalism of the poor', focusing on the global South but closely related to the 'environmental justice' movement in the United States.[32]

The thesis of the 'environmentalism of the poor' applies to India and also to Latin America, where it has been used since 1991. It does not assert that as a rule poor people or even indigenous peoples feel, think and behave as environmentalists. Rather, the thesis is that in the many resource extraction and waste disposal conflicts, historically and today, the poor are often on the side of the preservation of nature against business firms and the state. This behaviour is consistent with their interests and with their values. The environmentalism of the poor builds on the premise that the fights for human rights and the environment are inseparable.

In the environmentalism of the poor, as in environmental justice movements in general, it is important to recognize the contribution women make in poor communities, both rural and urban.[33] Women more often collect water, gather wood, look for medicinal plants, tend to domestic animals, and grow crops, and therefore they have greater knowledge and awareness of their community's direct dependence on the natural environment. This does not imply that women have an empathy with nature denied to men for biological reasons. The argument is based on social roles. In an urban setting, it is women who often take leading positions in environmental justice conflicts (in contrast to labour union struggles) as regards complaints against waste dumping, or air or water pollution. Women are often the main actors of environmental movements.

The environmentalism of the poor relates to actions and concerns in situations where the environment is a source of livelihood. This is reinforced by other values, such as the defence of indigenous territorial rights (appealing to Convention 169 of ILO or adivasi rights in India) or the claim to the sacredness of particular elements of nature (a mountain, a forest, or even a tree). When livelihood is threatened, those affected will be motivated to act provided that there is a sufficient degree of democracy and they are not suffocated by fear as is often the case. Indeed, a clean and safe environment is a need for all humans rather than a luxury good.[34]

In such conflicts, a variety of 'valuation languages' are deployed. Some of them were perhaps more powerful in the past (livelihood, sacredness) than in this era of the generalized market system where even 'the fetishism of fictitious commodities' is in the ascendant in schemes for payment for environmental services. One wonders, for instance, how effective it still is in India to oppose the sacredness of a 'sacred grove' against a mining project or a dam. Notice in India the attempt at compensation of damages in resource extraction conflicts by ascertaining the so-called net present value (in money terms) of the foregone products and services from forests.[35] This is a peculiarity of Indian state administration. Other valuation languages apart from money compensation, such as human rights, indigenous territorial rights, environmental justice against 'environmental racism', and even the Rights of Nature as in article 71 of the 2008 Constitution of Ecuador, are perhaps gaining in strength across the world. There is much scope for historical and comparative work on the 'valuation languages' deployed in environmental conflicts.

The Environmental Justice Atlas

In the EJAtlas we have 1,500 conflict cases by June 2015. We classify the conflicts in two ways, according to the:

1) ***Stage of the commodity chains*** at which they occur ***and*** their ***geographical reach*** (Table 9.2). One could easily fill in Table 9.2 exclusively with Indian and Latin American examples. Sometimes local conflicts become 'glocal', i.e. well known also outside the territory in question, as with the Dongria Kondh vs Vedanta in Odisha[36] or in Latin America, the Chevron-Texaco case in Ecuador.

2) ***The main commodity in question***, as in the following list.
   Nuclear: uranium extraction; nuclear power plants; nuclear waste storage.
   i. **Ores and building materials**: mineral extraction; mineral processing; tailings.
   ii. **Waste management**: e-waste and other waste import zones; ship-breaking; waste privatization; waste pickers; incinerators; landfills; uncontrolled dump sites; industrial; municipal waste.
   iii. **Biomass**: land-grabbing; tree plantations; logging; non-timber products; deforestation; agro-toxics; GMOs; 'biofuels'; mangroves vs shrimps; biopiracy and bio-prospection; intensive food production (monoculture and livestock); fisheries.
   iv. **Fossil fuels and climate justice / energy**: oil and gas extraction; oil spill; gas flaring; coal extraction; climate change related conflicts (glaciers and small islands); REDD/CDM; windmills; gas fracking.
   v. **Transportation and infrastructure**: megaprojects, high speed trains.
   vi. **Water management and hydric justice**: dams, water transfers, aquifers, hydroways, desalination.
   vii. **Biodiversity**: invasive species, damage to nature, conservation conflicts.
   viii. **Industrial and utilities conflicts**: factory emissions, industrial pollution.

Table 9.2 A classification of socio-environmental conflicts according to the stage of the commodity chains at which they occur and their geographical reach

Stage of the commodity chains	Geographical scope		
	Local	**National and Regional**	**Global**
Extraction	Resource conflicts in tribal areas, such as bauxite mining in Odisha, coal or uranium mining in Jharkhand, oil extraction in the Amazon of Ecuador or Peru or the Niger Delta.	Mangrove uprooting. Tree plantations for wood or paper pulp. Collapses of fisheries.	Worldwide search for minerals and fossil fuels at the 'commodity' frontiers. Bio-piracy. Attempts at regulation of 'corporate accountability'.
Transport and trade	Complaints against urban motorways or heavy traffic in rural mining areas because of noise, pollution, landscape loss.	Inter-basin water transport. Oil/gas pipelines (e.g. Burma to Thailand). No TAV movement (Italy). TIPNIS road (Bolivia).	Oil spills at sea. 'Ecologically unequal exchange' because of large South to North material flows.
Waste disposal and pollution, post-consumption	Conflicts over incinerators (dioxins) or VOCs, NOx, ozone, particulate matter.	Acid rain from sulphur dioxide. Nuclear waste disposal (Yucca Mountain, Nevada, USA; Gastre in Patagonia-Argentina). Ship dismantling (Alang-Sosiya, Chittagong).	CO^2, CFC: causes of climate change/ozone layer destruction/ocean acidification. POPs even in remote pristine areas. Claims for a 'carbon debt', climate justice.

It is laborious but easy to trace in India and Latin America many hundreds of examples of these types of conflicts, listing the specific commodities in question, the social actors involved, tracing their geographical distribution patterns over time, accounting for the reasons for the occasional successful outcomes (stopping projects). Partisans of green growth should have to explain how the social and economic institutions they defend, and the technologies they propose, would be able to solve the thousands of ecological distribution conflicts around the world by means other than political repression, violence, or 'criminalization' of activists. For instance, would compensatory revenue redistribution (facilitated by economic growth) be able to solve such conflicts?

Do indigenous groups in Latin America and India take part disproportionately in environmental conflicts?

This is one issue that we can begin to answer from the results of the EJAtlas. The answer seems to be 'yes'.[37] This is of relevance in order to trace an intellectual and political connection between global environmental justice and the US environmental justice movement on the 1980s that insisted so much on the struggle against 'environmental racism'.

Some results are given in Table 9.3. The database form includes a space to list social actors mobilizing in conflicts. Several actors can be listed simultaneously, including 'indigenous or traditional communities' and 'ethnically/racially discriminated communities'.

Where there are indigenous or traditional communities and ethnically discriminated communities (there is a certain overlap of both categories), their participation in the set of conflicts is seemingly larger than their relative number in the population as a whole. Thus, in South America, these communities are present in more than half the conflicts. In Europe, the four cases reported are in Scandinavia – Sami people.

One question to ask is whether the disproportionate participation of indigenous peoples in environmental conflicts (when they are present in the country in question) is explained by their location at the commodity frontiers or by the fact that transnational companies or governments target them because of their presumed low capacity to resist against political pressure. To repeat, interesting comparisons can

Table 9.3 Environmental conflicts and indigenous groups/ traditional communities in India, South America and Europe

	Number of conflicts in EJOLT Atlas	Participation of ethnically/racially discriminated communities *or* indigenous groups *or* traditional communities	Only ethnically/ racially discriminated communities	Only indigenous groups *or* traditional communities
South America (selected countries)	494	264	87	250
India	184	97	16	95
Europe (selected countries)	117	4	4	0
Africa (selected countries)	116	69	8	67

Source: EJOLT Atlas, www.ejatlas.org (as of 20 November 2014), in India, in selected South American countries (Argentina, Brasil, Colombia, Peru, Ecuador, Chile), in selected European countries (Finland, France, Germany, Italy, Serbia, Spain, Sweden) and in selected African countries (Madagascar, Mozambique, Nigeria, South Africa).

be made by applying the category of 'environmental racism' developed by the US environmental justice movement.

'Success' in environmental conflicts

Other types of analysis can be done. In the inventory of 1,259 cases (as of November 2014), 215 are reported as 'successes' in environmental justice, which often means that the investment project that triggered the conflict has been stopped. Table 9.4 shows the number of cases in the broad categories of conflicts.

There are differences in the 'success' rate (varying between 12 and 25 per cent), which we cannot explain at present. With more cases, one could try to see whether such 'deviations' from the average rate of 'success' of 17 to 18 per cent significantly depend for some reason on the commodities in question.

Table 9.4 Number of conflict cases and rates of success per selected commodity category in EJOLT inventory (as of November 2014)

Category	Total cases	'Success' cases
Mineral ores, building materials	281	58
Fossil fuels/climate change	230	27
Biomass extraction	216	31
Water management	180	28
Industry and utilities	100	20
Infrastructures and built environment	75	15
Waste management	66	15
Nuclear energy	46	8
Biodiversity conservation	36	8
Tourist recreation	29	5

The average rate of 'success' itself might also increase or decrease a little as more cases are brought into the EJAtlas. Perhaps 'success' of environmental justice is more easily achieved in some countries than others. If we reach an inventory of 3,000 cases worldwide by the end of 2018, we would dare predict that between 450 and 600 will be considered 'successes'. The database forms (which anybody can read on the EJAtlas webpage) provide space to explain the reasons why a conflict is considered a success, a failure, or a 'not sure' case in environmental justice. Inspection of this information would also help advance a theory of the meaning of 'success' (or failure) in conflicts on environmental injustice.

Finally, is ethnicity a factor in the rate of success? In the total number of conflicts in the inventory of 1,259 (at November 2014), in 580 indigenous, traditional and/or ethnically discriminated communities taking part, this is in 46 per cent, with the differences between Europe and other continents mentioned in the previous section. Of the total number of 'successes', 215, only in 91 do we have indigenous, traditional and ethically discriminated communities, which is a little over 42 per cent. Therefore ethnicity/indigeneity/'traditionality' does not seem to be a significant factor in explaining success or failure.

When we take only the social group 'ethnically/racially discriminated communities', we have a total of 196 conflict cases (out of 1,259), of which 47 are considered as 'successes', that is 23 per cent, which is not significantly higher than the overall rate of 18 per cent. Again, the hypothesis would be that ethnicity is not a factor either in achieving success or in suffering failure.

In general terms, one could ask not only about the factors that explain 'success' (the nature of the commodities in question, the social groups mobilizing, the political culture of the states and, importantly, the degree of democracy ...) but whether such rate of 'success' in environmental conflicts is or is not a factor helping to move the economy in a less unsustainable, more ecological direction. Moreover, in the EJOLT inventory there are many cases classified as 'not sure' (414), some of which are or have been very close to 'success'. So, a rate of 'success' (when there is a conflict) of environmental justice of 1/5 or perhaps even 1/4 is a plausible and at the same time an encouraging estimate.

Conclusions

The fundamental clash between economy and the environment comes from two facts. First, population growth. In the twentieth century population grew four times. It now seems that 'peak population' might be reached at about nine billion by 2050. Second, the social metabolism of industrial economies. Energy and materials are increasingly obtained from the 'commodity frontiers'. The growth in the number of resource extraction conflicts and also waste disposal conflicts (of which the most noticeable one is that arising from the production of an excessive amount of carbon dioxide) is explained to some extent by the changes in the social metabolism.

Other chapters of this book have outlined a critique of green growth. In this chapter we demonstrated with empirical analysis that economic growth in Latin America and India has not been green, and it is unlikely to be so. There has not been absolute dematerialization, and not even relative dematerialization. A consequence of this is, in our view, the increasing environmental conflicts. Latin America is perhaps reaching a peak in material extraction at a very high level while India will probably see it multiply by two or three in the next decades. Now, advocates of green growth argue that absolute dematerialization will take place, despite economic growth. The burden of proof falls on the eco-modernizers to convincingly show how absolute dematerialization would be possible in the future, despite the recent historical trends of social metabolism that we have discussed.

The 'environmentalism of the poor', or also popular environmentalism, livelihood ecology, liberation ecology and the movement for environmental justice (local and global) may help to move society and economy in the direction of social justice and ecological sustainability.

PART III: EMERGING ALTERNATIVES?

CHAPTER 10

Beyond 'development' and 'growth': the search for alternatives in India towards a sustainable and equitable world

Ashish Kothari*

Introduction: crisis and response

This chapter is written within the broad context of the ecologically unsustainable and deeply inequitable pathways that humanity has followed across the earth, as also the inadequacy and shortsightedness of many 'reformist' approaches towards being ecologically sustainable and more inclusive or equitable, including 'green growth' or the 'green economy' that are currently being pushed as part of the post-2015 sustainable development agenda. It does not go into detail on the above, given the substantial amount of literature already existing and a number of other chapters in this volume dealing with these issues. The chapter takes as its starting point the consequent search for alternatives that can provide for human well-being, equity and justice within planetary and ecological limits.

A more specific context for this chapter is what is happening in India (or, more broadly, South Asia). Behind the glitter and swagger of the twenty-first-century urban pockets that India proudly showcases, lie vast stretches of poverty, hunger, malnutrition, exploitation,

---

* Parts of this article are adapted from or based on Kothari 2014a: 62–72. On this version, useful comments were received from Joan Martinez-Alier, Daniela Del Bene, Manu Verghese Mathai, Gareth Dale and Jose A. Puppim de Oliveira. The author is also grateful to Aseem Shrivastava, whose collaboration in developing the idea of Radical Ecological Democracy while writing the book *Churning the Earth: The Making of Global India* has been invaluable.

inequality and ecological ruin. In a recent book, a colleague and I have provided detailed facts and figures, and extensive analysis, to show that India is decidedly on the path of ecological unsustainability, continued and new forms of impoverishment, and increasing inequalities, even while 'development' has benefited some of the middle classes and created an even more enriched upper class.[1] Growth in the post-1991 era of globalization in India, even when at fairly high rates, has not substantially increased net employment in the formal sector. India continues to occupy among the lowest positions in most global surveys of human development and social welfare, including UNDP's Human Development Index, and various measures on the gender gap, malnutrition and undernutrition, and hunger. In such a 'business as usual' scenario, we predict increasing ecological collapse and socio-economic inequity, and serious regional and class conflicts.

This is not to say that the situation in India is irretrievably dismal. Indeed, there are a number of exceptional initiatives by the state and civil society relating to poverty, environment, employment and empowerment, which are elements of a more sustainable and equitable future. However, at present these are submerged and overwhelmed by the sheer bulldozer effect of current macroeconomic development policies and related political governance structures. Substantial exploration at practical and conceptual levels is needed to overcome the present course and pursue holistic human well-being in tune with ecological finitude. What would such a future look like, and how would we get there?

Stories of the future: towards a Radical Ecological Democracy

In 2013, history was created in many parts of India, albeit without fanfare. Twelve village assemblies of the Dongria Kondh adivasis (indigenous group) in the state of Odisha decided, several of them by consensus, not to allow a multinational mining company to take over their lands; they cited sacredness of the land and forest, and their own notions of well-being, as the main reasons. In Mendha-Lekha, a Gond adivasis village in the state of Maharashtra, all the farmers voluntarily donated their private agricultural lands to the community, under an old law promoting the 'commons' that has almost never been used in the country. This followed a successful move by the village to claim control over forests surrounding it, reversing two centuries of colonial, state-centred control, and to declare 'tribal self-rule'. These are two of very many examples across India encompassing adivasis and non-adivasis rural communities (hunter-gatherer, agricultural, pastoral, fisher, and artisanal) that have, over the last two to three decades, demonstrated strong attempts at sustainable and equitable ways of achieving well-being. Increasingly collectives in urban areas too are experimenting with alternatives of various kinds.

These initiatives are a complex mix: of creating further spaces within the existing system and fundamentally challenging it, of retaining or regaining the best of tradition while discarding its worst, of synergizing old and new knowledge. Most of them point to a different set of principles and values than the ones on which the currently dominant economic and political structures are based. All of them have weaknesses and issues that need resolution, but they all show the potential of a different future for India. They point to a paradigm or vision of the future, which can be called Radical Ecological Democracy (RED) or eco-swaraj: *a socio-cultural, political and economic arrangement in which all people and communities have the right and full opportunity to participate in decision-making, based on the twin fulcrums of ecological sustainability and human equity.*[2]

Here, ecological sustainability is the continuing integrity of the ecosystems and ecological functions on which all life depends, including the maintenance of biological diversity as the fulcrum of life; human equity is a mix of equality of opportunity, access to decision-making forums for all, equity in the distribution and enjoyment of the benefits of human endeavour, and cultural security. RED is comprised of a set of intersecting elements or spheres, covering the political, economic, ecological, socio-cultural, and ethical and spiritual aspects of life. Each of these has multiple facets, explored below with the help of practical initiatives taking place in various parts of India.

Importantly, such a paradigm has emerged more from the lived experiences of grassroots movements and initiatives (many of which are described below). This is not to deny the influence of key ideologues, activists and figures of Indian and global history, both on me and on many of these initiatives, including of Buddha, Gandhi, Marx, Ambedkar, Tagore, and tribal or other traditional revolutionaries and rebels. In my own mind RED is an eclectic mix of all these, plus strands of deep ecology and social ecology from Western thought and action.

An alternative politics: power to communities

Decentralized, embedded political governance is one of RED's crucial elements. This goes well beyond the 'representative' democracy that countries such as India have adopted, towards more direct, radical democracy.

Decision-making starts from the smallest, most local unit, and builds to expanding spatial units. In India, the Constitution mandates governance by *panchayats* at the village and village cluster level, and by *ward committees* at the urban ward level. However, these are representative bodies, subject to the same pitfalls (albeit at smaller levels) that plague representative democracy at higher levels, including elite captures. It is crucial to empower the *gram sabha* (village assembly) in rural areas, and the area *sabha* (smaller units within wards) in cities, or another equivalent body where it is practical for all the adults of the individual hamlet or village or urban neighbourhood to participate in decision-making. All critical decisions relating to local natural resources or environmental issues should be taken at this level, with special provision to facilitate the equal participation of women and other underprivileged sections.

Mendha-Lekha village, mentioned above, adopts the principle of 'our government in Mumbai and Delhi, but we are the government in our village'. All decisions are taken by consensus in the full village assembly, based on information generated by *abhyas gats* (study circles). A struggle against a big dam that was to displace Mendha-Lekha and dozens of other villages, in the 1980s, brought to the villagers the importance of self-mobilization.[3] Since then the village has conserved 1,800 hectares of surrounding forest, and recently gained full rights to use, manage and protect it under the Forest Rights Act 2006, reversing a couple of centuries of colonial and post-colonial top-down governance of forests.[4] It has moved towards fulfilment of all basic requirements of food, water, energy and local livelihoods, including through the sustainable harvesting of bamboo from the forest.

In the state of Nagaland, a state government initiative called 'communitization' has devolved aspects of decision-making regarding health, education and power (e.g. salaries and transfers of teachers) to village and town communities.[5] Cities such as Bengaluru and Pune are exploring participatory budgeting, with citizens able to submit their priorities for spending to influence the official budgets. While this has a number of pitfalls and shortcomings, such as local elite dominance, and the fact that citizens still cannot *determine* spending priorities, civil society groups see it as a step towards decentralizing and embedding political governance.[6] In the Udaipur district of Rajasthan state, several villages facilitated by civil society groups have carried out detailed resource mapping and planning, and have mobilized to ensure that government budgets earmarked for them are spent in line with community-set priorities.[7]

But the local and the small scale cannot by themselves create the change we need other than on some local issues. Many operations need to be coordinated and managed at much larger levels, such as the railways and communication services. Many problems (toxics and pollution, desertification, climate change) are at scales much larger than the individual settlement, emanating from and affecting entire landscapes (and seascapes), countries, regions, and indeed the earth. The need for environmental governance at the global level is widely recognized and pursued on a range of issues. In a RED scenario, such larger level governance structures need to emanate from the basic decentralized decision-making units. These are envisioned as clusters or federations of villages and towns with common ecological features, larger landscape level institutions, and others that in some way also relate to the existing administrative and political units of districts and states (more on this below). Governance across states, and across countries, of course presents special challenges; there are a number of lessons to be learnt from failed or only partially successful initiatives such as the Kyoto protocol or sub-national regional initiatives such as river basin planning authorities in India.

Landscape and trans-boundary planning and governance (also called 'bioregionalism', or 'ecoregionalism', among other names) are exciting new approaches being tried out in several countries and regions. These are as yet fledgling in India, but some are worth learning from. For a decade, the Arvari Sansad (Parliament) in Rajasthan brought 72 villages in the state together, to manage a 400 sq km river basin through inter-village coordination, making integrated plans and programmes for land, agriculture, water, wildlife and development.[8] Its functioning has weakened in recent times, but it provides an important example to learn from. In the state of Maharashtra, a federation of Water User Associations has been handed over the management of the Waghad Irrigation Project, the first time a government project has been completely devolved to local people.[9]

Though communities (rural and urban) will be the fulcrum of the alternative futures, the state has a critical supporting and enabling role to play. It needs to retain, or rather strengthen, its welfare role for the weak (human and nonhuman), assist communities in situations where local capacity is weak, rein in business elements or others who behave irresponsibly towards the environment or people. It will have to be held accountable to its role as guarantor of the various fundamental rights that each citizen is supposed to enjoy under the Constitution of India, including through policy measures such as the Right to Information Act 2005. Finally, it will retain a role in larger global relations between peoples and nations.

Over time, however, nation-state boundaries may become far less divisive and important if genuine globalization (more on this below) is promoted; eventually they may become irrelevant. The increasing networking of peoples across the world, through both traditional means and new digital communications, could be a precursor to such a process. Cultural and ecological identities will become more important, but these too defined not so much as isolationist categories but as enriching diversity within the essential unity of humankind, a diversity to be celebrated, and with the openness of learning from and supporting each other.

Across all levels of decision-making above the smallest direct democracy unit, ways to ensure accountability of representatives have to be built in. Lessons could be learnt from ancient Greek and Indian democracies, and from ongoing experiments in Latin America.[10] These include highly constrained 'delegated' responsibility where representatives do not attain power independent of the constituency that has elected or selected them, but are subject to clear mandates given by the constituency, the right to recall, having to report back, etc. This will of course be more challenging at larger scales of decision-making where delegates or representatives are far away from the local units.

An alternative economics based on localization

Radical or direct democracy cannot work in isolation from the democratization of economic life. The second key element of RED is an economic system that acknowledges and respects ecological limits, places control over the means of production in the hands of communities, and empowers producers and consumers to democratically manage the economy as it relates to them.

Congruent with decentralized governance is economic localization, reversing the trend towards economic globalization. One of the principles of responsible governance is subsidiarity, in which those living closest to the resource (the forest, the sea, the coast, the farm, the factory, the urban facility, etc.) should be empowered to manage it. This is because it is assumed that they would have the greatest stake, and often the best knowledge, to manage it. Of course this is not always the case, for two centuries of government-dominated policies have effectively crippled community institutional structures, customary rules, and other capacities. There is also the issue of non-resident local communities having significant dependence on the local resource, e.g. in the case of nomadic or mobile pastoral peoples. But with such complexities built in, a move towards open localization of essential production, consumption, and trade, and of health, education and other services, is eminently possible if civil society organizations and the government sensitively assist communities. To give some live examples:

Sustainable agriculture using a diversity of crops has been demonstrated by thousands of farmers (including the most marginal, caste-discriminated women farmers) where the community groups Timbaktu Collective and Deccan Development Society work in Andhra Pradesh and Telangana, by communities working with Green Foundation in Karnataka, by farmers of the Beej Bachao Andolan, and the Jaiv Panchayat network of Navdanya.[11] Sustainable pastoralism has been sustained or revived among nomadic or resident pastoral communities with whom the group Anthra works.[12] Community conservation of forests, wetlands, grasslands, and coastal/marine areas, and also wildlife populations and species, is spread over several thousand sites in Odisha, Maharashtra, Uttarakhand, Nagaland, and other states.[13] Water self-sufficiency in arid, drought-prone areas has been demonstrated by hundreds of villages, through decentralized harvesting and strict self-regulation of use, such as in Alwar district of Rajasthan by Tarun Bharat Sangh, and in Kachchh by Sahjeevan and other groups.[14] In Bhuj town (Kachchh, Gujarat), groups such as Hunnarshala, Sahjeevan, Kutch Mahila Vikas Sangathan, and ACT, have teamed up to mobilize slum dwellers, women's groups, and other citizens into reviving watersheds and creating a decentralized water storage and management system, manage solid wastes, generate livelihood for poor women, create adequate sanitation, and provide dignified housing for all.[15] Here and in Bengaluru, Pune and other cities, increasingly vocal citizens are invoking the 74th Constitutional Amendment to urge for decentralized, local development planning and resource allocation through programmes such as participatory budgeting.[16]

Again, just as localized power is not adequate to deal with political relations at larger scales, localized economies cannot survive in isolation, especially in a world so intricately connected through economic relations. Parallel to political institutions at landscape and larger scales, there is a need to conceive of economics at scales different from the currently dominant structure. This includes trade and exchange conducted on the principles of democracy and fairness. Groups of villages, or villages and towns, could form units to further such economic democracy. For instance, in Tamil Nadu state, the dalit panchayat head of Kuthambakkam village, Ramaswamy Elango, envisages organizing a cluster of between 7–8 and 15–16 villages to form a 'free trade zone' or 'regional network economy', in which they will trade goods and services with each other (on mutually beneficial terms) to reduce dependence on the outside market and government. This way, the money stays back in the area for re-investment in local development, and relations among villages get stronger.[17] In the Nilgiris of Tamil Nadu, the initiative Just Change has brought together producers, consumers and investors into a single cooperative, enhancing the localization of exchanges that are benefiting several hundred families.[18]

Communities across larger landscapes could get together and prepare land/water use plans. Such plans, for each bioregion, could be combined into state and national plans, permanently putting the country's ecologically and socially most fragile or important lands into some form of conservation status (fully participatory and mindful of local rights and tenure). Such a plan would also enjoin towns and cities to provide as much of their resources from within their boundaries as possible, through water harvesting, rooftop and vacant plot farming, decentralized energy generation, and so on; and to build mutually beneficial rather than parasitic relations with rural areas from where they will still need to take resources. Such actions will spread where rural communities have a greater say in deciding what happens to their resources, and city-dwellers become more aware of the impacts of their lifestyles.

Such approaches provide massive opportunities for livelihood generation. There needs to be a renewed emphasis on labour-intensive industries and infrastructure, including handlooms and handicrafts, local energy projects, local access roads and communication lines, and others that people can be in control of, building on their own traditional knowledge or with easily acquired new skills. Jharkhand's state-created initiative, Jharcraft, has in less than a decade, enhanced the livelihoods of over 300,000 families with relatively simple inputs to empower the producers of silk cloth, cotton handlooms, metalcraft, tribal art, leatherwork, bamboo and cane furniture, and so on.[19] Another state government initiative, Kudumbashree in Kerala, has provided or enhanced livelihoods for 400,000 women in various local production or service units, though like many such successful large enterprises there are tensions created by political parties vying for control and unequal empowerment.[20] The social enterprise SELCO has enhanced livelihood and social conditions of over 150,000 families through decentralized solar power, provided by ensuring financial linkages that help the families ultimately pay for it themselves.[21]

Given the extent of land and water degradation in India, their regeneration, and consequent increase in productivity, could provide a huge source of employment, and create permanent assets for sustainable livelihoods. The Mahatma Gandhi National Rural Employment Guarantee Act (MGNREGA), one of the government's flagship programmes, as also other schemes such as the Jawaharlal Nehru National Urban Renewal Mission (JNNURM), could be further oriented towards such environment–employment combinations.[22]

RED also entails the democratization of the economic relations of production and consumption. This means decentralized production, which is in the control of the producer, linked to predominantly local consumption that is in the control of the consumer. India already has several dozen producer companies and cooperatives, of farmers, craftspersons, fishers, pastoralists and others; most of them run on democratic lines of decision-making and revenue-sharing. Apart from the Just Change initiative mentioned above, there are many others. This includes the Nowgong Agriculture Producer Company Ltd (NAPCL) in Madhya Pradesh, the Aharam Traditional Crop Producer Company (ATCPC) in Tamil Nadu, and the Dharani Farming and Marketing Cooperative Ltd in Andhra Pradesh, all examples of farmer-run companies encompassing several settlements, that enable producers to directly reach their markets; Qasab–Kutch Craftswomen's Producer Co. Ltd in Kachchh does the same for women working on embroidery, appliqué and patchwork.[23]

At several places in India where villages have been revitalized through locally appropriate development initiatives, rural–urban migration has slowed down and even got reversed. On a visit to Jharkhand state, I met families whose sons had come back from urban jobs to work in the village after Jharcraft (mentioned above) had enabled more secure, enhanced livelihoods. The Kudumbashree programme (also mentioned above) has reduced outmigration. Similar results are seen in villages such as Ralegan Siddhi and Hivare Bazaar in the state of Maharashtra, many in Dewas district of Madhya Pradesh where Samaj Pragati Sahayog is active, the village Kuthambakkam in Tamil Nadu, and others.

A close corollary to the discussion of economic localization is the nature of money. It may remain an important medium of exchange, but it needs to be much more locally controlled and managed rather than anonymously by international financial institutions and markets. Just Change, mentioned above, is making a beginning in this direction.

Considerable local trade could revert to locally designed currencies or barter, and prices of products and services even when expressed in money terms could be decided between givers and receivers rather than by an impersonal, non-controllable distant 'market'. A huge diversity of local currencies and non-monetary ways of trading and providing/obtaining services are already being used around the world.[24] Simultaneously, a host of localized, community-based banking and financing systems have also cropped up over the last couple of decades; these could begin to challenge the mega-concentrations that the big banks and financial institutions represent. None of this is going to be easy. The pervasive monetization of the economy even in so-called 'remote' parts of India is a massive challenge to such alternatives. But the continuation of barter-like exchanges in many parts of the country, a memory of the possibilities of this even where actually lost, and examples from other parts of the world provide the grounds for an increase in such alternative forms of exchange.

Reviving public control of the monetary and financial system, and reorienting financial measures such as taxation, subsidies and other fiscal incentives/disincentives to support ecological sustainability and related human security and equity goals are critical. A draft National Biodiversity Strategy and Action Plan produced in 2004 laid these out in detail, but they were never taken up as the Plan was rejected by the government as being too radical.[25] However, elements of this have come into a few recent Five-Year Plans at centre or state level, such as incentives for renewable energy, schemes to support organic farming, and tax breaks to urban neighbourhoods installing water harvesting and energy-saving technologies.

Equity and diversity: towards a just society

For localization to succeed, it is crucial to deal with the socio-economic exploitation and inequities embedded deep in the daily lives of Indians, arising both from tradition and from modernity, including in relations of caste, class, gender, ethnicity and others. Such inequities can indeed be tackled, as witnessed in the case of dalit women gaining dignity and pride through the activities of Deccan Development Society in Andhra, dalits and 'higher' castes interacting with much greater equality in the Kuthambakkam village of Tamil Nadu where mixed housing too has been promoted, and adivasis gaining recognition and equal status through 'self-rule' and other movements in central India. Initiatives like that of Maati Sangathan in Uttarakhand have mobilized and empowered women to resist domestic violence, gain independent livelihoods, and challenge male-dominated political processes. The group URMUL in Rajasthan has succeeded in enabling the girl child to access education and other services earlier denied to them by a highly patriarchal society.[26] Associations of waste pickers and hawkers such as the KKPKP in Pune and Hasirudala in Bengaluru and the National Hawkers Federation have provided substantial dignity to people otherwise socially shunned by the rest of society, by enhancing incomes, building relations with middle-class households, and showing that they are an essential part of the city.[27] Many alternative educational institutions are explicitly oriented towards creating the conditions of greater equality and equity. Several progressive policies and laws favouring the disprivileged (such as reserving positions in educational institutions and government jobs for women, 'lower' castes, and adivasis) have been important (even if inconsistent) tools for empowerment.

Being mindful of exploitative and iniquitous structures is important to avoid falling into another trap: that of revivalism, or promoting the 'golden past' as an ideal for the future. Some religious or faith groups, and even some environmental groups, are wont to project such a past, sandpapering the warts and blemishes that have been part of India's history. These also tend to be intolerant to other faiths and religions; the recent alliance between environmentalists and right-wing Hindu chauvinists around the campaign against the Tehri Dam in Uttarakhand, or the attempt to clean up the temple town of Vrindavan are examples of precisely what needs to be avoided.[28] This is especially crucial since a right-wing party, BJP, took power in Delhi in the 2014 elections.

Finally, a just society needs also to nurture and promote diversity: of cultures and languages, ideas, lifestyles, and so on. India is home to enormous socio-cultural diversity (including nearly 800 distinct languages, according to a recent Peoples' Linguistic Survey led by Prof. Ganesh Devy),[29] with close links to its biodiversity. Development and modernity have wiped out substantial parts of this diversity, but a number of initiatives at alternative living are successfully resisting this. The women of Deccan Development Society, for instance, regularly celebrate festivals and occasions related to all religions (including highlighting the links between cultural and biological diversity), and ensure that the students of their school Pachasaale are also imbibing respect for such diversity.

Knowledge democracy and ethics

The generation, transmission and use of knowledge and of ethical perspectives are crucial pillars of any society. RED envisages the dissolution of several boundaries that currently dominant forms of education, learning and research have created: between the 'physical', 'natural', and 'social' sciences, between these sciences and the 'arts', between 'traditional' and 'modern' knowledge, and so on. Ecological and human systems are not constituted by such neat boxes; landscapes are not amenable to easy boundaries between the 'wild' and the 'domesticated', the 'natural' and the 'human' (especially considering that humans are part of nature). The more we can learn and teach and transmit knowledge and conduct research in holistic ways, giving respect not only to specialists but also to generalists, the more we can understand nature and our own place in it.

A number of alternative education, learning and research initiatives attempt to do this: schools like *pachasaale* of the Deccan Development Society in Andhra Pradesh, the *jeevan shalas* ('life schools') of the Narmada Bachao Andolan, struggling to save the Narmada valley and its inhabitants from a series of mega-dams, and Adharshila Learning Centre in Madhya Pradesh; colleges like the Adivasi Academy at Tejgadh, Gujarat; open learning institutions like the Bija Vidyapeeth in Dehradun in Uttarakhand, Bhoomi College in Bengaluru, SECMOL in Ladakh, and Swaraj University in Udaipur.[30]

Many of the initiatives on alternative living also attempt to synergize various knowledge systems, emanating from local communities, formal scientific institutions, and others. Sustainable food production, water harvesting, appropriate shelter, and so on, are successfully achieved with such knowledge mixes. Several groups (e.g. those that are part of the Jan Swasthya Abhiyan) are working on public health systems that empower communities to deal with most of their health issues, through combining traditional and modern systems, and through strengthening the links between safe food and water, nutrition, preventive health measures, and curative care.

Finally, and equally important, RED would also promote, and in turn be strengthened by, a freeing of the personal and community spirit from the bounds of materialism and bigoted religiosity. Quests for improving oneself through spiritual means would be reinforced by the spirit of living and working in communities, and would in turn reinforce the community. These need to tread a careful line between those who believe that dedicating one's life to changing oneself is adequate (which can tend towards detachment from society), and others who feel that one's entire life needs to be dedicated to the collective (which can stifle personal space and creativity).

Meaningful globalization

RED is not to be construed as an argument against globalization per se. Throughout human history the flow of ideas, persons, services and materials among regions of the world have often enriched human societies. With its focus on localized economies, cultural diversity and ethical lifestyles, and the elimination of the homogenizing, road-rolling effect of global finance and development hegemonies, RED would actually make the flow of ideas and innovations at global levels much more meaningful, leading to enrichment of all cultures rather than of a few at the cost of most. To paraphrase Gandhi, globalization of this kind would enable the winds of all cultures to blow freely across peoples and regions, but not allow any one to sweep another into oblivion.

A most urgent need of such global exchange is to share the various ideas and visions of alternatives that are being discussed or practised across the world. India's adivasis and other local communities may find much that resonates with their own resistance modes and alternative worldviews, in the various versions of *sumak kawsay* or *buen vivir* ('good living') articulated by indigenous peoples of South America; put together, these could be a powerful antidote to the materialist growth oriented mindset of currently dominant system. The rich in India could learn from some of the *décroissance* or 'degrowth' processes or 'voluntary simplicity' initiatives in Europe and the US.

The state may be able to learn from the way Bhutan is attempting to employ the Gross National Happiness approach, or the kind of constitutional, legal and planning provisions articulated (though not necessarily well implemented) in the last few years in Ecuador, Venezuela and Bolivia, or the prominence given to sustainable farming and participatory science and technology in Cuba.[31]

More practically, India needs to build much better relations with neighbouring countries, based on our common ecological, cultural and historical contexts. Transboundary landscape and seascape management would be an example, including 'peace zones' oriented towards conservation where there are currently intense conflicts (e.g. the Siachen glacier between India and Pakistan). More globally, strengthening various treaties on peace, rights and the environment is a key agenda; these could dovetail into the new post-2015 Sustainable Development Goals framework, *if* it is based on sustainability and equity as core themes running across all goals.[32]

Principles and values

It is important to deduce the principles and values that emerge from ongoing initiatives in alternatives, which would form the bedrock for the RED framework. The following is a preliminary list. Clearly, they are different if not outrightly opposed to the principles displayed in today's capitalist or state-dominated economic and political systems (including their 'green economy' and 'green growth' narratives, which may incorporate some of these, but, without effectively building in *all* of them, remain trapped within the status quo):[33]

- The functional *integrity and resilience of the ecological processes and biological diversity* underlying all life on earth, respecting which entails a realization of the ecological limits of human activity, and enshrining the *right of nature* and all species to survive and thrive in the conditions in which they have evolved.
- *Equitable access* of all people, in current and future generations, to the conditions needed for human well-being (socio-cultural, economic, political, ecological, and in particular food, water, shelter, clothing, energy, healthy living and socio-cultural sustenance);

equity between humans and other elements of nature; and social, economic and environmental justice for all.

- The *right of each person and community to participate* meaningfully in crucial decisions affecting her/his/its life, and the enabling conditions for such participation, as part of a radical, participatory democracy.
- Linked to the above, governance based on *subsidiarity and ecoregionalism*, with local rural and urban communities (small enough for all members to take part in face-to-face decision-making) as the fundamental unit of governance, linked with each other at bioregional, ecoregional and cultural levels into landscape/seascape institutions that are answerable to these basic units.
- The *responsibility* of each citizen and community to ensure meaningful decision-making that is based on the twin principles of ecological integrity and socio-economic equity.
- Respect for the *diversity* of environments and ecologies, species and genes, cultures, ways of living, knowledge systems, values, economies and livelihoods, and polities, in so far as they are in consonance with the principles of sustainability and equity.
- *Collective and cooperative thinking and working* founded on the socio-cultural, economic, and ecological commons, respecting both common custodianship and individual freedoms and innovations within such collectivities.
- The ability of communities and humanity, as a whole, to respond, adapt and sustain the *resilience* needed to maintain ecological sustainability and equity in the face of external and internal forces of change.
- The inextricable *interconnectedness* among various aspects of human civilization, and therefore among any set of 'development' or 'well-being' goals: environmental, economic, social, cultural and political.
- Individual and collective worldviews of *simplicity* and *enoughness*, with *satisfaction* and *happiness* derived from the quality of relationships starting with the most proximate ones within the family, among neighbours, friends, colleagues, the wider community and ultimately the rest of nature and humanity, and from the pursuit of learning and spiritual wisdom, rather than from ever-increasing material accumulations.

It is important to note that these principles and values need to go together, in an integrated manner, else there is the risk of falling back on a piecemeal and failed approach to sustainability and equity – such as the one being attempted by the green growth discourse. In particular, the first three of the above principles are often articulated as part of neoliberal democracies, but their true implementation depends on incorporating the remaining principles. It is simply not possible for capitalist or state-dominated regimes to pursue the full set of these principles without contradicting their own fundamental characteristics.

This list of principles will undoubtedly be added to on the evolutionary path that RED takes, for any such pathway must be a continuous dialogue among human beings, and between humanity and the rest of nature. Nor is RED *the* solution or blueprint, but a framework deduced from a great variety of initiatives pursuing alternatives reflective of the diversity of human and other life.

Challenges and opportunities for the transformation

For its wider implementation, RED calls for massive mindset, structural and behavioural shifts. It faces serious challenges including inadequate understanding of the impacts of human activities on the environment, and of the workings of nature, continuing tension between various knowledge systems hampering synergistic innovation, a political and bureaucratic leadership that for the most part lacks ecological literacy, unaccountable state and corporate power, and corruption of various kinds, continued militarization of the subcontinent and the vested interests that the military represents, and a feeling of 'helplessness' or apathy among the general public.

But in India as in many other parts of the world, there are many signs that a transformation is possible over the next few decades. These include a marked increase in practical initiatives that attempt to be ecologically sustainable (e.g. conversion from conventional to organic farming), equitable and just (e.g. in reclaiming community rights to resources, and women's access to decision-making) ways of meeting needs and aspirations. They include also strong resistance by communities and civil society against the imposition of destructive 'development' projects and processes, and the commercialization of life and knowledge, such that at any given moment dozens of dams, mines, highways, industries, and attempts to steal biodiversity are unable to move ahead or are abandoned. Then there are the attempts at advocacy resulting in progressive policies that expand democratic and sustainability spaces, useful in providing platforms for more fundamental transformation (with possibly the best example being the Right to Information Act 2005, a landmark legislation that grants citizens the right to access information from and relating to most government and government-aided agencies).

Aiding the above are technological innovations that make human life not only less dreary but also more ecologically sensitive, in industrial and agricultural production, energy, housing and construction, transportation, household equipment, and others, often building on traditional technologies. Also supportive are financial incentives for ecologically more sensitive practices, such as schemes that over a dozen states in India have for promoting organic farming; and awareness and concern regarding ecological and social equity issues, as such issues get integrated into educational, media and other forums.[34]

Who will be the primary agents of transformation?

Peoples' movements and civil society organizations, mostly in the non-party political sector (including progressive worker unions in the formal and informal sector), lead several of the initiatives mentioned above. Such movements and organizations are likely to continue being the main change-makers into the near future, especially those among them that are part of, or are facilitating, the empowerment of rural and urban communities. At times sections and individuals within government, political parties and academic institutions have taken the lead, or helped communities and civil society organizations, and it is important to continue to push for more radical changes within such institutions.

Over time several political parties will feel pressure from their constituencies, as power becomes decentralized, to reorient their focus to issues of sustainability and equity. The more progressive sections within them will grasp the opportunities to push from within. So will business, facing pressure from consumers, but I don't foresee the private sector in its current dominant form remaining, since, in a RED scenario, organizations with profits as their major motive will not have a place; they will be replaced by producer companies (i.e. farmers, artisans, industrial workers, and so on, who organize and share the means of production and distribution), the public sector (managed by the state but under full democratic control), and the emerging category of 'social enterprise' (when it is genuinely public-oriented). International agencies, themselves pressurized from increasingly vocal and active communities in relevant countries and regions, too will play a role, with environment and human rights treaties gaining ground, and multilateral/bilateral aid agencies being reformed towards the new values.

How can the state itself be transformed to play its role as guarantor of rights, facilitator of communities, and regulator of industry, in so far as such a role may be needed in the interim pathways towards a RED future? There are no easy answers here. The experience of the movement for public access to information in India suggests that, under public influence or sometimes on its own accord through enlightened officials and politicians, the state can bring in progressive policies (in this case, the Right to Information Act) that greatly expand democratic and welfare spaces. And perhaps some lessons will be learnt from the ongoing experiments in decentralized governance in Latin American countries such as Venezuela. But these are all ultimately limited by the current nature of the state, as seen for instance in the resistance to allow the RTI Act to be used to expose the full extent of crony capitalism in India, or for instance in the subversion of decentralized governance when it comes to extractive industry in Latin America.[35] Each country or region will have to find its pathways of a more accountable state. This is more likely to happen as mobilization at grassroots level grows in number and quality of its engagement. Peoples' movements will also have to recognize the fine line between policy-based expansion of democratic spaces that aid fundamental transformation, and those, like green growth, that the state uses to soften or even co-opt peoples' movements.

One significant factor in the transformation, globally, could be the growing knowledge that we are part of one earth. For perhaps the first time in history, not in small part due to the climate crisis, a truly global consciousness is emerging. As more and more peoples' forums for regional and global interaction increase (2014 alone has at least half a dozen global forums on well-being and alternatives to development, and will see significant civil society mobilization around the post-2015 goals), this consciousness will be a basis for enlightened action. The 'sandwich' effect of grassroots mobilization and global consciousness and action is likely to be crucial in changing the way governments (stuck in between) behave. Such change will of course not happen without encountering resistance and backlash from the powers-that-be, to withstand and resist which it is crucial to strengthen networking and solidarity across movements at all levels.

A recent move to bring together practitioners and thinkers of alternatives in India is the Vikalp Sangam ('Alternatives Confluence'), which combines documentation and outreach, gatherings and other processes at regional and national levels.[36]

Finally, the transformation of the self, deepening self-enquiry and advancing spiritual growth is a crucial component of RED.[37] Many individual attributes would have to be amplified in all learning and educational pursuits. The ability to see oneself as a human being with inalienable human dignity, immense capability, intrinsic rights and responsibilities towards other human beings who are equal in dignity, and towards nature more broadly, is critical. Similarly the opportunity to connect to nature outside while understanding that each of us is part of nature and the capacity to engage in the qualitative pursuit of happiness (social relations, broadening and deepening one's knowledge, being with nature) rather than mindlessly going after material accumulation needs greater appreciation. These have to go hand in hand with social transformation. Engaging in social movements helps in individual change, e.g. by instilling an acute awareness of the 'other' and a sense of responsibility towards such others. In turn, personal self-reflection and spiritual or ethical growth help more meaningul engagement with social causes as they enhance understanding and empathy with others and provide people with the confidence to work in collectivities.

Conclusion: India and the rest of the world

If well-being is about having secure ways of meeting basic needs, being healthy, having access to opportunities for learning, being employed in satisfactory and meaningful tasks, having good social relations, and leading culturally and spiritually fulfilling lives, there is no reason this has to be achieved through ecological devastation, and no reason why only some humans get to enjoy it. Human well-being can be achieved without endangering the earth and ourselves, and without leaving behind half or more of humanity.

No country or people can undertake such a massive transformation on its own. But the peoples of the Indian subcontinent are perhaps strongly placed to take a lead on many aspects of it, for a variety of reasons: its continued ecological and cultural diversity (substantial parts of which still remain), thousands of years of history (including ancient democratic practices), adaptation, and resilience in the face of multiple crises, the continued existence of myriad lifestyles and worldviews including of ecosystem people who still tread the most lightly on earth, the powerful legacy of Buddha, Mahavir, Gandhi, Tagore, Ambedkar, Aurobindo and other progressive thinkers including many in the modern era following these giants or learning from outside scholars and revolutionaries like Marx, the equally important legacy of rebels and activists and poets from among adivasis, dalits, and other subordinated sections of Indian society, the solid base of civil society activism and relatively free media, the many peoples' movements of resistance and reconstruction, an increasingly vocal home-grown version of feminism, and the equally numerous opportunities for spiritual transformations of the self.

Yet again, though, India will succeed in the transition to a sustainable and equitable world only if it also engages with other peoples. As mentioned above, a number of indigenous and civil society movements are coming up around the world, with alternative frameworks and practices that we can learn from and contribute to. Through its history Indian peoples have exchanged ideas and worldviews and materials with other peoples of the world; it has challenged, taught and learnt from other peoples; it will need to do all this and more, at even more intense levels, if humanity is to transcend its greatest crisis and emerge as a wise, gentle custodian of the earth.

CHAPTER 11

Reconsidering growth in the greenhouse: the Sustainable Energy Utility (SEU) as a practical strategy for the twenty-first century

Job Taminiau and John Byrne

Introduction

Satellite imagery of our planet by nightfall depicts human triumph and progress as extensive, and sophisticated networks of artificial lighting are visible from space, illuminating modern development – a phenomenon which was invisible only 100 years ago. Implemented at such a scale and intensity that naturally starlit skies have been placed outside common experience for many, the widespread use of electricity illustrates human dominance over nature, the power of technology and capital, and the astonishing expansion of modernity. Globalization of the Modern Model has delivered significant benefits as, for instance, modern energy development has provided millions of people with critical services such as sanitation and healthcare, clean water, reliable and efficient lighting, heating and cooling, cooking, mechanical power, transport and telecommunications. The success of modernization is so highly regarded that national governments have promised the spread of the Modern Model as a political objective. Indeed, the Millennium Development Goals (MDGs) can only be delivered through the development of energy.[1]

However, the powerful imagery of the 'World by Night' produced by the National Aeronautics and Space Administration (NASA) reveals, at the same time, a developmental and social dilemma of modern success. The visualization depicts both those with access to lighting options and its associated services and also the privileged character of modern development, despite the invention of the light bulb over a century ago. In fact, two billion human beings, almost one-third of the planet's population, cannot afford or reliably access electrical energy services.[2] This persistent problem of energy poverty traps billions of people who cannot participate in a wide range of social and economic activities. The trap is especially harmful for those who find themselves excluded from even the basic benefits of potable water, education (for example, lighted classrooms) and healthcare (e.g. refrigerated medicine cabinets). Closing the chasm between the energy rich and the bottom billion represents a formidable challenge for the Modern Model.

This social dilemma is compounded by an ecological dilemma that has been the companion of industrial development since the start of the Industrial Revolution and which prevents business-as-usual development patterns as human society moves through in the twenty-first century. The 'World by Night' imagery discloses one example of the ecological significance of modern development as light pollution's victory over the night's sky is emblematic of humanity's capability to alter global environments and encroach upon natural frontiers. The concept of the 'Anthropocene' offers the realization that human activity now rivals geological processes and energy flows in shaping the planet's natural history.[3] The exponentially increasing natural resource use and activity levels by humanity that characterize the Anthropocene is expected to produce significant ecological consequences as its effluences strain and overshoot 'planetary boundaries'.[4] As such, the aspiration of the world's energy poor to be fairly treated and join the world's energy rich on the pathway to greater prosperity challenges ecosystem health so long as the wealthy refuse to cut back on natural resource consumption. As Herman Daly pointed out long ago, 'sustainable growth' is an oxymoron which pushes the poor into a perennial politics of blame for seeking development while elites enjoy luxury rationalized by an ideology of 'angelized GDP'.[5] This confrontation highlights in-built injustice in the modernized ecosystem and further underscores the need to change the operating principles of societal development if human civilization is to be consistent with long-term ecological viability.

The green growth rescue?

A recently heralded strategy to alleviate these dilemmas of the Modern Model is the reconstruction of the global economy on principles of 'green growth'. This concept, originally limited to notions of 'eco-industry' growth, is now being applied to signal an economy-wide transformation process. The strategy continues the modern premise that economic expansion is capable of erasing inequality but modifies the ecological footprint of development by an appeal to smarter technology and resource management: 'green growth is about making growth processes resource-efficient, cleaner and more resilient without necessarily slowing them.'[6] As long as social and political architectures continue to encourage and prioritize the 'green' principles of economic growth, the strategy promises continuous enhancements of the living conditions of both poverty stricken and wealthy communities alike. The shift to a green energy system fuelled by renewable energy as an infinite (or, at least, long-lasting) supply to energize continued growth is a critical technological and management component in the green growth strategy in order to circumvent negative climate change consequences. As such, there are two shared premises of the several green growth narratives now in use: 1) confidence in green energy architectures to deliver endless economic expansion; and 2) belief in the curative properties of green growth to persistent problems of poverty and inequality.

The green growth pathway has found widespread support and acclaim. For instance, in a 2009 Declaration on Green Growth, the Organisation for Economic Co-operation and Development (OECD) affirmed its commitment to green growth 'as part of our response to the current crisis and beyond, acknowledging that "green" and "growth" can go hand-in-hand'.[7] South Korea's National Strategy for Green Growth similarly offers a notable example of the strategy with the commitment to build the next phase of development on green principles to propel this 'Asian miracle'.[8]

The analytical benefit provided by this optimistic strategy is the alliance between short-term economic benefits and election-cycle drive political agendas with long-term ecological progress and viability. As a development paradigm, the green growth strategy promises the management of ecological harm within reasonable boundaries while continuously expanding the services and benefits offered by the Modern Model to ever more people. In effect, and similar to classic re-dimensioning efforts of economic thought, green growth seeks to account for environmental degradation within economic growth frameworks.

But, can successful implementation of green growth principles resolve conflicts between economic growth and environmental sustainability? And can poverty and inequality be systematically addressed by 'doubling down' on the promise of growth? Additionally, proponents have not explained why the astonishing economic growth of the twentieth century has left 2 billion people with little or no access to technologies invented over one hundred years ago. Why is it plausible to believe that green technologies have curative properties to treat poverty and inequality which their industrial forebears did not? Improvements in energy and carbon productivity – where higher levels of economic activity are produced against lower environmental pollution or energy use in a relative sense – are cited in support of green growth, compelling some to argue for the 'bottomless well' of human ingenuity and innovation.[9] Another line of support brought forward is the rising penetration of renewable energy in total primary energy supply. Indeed, year-on-year growth of green energy technology options such as wind and solar has been impressive: annual capacity growth rates have continually surpassed 40 per cent for photovoltaic (PV) energy; and compound US annual growth rates for solar PV over the last ten years is an impressive 65 per cent.[10]

Evaluating the 'greenshift' as a means to alleviate energy poverty

A 'greenshift' of the modern energy regime is proposed as the way to cleanse growth aspirations of their negative ecological consequences. The challenge is formidable: the Energy Information Administration (EIA) projects that world energy use will amount to 820 quadrillion British Thermal Units (BTUs) in 2040, up from the 630 quadrillion BTU level in 2010 (a 56 per cent increase in energy consumption).[11] Proposals to address this challenge range from 'dash for gas' transitional strategies, nuclear revivalism, 'clean coal' pursuits, and renewable energy futures.[12] Proponents find solace in the fact that other technologies, such as the information and telecommunications sector have successfully scaled similar transformation challenges in previously unpractised short timeframes.

However, the energy regime of the Modern Model reveals a potential social complication: energy development principles were structured in favour of increasingly large-scale and centralized technologies that could provide massive amounts of energy – what Amory Lovins depicted as the 'hard path' of development.[13] Indeed, a celebrated trend within the green energy sector's rapid growth is the shift to large-scale applications of renewable energy, substantiating calls for green 'Manhattan Projects'. Propelled by principles of economies of scale and efficiency improvements – and supported by sometimes generous financial policy support – dreams of 10, 15, 20 megawatt (MW) wind turbines lead to a championing of the industry along the lines of 'bigger is greener' or, perhaps, a 'small is stupid' mentality. Energy infrastructure data maintained by the US Federal Energy Regulatory Commission (FERC) offers an example of this trend (Figure 11.1).

Figure 11.1 Index of energy infrastructure data from FERC reporting annual solar PV installations and capacity additions

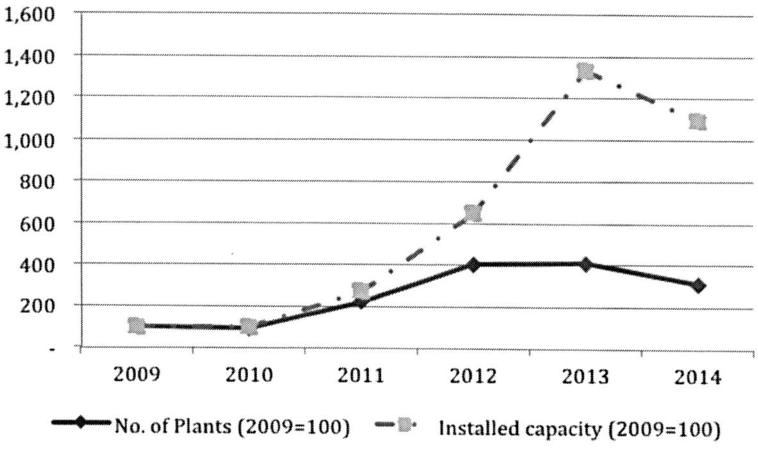

Source: Federal Energy Regulatory Commission. Energy Infrastructure updates. Available at: www.ferc.gov/legal/staff-reports.asp.

Proponents of this energy future ignore that current constructs provide for such 'bigger is greener' and 'more is better' claims along existing consumption–production and nature–society relations: such a course of action could negate the social promise that was thought to be inherent to sustainable energy and, in fact, could become simple 'life extension projects'[14] for the modern energy project. As 'Big Wind', 'Big Solar' and others are integrated into the existing structure of 'Giant Power', promises of a democratized energy world and notions of 'energy for all' evaporate and are replaced by an economic rationalism of expansion and growth. Decentralized and horizontal outgrowth of energy, allowing for innovative energy access and new end-user relationships to energy based on individual contexts, are challenged by 'Giant Power' constructs that function around centralized, oligopolistic and hierarchical energy geographies and economics. The result is an inherently modernist endeavour: environmental narratives are seamlessly incorporated into the modernization project. Self-criticism is only applied to the 'end-of-pipe' consequences of current social relations to the environment – i.e. modernity's pollution consequences – rather than challenging the corporate character of energy development, the class differences that substantiate capitalist expansion and community fragmentation, or existing patterns of inequality.[15]

Questioning equality as a construct of growth

A discourse of political expression is available to civil society to communicate preferential development routes or direct prioritization of the political agenda in liberal democracies, at least at the conceptual level.[16] However, demands for change by civil society are frequently parried by pointing to a lack of 'political will' to address the issue at hand. The climate change discourse offers an example: the Yale Project on Climate Change Communications has found that a majority of Americans (70 per cent) think climate change should be a 'very high' (16 per cent), 'high' (26 per cent) or 'medium' (29 per cent) priority[17] but US political power, in contrast, has consistently been applied in an effort to reduce the effectiveness and stringency of global commitments to climate change mitigation. A 'reality gap' between rhetoric and actual action is apparent.[18]

Institutions and social relationships of the Modern Model have evolved around the continuing support of a model of capital accumulation and corporate power. A case can thus be made that the voice of civil society is pre-empted by a political and corporate discourse in favour of this model.[19] Political legitimacy, at least in part, depends on how well political action facilitates the 'general interest of capital'.[20] Political adages – such as 'green growth' – which are rapidly and easily accepted by existing political and economic architectures, as evidenced by the widespread political support positioned at its foundation, are therefore unlikely to deliver fundamental change.

In effect, the corporatist ideology establishes a state of 'autonomous' technology and capital which evaluates alternative development pathways against the established status quo, resulting in a preservation of its own existence. Civil society's identity is reduced to a 'consumer democracy' in which end-users of energy's dominant means to influence entrepreneurial and capitalistic activity are limited to their daily vote on the means of production through the global marketplace. With the marketplace as the main depository of social and political governance, civil society's voice is fragmented, marginalized and alienated through a process coined by Lewis Mumford as the 'democratic-authoritarian bargain':

> Under the democratic-authoritarian social contract, each member of the community may claim every material advantage, every intellectual and emotional stimulus he may desire, in quantities hardly available hitherto even for a restricted minority: food, housing, swift transportation, instantaneous communication, medical care, entertainment, education. But on one condition: that one must not merely ask for nothing that the system does not provide, but likewise agree to take everything offered, duly processed and fabricated, homogenized and equalized, in the precise quantities that the system, rather than the person, requires.[21]

The Modern Model's capitalist reflex to environmental degradation is made apparent in the carbon market policy model. Driven by principles of cost-effectiveness, efficiency and flexibility, the carbon market model aligns with modern political economy dynamics and is especially suited for large-scale, transnational corporations.[22] Recent surveys, however, show an emerging force, applied by 'green' corporations, to *enhance* action levels and push for more stringent negotiation outcomes in order to advance their business position.[23] Expressions by incumbents at the heart of the 'carbon economy', however, are likely to slow down this process.

More fundamentally, the positioning of science, technology and markets as the means to liberate society from natural constraints produces a nature–society relationship which will not yield to absolute natural boundaries. The drive to maximize growth patterns and sustain capital accumulation instead seek to 'bend' ecological thresholds, translating sustainability rules into efficient applications of science, technology and economics in an attempt to tie economic and technical efficiency to the ethical notion of equality. Ethical value, in this management system of commodification, only surfaces through its transformation into abstract units with exchange value. The result is a juxtaposition of technological and management capability and ethical virtue: 'Carbon emissions become an electronically tradable unit on a trader's screen displaying (only) the current price and volume traded. This virtualization of carbon simultaneously embodies the moral character, or the virtue, of the commodity being traded.'[24]

The blending of virtue with technological and management capability inserts the logic that every improvement in technological and managerial application delivers a normative benefit. Effectively, the commodification of the environment can be seen as a pursuit of making climate change *itself* efficient: the carbon price now becomes the dominant guiding mechanism whether climate change mitigating actions should be performed as marginal decision-making processes determine whether the reduction of one more unit of emission reductions is efficient. This notion was coined 'efficient global warming' by one of the authors.[25]

These considerations expose a critical weakness in growth-based strategies: the relationship between society, nature and economy – other than commonly represented 'triangles' of sustainable development which suggest economic activity, nature and society have independent components – is one of fundamental integration. In order to account for the fundamental nature of 'planetary boundaries',[26] a principle of sufficiency thus needs to be inserted beyond which growth in an absolute sense is no longer pursued. The empirical record for *absolute* decoupling – impact decreases in absolute terms even as economic growth continues – however, is far from robust.[27] Evidence of relative decoupling is unsurprising as profit-maximization strategies continually seek to gain additional value from each unit of input, but absolute decoupling represents a more fundamental notion: limiting expansion to stay within absolute, non-market boundaries of the natural system. Studies on environmental dependency suggest that the empirical record to support decarbonization or dematerialization along lines of 'absolute decoupling' is weak.[28] Additionally, a growing body of literature continues to critique the position that economies can grow their way out of environmental harm to the point where the position has become largely untenable.[29] Indeed, it appears that only economic crisis has been able to materially affect the rising pattern of global greenhouse gas emissions. However, investigations into the effects of such downturns on global emissions suggest that the effect is not only short-lived but also marginal.[30]

Cornucopian promises of equality, therefore, rationalize the weakening of the fundamental nature of ecological limitations and their social inequality consequences. In fact, absolute restraint in line with ecological limits is considered irrational unless market efficiency, in the form of for instance a carbon price, dictates such change. The fundamental and ethical character of ecological limitations is further eroded as technological and managerial capability improves. Equality as a construct of growth therefore fails to materialize as business-as-usual extrapolations demonstrate the unworkable energy and environmental future of the modern energy regime.[31, 32] The need for a different pathway is apparent.

Moving beyond green growth rhetoric

Lewis Mumford, in his description of the 'democratic-authoritarian bargain', early on recognized the consequences and implications of society's devotion and allegiance to Modern Model politics and envisioned a new pathway with which to approach technology, capital and societal development:

> [W]e had better map out a more positive course: namely, the reconstruction of both our science and our technics in such a fashion as to insert the rejected parts of the human personality at every stage of the process. This means gladly sacrificing mere quantity in order to restore qualitative choice, shifting the seat of authority from the mechanical collective to the human personality and the autonomous group, favoring variety and ecological complexity, instead of stressing undue uniformity and standardization, above all, reducing the insensate drive to extend the system itself, instead of containing it within definite human limits and thus releasing man himself for other purposes. We must ask [...] what is good for man: not machine-conditioned, system-regulated, mass-man, but man in person, moving freely over every area of life.[33]

A workable strategy will need to improve the human condition while decoupling economy and energy in an absolute sense in an effort to observe fundamental ecological and social limitations. Insensate expansion, powered by the misguided assumption that such a process opens opportunities for all, can no longer be positioned as the objective of strategies of change. Instead, recognizing Steinberger and Roberts' finding that energy and carbon decouple from human needs at higher living standards,[34] strategic consideration needs to be applied towards the fulfilment of actual needs rather than the continuous expansion of supply. For energy, a new strategy that *matches* energy supply to human needs can represent Mumford's new positive course.[35]

The currently dominant governor of energy supply in the Modern Model is the conventional energy utility. Conventional energy utilities have evolved and thrived in the Modern Model's centralized, high-throughput energy regime, and their decision-making procedures reflect this origin. For instance, utility revenues are dependent on energy sales, requiring cost recovery mechanisms to offset decreased revenues and the cost of 'stranded assets' when energy efficiency programmes successfully reduce energy use. Also, the integration of onsite and small-scale renewable energy generation contradicts the architectural logic of modern utility systems. These limitations require modification if a conventional energy utility is to excel in an energy regime designed to reduce energy use and generate remaining energy use from renewable energy sources. Ongoing discussion is taking place on the shape and functioning of such an institution. These 'Utility 2.0' discussions have produced innovative business models. A commonly cited model is the energy service utility, two US examples of which are the Energy Trust of Oregon and Efficiency Vermont; institutions that seek to deliver energy services to customers rather than electricity sales. Conceptually, however, these examples do not pursue paradigmatic change as they carve out energy service markets in parallel operations with conventional energy utilities.[36] Additionally, these models are often dependent on funds from conventional utilities to underwrite their investments.

To fulfil Mumford's vision, a more fundamental strategy is required. A pathway of strategic social change that positions livelihood-centred energy and economic development and participatory governance at centre stage through the deployment of transformative social innovations – a process of 'Social Change 2.0' if you will – is needed to establish a collaborative playing field, empower people, transform dysfunctional social systems and produce infrastructure-scale change.[37] Here, we discuss the Sustainable Energy Utility (SEU) as a viable and practical model to fulfil Mumford's vision and advance equality and sustainability.

The Sustainable Energy Utility (SEU)

Designed to redraft the energy–economy–environment–society relationship, the SEU can be put forth as one answer to the challenges raised to green growth. At its core, the SEU promotes energy economy restructuring along principles of sufficiency, dialling back energy use where possible and using onsite renewable energy where needed. Its other innovative characteristics emerge when considering: a) how the SEU engages the community in which it functions; b) how it positions the value inherent in all communities; and c) how it attracts financial support to deliver infrastructure-scale change.

The SEU and community trust

Unlike accepted conceptualizations of the individual as reactive 'end-users' or 'consumers', the SEU views people and communities as self-organizing, proactive, self-reflecting and self-regulating. Positioned as a 'community utility', the SEU empowers residents and businesses to embark on a future of sustainable energy, moving beyond limited conceptualizations of 'prosumers' and towards sustainable citizens.[38] SEU performance, as such, is judged on its capacity to realize public benefits, foster social acceptance and maintain social engagement, and is evaluated by the community it serves.[39] Indeed, without community participation and trust, the SEU model ceases to exist. Allowing for community-designated environmental, social and governance objectives, the SEU reconstitutes the contemporary technocratic energy development model that prioritizes the voice of experts of technical acumen – paid for by community members through their energy bills – rather than making energy experts subservient to community goals.[40]

Participants in SEU programmes indicate their energy service needs and advanced investment-grade energy audits determine where improvements can take place and what energy reduction measures and technologies are suitable for the participant. The results of these assessments are documented in a) a long-term guaranteed savings agreement between the energy service corporations (ESCOs), the participant, and the SEU outlining the energy savings available and contractually guaranteeing their materialization, b) a payment agreement between the SEU, debt issuer and the participant outlining a payment schedule where debt service payments and remaining utility bill payments together do not exceed the utility bill payments prior to the installation of energy-saving measures, and c) a programme agreement between debt issuer, participant, SEU and ESCOs that outlines the functioning of the overall programme. Critically, energy savings are denominated in dollar amounts, providing security and clarity to all programme participants. Community trust is strengthened further as the programme is customizable to local conditions (e.g. repayment terms, energy saving measures), the participant incurs no upfront capital costs, the participant owns all improvements and associated benefits, net savings accrue to public participants, monitoring and verification protocols support participant goals (if monitoring and verification report energy saving shortfalls, the ESCO is held responsible under the guaranteed savings agreement and will need to remedy the performance shortfall or provide compensation), and low cost capitalization (see below) is available by taking advantage of community pooling and transaction standardization. The SEU thus becomes a trusted advisor of the community as it provides independent, objective monitoring and verification of investment performance and identifies actions needed to comply with the contractual savings guarantee throughout the long-term duration of the programme (20–25 years per contractual engagement).

The SEU and the commonwealth

Drawing from Amory Lovins' concept of the 'negawatt',[41] the SEU's core value proposition is that it is more cost-effective to reduce energy use through conservation and efficiency efforts than to expand energy supply to meet rising demand. The promise of cost reductions realized by lowering the utility bill in this manner can be aggregated across the entire community, yielding a substantial wealth of energy use reduction potential. The 'commonwealth' – the ongoing mutual promise to share the costs and benefits of building an energy scheme that uses less – is applied to underwrite the energy use reduction measures and investment costs and attract financial capital from the capital markets. Community investments in this manner promote collective gains such as improved public health and biodiversity recovery. Providing any remaining energy use with renewable energy sources provides the additional benefit of constructing an enduring commonwealth. The SEU thus provides for a practical strategy by investing in less use, funded by the difference between waste and conservation and, for large investments where up-front capital costs are substantial, drawing from the substantial wealth of the commons. Future expansion costs for additional energy capacity or remediation and restoration infrastructures are avoided.

Positions of limiting energy supply or growth are commonly criticized as 'backward' or risking 'degrowth'. However, focusing on energy service delivery rather than energy supply is by no means a recipe for social decline. Indeed, significant benefits can be accrued with the effective deployment of the commonwealth. For instance, a recent publication by the International Energy Agency (IEA) reports a global \$115 trillion fuel saving opportunity residing within decarbonization strategies.[42] Similarly, a \$279 billion investment could yield $1 trillion in return in energy savings within the US building sector over a ten-year period[43] and annual US non-transportation energy efficiency potential equates to $1.2 trillion in energy savings against an initial $520 billion investment corresponding to about 1.1 gigatons of greenhouse gas emission reductions.[44] Much of this potential remains untapped. The final innovation of the SEU is its capitalization approach and practical strategy with which to unlock the commonwealth.

The financial identity of the SEU strategy

The commonwealth, i.e. its energy savings potential, is deployed by the SEU in an innovative and practical strategy to overcome oft-cited barriers to successful energy efficiency and conservation efforts such as high upfront costs, limited capital availability, and the need to maintain ratepayer protection. Additionally, the deployment of the commonwealth in this manner, pooling together community savings options in infrastructure-scale investment opportunities, allows for a reduction in the cost-of-capital by engaging the capital markets. These New Energy Economics leverage financial capital from a variety of sources (philanthropic, energy and carbon auction markets, crowdfunding,[45] etc.) but an especially innovative approach is the deployment of tax-exempt revenue bonds that access the private capital market.

Figure 11.2 demonstrates how commonwealth resources can be used to pay back the bond debt service throughout the maturity of the bond. A community participant's energy use and utility costs, through the deployment of energy efficiency, conservation and renewable energy measures can thus be reduced without a financial commitment from the community participant other than the promise to pay back the debt service (which is paid for by the energy savings). Debt service repayment is ensured through the guaranteed savings agreement with the ESCOs pledging contractual monetary savings to the public participant. This is an important element: unlike other approaches to energy savings, commonly expressed in energy terms such as kilowatt hours, the monetization of energy savings delivers transparency and clarity to investors and community participants alike. Guaranteed savings agreements are possible as the SEU leverages the significant commonwealth towards those that install the energy savings measures, negotiating favourable contracts with lower prices and guarantees. The combined value of the commonwealth resource opens up this option as the energy service contractors are eager to tap into this market and will thus back up their installation measures with promises of guaranteed savings. Finally the use of standardized and transparent contractual arrangements for all participants further strengthens the credit worthiness, as these documents have established a solid track record in other types of arrangements elevating private market trust.

Figure 11.2. Example illustration of the application of the Commonwealth principle for a programme participant

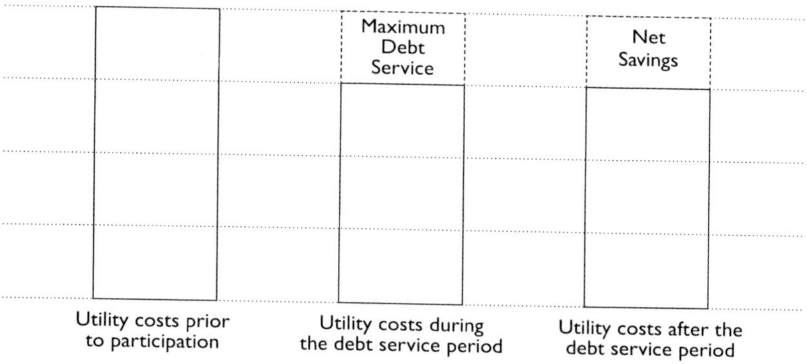

Source: Citi (2011). *Delaware Sustainable Energy Utility – Energy Efficiency Revenue Bonds. Series 2011: Post-Pricing Commentary*. New York, NY: Citigroup.

Green growth and the Sustainable Energy Utility (SEU)

The difference between the green growth narrative and the narrative represented by institutional innovations like the SEU is paradigmatic: optimal growth versus sustainability.[46] For instance, fundamentally, *matching* energy supply to be directly in line with energy service needs is wholly different compared to providing ever-growing energy supply options to satiate unending demand. Similarly, where marginal decision-making processes – which decide whether action should be undertaken based on the marginal addition of one extra unit of action – can suffer from rebound effects as energy efficiency measures make the use of additional energy easier and more attractive,[47] infrastructure-scale system transformation along guaranteed savings for 20–25 years provides long-lived, system change. On top of that, the positioning of the SEU as a community utility, drawing from the commonwealth and reliant on community trust, changes the end-user relationship to energy from one of consumer to one of empowered sustainable citizen – indeed, the application of the SEU model changes the public or commons character of energy–society relations as a whole. It's difficult to imagine how this change enables privatization to return in the form of spending to have more.

Renewable energy applications under SEU models serve to provide remaining energy use after energy savings measures have been implemented. Positioning energy supply options in this manner counteracts earlier mentioned consequences of a 'greenshift' under growth processes as the context-specific nature of participants' energy profiles dictates diversity through customer-sited energy applications rather than uniformity and centralization. The provision of just enough energy supply options to meet remaining energy demand furthermore directly counteracts mentalities of 'more is better', 'bigger is greener', and 'small is stupid' and, instead, celebrates restraint. Finally, the fact that energy systems put in place by SEU programmes are owned by the community (i.e. the programme participants) shifts away from the corporate character of large-scale and centralized energy development and, instead, celebrates a commons-based character of energy supply.

Equality as a construct of the commons establishes benefits out of reach for growth-based equality pursuits in at least three ways. First, unequal consequences of planetary boundary overshoot – such as climatic change – are addressed by creating a system that thrives by explicitly staying within such boundaries. This change equalizes the position of the powerful with those of the 'other' (other places, other peoples, other times). Moreover, rather than seceding control to bureaucratic and technical experts, SEU models empower people to control their own energy futures as community participants articulate the energy service needs they require. Finally, equality as a construct of the commons allows for resource efficiency in an absolute sense to occur where welfare benefits are realized with lower energy use in an absolute sense – a process that can continue as energy saving technologies progress.

Practical SEU application

The transformative power of the SEU approach is illustrated by its first application by the Delaware SEU in the United States. The issue of the state-wide tax-exempt bond issue realized a $72.5 million financing in sustainable energy capital from the private market, sufficient to invest in energy saving measures that deliver a guaranteed $148 million energy saving.[48] The $37 million premium benefits the agencies and institutions of the state of Delaware that participate in the programme, lowering the cost-of-government (Figure 11.3). Indeed, the Delaware SEU, applying its 'social change 2.0' framework, outpaces the results of 'Utility 2.0' counterparts such as Energy Efficiency of Vermont and Energy Trust of Oregon.[49]

Figure 11.3 Overview of the Delaware SEU Sustainable Energy Bond issue's costs and guaranteed savings

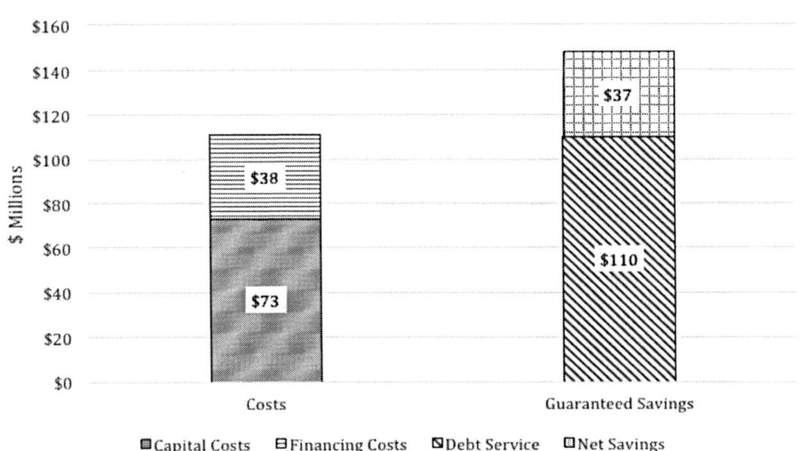

Source: Citi, *Energy efficiency revenue bonds.*

The transformational power of this strategy has received endorsements from the US White House and the Asian Development Banks and the SEU model experiences active diffusion within the US and around the world.[50] To facilitate diffusion, the Foundation of Renewable Energy and Environment (FREE) provides knowhow and advice to organizations across the US and internationally to take advantage of the SEU model. For instance, the Sonoma County Water Agency (SCWA) in California is set to release a $30–$50 million bond issue for Sonoma County. Interestingly, this bond issue innovates beyond earlier iterations of SEU bonds as it includes material- and water-savings potential available in the community. A partnership with the California Statewide Communities Development Authority (CSCDA) seeks to provide outgrowth of the application to the entire state of California, which would significantly advance the SEU concept. Similarly, a recent launch by the Pennsylvania Treasury in collaboration with FREE of the Sustainable Energy Finance Program is a further example of the diffusion of the SEU model. Finally, through the partnership between FREE and Applied Solutions (an agency dedicated to serving community needs in all US jurisdictions), many more communities throughout the US are being engaged and informed about the SEU concept and promise.

The Delaware SEU example offers a guide to how the SEU model can unlock significant energy savings when applied in a comprehensive strategy: a national application of the model in the US along the same lines as described in this chapter would present a $25 billion energy investment market in the public sector alone (i.e. applying the model in municipalities, universities, schools and hospitals). When applied at this level, approximately 300,000 additional green jobs and 225 million metric tons of greenhouse gas emission reduction could be realized.[51] Indeed, considerable opportunity exists for such a strategy as the SEU model would outperform current programmes with similar objectives by a factor of six.[52]

Pursuing 'Social Change 2.0' in the twenty-first century

As Mumford says, we need to consider whether we advance strategies that are good for 'machine-conditioned, system-regulated, mass-man' or whether we pursue and develop strategies that align with 'man in person'.[53] We offer that the SEU model is representative of this strategic pursuit. The proposals under the green growth narrative – the end-of-pipe greening of existing unequal and hierarchical energy geographies, the reliance on resource efficiency when faced with absolute growth, and the conceptualization of community members as energy consumers along the democratic-authoritarian bargain – are challenged by this new commons-based paradigm arguing for the reallocation of capital to serve the public benefits of equality, sustainability and justice. As such, the SEU model is paradigm shift-inducing as it competes – both politically and economically – with the existing utility framework.

The 'Social Change 2.0' strategy, of which the SEU model is a part, is proposed as the way forward. In the energy and climate space, the SEU shows a practical articulation of this strategy by matching supply to energy service needs and empowering the community landscape. By doing so, it prioritizes the position of energy efficiency and conservation – now too often considered a 'fifth fuel' afterthought in supply-dominated energy geographies. To prioritize energy saving within the supply-dominated business model, like that of the conventional energy utility, requires extensive regulatory frameworks and rate-recovery mechanisms yielding the paradoxical outcome that, despite frequent affirmations of the cost effectiveness of energy saving compared to energy production, end-users are subjugated to rent-seeking behaviour – they pay more for less. The value proposition that the SEU model maintains moves away from this conceptualization and instead creates a practical strategy to unlock existing community value of future energy savings and leverages this resource to realize infrastructure-level investments in measures that cost-effectively result in energy-use dial-back.

The Social Change 2.0 strategy injects human personality into (energy) development agendas as it supports social innovations like the SEU. Fundamentally, such a strategy repositions the community away from the conceptualization of the 'individual as beneficiary' – enjoying all that is provided but without influence – and towards the notion of the 'individual as author' where individuals and communities democratically govern their own energy future. As the movement actively labours to accelerate the diffusion of the SEU model throughout the US and globally, its promise of advanced prosperity, restructured ecology–energy–society relations, and energy provision to meet energy service needs becomes clear. A twenty-first-century sustainability paradigm that seriously considers both the need to advance equality while maintaining the long-term ecological viability is within our reach.

CHAPTER 12

Alternatives to green growth? Possibilities and contradictions of self-managed food production

Steffen Böhm, Maria Ceci Araujo Misoczky, David Watson and Sanjay Lanka

Introduction

It is now widely understood that the 'green growth' economic policy agenda is pervaded by serious shortcomings, inconsistencies and contradictions. Many companies' CSR reports, NGOs' sustainability action plans and governments' climate change white papers are often not worth the FSC-labelled paper they are written on, given that they regularly fail to question the unsustainable bases of capitalism: accumulation, reproduction and economic growth. As many contributions to this book show vividly, 'green growth' is, at best, the naïve belief in the possibilities of capitalism to green itself; at worst, it is the latest ideological reshaping of the hegemony of capital without addressing its intrinsic unsustainability.

The call for alternatives to capitalism has existed ever since its emergence. Yet, in recent years, it has been increasingly argued that such 'alternatives already exist, and that many of the resources and ideas we need are already available to us'.[1] 'It is by looking at the cracks and gaps within capitalism that we begin to see' that our current, globally operating, socio-economic system is anything but, encompassing many local differences and alternatives.[2] In these cracks and gaps, it is argued, many experiment with alternative 'relations of production and exchange that do not follow the logic of capital accumulation'.[3] Such alternative practices include workers cooperatives, alternative currencies and trading systems, local food initiatives, and community-supported agricultural schemes, to name but a few. Parker *et al.* and Gibson-Graham *et al.* describe many of these alternative practices, calling for a continued 'insurgent entrepreneurship' that could give rise to blueprints for new, more sustainable, communities.[4]

In this chapter, we review three such self-proclaimed alternatives, focusing specifically on the political economy of food and agriculture, given that food production plays such a fundamental role in the emergence and maintenance of capitalism and, at the same time, the reproduction of life. In fact, we argue with Moore that 'green growth' has been the defining mode of the organization of capital's political economy ever since its rise, precisely because of the centrality of the food–capital nexus.[5] Moore argues that neoliberal capitalism has found it, and will continue to find it, increasingly difficult to produce cheap food at a decent enough quality and quantity to feed a rapidly growing world population. This production crisis, coupled with the environmental and social crisis that has always been part and parcel of the capitalist system, has given rise to a range of productive, organizational practices that attempt to overcome some of the perverse consequences of this crisis.

We will discuss three specific case studies from different parts of the world, which could be considered part of the attempts to resist the capitalist agri-food system, working towards possible alternatives. Namely, we will explore agroecological practices in food-growing cooperatives in India, local food communities in the UK and organic food production related to the Landless Workers Movement (the MST) in Brazil. In many ways, we need to celebrate these attempts, as all of them have tried to address the fundamental unsustainability of the capitalist agri-food system, exploring and experimenting with alternative practices and discourses of food production.

However, we would do the social movements for alternative political economies a disservice if we simply celebrated these initiatives without critically engaging with them. We believe there is a need to critically evaluate the very working practices of these intended alternative production projects and the way they are often connected within the (global) economy. While, at face value, these projects might look alternative (green, more sustainable, more ethical, etc.), the reality is often more complex, with many contradictions at work, precisely because they sit within the inescapable web of socio-economic capitalist relations. We will argue that in many ways these so-called 'alternatives' are part and parcel of capital's continuous attempts to find new ways of accumulation and legitimization.

Green (food) growth as capitalism's world-ecology

The global agri-food system is one of the fastest growing industries in the world and it plays an immensely important role for the expansion and metabolic reproduction of the capitalist system. While global food production has tripled since the 1960s, and global agri-food companies play an increasingly central role in the global food value chain, delivering healthy profits to their shareholders, the system does not produce positive outcomes for all. In fact, the global agri-food system is in crisis.[6]

About a billion people do not have access to the minimum amount of daily calories needed for survival.[7] While hunger is a persistent problem, levels of obesity continue to rise.[8] This is not limited to the so-called developed world; countries in the South too are struggling to cope with rising levels of obesity, even though chronic hunger persists in the same context.[9] Since the 2008 financial crisis, many people have experienced food insecurity, because of rapidly rising food prices, signalling the reversal of a long-term trend of falling prices.[10]

The majority of food produced and consumed in countries of the so-called developed world is manufactured within an industrial setting, using standardized methods of production. While it produces negative outcomes for workers at all levels of the global food supply chain, it also produces negative health outcomes for consumers, known as 'Western diseases' such as hypertension, diabetes, cancer and obesity.[11] The same processes of industrialization that have contributed to reduced food costs for consumers have had very real costs for the environment, such as degradation of land, salinization and contamination of water supplies, biodiversity loss and increased carbon emissions.[12] The highly complex processes of food production and supply, which are largely obscured to the consumer, have left them open to abuse, or misuse, as exemplified by the recent 'horse meat scandal' that gripped Europe in 2013.[13]

Following O'Connor, some critical commentators argue that the capitalist agri-food system produces these negative outcomes for society and nature, given capital's tendency to continuously undermine its own resources and mode of production.[14] Jason Moore argues that such a perspective relies on a false capital–nature dichotomy. Instead, he begins 'from the premise that capitalism does not act upon nature so much as develop through nature–society relations'.[15] He envisages capital as a 'world-ecology'. According to Moore's understanding, capitalist relations do not produce crisis; rather they are constitutive of crisis. Moore identifies various junctures in the history of capitalism whereby such crises have prompted significant changes in the modes and locus of capital accumulation.[16] Critical to solving these crises has been the opening of new frontiers, enabling appropriation of more of nature's (extra human and human) 'free gifts'. This includes the agricultural land of the new world as well as the slaves put to work upon it, which both contribute to increased yields at a reduced (financial) cost and in doing so provide a cheap source of energy to feed labour elsewhere.[17] The history of capitalism then becomes a series of self-induced crises, which are temporarily overcome through the creation of new frontiers and socio-technical innovation, so that capitalism is both cause and effect of its own crises.[18]

In this way, one could say that 'green growth' has always been part of the very nature of the capitalist system and the concept simply represents a reframing of this relationship. It is not an invention of the Rio+20 conference, UNEP, Korea, or other hegemonic actors. Moore's approach underlines how the rise of capitalism and its continued reproduction has always had a close relationship to the industrialization and expansion of the food system. Ever since the enclosure of the commons simultaneously threw millions of peasants off the land and millions of 'free labourers' into the realms of factory work, the capitalist system has depended on the simultaneous revolutionizing of food production and distribution. The slavery system, the plantation system, the 'green revolution', the more recent GM revolution: these have all been important junctures of capitalism's 'green growth'.

The growth of the capitalist global agri-food system has always had a contradictory relationship with peasants and smallhold farmers. On the one hand, as noted above, capital's industrialization has forced millions of peasants and farmers off their land, enslaving them directly or, through dispossession, forcing them to become workers in cities. On the other hand, capitalism still needs these smallholders to feed the population. While the industrial agri-system uses 70 per cent of agricultural resources to provide 30 per cent of the world's food, smallhold farmers produce the remaining 70 per cent using only 30 per cent of the resources.[19] Industrial agriculture hence aims to 'win over' smallhold farmers, luring them into new production systems that involve high cost inputs such as genetically modified (GM) seeds, fertilizers, and pesticide/herbicide, which are the commodities that produce the highest surplus value for multinational agri-businesses.[20]

This industrial form of food production replaces local markets and local cultures that have traditionally been places of crop diversity, promoted through the ingenuity of farmers to evolve new breeds through the conservation of seeds and plant varieties.[21] Small and marginal farmers are faced with a dependence on the technologies of the green/industrial revolution and domination by development strategies of governments from around the world that subsidize large agri-businesses.[22] One of the outcomes is that small farmers fall into debt, as they become dependent on governmental or agri-business credits that they cannot repay with the incomes they generate.[23] As a result, small farming communities and their food production practices become ever more marginalized, losing their voice and visibility.[24] As global markets take over from local markets, diversity is replaced by monocultures.[25]

The industrial method of farming is actively promoted by the large transnational corporations (TNCs), governments and civil society organizations alike, accompanied with the rhetoric of a responsible and sustainable approach to business.[26] As we have argued, the recent emergence of the 'green growth' agenda is just the latest round of capital's attempt to reorganize and 'restyle' its relationship to nature, on which it depends for its own reproduction. While the 'green growth' discourse argues for the possibility of finding a harmonious way of integrating the environmental, social and economic aspects of sustainable development, its reality is full of contradictions.[27]

Calling for agroecological alternatives, and their limits

Given the above-outlined crises of the global agri-food system, a range of so-called agroecological techniques, combined with more localized agri-food chains, are increasingly seen as part of the solution.

Agroecology is 'the integrative study of the ecology of the entire food system, encompassing ecological, economic and social dimensions'.[28] The focus of agroecology is the entire food system, taking into consideration the production of food, its processing and transportation, the role played by financial intermediaries, marketing and finally how it is consumed.[29] The livelihoods of farmers, including their families and the communities that they live in, are essential for the sustainable existence of agricultural systems.[30] Livelihood is defined as the multiple resources and capabilities that people utilize to make a living, and biodiversity plays a crucial role in making agroecology successful and sustainable in the long run.[31] Hence, agroecology is a growing practice that considers the holistic relationship between all important biophysical, technical and socio-economic components of farming systems, aiming to sustain yields while minimizing the negative environmental and socio-economic impacts of modern, large-scale farming techniques.

There is a lot of promise in agroecological practices, which have been successfully used by smallhold farming and local food-growing communities throughout the world.[32] Yet, these alternatives to global agri-business are not without contradictions and shortcomings, as a number of authors have highlighted recently. Bernstein, for example, is sceptical about agroecological smallholders being able to feed a growing urban population, effectively necessitating the continuing expansion of industrialized, unsustainable farming techniques.[33] Along similar lines, Jansen argues that agroecological farmers are often integrated into capital's global supply chains in various ways.[34] Fidler emphatically claims that the local food movement in the US is a 'capitalist, individualist, and limited response to critiques of agriculture and lacks an ideological center of gravity and large-scale vision of reform. It fails to address the problems capitalist agriculture creates for the environment and for agricultural labor, central concerns for Marx.'[35] Equally, Boillat *et al.*'s implicit claim is that a truly different agricultural future can only be accomplished within what they call 'self-managed socialism', i.e. not within a capitalist context.[36]

What these critiques have in common is a concern for connecting the local, often more sustainable, realities of agroecological practices to the global unsustainability of the global agri-food system, often controlled and managed by large multinational companies. As Jansen makes clear, the dialectical critique of local–global relations reveals that the continuous crises of global capital necessitate the investment of existing profits into new accumulation opportunities (what Marx called 'expanded reproduction') as well as what Harvey called 'accumulation by dispossession' – the often violent expropriation of land and spaces of all kinds by capital. In this sense, once 'alternative' agroecological practices are lucrative and show potential of surplus value production they are immediately incorporated into the accumulation practices of capital.[37]

Let us now introduce and discuss three alternative food-growing programmes to expand on this critique further, illustrating the workings of global capitalism within the contemporary food system.

India

Although agriculture is still dominated by smallholders in India, farmers are increasingly dependent on globally operating seed and chemical companies. As mentioned above, debt is an increasing problem for smallholder farmers, as can be seen in the case of Andhra Pradesh, a state in India where about 82 per cent of farmers are in debt, which is taken on to buy the inputs needed for cash crop cultivation under the urging of the government.[38] This is due to a decline in traditional farming techniques in India which were based on the concept of intercropping, where a combination of different crops were grown together in such a way that some of them provided the essential sustenance for the soil.[39]

The Haryali project is an agroforestry programme in Andhra Pradesh that is built on the principle of bringing back the traditional farming techniques using intercropping and the environmental services provided by biodiversity. The project's scope is to plant around 6 million saplings during a five-year period on 6,000 hectares, giving a local coffee-growing cooperative the chance to diversify their production, with the hope of making them more independent from fluctuating global coffee prices and positively contributing to their livelihood.

The project has been approved by the government of India and certified by the UNFCCC under the Clean Development Mechanism (CDM), as its trees will also help to reduce global greenhouse gas emissions. The Haryali project is implemented by farmers belonging to the *Chinna Sannakara Girijana Ryotu Paraspara Sahayaka Sangham* or The Small and Marginal Tribal Farmers Mutually Cooperative Society (SAMTFMACS) under the coordination of the Naandi Foundation. It is a partnership between SAMTFMACS, Naandi Foundation, the Livelihoods Group led by Danone, the French multinational company, and the Indian multinational corporation Mahindra & Mahindra.

SAMTFMACS was formed in 2007 as a coffee processing and marketing enterprise with the goal of improving the livelihoods of the tribal communities of the Paleru Integrated Tribal Development Agency (ITDA) and has a membership of over 11,000 smallhold farmers who depend upon growing coffee as a primary source of income. Since high-quality coffee is shade grown, the members of SAMTFMACS, under the leadership of the Naandi Foundation, came up with the idea of creating shade for their coffee using fruit trees. Given that trees sequester carbon, this enables the community to earn some extra money from selling carbon credits to the international market. In addition, as the fruit trees mature they will provide an alternate source of revenue for the farmers that will enable them to diversify their livelihoods from a dependence on coffee alone.

The goal of providing sustainable development through sustainable livelihoods is at the core of the design and implementation of this project. As such, it can be seen as an alternative to dominant CDM practices that have been critiqued for having a focus on providing cheap carbon credits for the biggest polluters in the global North while not providing enough sustainable development for the communities that are a part of the project.[40] Most CDM projects have contributed to the destruction of the environment and little to the livelihoods of local populations. Further, in projects of afforestation, CDM projects have seen the use of large monoculture plantations, where the local people are treated as 'encroachers'.[41]

Having said that, it is important to analyse the political economy of the Haryali project, understanding the vital role large multinational companies, namely Danone and Mahindra & Mahindra, and a corporate and government-funded NGO, Naandi Foundation, play. Dependency is cemented, rather than questioned, by this project. The SAMTFMACS cooperative seems largely dependent on the Naandi Foundation, which itself is funded by Mahindra & Mahindra and the Indian state. The farmers of the cooperative have very little, if any, control over the management of the value chain of the coffee and the marketing of fruits produced as part of the Haryali project. The project provides vital legitimating functions for both Danone and Mahindra & Mahindra, and is used for marketing and public relations opportunities by these two multinational companies.

United Kingdom

In highly industrialized countries, the critique of, and resistance to, the food system has been rife, with growers, consumers and activists searching for a range of alternative ways of growing and distributing food. A key component of this alternative movement has been towards more localized food, which is a growing sector in the UK. Projects such as community-supported agriculture (CSA), box schemes, allotments and community gardens are promoted as a means to revitalize local communities, supply healthier food and improve agricultural sustainability.

The ability of local food systems to 'short-circuit' long complex supply chains typically realized in the conventional food system has been proclaimed as one of their beneficial attributes.[42] Direct agricultural markets are central to this ability, creating a space where consumer and producer interact 'face-to-face' in an arena of exchange that is imbued with more social meaning than conventional retail spaces.[43] Beyond this, they also play a key role in enabling rural producers to capture a greater share of value from the exchange of their products.[44] As such, they have been seen as an important tool for rural development. This usually depends on the existence of a niche market, such as 'organic' or 'local', which producers have been encouraged to turn towards, diversifying production to remain viable.[45] However, such niches often remain entangled in conventional structures, so they cannot escape the logic that governs the inequalities and contradictions of the food and agricultural market.

Direct agricultural markets such as farmers markets form a different setting than supermarkets, bringing together producers and consumers in an interaction that is absent from conventional retail structures, yet they do not challenge the commodification of food.[46] Community Supported Agriculture (CSA) constitutes a distinctive form of alternative, whereby consumers share the risks and rewards of production with the producer/s.[47] CSA marks a significant departure from conventional economic exchange, typically involving purchasing a 'share' in a farm and receiving a regular harvest in return and might also include a work commitment.[48] This enables people to produce directly to meet some of their needs instead of meeting them all via the market and production structured by waged labour, thereby counteracting the abstraction and alienation of capitalist labour. This is not restricted to CSA, occurring in community gardens, allotments, private gardens, wherever the opportunity for such direct work exists and the forces of capital are not exerted. That such opportunities exist in 'everyday life' should not convince us that there is nothing alternative about CSA or other food initiatives but does underline how the value relations that define so many aspects of life under the dominant market practices are not totalizing.

CSAs define production as a shared goal entailing a deeper commitment than typical economic transactions. Besides exposing consumers to the same risks and rewards experienced by producers, this also goes some way to creating a community tying people together with a shared interest but also through shared work.[49] The kind of work undertaken in these spaces is also significant. In a study of allotments, Schoneboom describes 'the novel self-directed, sensation of tangible labour' which 'provides an antidote to intangible knowledge or service work'.[50] While these spaces can challenge prevailing market structures, they can also prop them up by supporting the conditions of production; acting as a refuge for stressed workers to recover from the strains of paid work and providing for workers' material needs, allowing wages to be kept lower.[51] CSA also brings consumers more directly into contact with the process of food production and thereby connecting them to the land bridging the metabolic rift created in the conventional food system.[52] Other forms of food production/distribution can bring people closer to production but few directly connect people to the land through production.

Despite the positive impacts at a local level, it would be naïve to suggest that the 'alternative' practices discussed here have the power to wholly dismantle capitalism by themselves. Yet they do highlight how resistance can be articulated in everyday life. Even though we must acknowledge limitations, we also need to retain an appreciation for non-capitalist values and practices that reside within capital's dominant framework if we are to envisage a wholesale transformation of society.

Brazil

The Landless Workers Movement (Movimento dos Trabalhadores Sem Terra, or MST) emerged in Rio Grande do Sul in 1979 and is broadly considered as one of the most influential social movements in Latin America. In the following paragraphs, we will engage with a critical appraisal of MST's trajectory, moving from cooperatives to family agriculture. This critical appraisal does not ignore the importance of the movement but values the need of highlighting its contradictions. In the words of Harvey: 'Contradictions are by no means all bad [...]. They can be a fecund source of both personal and social change from which people merge far better off than before.'[53]

In its 30 years of existence, the MST struggle has won title to 7.5 million hectares of land, on which 370,000 families now live. Between 1987 and 1989, the MST invested in the development of different associations of producers. For the MST, the Cooperativas de Produção Agropecuária (CPAs, Agricultural Production Cooperatives) would bring together the collective organization of production with market insertion strategies, enabling the economic viability of the settlements.[54] Until 1992, organizational 'laboratories' were created in several states to support the formation of production cooperatives.[55] The laboratories were constituted by short courses, designed to 'stimulate the division of labour and collectivism, creating sectors of activities and production, to enhance productivity and improve economic outcomes'.[56] In 1992, there were 55 cooperatives of production and commercialization.[57] This expansion has to be considered in association with the creation, in 1985, of the Special Credit Program for Agrarian Reform (Programa de Crédito Especial para a Reforma Agrária – Procera) run by the federal government and providing annual production loans and one-off loans for investment. Procera privileged collective loans.[58]

However, 'many settlements opted for the opposite extreme: family farms without any collaboration between the settlers'. Consequently, 'the leadership of the MST acknowledged that collectivism could not be enforced uniformly and, thereafter, allowed settlements to organize production as they wished'.[59] From then on, the MST started to build a different identity oriented towards agroecological production. The first experiences of agroecological production occurred in 1993. Another event that led to this reorientation was the substitution of Procera by another governmental credit policy: the National Program to Strengthen Family Farming (Programa Nacional de Fortalecimento da Agricultura Familiar – Pronaf), created in 1995.[60]

Agroecological production was part of a strategic turn informed by contextual changes: increase in the number of families owning the land, militants' resistance against cooperatives, changes in credit public policies, growing market demand for agroecological food and the dissemination of the sustainability discourse. Another aspect to be considered was the fact that, in 1996, the MST became a member of Via Campesina, which includes in its programme agroecology and sustainability.

It is obvious that the movement's strategy becomes more and more dependent on a successful insertion into the market to guarantee the survival of the producers as well as the payment of credit loans. Harvey has already indicated the limits of 'non-capitalist forms or labour organization', such as workers cooperatives, because their aim 'is still the production of exchange values'.[61] Therefore, it cannot come as a surprise that in the Food Security and Sovereignty Panel during the Rio+20 Conference, the leaders of the MST proudly announced the sale of 15 tons of organic rice to Grupo Pão de Açúcar, a supermarket chain controlled by the Casino Group, a large French multinational company.[62]

The discussion of some of these intended alternatives does not disregard the fact that very important changes have been achieved for the actual organization of MST and, especially, for the survival of the producers. Yet, the point we are making is that this could not have been accomplished without these small-scale producers inserting themselves into existing market relations, including the financial system mediated by governmental credit programmes. These former landless workers became small agricultural producers and, as such, their aims have obviously changed. The important point to highlight here is that, despite the value of this kind of practice for all those involved, it cannot be considered as an alternative to the existing, dominant agricultural model. Food sovereignty cannot be achieved by increasing the price of healthy organic food – a consequence of companies selling it and their need of profit. It also cannot be considered as an alternative because it is fully integrated into the existing division of labour between small producers and agri-businesses in the Brazilian political economy of food production.

Limits of alternatives to green growth capitalism

In recent years, a politics has taken hold around the world that argues that capitalism has many cracks and gaps, having failed to commodify everything.[63] Gibson-Graham *et al.*, in line with popular social movements, such as the Transition Town movement, have argued for a pragmatic 'do-it-yourself'-style approach, taking very practical steps towards taking back the economy without waiting for 'the revolution'.[64] This is based on an 'anti-essentialist', pragmatist understanding of politics that emphasizes 'the contingency of social outcomes rather than the unfolding of structural logics'.[65] What Gibson-Graham and colleagues are trying to do is, through the sheer performative power of their knowledge, to create a new world of socio-economic alternatives to crisis prone global capitalism.[66]

In this chapter, we have shown the limits of such a performative approach to wishing along alternatives, arguing that the dynamics of accumulation and legitimation continuously drive capital to incorporate or neutralize the most promising alternative politico-economic strategies of social movements. In the above-discussed Indian case, we can see how agroecological food production practices, which are widely seen as radical alternatives to the unsustainabilities and exploitative nature of the global agri-food system, are captured by NGOs and businesses to provide legitimation for Danone and Mahindra & Mahindra, two important multinational corporations. The agroecological Haryali project has become entangled in the corporate discourses of CSR and sustainability. While under different socio-economic relations the project might indeed contribute towards the development of independent livelihoods of local, smallhold farmers, our case analysis has argued that, in fact, new sets of dependencies have been established, which must be regarded as regressive rather than progressive. Although the Haryali project provides a legitimation function for corporate actors, as well as the Indian state, it can also be understood as an important testing ground for how to address the crisis and 'metabolic rift' tendencies of the global capitalist agri-food system.

The theory of 'metabolic rift' has provided a critique of human interaction with nature under capitalist relations of production and the damaging consequences of this. Marx considered the 'metabolic' interaction between man and nature to be fundamental in order to meet the needs of human existence and therefore in defining the nature of labour.[67] Capitalist labour structures engender 'the separation of social production from its natural biological base', creating a rift in the social and ecological metabolism, or exchange, between humans and nature.[68] For example, the importation of guano (bird droppings) as a soil improver in nineteenth-century Europe became a necessity as more intensive agricultural methods began to exhaust the soil. As these stocks themselves ran low, industrial agriculture turned to the emerging synthetic fertilizer industry.[69] These crises are emblematic of 'capitalism's antagonistic relation to the environment' and the metabolic rift it creates between humans and nature, and is intensified by modern agriculture.[70]

Arguably, we can see more agroecological and other sustainable methods of food production as an attempt to address this very rift. The Haryali project experiments with new ways of diversification, away from monocultures towards a system that makes local smallhold farming communities more sustainable and independent of global, fluctuating coffee prices. Yet, the market is never far away from the considerations of this agroecological project. Rather than forging new, non-capitalist social and economic relations, the aim is always about how to make the best of existing market conditions and how to make the market work for these food-growing cooperatives.

The ecological rift is hence always also a social rift, stemming from the alienation embodied in the structures of labour and exchange under capitalism; we can see a response to this in the MST case. Although, its abandonment of political objectives aimed at restructuring the nature of work and production in favour of a more agroecological focus makes it more vulnerable to appropriation by the market, precisely because this very market increasingly calls for 'organic', 'local' and other, more sustainably and ethically produced agricultural products. MST's deal with the French Casino Group establishes not only a relationship characterized by dependency. It will also shape the social, economic and ideological relations within the MST for years to come. MST farmers will increasingly see themselves as service providers that respond to market demands, rather than working towards the production of new socio-economic subjectivities. The increasingly regressive politics of the MST also becomes visible in the current political crisis involving the Workers Party leadership in Brazil. Being dependent on public subsidies, the MST has been a key organizer of recent demonstrations in support of the president, whose administration faces accusations of corruption. These demonstrations were coordinated in a meeting in São Paulo with former President Lula.[71]

Struggles for alternatives are hence embedded in a paradox between resistance and reinforcement. This also becomes visible in the local food case from the UK. In contrast to the cases from India and Brazil, the UK case is not about meeting the subsistence needs of smallhold farmers. Rather, local food projects in so-called developed countries are often seen as the preserve of the middle class.[72] Similarly, consumption of local food is seen less as a political statement and more as a luxury for middle class consumers.[73] It is precisely this demand by the well-off middle classes for 'organic' and 'local' food that might be dialectically related to the dynamics faced by smallhold farmers in Brazil, India and elsewhere. Arguably, though, the instances where consumers are drawn into production of organic local food rather than just demanding it, such as CSAs, move closer to articulating an alternative to the market than those small-scale farmers who remain wedded to it.

The local food case from the UK exhibits another aspect of reproduction that is also worth considering here. Many feminists have argued for some time that alternative market and non-market relations, such as household work, including food growing, preparation and cooking, have played a vital role in how workers are able to reproduce their labour power that is then harnessed by for-profit enterprises. Fraser has recently reiterated the point that capitalism's 'hidden abode' should not only be seen as economic category.[74] The secret of capitalism's 'success' does not only lie in the way production is structured. That is, according to Fraser, capitalism is not limited to the sphere of markets and economic relations but also depends upon non-marketized or alternative elements of life.[75]

Production is made possible by the processes that ensure social reproduction of the workforce; much of this activity – for example schooling and childcare – goes on outside of the market and does not take the form of waged labour although it is crucial to ensuring wage labour can take place and thereby enable accumulation for capitalism to function. The enthusiasm for 'grow your own' and local food in the UK might be interpreted as signs of resistance but they also provide space for people to renew their physical and mental capacities so they can re-enter the cycle of consumption they are seeking to escape.

We can see how the 'alternatives' introduced in this chapter can be seen as attempts to respond to capitalism and its contradictions. That is, to some extent at least, they all seek to address elements of crises in the social, natural and political conditions of existence, which have been continuously undermined by capital's own drive. In this sense, we could argue that by attempting to counteract its self-induced failings they only continue to prop it up. However, capitalism is a socio-economic framework riddled by contradiction and it would be unfair to dismiss alternatives offhand because they are simply not revolutionary enough.

They do, however, need to be scrutinized. The words of Mészáros serve as a clear reminder.[76] He says that 'capital [should] be overcome in its totality from its relations, or else its way of social metabolic reproduction, which dominates everything, won't be able to be moved even in relation to relatively less important matters'. In the same direction, recent history has shown that the working class made little progress towards building its class autonomy and independence, since, sometimes it remains vulnerable to state cooptation and/or sometimes it submits itself to the cumulative and expansionist imperatives of capital.[77] Similarly, Moore's analysis of the evolution of feudalism to capitalism highlights that transition of this scale is far from consonant, noting that although capitalism's ability to evolve through crises attests to its durability, this process also moves us closer towards a terminal crisis.[78]

To recognize these limits does not mean that we dismiss these productive and organizational practices as irrelevant. By means of these practices, social groups are reproducing themselves; they are creating less competitive human relations and living the possibilities of cooperation. However, to value the significance of these experiences for those involved cannot obscure the fact that they lack the potential to transform the existing political economy of food production altogether. The dialectic resides in the need to value these practices and, at the same time, to criticize their intrinsic limits.

NOTES

Introduction

1 OECD (1972) Recommendation of the council on guiding principles concerning international economic aspects of environmental policies. May. Council Document no. C(72)128. Paris: Organisation for Economic Co-operation and Development.
2 Grober, U. (2010) *Die Entdeckung der Nachhaltigkeit: Kulturgeschichte eines Begriffs*, Kunstmann, 261.
3 Lélé, S. (1991) 'Sustainable Development: A Critical Review', *World Development* 19(6): 607–621.
4 Bill Adams, quoted in Payne, A. and Phillips, N. (2010) *Development*, Polity, 133.
5 Rist, G. (2008) *The History of Development: From Western Origins to Global Faith*, 3rd edn, Zed, 182, 194.
6 Lynne Chester, reviewing *Sustainable Capitalism: A Matter of Common Sense* by John E. Ikerd, in *Review of Radical Economics*, 2011.
7 Kenis, A. and Lievens, M. (2015) *The Limits of the Green Economy: From re-inventing capitalism to re-politicising the present*, Routledge.
8 Peck, J., Theodore, N. and Brenner, N. (2010) 'Postneoliberalism and its Malcontents', *Antipode* 41(1).
9 At Rio+20, however, some Latin American countries resisted the green growth discourse, arguing that the 'commoditization' of the environment was not an acceptable alternative, and the green economy was not prioritized in the conclusions of the final regional document. Puppim de Oliveira, 2012.
10 John Crowley, personal communication.
11 See e.g. Stern, N. (2006) *The Economics of Climate Change*, Cambridge University Press.
12 Smith, A. (1993) [1776] *The Wealth of Nations*, Oxford University Press, 81.
13 Stiglitz, J.E., Sen, A. and Fitoussi, J.-P. Report by the Commission on the Measurement of Economic Performance and Social Progress, 2009, www.stiglitz-sen-fitoussi.fr/documents/rapport_anglais.pdf (accessed 6 April 2015).
14 Wilkinson, R. and Pickett, K. (2009) *The Spirit Level*, Allen Lane, 215.
15 Weil, D. (2009) *Economic Growth*, 2nd edn, Pearson, 491.
16 Panayotou, T. (1993) *Empirical Tests and Policy Analysis of Environmental Degradation at Different Stages of Economic Development*. Working Paper

WP238, Technology and Employment Programme, International Labour Office, Geneva. Beckerman, W. (1992) 'Economic growth and the environment: Whose growth? Whose environment?' *World Development* 20: 481–496.

17 Daly, quoted in Sunderlin, W. (2003) *Ideology, Social Theory and the Environment*, Rowman & Littlefield, 170.

18 Sunderlin, W. (2003) *Ideology, Social Theory and the Environment*, Rowman & Littlefield, 161.

19 Stern, *Climate Change*.

20 Dietz, T., Rosa, E.A. and York, R. (2012) 'Environmentally efficient well-being: Is there a Kuznets curve?' *Applied Geography* 32: 21–28.

21 Buttel, F.H. (2000) Ecological modernization as social theory. *Geoforum* 31: 57–65; Mol, A.P.J. and Spaargaren, G. (2000) 'Ecological modernization theory in debate: A review', *Environmental Politics* 9(1): 7–49.

22 York, R. and Rosa, E.A. (2003) 'Key challenges to ecological modernisation: Institutional efficacy, case study evidence, units of analysis, and the pace of eco-efficiency', *Organization & Environment* 16(3): 273–288.

23 Wiedmann, T.O., Schandl, H., Lenzen, M., Moran, D., Suh, S., West, J. and Kanemoto, K. (2013) The material footprint of nations. *Proceedings of the National Academy of Science* USA. Retrieved 4 October 2013 from doi: 10.1073/pnas.1220362110

24 Jevons, W. (1865) *The Coal Question: An Inquiry Concerning the Progress of the Nation, and the Probable Exhaustion of Our Coal-Mines*, www.eoearth.org/article/The_Coal_Question:_Of_our_Consumption_of_Coal.

25 By 'comparatively safe' we mean less likely to trigger 'nonlinear tipping elements'. See Klein, N. (2014) *This Changes Everything: Capitalism vs the Climate*, Simon & Schuster; Lynas, M. (2008) *Six Degrees: Our Future on a Hotter Planet*, Harper.

26 UN (2012) 'Green Growth', http://sustainabledevelopment.un.org/index.php?menu=1447.

27 Shin, Hyon-hee (2013) 'South Korea ditching "green growth"', *The Korea Herald* (online). Published on 30 March. 2013. www.asianewsnet.net/South-Korea-ditching-green-growth-44753.html (accessed on 27 August 2013).

28 Glemarec, Y. and Puppim de Oliveira, J. (2012) 'The role of the visible hand of public institutions in creating a sustainable future', *Public Administration and Development* 32(3).

29 www.climate-change-jobs.org/ http://climatejobs.org.za/.

30 UN ECLAC – United Nations Economic Commission for Latin America and the Caribbean (2011) Conclusions of the Latin American and Caribbean Regional Meeting Preparatory to the United Nations Conference on Sustainable Development (Santiago, 07–09 September, 2011). Downloaded from www.cepal.org/noticias/paginas/5/43755/RIO+20_working_draft_9_Sept_-_5.50_pm_limpio.pdf on 25 February 2015.

Chapter 1

1 Energy efficiency is to a large extent also a function of enhanced material and resource efficiency.

2 See UNEP (2011) *Towards a Green Economy: Pathways to Sustainable Development and Poverty Eradication.* Nairobi/Geneva, 2–3, and The Global Commission on the Economy and Climate (2014). *Better Growth, Better Climate: The New Climate Economy Report.* World Resources Institute. Washington, DC. Available at: http://newclimateeconomy.report/.

3 Conversely, The New Climate Economy Report simplistically supposes that 'structural and technological changes unfolding in the global economy, combined with multiple opportunities to improve economic efficiency, now make it possible to achieve both better growth and better climate outcomes' (Global Commission on the Economy and Climate, 15).

4 IPCC (2007a) Climate Change 2007: The Physical Science Basis. Cambridge University Press. Available at: www.ipcc.ch/publications_and_data/publications_ipcc_fourth_assessment_report_wg1_report_the_physical_science_basis.htm.

5 IPCC (2014) Climate Change 2013: The Physical Science Basis (Working Group 1). Summary for Policy Makers. Available at: www.climatechange2013.org/images/report/WG1AR5_SPM_FINAL.pdf.

6 IPCC (2007b) Climate Change 2007: Mitigation of Climate Change. Cambridge University Press. Available at: www.ipcc.ch/publications_and_data/publications_ipcc_fourth_assessment_report_wg3_report_mitigation_of_climate_change.htm.

7 PricewaterhouseCoopers (2013) Busting the carbon budget. Low Carbon Economy Index 2013. London. Available at: www.pwc.co.uk/sustainability-climate-change. PricewaterhouseCoopers (2014). 2 degrees of separation: ambition and reality. Low Carbon Economy Index 2014. London. Available at: www.pwc.co.uk/sustainability-climate-change.

8 The estimates for carbon intensity dynamics by PwC are very conservative and at the lower end of the scale, because PwC analysis only considers energy-related carbon emissions, not the majority of emissions from agriculture and additional emissions from reaching trigger points of climate change. See PricewaterhouseCoopers (2012). Too late for two degrees? Low Carbon Economy Index 2012. London: 12.

9 Ibid.

10 Ibid.

11 World Bank (2015) Decarbonizing Development: Three Steps to a Zero-Carbon Future. Study prepared by Fay, M., Hallegatte, S., Vogt-Schilb, A., Rozenberg, J., Narloch, U. and Kerr, T. Washington D.C. Available at: www.worldbank.org/content/dam/Worldbank/document/Climate/dd/decarbonizing-development-report.pdf.

12 OECD (2012) OECD Environmental Outlook to 2015. Paris. Available at: http://dx.doi.org/10.1787/9789264122246-en.

13 Pielke, R. (Jr) (2010) *The Climate Fix: What Scientists and Politicians Won't Tell You About Global Warming*, Basic Books, New York.

14 McKinsey Global Institute (2008) The carbon productivity challenge: Curbing climate change and sustaining economic growth. Available at: www.mckinsey.com/mgi/reports/pdfs/Carbon_Productivity/MGI_carbon_productivity_full_report.pdf.

15 Relative decoupling implies that the growth of GHG emissions is slower than GDP growth, which does not check GHG emission growth. The environmental

impact of relative decoupling can even be negative if the marginal ecological cost of scarce ecological resources outpaces the reduction in ecological input use per unit of GDP. (See Paech, N. (2012). Grünes Wachstum? Vom Fehlschlagen jeglicher Entkopplungsbemühungen: Ein Trauerspiel in mehreren Akten. In: Sauer T, Ökonomie der Nachhaltigkeit – Grundlagen, Indikatoren, Strategien. Metropolis Verlag, Munich.)

16 Since the 1970s, refrigerators and freezers in the United States, for instance, have increased in size by a third, while consuming two-thirds less energy at one-third the price. For more information: www.c2es.org/technology/fact sheet/ResidentialBuildingEnd-Use.

17 A significant reduction in energy and material intensity of modern lighting systems is linked to three recent developments: (i) the development of new energy-efficient lighting equipment; (ii) utilization of improved lighting design practice; and (iii) improvements in lighting control systems. Energy and material efficiency gains are estimated to be in the order of a factor of 4–8, caused by lower energy consumption and longer life time (http://energy.gov/energy saver/ articles/led-lighting).

18 For an overview of the picture in other sectors, such as the building sector, cargo transport and air traffic, see Exner, A., Lauk, C. and Kulterer, K. (2008) *Die Grenzen des Kapitalismus: Wie wir am Wachstum scheitern*. Vienna, 49–54.

19 Improvements in fuel efficiency have also been handicapped by increased purchases of so-called sport utility vehicles (SUVs), which are 10 to 50 per cent heavier than normal passenger vehicles and thus tend to have a higher fuel consumption (estimated at 25 per cent or more). The average weight of passenger cars has also increased in the last few decades. The weight of Volkswagen's popular Golf model, for instance, has virtually doubled since its launch in 1974. ADAC (2014) Motorwelt, No. 8. Available at: www.adac.de, 25.

20 European Environment Agency (2010) The European Environment State and Outlook 2010: Consumption and the Environment. Copenhagen. Available at: www.eea.europa.eu/soer/europe/consumption-and-environment.

21 According to Schmidt-Bleek, F. (2014) *Grüne Lügen* (Green Lies), Ludwig Publishers, Munich: 137 and 169, the ecological rucksack of IT equipment is generally ten times as high as for other products.

22 But even in this regard, there are exceptions. In German online commerce, for instance, recent analysis suggests that there are more parcels returned from customers to online traders after purchase than the mailing of parcels among private individuals in the country, causing additional transport and fuel consumption.

23 For more information, Alcott, B. (2012) 'Mill's scissors: structural change and the natural-resource inputs to labour', *Journal of Cleaner Production* 21, 83–92.

24 Just one illustration: to meet global electricity consumption by (solar) photovoltaic panels in 2030 would require a consumption of copper of 100–200 million tons; this compares to a recent global copper production level of about 15 million tons per annum. Similar scenarios apply to rare earths and some heavy metals. What is more, their production is highly environmentally and/or socially problematic (Exner *et al.*, *Die Grenzen*: 68, 69, 72). See Achzet, B., Zepf, V. and Reller, A. (2011) The role of raw materials in current and emerging energy tech-

nologies. Paper presented at the World Resources Forum 2011, Davos, 19–21 September. Available at: www.worldresourcesforum.org; Bleischwitz, R., Bahn-Walkowiak, B., Ekardt, F., Feldt, H. and Fuhr, L. (2012) International Resource Politics: New challenges demanding new governance approaches for a green economy. Discussion Paper on Ecology, No. 36, Heinrich Böll Fundation and Wuppertal Institute for Climate, Environment and Energy.

25 Estimates of land requirements for biofuels vary widely, but mainly depend on the type of feedstock, geographical location, and level of input and yield increase. The massive scale of land requirements for meeting biofuel blending targets, however, poses a serious competitive challenge for land for food-crop production. To replace 10 per cent of global transport fuel demand by first generation biofuels in 2030 would require the equivalent of no less than 8 to 36 per cent of current global cropland, including permanent cultures (UNEP (2009), *Towards Sustainable Production and Use of Resources: Assessing Biofuels*. Paris).

26 Hänggi, M. (2011) *Ausgepowert – Das Ende des Ölzeitalters als Chance* (out of power – the end of the oil age as an opportunity). Rotpunktverlag, Zurich.

27 Röpke, L. and Lippelt, J. (2011) *Kurz zum Klima: Sichere und umweltfreundliche Stromversorgung – ein Zielkonflikt?* (Climate in Brief: Secure and environmental friendly electricity supply – a conflict of goals?). Ifo Schnelldienst, 64(2): 32–34. Available at: www.cesifo-group.de.

28 Sarkar, S. (2009) *The Crises of Capitalism*, Cologne: 316–318, and Rundgren, G. (2012) *Garden Earth: From hunter and gatherer to capitalism and thereafter*. Regeneration, Uppsala, chapter 6.

29 Exner *et al.*, *Die Grenzen*: 60–79.

30 Hall, A.S., Balogh, S. and Murphy, D.J.R. (2009) 'What is the minimum Energy Return on Investment that a sustainable society must have?' *Energies*, 2. Available at: www.mdpi.com/journal/energies. See also Taminiau and Byrne, Chapter 11 of this volume.

31 MacKay, D.J.C. (2009) *Sustainable Energy – without the hot air*, Cambridge, United Kingdom. Available at: www.withouthotair.com.

32 For in-depth analysis, see Hoffmann, U. (2011) Some Reflections on Climate Change, Green Growth Illusions and Development Space. UNCTAD Discussion Paper, No. 205: 4–5.

33 Jevons, W.S. (1906 [1865]) *The Coal Question: An Inquiry Concerning the Progress of the Nation, and the Probable Exhaustion of Our Coal-Mines*, Macmillan, London.

34 Santarius, T. (2012) *Der Rebound-Effekt: Über die unerwünschten Folgen der erwünschten Energieeffizienz. Studie zur Impulse zur Wachstums Wende.* Wuppertal Institute on Climate, Environment and Energy. Wuppertal. Available at: www.santarius.de/wp-content/uploads/2012/03/Der-Rebound-Effekt-2012.pdf.

35 Rundgren, *Garden Earth*.

36 Foster, J.B., Clark, B. and York, R. (2010) 'Capitalism and the Curse of Energy Efficiency: The Return of the Jevons Paradox', *Monthly Review* 62, No. 06 (November). Available at: http://monthlyreview.org/2010/11/01/capitalism-and-the-curse-of-energy-efficiency.

37 Santarius, *Der Rebound-Effekt*.

38 On 24 September 2014, the day that followed the UN Climate Summit 2014, the European Parliament's environment committee voted in favour of giving away free carbon permit allowances, equivalent to 5 billion euro, to a select group of heavy industries in the EU, in an effort to discourage them from moving production abroad to countries with lower environmental standards. Carbon prices in the European Emissions Trading Scheme were above 30 euro/t in 2008, but dropped to a mere 7 euro/t in December 2014. While the European Commission plans to reform the current system, analysts predict that carbon prices will not rise to much more than 10 euro/t by 2020. ICTSD (2014). International Centre for Trade and Sustainable Development, *Bridges Weekly 18*(31) (25 September), Geneva: 13–14.
39 Pielke, *Climate Fix*.
40 Bleischwitz *et al.* International Resource Politics.
41 All too often the mistake is made of calculating ecological gains of new products only based on their ecological footprint during the lifetime of the concerned product, while ignoring the ecological rucksack caused by the material that is used in the production of the new good. As regards cars, lifetime fuel consumption and related carbon emissions account for only 20 per cent of the total ecological impact of a car (Schmidt-Bleek, *Grüne Lügen*, 81).
42 Aichele, R. and Felbermayr, G. (2011) 'Carbon footprints', *IFO Schnelldienst* 64(21): 11–16. Munich. Available at: www.cesifo-group.de.
43 As pointed out by Schmidt-Bleek, we are in the paradoxical situation that never in history have we practised so much environmental policy, yet the extent of environmental damage keeps rising (Schmidt-Bleek, *Grüne Lügen*: 38).
44 It is beyond the scope of the analysis in this chapter to elaborate on the key issues that delay and hamper progress in international climate change negotiations, particularly in the UNFCCC.
45 Cited in Kriener, M. (2011) Die Nackenschläge von Durban (the setbacks of Durban). *ZeO2*, 24 December. Available at: www.zeozwei.de.
46 The level of total public and private investment in EU countries has decreased every year since the 2008 crisis and in 2013 was 15 per cent below the investment volume of the pre-crisis level (*Die Zeit*, No. 31, 2014, 26).
47 Kallis, G. (2011) 'In Defence of Degrowth', *Ecological Economics* 70: 878. One should not overlook the conflicts and complexities in internalization of costs, especially for complicated systems, like agriculture. By way of illustration, one can reduce methane emissions by culling cows, but then biodiversity of many landscapes will be devastated.
48 Lockwood, M. (2011) The limits of environmentalism – Part 4. Available at: http://politicalclimate.net/2011/03/25/the-limits-to-environmentalism-4./.
49 Green, D. (2011) 'Can democracies kick the growth habit?' Power Blog of Oxfam International. Available at: www.oxfamblogs.org/fp2p/?p=2920.
50 Cf. Bluemling and Yun (Chapter 5 of this volume) and Mahnkopf (Chapter 6).
51 Tienhaara, K. (2009) A tale of two crises: What the global financial crisis means for the global environmental crisis. Global Governance Working Paper, No. 37. Amsterdam. Available at: www.glogov.org/images/doc/WP37.pdf.
52 Nair, C. (2011) *Consumptionomics. Asia's Role in Reshaping Capitalism and Saving the Planet*, Infinite Ideas Ltd, Oxford.

53 Randers, J. (2013) Presentation at the conference on Sustainability – Responsibility for a Finite World, Göttingen, Germany. 22 November. Reproduced in: *Blickpunkt Zukunft*, 34: 60. Available at: www.blickpunkt-zukunft.com.
54 For analysis, see Adler and Schachtschneider (2010), 67.
55 Jackson, *Prosperity*.
56 This would also encourage longevity of products, their re-use, repair and recycling.
57 For an elaborate analysis, see: Fatheuer, T, Fuhr, L, Unmüssig, B (2015). Kritik der Grünen Ökonomie, Oekom Verlag, Munich.
58 In a recent report ('Decarbonizing Development'), even the World Bank emphasizes that 'it is ... critical to use the savings or new proceeds generated by climate policies to compensate poor people, promote poverty reduction, and boost safety nets'.
59 Adler, F. and Schachtschneider, U. (2010) *Green New Deal, Suffizienz oder Ökosozialismus? Konzepte für gesellschaftliche Wege aus der Ökokrise*, Oekom Verlag, Munich.
60 Loske, R. (2011) *Abschied vom Wachstumszwang. Konturen einer Politik der Mäßigung*, Basilisken Presse, Rangsdorf, Germany. Some alternative indicators already exist, such as the Genuine Progress Indicator, the Happy Planet Index or the Index of Sustainable Economic Welfare. The latter, calculated for Germany for the period 1990 to 2009, for instance, showed an increase of 6 per cent, whereas conventional GDP increased by 11 per cent. See Hoffmann ('Some Reflections') and Pinzler, P. (2013) Gutes Leben, neu berechnen. *Die Zeit*, No. 4 (17 January), 23.
61 Nair, *Consumptionomics*.
62 There are already the contours of serious conflicts in the 'sharing economy'. Large internet platforms for taxi or hotel/guest room services, for instance, are increasingly dominant, and encourage expansion of the use of such services, leading to increased, rather than reduced, material and energy consumption. Furthermore, there is the risk that these internet platforms create precarious working or contractual conditions and challenge basic requirements of public safety. Cf. Loske, R. (2014) Aufwachen bitte. Überlasst die Sharing-Ökonomie nicht den Internetriesen. *Die Zeit*, No. 43 (16 October), 27.
63 The word 'catastrophe' is of Greek origin (*katastrophé*). It means 'a drastic turnaround'. In other words, a catastrophic situation might also offer opportunities for change.
64 Randers, J. (2012) 2052: A Global Forecast for the Next 40 Years. June. Available at: www.2052.info.
65 This, however, also implies that most developing countries may have little prospect for developmental catch-up with the North and that poverty levels largely remain unchanged.
66 The downside of lower economic growth under the Randers scenario is that there will only be some 5 billion middle class people in the world by 2050; the rest of the population would be poor, i.e. there would be more poverty than there would otherwise have been.
67 See Schramm, S. (2014) Unser umtriebiges Element. *Die Zeit*, No. 40, 37–38.

Chapter 2

1 European landmarks of this literature include Clare, J. (1997) *John Clare: Everyman's Poetry*, J.M. Dent; Thompson, E.P. (1967) 'Time, Work-Discipline and Industrial Capitalism', *Past and Present XXXVIII*: 56–97 and (1980) *The Making of the English Working Class*, Penguin; and Polanyi, K. (2001) *The Great Transformation: The Political and Economic Origins of Our Time*, Beacon Press. Two recent Latin American explorations are Boelens, Rutgerd, Jaime Hoogesteger and Jean Rodriguez de Francisco (2014) 'Commoditizing Water Territories: The Clash between Andean Water Rights Cultures and Payment for Ecosystem Services', *Capitalism Nature Socialism XXV*(3): 84–102 and Grandia, L. (2012) *Enclosed: Conservation, Cattle and Commerce among the Q'eqchi Maya Lowlanders*, University of Washington Press.

2 Marx, K. (1990) *Capital*, Vol. I, trans. Ben Fowkes, Penguin, 638.

3 Moore, J.W. (2014) 'The Capitalocene, Part II: Abstract Social Nature and the Limits to Capital', available at www.jasonwmoore.com/Essays.html, 36.

4 Henderson, G. (2004) '"Free" Food, the Local Production of Worth, and the Circuit of Decommodification: A Value Theory of the Surplus', *Environment and Planning D: Society and Space XXII*(4): 507.

5 See also Fraser, N. (2014) 'Behind Marx's Hidden Abode: For an Expanded Conception of Capitalism', *New Left Review LVI*: 55–72.

6 Moore, J.W. (2014) 'Cheap Food and Bad Climate: From Surplus Value to Negative-Value in the Capitalist World-Ecology', available at www.jasonwmoore.com/Essays.html, 20.

7 Moore, J.W. (2014) 'The Capitalocene, Part II: Abstract Social Nature and the Limits to Capital', available at www.jasonwmoore.com/Essays.html, 7.

8 Moore, J.W. (2011) 'Wall Street is a Way of Organizing Nature: An Interview with Jason Moore', *Upping the Anti: A Journal of Theory and Action XII*: 46.

9 McMichael, P. (2009) 'A Food Regime Genealogy', *Journal of Peasant Studies XXXVI*(1): 139–169. As Nancy Fraser notes, the 'co-construction of "care" as a noncommodity' has long been another accompaniment of the co-construction of labour power as a commodity: Fraser, 'Hidden Abodes', 9.

10 E.g., Pyne, S.J. (2000) *Vestal Fire: An Environmental History, Told Through Fire, of Europe and Europe's Encounter with the World*, University of Washington Press.

11 Scott, J.C. (2012) *Two Cheers for Anarchism: Six Easy Pieces on Autonomy, Dignity, and Meaningful Work and Play*, Princeton University Press, 48.

12 Anderson, B. (1998) *The Spectre of Comparisons: Nationalism, Southeast Asia, and the World*, Verso. 'Forest cleansing' continues today in many nonofficial or semi-official guises as well. See Lohmann, L. (1999) 'Forest Cleansing: Racial Oppression in Scientific Nature Conservation', The Corner House.

13 Crosby, A.W. (1997) *The Measure of Reality: Quantification in Western Europe, 1250–1600*, Cambridge University Press; Edgerton, S.Y. (1976) *The Renaissance Rediscovery of Linear Perspective*, Basic Books; Latour, B. (1986) 'Visualization and Cognition: Thinking with Eyes and Hands', in H. Kuklick (ed.) *Knowledge and Society: Studies in the Sociology of Culture Past and Present*, JAI Press, 1–40.

14 Biggs, M. (1999) 'Putting the State on the Map: Cartography, Territory, and

European State Formation', *Comparative Studies in Society and History XLI*(2): 377.

15 Green, L. (2013) 'The Day-World *Hawkri* and Its Topologies: On Palikur Alternatives to the Idea of Space', in Green, Lesley (ed.) *Contested Ecologies: Dialogues in the South on Nature and Knowledge*, Human Sciences Research Council Press, 78.

16 Blomley, N. (2007) 'Making Private Property: Enclosure, Common Right and the Work of Hedges', *Rural History XVIII*(1): 1–21.

17 McRae, A. (1996) '"To Know One's Own": The Discourse of the Estate Surveyor', in *God Speed the Plough: The Representation of Agrarian England, 1500–1660*, Cambridge University Press, 169–197.

18 Smith, N. (2010) *Uneven Development: Nature, Capital and the Production of Space*, Verso, 123. See also Anderson, B. (1983) *Imagined Communities: Reflections on the Origins and Spread of Nationalism*, Verso, 170–171.

19 Latour, 'Visualization and Cognition'; Eisenstein, E. (1979) *The Printing Press as an Agent of Change*, Cambridge University Press.

20 Green, 'The Day-World *Hawkri*'.

21 Gurevich, A.J. (1976) 'Time as a Problem of Cultural History', in Gardet, L. (ed.) *Cultures and Time*, UNESCO Press, 241.

22 Szamosi, G. (1986) *The Twin Dimensions: Inventing Time and Space*, McGraw Hill, 100–111.

23 Bastian, M. (2012) 'Fatally Confused: Telling the Time in the Midst of Ecological Crises', *Environmental Philosophy IX*(1): 23–48; Crosby, *Measure of Reality;* Glennie, P. and Thrift, N. (2009) *Shaping the Day: A History of Timekeeping in England and Wales 1300–1800*, Oxford University Press; Zerubavel, E. (1982) 'The Standardization of Time: A Sociohistorical Perspective', *American Journal of Sociology LXXXVIII*(1): 1–23; Schivelbusch, W. (2004) *The Railway Journey: The Industrialization of Time and Space in the Nineteenth Century*, University of California Press.

24 The Corner House (2014) *Energy, Work and Finance*, The Corner House; Smith, Crosbie and M. Norton Wise (1989) *Energy and Empire: A Biographical Study of Lord Kelvin*, Cambridge University Press.

25 Bryan, D. and Rafferty, M. (2014) 'Financial Derivatives as Social Policy beyond Crisis', *Sociology 48*(5): 887–903.

26 Sack, R.D. (1986) *Human Territoriality: Its Theory and History*, Cambridge University Press, 78. This struggle has never been completed, for example in Brazil, where constitutional requirements that land have a social function are used by the Movimento dos Trabalhadores Rurais Sem Terra to justify land occupations involving hundreds of thousands of families. Thanks for this reminder to Winnie Overbeek.

27 Prudham, S. (2008) 'The Fictions of Autonomous Invention: Accumulation by Dispossession, Commodification and Life Patents in Canada' in Mansfield, B. (ed.) *Privatization: Property and the Remaking of Nature-Society Relations*, Blackwell, 26.

28 Huxley, A. (1936) 'Time and the Machine', in *The Olive Tree*, Chatto and Windus, 122.

29 Illich, I. (2006) 'The Social Construction of Energy', *New Geographies II*: 11–19; Robert, J. (2006) 'Alternatives and the Technogenic Production of Scarcity', *New Geographies II*: 134–138.

30 Altvater, E. and Geiger, M. (2013) 'Exiting the Multiple Crises through Green Growth?' in Exner, A., Fleissner, P., Kranzl, L. and Zittel, W. (eds) *Land and Resource Scarcity: Capitalism, Struggle and Well-Being in a World without Fossil Fuels*, Routledge, 17.
31 Galison, P. (2003) *Einstein's Clocks, Poincare's Maps*, Sceptre.
32 Wainwright, J. and Barnes, T. (2009) 'Nature, Economy, and the Space–Place Distinction', *Environment and Planning D: Society and Space XXVII*, 966–986.
33 Equivalence among human beings, nicely writes David Graeber, 'only seems to occur when people have been forcibly severed from their contexts, so much so that they can be treated as identical to something else ... Any system that reduces the world to numbers can only be held in place by weapons' (Graeber, D. [2010] *Debt: The First 5000 Years*, Melville, 386).
34 'Calling it quits' is of course a capitalist idealization. Wage disputes are never just about numbers but also encompass complex and multiple resistances to this type of formatting (Mann, G. [2007] *Our Daily Bread: Wages, Workers and the Political Economy of the American West*, University of North Carolina Press). This is even more obvious with fines handed down in tort cases (O'Neill, John [forthcoming] 'The Price of an Apology: Justice, Compensation and Rectification', *Cambridge Journal of Economics*). Substantive statements of equivalence in economics and law tend to be performative utterances.
35 Quine, W. v. O. (1960) *Word and Object*, MIT Press.
36 Viveiros de Castro, E. (2004) 'Perspectival Anthropology and the Method of Controlled Equivocation', *Tipití II*(1): 3–22.
37 Donald Davidson has noted how the workability of different 'manuals' of linguistic equivalences assigning different distributions of 'meaning' and 'belief' to a subject ultimately throws the whole scheme/content dualism into doubt: 'there is no such thing as a language, not if a language is anything like what many philosophers and linguists have supposed' (Davidson, D. [2005] *Language, Truth and History*, Oxford University Press. 107). See also Davidson, D. (1991) *Inquiries into Truth and Interpretation*, Oxford University Press and Verran, H., 'Engagements between Disparate Knowledge Traditions: Toward Doing Difference Generatively and in Good Faith' in Green, Lesley (ed.) *Contested Ecologies: Dialogues in the South on Nature and Knowledge*, Human Sciences Research Council Press, 154–155.
38 Wainwright and Barnes, 'Nature, Economy', 977.
39 Quoted in McRae, 'To Know One's Own', 182.
40 Lohmann, L. (2015) 'What is Nature? Does Nature Have Rights?', The Corner House.
41 McNally, D. (2003) 'Beyond The False Infinity of Capital: Dialectics and Self-Mediation in Marx's Theory of Freedom', in Albritton, R. and Simoulidis, J. (eds) *New Dialectics and Political Economy*, Palgrave Macmillan, 12.
42 Marx, *Capital*, 526. As George Caffentzis stresses, there can be no capitalist value without the possibility of worker refusal (Caffentzis, G. (2013) *In Letters of Blood and Fire*, PM Press).
43 McNally, 'False Infinity', 12.

44 Ingold, T. (2000) 'To Journey along a Way of Life: Maps, Wayfinding and Navigation', in Ingold, T., *The Perception of the Environment: Essays on Livelihood, Dwelling and Skill*, Routledge, 219–42.

45 Burawoy, P. (1980) *Manufacturing Consent: Changes in the Labour Process Under Monopoly Capitalism*, University of Chicago Press; Willis, P. (1977) *Learning To Labour*, Ashgate; Spittler, G. (2009) 'Contesting the Great Transformation: Work in Comparative Perspective', in Hann, C. and Hart, K. (eds) *Market and Society: The Great Transformation Today*, Cambridge University Press, 160–174; Zizek, S. (1997) *The Plague of Fantasies*, Verso.

46 Haug, E.G. and Taleb, N.N. (2010) 'Option Traders use (Very) Sophisticated Heuristics, Never the Black–Scholes–Merton formula', available at http://ssrn.com/abstract=1012075.

47 McCloskey, D.N. (1998) *The Rhetoric of Economics*, University of Wisconsin Press, 95–97.

48 Anker, P. (2001) *Imperial Ecology: Environmental Order in the British Empire, 1895–1945*, Harvard University Press; Gane, N. (2006) 'When We Have Never Been Human, What Is to Be Done?: Interview with Donna Haraway', *Theory, Culture and Society XXIII*(7–8): 135–158; Lohmann, L., 'Neoliberalism's Climate', forthcoming in Springer, Simon, Kean Birch and Julie MacLeavy (eds) *Handbook of Neoliberalism*, Routledge.

49 Büscher, B. (2014) 'Nature on the Move I: The Value and Circulation of Liquid Nature and the Emergence of Fictitious Conservation', in Büscher, B., Dressler, W. and Fletcher, R. (eds) *NatureTM Inc.: Environmental Conservation in the Neoliberal Age*, University of Arizona Press, 183–204.

50 In *de re* valuation, what is valued is a particular thing; in *de dicto* valuation, what is valued is whatever falls under a description. Thanks to John O'Neill for pointing out the applicability of this distinction to the trade in ecosystem services.

51 Tucker, G., Allen, B., Conway, M. *et al.* (2013) 'Policy Options for an EU No Net Loss Initiative: Report to the European Commission', Institute for European Environmental Policy; Business and Biodiversity Offsets Programme (2014) 'To No Net Loss of Biodiversity and Beyond: A Summary of Discussions at the Conference, 3–4 June', BBOP.

52 See, e.g., www.geoengineeringmonitor.org/2015/06/net-zero-is-not-zero-the-g7s-dystopian- decarbonization/.

53 Helm, D. (2014) 'Taking Natural Capital Seriously', *Oxford Review of Economic Policy XXX*(1): 109–125.

54 Robertson, M.M. (2007) 'Discovering Price in All the Wrong Places: The Work of Commodity Definition and Price under Neoliberal Environmental Policy', *Antipode XXXIX*(3): 507.

55 The useful phrase 'hybrid labour' is due to Alyssa Battistoni.

56 MacKenzie, D. (2009) 'Making Things the Same: Gases, Emissions Rights and the Politics of Carbon Markets', *Accounting, Organizations and Society XXXIV*(3–4): 440–455.

57 Ross, T. (2014) 'Owen Paterson Alarms Campaigners with Plan to Build on Ancient Woods', *Daily Telegraph*, 5 January.

58 Arrighi, G. (2009) *The Long Twentieth Century: Money, Power and the Origins of Our Time*, Verso.

59 Lane, R. (2014) 'Resources for the Future, Resources for Growth: The Making of the 1975 Growth Ban' in Stephen, B. and Lane, R. (eds), *The Politics of Carbon Markets*, Routledge, 27–50.
60 Anker, *Imperial Ecology*.
61 As Bruno Latour writes, capitalism 'is not to be used to explain the evolution of science and technology': efforts to 'describe the scientist as a capitalist' take for granted an untenable 'division between mental and material factors' ('Visualization', 31–32). Capital has 'no singular logic, no essence', Timothy Mitchell observes. 'It survives parasitically ... taking up residence in human bodies and minds, or in sugar cane or private property, drawing its energies from the chemistry of others, its forces from other fields, its momentum from others' desires' (Mitchell, T. [2002] *Rule of Experts: Egypt, Techno-Politics, Modernity*, University of California Press. 303). As Geoffrey Bowker stresses, commodification, representation, organization, infrastructure and nature have to be looked at together.
62 Aries Consortium (2009) 'The ARIES Project: Artificial Intelligence for Ecosystem Services', quoted in Sullivan, Sian (2010) '"Ecosystem Service Commodities" – A New Imperial Ecology? Implications for Animist Immanent Ecologies, with Deleuze and Guattari', *New Formations: A Journal of Culture/Theory/Politics LXIX*, 120).
63 Bowker, G. (2005) *Memory Practices in the Sciences*, MIT Press, 205.
64 Kob, J. (2015) 'Getting the Trembling Mountain to the Market: A History of Catastrophe Modelling and the Emergence of a New Disaster Risk Market', paper presented at the Financialization of Nature Conference, University of Sussex, 19–20 March.
65 Economist advocates of cap and trade systems tend to criticize grandfathering as an inefficient anomaly, usually insisting that emissions allowances should be auctioned instead and the rents shunted to the auctioneer (usually the state). It is significant that this theoretical insistence has never had much of an impact on practice.
66 Quoted in Nicholls, M. (2011) 'EcoSecurities Co-Founder Launches Brazilian Environmental Exchange', *Environmental Finance*, 20 December.
67 Huws, U. (2011) 'Crisis as Capitalist Opportunity: The New Accumulation through Public Service Commodification', *Socialist Register* 2012: 64–84.
68 The phrase is due to the Centre for Research on Socio-Cultural Change.
69 See, e.g., McCarthy, J. (2007) 'Privatizing Conditions of Production: Trade Agreements as Neoliberal Environmental Governance', in Heynen, N., McCarthy, J., Prudham, S. and Robbins, P. (eds), *Neoliberal Environments: False Promises and Unnatural Consequences*, Routledge.
70 Kay, K. (2015) 'A Hostile Takeover of Nature? Placing Value in Conservation Finance', paper presented at the Financialization of Nature Conference, University of Sussex, 19–20 March.
71 Dempsey, J., personal communication.
72 Robertson, 'Discovering Price'.
73 Henderson, '"Free" Food', 507. See also Boelens *et al.*, 'Commoditizing Water Territories'.
74 Confédération Paysanne [Via Campesina France] (2014) 'Statement against Climate-Smart Agriculture', 18 September.

75 It may at first seem counterintuitive that a forest-that-supposedly-would-otherwise-be-destroyed is materially distinguishable from a forest commons in the same place and containing the same nonhuman biota. Diachronically, however, the two feature different sets of relationships between those biota and the humans associated with them; and those relationships will eventually result in different biota as well.

76 Fairhead, J., Leach, M. and Scoones, I. (2012) 'Green Grabbing: A New Appropriation of Nature?', *Journal of Peasant Studies XXXIX*(2), 237–261; Oakland Institute (2014) *The Darker Side of Green: Plantation Forestry and Carbon Violence in Uganda*, Oakland Institute.

77 Lohmann, L. (2009) 'Toward a Different Debate in Environmental Accounting: The Cases of Carbon and Cost–Benefit', *Accounting, Organizations and Society XXXIV*, 499–534 and Lohmann (2012) 'The Endless Algebra of Climate Markets', *Capitalism Nature Socialism XXII*(4): 93–116.

78 Holm, P. (2007) 'Which Way is up on Callon?', in MacKenzie, D., Muniesa, F. and Siu, L. (eds) *Do Economists Make Markets? On the Performativity of Economics*, Princeton University Press, 239.

79 Amann, M. and Wagner, F. (2014) 'A Flexibility Mechanism for Complying with National Emission Ceilings for Air Pollutants', Specific Contract No. 070307/2013/666175/FRA/ENV.C.3 implementing Framework contract No ENV.C.3/FRA/2013/0013-IIASA of DG-Environment of the European Commission, International Institute for Applied Systems Analysis.

80 Robertson, M.M. (2012) 'Measurement and Alienation: Making a World of Ecosystem Services', *Transactions of the Institute of British Geographers XXXVII*, 394.

81 Ibid.

82 Fraser, 'Hidden Abode', 57.

83 Thanks for very helpful discussion and comments to Gareth Dale, Jutta Kill, Winnie Overbeek, Jessica Dempsey, Nick Hildyard, Morgan Robertson, Romain Felli, Sarah Bracking, Manu Mathai and Jose Puppim de Oliveira.

Chapter 3

1 Foucault, M. (1993) 'About the beginning of the hermeneutics of the self', *Political Theory* 21(2): 204.

2 Myung-bak, L. (2008) 'A great people with new dreams', *Korean Presidential Speech*, August 15. Retrieved 8 June 2014 from www.korea.net/Government/Briefing-Room/Presidential-Speeches/view?articleId=91000&pageIndex=9.

3 Hansen, J. (2011) *Storms of My Grandchildren: The truth about the coming climate catastrophe and the chance to save humanity*, New York, Bloomsbury; Stern, N. (2006) *The Stern Review of the Economics of Climate Change*, Cambridge, Cambridge University Press; Bloomberg, M., Paulson, H. and Steyer, T. (co-chairs) (2014) *Risky Business: The economic risks of climate change in the United States*. Retrieved 28 June 2014 from http://riskybusiness.org/uploads/files/RiskyBusiness_PrintedReport_FINAL_WEB_OPTIMIZED.pdf.

4 Clark, L.P., Millet, D.B. and Marshall, J.D. (2014) 'National patterns in environmental injustice and inequality: outdoor NO2 air pollution in the United States', *PLOS One* 9(4) (April e94431): 1–8; Pacheco, T. (2008) 'Inequality,

environmental injustice, and racism in Brazil: beyond the question of color', *Development in Practice* 18(6) (November): 713–725.

5 Bullard, R.D. editor (2003) *Just Sustainabilities: Development in an Unequal World*, Cambridge, MIT Press; Bullard, R.D. (2005) *The Quest for Environmental Justice: Human Rights and the Politics of Pollution*, San Francisco, Sierra Club Books; United States Environmental Protection Agency (2014) 'Environmental justice program and civil rights'. Retrieved 10 October 2014 from www.epa.gov/region1/ej/.

6 Piketty, T. (2014) *Capital in the Twenty-First Century*, Cambridge, Belknap at Harvard University Press.

7 Organisation for Economic Co-operation and Development (OECD) (2011) *Towards Green Growth*, 13. Retrieved 10 May 2014 from www.oecd.org/dataoecd/37/34/48224539.pdf; see also World Bank (2012), *Inclusive Green Growth: A Pathway to Sustainable Development*. World Bank. Retrieved 10 May 2014 from http://issuu.com/world.bank.publications/docs/9780821395516.

8 Economic and Social Commission for Asia and the Pacific (ESCAP), Asian Development Bank (ADB), and United Nations Environment Program (UNEP) (2012) *Green Growth, Resources and Resilience: Environmental Sustainability in Asia and the Pacific*. United Nations and Asian Development Bank Publication, Bangkok. Retrieved 6 June 2014 from www.adb.org/sites/default/files/green-growth-resources-resilience.pdf; World Bank (2012), *Inclusive Green Growth: A Pathway to Sustainable Development*. World Bank. Retrieved 10 May 2014 from http://issuu.com/world.bank.publications/docs/9780821395516.

9 Stern, *Stern Review*; World Bank, *Inclusive*.

10 Economic and Social Commission for Asia and the Pacific (ESCAP), Asian Development Bank (ADB), and United Nations Environment Program (UNEP) (2012). *Green Growth, Resources and Resilience: Environmental Sustainability in Asia and the Pacific*. United Nations and Asian Development Bank Publication, Bangkok: iii. Retrieved 6 June 2014 from www.adb.org/sites/default/files/green-growth-resources-resilience.pdf.

11 ESCAP/ADB/UNEP, *Green Growth*.

12 World Bank, *Inclusive*.

13 ESCAP/ADB/UNEP, *Green Growth*.

14 ESCAP/ADB/UNEP, *Green Growth*.

15 Foster, J.B., Clark, B. and York, R. (2010) *The Ecological Rift: Capitalism's War on the Earth*, New York, Monthly Review Press; O'Connor, J. (1998) *Natural Causes: Essays in Ecological Maxism*, London, Guilford Press, 234–251; Parr, A. (2013) *The Wrath of Capital: Neoliberalism and Climate Change Politics*, New York, Columbia University Press, 19–21.

16 Piketty, *Capital*, 25.

17 Piketty, *Capital*, 25.

18 Piketty, *Capital*, 23.

19 Piketty, *Capital*, 26.

20 Piketty, *Capital*, 25.

21 Piketty, *Capital*, 1.

22 Harvey, D. (2005) *A Brief History of Neoliberalism*, Oxford, Oxford University Press, 187.
23 Klein, N. (2007) *The Shock Doctrine: Disaster Capitalism*, New York, Picador.
24 Peck, J. (2010) *Constructions of Neoliberal Reason*, Oxford, Oxford University Press, 28; Mirowski, P. (2014) *Never Let a Serious Crisis Go to Waste*, London, Verso, xi.
25 Harvey, *Neoliberalism*, 183.
26 Mirowski, *Serious Crisis*, xiv.
27 Open Secrets (2014) 'Lobbying Database'. Center for Responsive Politics. Retrieved 1 June 2014 from www.opensecrets.org/lobby/.
28 Wolf, M., Haar, K. and Hoedeman, O. (2014) *The First Power of the Financial Lobby: A survey of the size of the financial lobby at the EU level*. April. Corporate Europe Observatory, The Austrian Federal Chamber of Labour, and the Austrian Trade Union Federation, 15. Retrieved 6 June 2014 from http://corporateeurope.org/sites/default/files/attachments/financial_lobby_report.pdf.
29 Grice, A. (2013) 'Energy rip-off: 'Big Six' firms too close to ministers, says Ed Miliband'. *The Guardian*. Monday 7 October. Retrieved 22 June 2014 from www.independent.co.uk/news/uk/politics/energy-ripoff-big-six-firms-too-close-to-ministers-says-ed-miliband-8862740.html.
30 Notice of Arbitration (2013) Lone Pine Resources Inc. versus the Government of Canada, September 6. Retrieved 1 June 2014 from www.international.gc.ca/trade-agreements-accords-commerciaux/assets/pdfs/disp-diff/lone-02.pdf.
31 Bluemling and Yun, Chapter 5 of this volume.
32 Cited in Jeong-su, Kim (2013) 'The environmental fallout of the Four Major Rivers project', *The Hankyoreh*, August 13. Retrieved 8 June 2104 from www.hani.co.kr/arti/english_edition/e_national/598190.html.
33 Mirowski, *Serious Crisis*, 192
34 Myung-bak, 'great people'; Myung-bak in Snyder, Scott (2012) 'Assessing the Global Green Growth Institute (GGGI) and the Sustainability of South Korea's Contribution', *Council on Foreign Relations*, 6 November. Retrieved 1 December 2014 from http://blogs.cfr.org/asia/2012/11/06/assessing-the-global-green-growth-institute-gggi-and-the-sustainability-of-south-koreas-contribution/.
35 World Bank, *Inclusive*.
36 Foucault, M. (1991) 'Questions of method'. *The Foucault Effect: Studies in Governmentality*. Edited by Graham Burchell, Colin Gordon and Peter Miller. Chicago, University of Chicago Press, 79.
37 Foucault, M. (1982) 'The Subject and Power', *Critical Inquiry* 8(4) (Summer): 790.
38 Foucault, M. (2010 [1979]) *The Birth of Biopolitics: Lectures at the College de France 1978–79*, trans. Graham Burchell (New York: Palgrave Macmillan), 186.
39 Meadway, J., Chapter 4 of this volume.
40 Hayek, F. (1944) *The Road to Serfdom*, Chicago, Chicago University Press, 27.
41 Mirowski, *Serious Crisis*, 8–9.

42 ESCAP/ADB/UNEP, *Green Growth.*
43 ESCAP/ADB/UNEP, *Green Growth.*
44 Evans, B. and Reid, J. (2014) *Resilient Life: The Art of Living Dangerously*, Cambridge: Polity.
45 Evans and Reid (2014) *Resilient Life*, 1.
46 Hallegatte, S., Heal, G., Fay, M. and Treguer, D. (2011) 'From Growth to Green Growth: A Framework', *Policy Research Working Paper*. WPS5872. The World Bank Sustainable Development Network. Office of the Chief Economist. November: 2.
47 Hallegatte *et al.*, 'Growth to Green Growth'.

Chapter 4

1 Jackson, T. (2009) *Prosperity without Growth*, London: Sustainable Development Commission.
2 Jackson, *Prosperity*, 49.
3 Jackson, *Prosperity*, 54.
4 Coote, A., Franklin, J. and Simms, A. (2010) *21 Hours*, London: New Economics Foundation.
5 Schumacher, E.F. (1973) *Small Is Beautiful*, London: Blond and Briggs.
6 Latouche, S. (2009) *Farewell to Growth*, Cambridge: Polity Press.
7 Martinez-Alier, J. (2009) 'Socially sustainable economic de-growth', *Development and Change* 40(6): 1099–1119; Schneider, F., Kallis, G. and Martinez-Alier, J. (2010) 'Crisis or opportunity? Economic degrowth for social equity and ecological sustainability', *Journal of Cleaner Production* No. 18; and Joan Martinez-Alier et al. in this volume (Chapter 9).
8 Mill, J.S. (1848) *Principles of Political Economy with Some of their Applications to Social Philosophy*, London, 514–515.
9 Mill, *Principles*, 483.
10 Edge, R.M. and Gurkaynak, R.S. (2011) 'How useful are estimated DSGE forecasts?', Finance and Economics Discussion Series, Washington, D.C.: Federal Reserve Board, 17.
11 Samuelson, P.A. (1966) 'A summing up', *Quarterly Journal of Economics 80*(4).
12 Galbraith, J. (2014) 'A *Kapital* for the twenty-first century?', *Dissent*, Spring 2014.
13 Stiglitz, J.E., Sen, A. and Fitoussi, J.-P. (2009), *Report by the Commission on the Measurement of Economic and Social Progress*, Paris.
14 Bellamy Foster, J., Clark, B. and York, R. (2009) 'The Midas Effect: a critique of climate change economics', *Development and Change* 40(6).
15 Ehrlich, P.R. and Holdren, J.P. (1971) 'Impact of Population Growth', *Science 171*(3977): 1212–1217.
16 Rezai, A., Taylor, L. and Mechler, R. (2013) 'Ecological macroeconomics: an application to climate change', *Ecological Economics 85*: 69–76.
17 Graziani, A. (1979) 'L'analisi marxista e la struttura del capitalismo contemporaneo', *Storia del marxismo. IV: Il marxismo oggi*. Turin: Einaudi. Quoted in Bellofiore, Ricardo (2010), 'Marx and Sraffa: a reopening of the debate', working paper, Dipartimento di Scienze Economiche 'Hyman P. Minsky' Università di Bergamo.

18 Waring, M. (1988) *If Women Counted: a new feminist economics*, San Francisco: Harper and Row.
19 Ricardo, D. (1821) *On the Principles of Political Economy and Taxation*, London, 15.
20 Marx, K. (1970) *Marx/Engels Selected Works*, Vol 3, Moscow: Progress Publishers, 13.
21 Kalecki, M. (1943) 'Political aspects of full employment', *Political Quarterly* 14:4.
22 Böhm-Bawerk, Eugen von (1949) *Karl Marx and the Close of His System*, New York: Augustus M. Kelley.
23 Sraffa, P. (1960) *Production of Commodities by Means of Commodities: prelude to a critique of political economy*, Bombay: Vora & Co.
24 For a representative selection, see Teulings, Coen and Richard Baldwin, eds (2014) *Secular Stagnation: facts, causes, and cures*, London: Centre for Economic Policy Research.
25 Mill, *Principles*, 302–3.
26 Mill, *Principles*, 305.
27 Kovel, J. (2011) 'Five Theses on Ecosocialism', thesis 3, http://ecosocialisthorizons.com/2011/11/five-theses-on-ecosocialism/.

Chapter 5

1 ADBInstitute (2013) *Low-Carbon Green Growth in Asia – Policies and Practices*, Asian Development Bank.
2 For an overview of definitions, see: Allen, C. and Clouth, S. (2012) *A Guidebook to the Green Economy*, Issue 1, UNDESA (United Nations Division for Sustainable Development), August 2012, www.uncsd2012.org/content/documents/528Green%20Economy%20Guidebook_100912_FINAL.pdf, retrieved 26 July 2013, 63f.
3 ADBInstitute, *Low-Carbon Green Growth*; Hallegatte, S., Heal, G., Fay, M. and Treguer, D. (2011) *From Growth to Green Growth*. The World Bank, Policy Research Working Paper no. 5872; RoK (Republic of Korea) (2010) *Framework Act on Low Carbon, Green Growth*. Ministry of Government Legislation; UNESCAP (United Nations Economic and Social Commission for Asia and the Pacific) (2010) *Preview – Green Growth, Resources and Resilience. Environmental sustainability in Asia and the Pacific*. United Nations Publication. www.unescap.org/esd/environment/flagpubs/ggrap/documents/Green%20Growth-16Sept%20%28Final%29.pdf, viewed 29 July 2013; G8 (2009) *G8 Leaders Declaration: Responsible Leadership for a Sustainable Future*. www.g8.utoronto.ca/summit/2009laquila/, retrieved 8 August 2013.
4 ADBInstitute, *Low-Carbon Green Growth in Asia*; OECD (2011) *Towards Green Growth: Monitoring Progress – OECD Indicators*. www.oecd.org/greengrowth, retrieved 20 August 2013; UNESCAP, *Preview – Green Growth, Resources and Resilience*.
5 OECD, *Towards Green Growth*; RoK, *Framework Act*; Ianchovichina, E. and Lundstrom, S. (2009) *Inclusive Growth Analytics – Framework and Application*. Policy Research Working Paper 4851. World Bank, Economic Policy Division, Economic Policy and Debt Department; G8, G8 Leaders Declaration; Lee, M.-B. (2008) 'A great people with new dreams'. Presidential Speech

by Lee Myung-bak on the 63rd anniversary of national liberation and the 60th anniversary of the founding of the Republic of Korea. www.korea.net/Government/Briefing-Room/Presidential-Speeches/view?articleId=91000, viewed 8 August 2013.

6 See e.g.: Hallegatte *et al.*, *From Growth to Green Growth* and UNESCAP, *Preview – Green Growth*.

7 OECD, *Towards Green Growth*, 5.

8 Van den Bergh, J.C.J.M. (2011) 'Environment versus growth – a criticism of "degrowth" and a plea for "a-growth"', *Ecological Economics* 70(5): 881–890; and Birgit Mahnkopf in this volume (Chapter 6).

9 See also Ricardo Abramovay in this volume (Chapter 7).

10 See: Rist, G. (2006) *The History of Development – from Western Origins to Global Faith*, Zed Books, 2nd edition.

11 Blaxekjaer, L. (2012) 'The Emergence and Spreading of the Green Growth Policy Concept', paper prepared for the Earth System Governance Conference, Lund University, 18–20 April 2012.

12 Yun, S.-J. (2010) 'Not So Green: A Critique of South Korea's Growth Strategy', *Global Asia*, 22 June 2010. See also: Yun, S.-J. (2009) 'UNEP should engage in independent research', *The Hankyoreh*, 27 August 2009, http://english.hani.co.kr/arti/englishedition/eopinion/373377.html, viewed December 2013.

13 ADBInstitute, *Low-Carbon Green Growth in Asia*.

14 See: Yoon, S. (2010) 'President Lee, OECD Secretary-General discuss cooperation for G20'. *KOREA.net*, 26 October 2010. http://m.korea.net/english/NewsFocus/Policies/view?pageIndex=43&articleId=83606, viewed 5 July 2014; Young, S. (2012) 'Green Growth, Sustainable Development, Architecture for Green Growth and Korea's Aspiration as a Hub for Global Green Growth', Keynote Speech at the Workshop 'Strengthening Planning and Implementation Capacities for Sustainable Development in Post-Rio Context', Incheon, Korea, 14–16 November 2012, UN Office for Sustainable Development. www.unosd.org/content/documents/80UNOSD_Workshop_Keynote_Speech_on_GG&SD_SgY.pdf, viewed 5 July 2014.

15 2014 UNEP Newscentre (2014) 'Zayed International Prize for the Environment Honours Top Environmentalists', UNEP News Centre, 3 February 2014, www.unep.org/NEWSCENTRE/Default.aspx?DocumentID=2762&ArticleID=10705, viewed 5 July 2014.

16 Zayed Prize (2010) 'Winners Fifth Cycle', Zayed International Foundation for the Environment, www.zayedprize.org.ae/winners5.html, viewed 3 July 2014.

17 Carter, N. (2007) *The Politics of the Environment – Ideas, Activism, Policy*, second edition, Cambridge University Press; Rist, G. (1997) 'The environment, or the new nature of "development"'. In: G. Rist, *The History of Development: From Western Origins to Global Faith*, Zed Books, 171–196.

18 Rist, 'The environment'.

19 Rist, 'The environment', 188.

20 Princen, T. and Finger, M. (1994) *Environmental NGOs in World Politics – Linking the Local and the Global*, Routledge.

21 UNCED (United Nations Conference on Environment and Development) (1992a) *AGENDA 21*. Rio de Janeiro, Brazil, 3 to 14 June 1992, http://

sustainabledevelopment.un.org/content/documents/Agenda21.pdf, viewed 9 August 2013. See also: Carter, *The Politics of the Environment*, 311.

22 Lafferty, W.M. and Eckerberg, K. (2009) *From Earth Summit to Local Agenda 21 – Working towards Sustainable Development*, 2nd edition, Earthscan.

23 Rist, 'The environment'.

24 Redclift, M. (1987) *Sustainable Development – Exploring the Contradictions*, Methuen.

25 We use Antonio Gramsci's understanding of 'civil society' as the institutions and organizations that act as intermediary between economy and the State.

26 Papadakis, K. (2006) 'Socially sustainable development and participatory governance – legal and political aspects', International Institute for Labour Studies Geneva Discussion Paper Series No. 166, IILS Publications, 1.

27 See e.g. Selman, P. (2000) 'A sideways look at Local Agenda 21', *Journal of Environmental Policy & Planning* 2(1): 39–53; Fidelis, T. and Moreno Pires, S. (2009) 'Surrender or resistance to the implementation of Local Agenda 21 in Portugal – the challenges of local governance for sustainable development', *Journal of Environmental Planning and Management* 52(4): 497–518; Olsson, J. (2009) 'Sustainable development from below – institutionalising a global idea-complex', *Local Environment: The International Journal of Justice and Sustainability* 14(2): 127–138.

28 Blaxekjaer, 'The Emergence and Spreading'.

29 See: UNESCAP (2006) 'Green Growth at a Glance – The Way Forward for Asia and the Pacific', United Nations 2006, ST/ESCAP/2407.

30 UNESCAP, 'Green Growth at a Glance'.

31 UNESCAP, 'Green Growth at a Glance', 8.

32 UNESCAP, 'Green Growth at a Glance', 9.

33 UNESCAP, 'Green Growth at a Glance', 37.

34 UNESCAP, 'Green Growth at a Glance', 48.

35 See: Ekins, P. (2000) *Economic Growth and Environmental Sustainability – The Prospects for Green Growth*, Routledge.

36 Lee, M.-B., 'A great people with new dreams'.

37 Lee, M.-B., 'A great people with new dreams'.

38 Yun, S.-J., 'Not So Green'.

39 Lee, J.-H. and Yun, S.-J. (2011) 'A Comparative Study of Governance in State Management: Focusing on the Roh Moo-hyun Government and the Lee Myung-bak Government', *Development and Society* 40(2): 302.

40 Yun, S.-J., 'Not So Green'.

41 UNESCAP (n.d.) 'Green New Deal. Fact Sheet, Low Carbon Green Growth Roadmap for Asia and the Pacific', www.unescap.org/sites/default/files/32.%20FS-Green-New-Deal.pdf , accessed 8 July 2014.

42 Yun, S.-J., 'UNEP should engage'.

43 Yun, S.-J. (2014) 'Experts' Social Responsibility in the Process of Large-Scale Nature-Transforming National Projects: Focusing on the Case of the Four Major Rivers Restoration Project in Korea', *Development and Society* 43(1): 120.

44 RoK (Republic of Korea) (undated) *The River Revitalization of Korea – The Four Rivers Restoration Project. Investing in a safe and sustainable Korea, now and in the future*, Republic of Korea, www.4rivers.go.kr/eng, retrieved 11 August 2013.

45 Yun, S.-J., 'Experts' Social Responsibility'.
46 Yun, S.-J., 'Experts' Social Responsibility'.
47 Lawrence, P., Meigh, J. and Sullivan, C. (2002) 'The Water Poverty Index: an International Comparison', Keele Economics Research Papers. Keele University, UK. Available from http://core.kmi.open.ac.uk/download/pdf/9308992.pdf, viewed 22 October 2014.
48 Yun, S.-J., 'Experts' Social Responsibility'.
49 Yun, S.-J., 'Experts' Social Responsibility', 110.
50 Yun, S.-J., 'Experts' Social Responsibility'.
51 See Yun, S.-J., 'Experts' Social Responsibility'.
52 Yun, S.-J., 'Experts' Social Responsibility', 120.
53 Normile, D. (2010) 'Restoration or Devastation?', *Science*, 26 March 2010, *327*: 1569–1570.
54 The Kyunghyang Shinmun (2013) 'How about an inspection of BAI's inspection of the Four Major Rivers project?', *The Kyunghyang Shinmun*, 12 July 2013. Available from http://english.khan.co.kr/khan_art_view.html?code=790101&artid=201307121039097, viewed 9 August 2013. See also Stedman, L. (2013) 'Republic of Korea: Audit claims extensive Four Rivers project problems', *Water 21*, Main news stories, 22 January 2013. www.iwapublishing.com/template.cfm?name=news1448.
55 Van Eynde, S., Bluemling, B. and Bruyninckx, H. (2014) 'Explaining "low carbon development" in Asia – the case of China'. In: P. Harris and Lang, G. (eds), *Society and Environment in Asia*, Routledge, 404–422.
56 Yun, S.-J. (2012) 'Nuclear power for climate mitigation? Contesting frames in Korean newspapers', *Asia Europe Journal*, No. 1001/2012: 57–73.
57 Ministry of Trade, Industry and Energy (2014) 'The 2nd National Basic Energy Plan', in Korean.
58 Yun, S.-J., 'Experts' Social Responsibility'.
59 Bretton Woods Project (2012) 'World Bank's "green growth" approach denounced', *Update 81*, Bretton Woods Project, 3 July 2012. www.brettonwoodsproject.org/greengrowth81.
60 Daly, H. (1992) 'Sustainable Growth – An Impossibility Theorem', in John Dryzek and Schlosberg (eds), *Debating the Earth: The Environmental Politics Reader*, Oxford University Press, 285.
61 Methmann, C.P. (2010) '"Climate Protection" as Empty Signifier: A Discourse Theoretical Perspective on Climate Mainstreaming in World Politics', *Millennium – Journal of International Studies 39*: 364.
62 Principle 12 of the Rio Declaration: 'States should cooperate to promote a supportive and open international economic system that would lead to economic growth and sustainable development in all countries, to better address the problems of environmental degradation' (UNCED 1992).
63 See UNCED (United Nations Conference on Environment and Development) (1992b) 'Rio Declaration on Environment and Development', Rio de Janeiro, Brazil, 3 to 14 June 1992. www.unep.org/Documents.Multilingual/Default.asp?documentid=78&articleid=1163, viewed 9 August 2013.
64 Daly 'Sustainable Growth'.
65 Ekins, *Economic Growth and Environmental Sustainability*, 61.

66 Herrik and Kindleberger (1983), 21, as cited in Barbier, E.B. (1987) 'The Concept of Sustainable Economic Development', *Environmental Conservation 14*(2): 101.
67 Barbier, 'The Concept of Sustainable Economic Development', 101.
68 Ekins, *Economic Growth and Environmental Sustainability.*
69 De Janvry, A. and Sadoulet, E. (2011) 'Subsistence farming as a safety net for food-price shocks', *Development in Practice 21*, 472–480.
70 Stiglitz, J.E., Sen, A. and Fitoussi, J.-P. (2009) 'Report by the Commission on the Measurement of Economic Performance and Social Progress', www.stiglitz-sen-fitoussi.fr/documents/rapport_anglais.pdf, retrieved 9 August 2013.
71 UNDP (2013) 'Humanity Divided – Confronting Inequality in Developing Countries', Bureau for Development Policy, United Nations Development Programme. www.undp.org/content/dam/undp/library/Poverty%20Reduction/Inclusive%20development/Humanity%20Divided/HumanityDivided_Full-Report.pdf, viewed 8 July 2014.
72 Stiglitz *et al.*, 'Report by the Commission', 7.
73 Stiglitz *et al.*, 'Report by the Commission', 11.
74 Stiglitz *et al.*, 'Report by the Commission', 11, emphasis omitted.
75 Stiglitz *et al.*, 'Report by the Commission', 11, emphasis omitted.
76 Ekins, P. (1993) '"Limits to growth" and "sustainable development" – grappling with ecological realities', *Ecological Economics 8*: 272.
77 UNESCAP, *Preview – Green Growth.*
78 Korea Energy Economics Institute (2013) *Energy Info Korea*, Gyeonggido, Yang-hoon Sonn, www.keei.re.kr.
79 IEA (2013) '*2013 Key World Energy Statistics* www.iea.org/publications/free-publications/publication/KeyWorld2013.pdf, retrieved 8 August 2013.
80 Blaxekjaer, 'The Emergence and Spreading'.
81 Statistics Korea (2012) 'Korea's Green Growth – based on OECD Green Growth Indicators', http://sri.kostat.go.kr, viewed 20 August 2013.
82 Bluemling, B., Yang, H. and Pahl-Wostl, C. (2007) 'Making water productivity operational – A concept of agricultural water productivity exemplified at a wheat–maize cropping pattern in the North China plain', *Agricultural Water Management 91*: 11–23.
83 Sachs, W. (1999) *Planet Dialectics – Exploration in Environment & Development*, Zed Books.
84 Princen, T. (2005) *The Logic of Sufficiency*, MIT Press.
85 See Yun, S.-J., 'Not So Green'; Yun, S.-J., 'UNEP should engage'; ADBInstitute, *Low-Carbon Green Growth.*
86 Yun, S.-J., 'UNEP should engage'.
87 Shin, H.-H. (2013a) 'Park ditches "green growth" in environmental policy shift', *The Korea Herald*, 28 March 2013, viewed 23 September 2014, www.koreaherald.com/view.php?ud=20130328000986.
88 See Adrian Parr in this volume (Chapter 3)
89 ADBInstitute, *Low-Carbon Green Growth*; Reuters (2011) 'Green Growth, South Korea's National Policy, Gaining Global Attention', *Reuters*, U.S. edition, 26 January 2011, viewed 23 September 2014; World Bank (2012) 'Korea's Global Commitment to Green Growth', *The World Bank News*,

5 May 2012, viewed 23 September 2014, www.worldbank.org/en/news/feature/2012/05/09/Korea-s-Global-Commitment-to-Green-Growth.

90 Shin, H.-H., 'Park ditches "green growth"'.

91 Kim, S.-Y. and Thurbon, E. (2014) 'Green Growth – rebooted in South Korea, booted out in Australia'. *The Conversation*, 6 February 2014, http://theconversation.com/green-growth-rebooted-in-south-korea-booted-out-in-australia-22243, viewed 23 September 2014; Shin, H.-H. (2013b) 'Korea eyes era of "green growth 2.0"', *The Korea Herald*, 10 November 2013, viewed 8 October 2014. www.koreaherald.com/view.php?ud=20131110000342.

92 Shin, H.-H., 'Korea eyes era'.

93 Banerjee, P. and Sood, A. (2012) 'The Political Economy of Green Growth in India', Occasional Paper Five, *Social Dimensions of Green Economy and Sustainable Development*, April 2012. United Nations Research Institute for Social Development, Friedrich Ebert Stiftung. http://www.fes-globalization.org/geneva/documents/5%20UNRISD%20Banerjee.pdf, retrieved 08 October 2014, iii.

94 Loher, J.F. (2012) 'Domestic Climate Change Governance in East Asia – A Comparative Analysis of Japan, China and South Korea', *Vienna Journal of East Asian Studies* 3, 73–107.

95 Lash, S. (1994) 'Reflexivity and its Doubles: Structure, Aesthetics, Community', in: U. Beck, A. Giddens, S. Lash, *Reflexive Modernization – Politics, Tradition and Aesthetics in the Modern Social Order*, Stanford University Press, 112.

96 See Mahnkopf, 'Can green growth rescue capitalism'.

Chapter 6

1 Löfstedt, R. (2004) 'The Swing of the Regulatory Pendulum in Europe: From Precautionary Principle to (Regulatory) Impact Analysis', *Journal of Risk and Uncertainty* 28(3), 237–260.

2 Stern, N. (2006) *The Economics of Climate Change*, Cambridge University Press.

3 EC (2010) *Europe 2020 – A strategy for smart, sustainable and inclusive growth*, COM(2010)2020final, Brussels; http://ec.europa.eu/eu2020/pdf/COMPLET%20EN%20BARROSO%20%20%20007%20-%20Europe%202020%20-%20EN%20version.pdf; EC (2011a) *A resource-efficient Europe – Flagship initiative under the Europe 2020 Strategy*, COM(2011)21, Brussels; http://ec.europa.eu/resource-efficient-europe/pdf/resource_efficient_europe_en.pdf; EC (2012) *Energy roadmap 2050*, Luxembourg; https://ec.europa.eu/energy/sites/ener/files/documents/2012_energy_roadmap_2050_en_0.pdf.

4 EC (2011b) *Energy 2020, A strategy for competitive, sustainable and secure energy*; http://ec.europa.eu/energy/strategies/2010/2020_en.htm.

5 REN 21 (Renewable Energy Policy Network for the 21st Century) (2014) *Renewables 2014. Global Status report*; www.ren21.net/ren21activities/globalstatusreport.aspx.

6 See Hertwich, Edgar *et al.* (2013) *Integrated life-cycle assessment of electricity-supply scenarios confirms global environmental benefit of low carbon technologies*; Proceedings of the National Academy of Sciences of the USA;

www.pnas.org/cgi/doi/10.1073/pnas.1312753111; Fizaine, F. and Court, V. (2014) *Energy transition towards renewable and metal depletion: an approach through the EROI concept*, Working paper from Chaire Economie du Climate; www.ecopapers.repec.org.

7 Hall, C., Lambert, J. and Balogh, S. (2014) 'EROI of different fuels and the implications for society', *Energy Policy* 64: 150.

8 The concept of EROI (Energy Return On Investment), alternatively called EROEI (Energy Return On Energy Invested), is a 'means of measuring the quantity of various fuels by calculating the ratio between the energy delivered by a particular fuel to society and the energy invested in the capture and delivery of this energy', Hall *et al.*, 'EROI', 142.

9 See Fizaine and Court, 'Energy transition', who are able to demonstrate that the energy requirements associated to metal extraction could have a not-too-far impact on the capacity of these 'green' technologies to deliver net energy to society.

10 Both wind and solar electricity production involve a comparatively high demand for non-energetic raw materials such as copper, iron, bauxite or rare earth oxides, of which some are close to peak production. This holds true particularly for copper, which as an electrical conductive material is needed not only for renewable energy technologies but also for many other technological applications (above all in the telecommunication sector and the armament industry). See Bardi, U. (2013) *Der geplünderte Planet. Die Zukunft des Menschen in Zeiten schwindender Ressourcen*, Oekom; Bleischwitz, Raimund, Bahn-Walkowiak, Bettina, Eckardt, Felix, Feldt, Heidi and Fuhr, Lili (2012) *International Resource Politics. New challenges demanding new governance approaches for a green economy*, Berlin: Heinrich Böll Foundation; Klare, M. (2012) *The Race for What's Left. The global scramble for the world's last resources*, Metropolitan Books; Exner, A., Feissner, P., Kranzl, L. and Zittel, W. (2013) *Land and Resource Scarcity. Capitalism, struggle and well-being in a world without fossil-fuels*, Routledge; PBL Netherlands Environmental Assessment Agency (2011) *Scarcity in a Sea of plenty? Global resources scarcities and policies in the European Union and the Netherlands*, The Hague; www.pbl.nl/sites/default/files/cms/publicaties/500167001_0.pdf.

11 EC (2008) *The Raw Materials Initiative. Meeting our Critical Need for Growth and Jobs in Europe*; http://ec.europa.eu/enterprise/sectors/metals-minerals/files/sec_2741_en.pdf; EC (2011c) *Tackling the Challenges in Commodity Markets and on Raw Materials*; http://eur-lex.europa.eu/LexUriServ/LexUriServ.do?uri=COM:2011:0025:FIN:en:PDF.

12 EC (2014) *A policy framework for climate and energy in the period from 2020 to 2030*; http://ec.europa.eu/energy/doc/2030/com_2014_15_en.pd

13 There will be an annual cap on new installations; for new 'clean' energy projects a tendering model will be introduced that will raise the risks for smaller business and offshore wind will have higher feed-in tariffs than other forms of 'clean energy'.

14 See Mahnkopf, B. (2013) *Peak Everything – Peak Capitalism? Folgen der sozial-ökologischen Krise für die Dynamik des historischen Kapitalismus*, Working Paper 02/2013 DFG-KollegforscherInnengruppe Postwachstumsgesellschaften,

Friedrich Schiller Universität Jena; www.kolleg-postwachstum.de/sozwgmedia/dokumente/WorkingPaper/wp2_2013.pdf; Mahnkopf, B. (2014) 'Peak Capitalism'? Wachstumsgrenzen als Grenzen des Kapitalismus, in: *WSI-Mitteilungen* 7/2014: 505–512; Dale, G. (2012) 'The growth paradigm: a critique', *International Socialism* 134, March 2012; http://isj.org.uk/index.php4?id=798; and particularly Jame Meadway in this volume (Chapter 4).

15 Marx, K. (1970) *MEW 23: Das Kapital. Kritik der politischen Ökonomie*, Erster Band, 169.

16 Foster, B., Clarke, B. and York, R. (2010) *The Ecological Rift – Capitalism's War on the Earth*, Monthly Review Press.

17 Altvater, E. and Mahnkopf, B. (2007) Grenzen der Globalisierung. Ökonomie, Ökologie und Politik in der Weltgesellschaft, 7th edn, Westfälisches Dampfboot, Chapter 4.

18 See Altvater, E. (2005) *Das Ende des Kapitalismus wie wir ihn kennen*, Westfälisches Dampfboot.

19 Marx, K. (1970) *MEW 23: Das Kapital, 630–635.*

20 According to the calculations presented in Carbon Tracker (2013) *Unburnable carbon 2013: wasted capital and stranded assets*, http://carbontracker.live.kiln.it/Unburnable-Carbon-2-Web-Version.pdf, these reserves had a share value of $4 trillion in 2012 and serviced $1.27 trillion in outstanding corporate debt over the same period.

21 Bardi, *Der geplünderte Planet;* Diederen, Andre (2009) *Metal minerals scarcity: A call for managed austerity and the elements of hope*, in: *The Oil Drum: Europe*; www.theoildrum.com/node/5239; Energy Watch Group, *Uranium Resources and Nuclear Energy*.

22 Heinberg, R. (2010) *Peak Everything. Waking up to the Century of Declines*, New Society Publishers, 246.

23 Foster, B., Clarke, B. and York, R. (2010) *The Ecological Rift – Capitalism's War on the Earth*, Monthly Review Press.

24 Polanyi, K. (2001) *The Great Transformation. The Political and Economic Origins of Our Time*, Beacon Press.

25 See, among others, Larry Lohmann in this volume (Chapter 2); Sullivan, S. (2011) *Banking Nature? The financialisaton of environmental conservation*, Open Anthropology Cooperative Press; http://openanthcoop.net/press/http:/openanthcoop.net/press/wp-content/uploads/2011/03/Sullivan-Banking-Nature.pdf; McAfee, K. (2012) 'Nature in the Market-World: Ecosystem Services and Inequality', *Development* 55(1): 25–33.

26 Cooper, M. (2010) 'Turbulent worlds: Financial markets and environmental crisis', *Theory, Culture & Society* 27(2–3): 167–190.

27 See ILO (2013) *Global Employment Trends 2014*, ILO; Piketty, T. (2014) *Capital in the Twenty-First Century*, Harvard University Press; UNDP (2014) *Human Development Report 2014: The Age of Vulnerability*, UNDP.

28 Moore, J.W. (2015) *Capitalism in the Web of Life: Ecology and the Accumulation of Capital*, Verso (forthcoming)

29 For the difference between scarcity and shortages see Elmar Altvater's comments on James O'Connor's concept of an 'underproduction crisis'; see Altvater, E. (1993) *The Future of the Market. An Essay on the Regulation of Money and Nature after the Collapse of Actually Existing Socialism*, Verso, 218–222.

Chapter 7

1 Dauvergne, P. and Lister, J. (2013) *Ecobusiness: a Big Brand Takeover of Sustainability*, MIT Press.

2 Smil, V. (2014) *Making the Modern World. Materials & Dematerialization*, Wiley. Berdi, Ugo (2014) *Extracted. How the Quest for Mineral Wealth is Plundering the Planet*, Chelsea Green Publishing. UNEP (2014) *Decoupling 2: technologies, opportunities and policy options. A Report of the Working Group on Decoupling to the International Resource Panel.* www.unep.org/resourcepanel/Portals/24102/PDFs/IRP_DECOUPLING_2_REPORT.pdf, consulted on 2 July 2015.

3 GreenBiz Group and Trucost (2015) *State of Green Business 2015*. www.greenbiz.com/report/state-green-business-report-2015, last viewed 3 April 2015.

4 Jackson, T. (2009) *Prosperity without Growth. Economics for a Finite Planet*, Routledge.

5 UNEP (2011) *Decoupling natural resource use and environmental impacts from economic growth. A Report of the Working Group on decoupling to the International Resource Panel.* www.unep.org/resour-cepa- nel/decoupling/files/pdf/decoupling_report_english.pdf, last viewed 29 September 2014, consulted on 2 July 2015.

6 www.uncsd2012.org/content/documents/BRAZIL%20Submission%20%20English%201.11.11doc.pdf. For an analysis of this document, see Abramovay, R. (2012) 'Inequalities and limits should be at the core of Rio+20'. *Estudos Avançados* 26(74) www.scielo.br/pdf/ea/v26n74/en_a03v26n74.pdf, last viewed 2 February 2015.

7 Souza Jr. Carlos, João Siqueira, Júlia Ribeiro and Márcio Sales (2013) Deforestation and forest degradation in the Amazon Biome. IMAZON_http://imazon.org.br/PDFimazon/Ingles/other_publications/MAPA_13mar2013_ingles.pdf, last viewed 27 February 2015. Tollefson, J. (2015) 'Stopping deforestation: Battle for the Amazon', *Nature* 520: 20–23, 2 April. www.nature.com/news/stopping-deforestation-battle-for-the-amazon-1.17223, consulted on 2 July 2015.

8 http://en.wikipedia.org/wiki/Movimento_Passe_Livre, consulted on 2 July 2015.

9 Singer, A. (2013) 'Brasil, junho de 2013: Classes e ideologias cruzadas'. *Novos Estudos CEBRAP*, número 97, novembro, www.scielo.br/scielo.php?pid=S0101-33002013000300003&script=sci_arttext&tlng=es, consulted on 2 July 2015.

10 Rocha, S. (2013) 'Pobreza no Brasil. A Evolução de Longo Prazo (1970–2011). XXV Fórum Nacional (Jubileu de Prata – 1988/2013) O Brasil de Amanhã. Transformar Crise em Oportunidade. Rio de Janeiro, 13–16 de maio de 2013 www.forumnacional.org.br/pub/ep/EP0492.pdf, consulted on 25 September 2014.

11 Barros, R., Mendonça, R. and Tsujada, R. (2011) "Portas de saída, inclusão produtiva e erradicação da extrema pobreza no Brasil" in Portas de saída, inclusão produtiva e erradicação da extrema pobreza no Brasil. Secretaria de Assuntos Estratégicos da Presidência da República, www.sae.gov.br/site/wp-content/uploads/Portas-de-erradica%C3%A7%C3%A30-da-extrema-pobreza.pdf, consulted on 2 July 2015.

12 OXFAM (2014) 'Working for the Few. Political capture and economic inequality'. Oxfam Briefing Paper 178 www.oxfam.de/sites/www.oxfam.de/files/bp-working-for-few-political-capture-economic-inequality-200114-summ-en-oxfam.pdf, consulted on 25 September 2014.

13 Ferreira, F., Messina, J., Rigolini, J., López-Calva, L.-F., Lugo, M.A. and Vakis, R. (2013) *Economic Mobility and the Rise of the Latin American Middle Class*. Washington, DC: World Bank. doi: 10.1596/978-0-8213-9634-6. License: Creative Commons Attribution CC BY 3.0 https://openknowledge.worldbank.org/bitstream/handle/10986/11858/9780821396346.pdf, consulted on 2 July 2015, ix.

14 Ferreira *et al.*, *Economic Mobility*, 12.

15 Menezes Filho, Naércio and DianaNuñez (2012) 'Estimando os Gastos Privados com Educação no Brasil'. Policy Paper 03 Insper, www.insper.edu.br/wp-content/uploads/2013/01/Estimando-os-gastos-privados-com-educa%C3%A7%C3%A3o-no-Brasil.pdf, consulted on 29 September 2014. Casa do Saber, Fundação Aprendiz, Fundação Bradesco, Fundação Educar, Instituto Ecofuturo, Instituto Natura, Instituto Unibanco and Parceiros da Educação (s/d) 'A Transformação da Qualidade da Educação Básica Pública no Brasil' www.parceirosdaeducacao.org.br/evento_propostas/pdf/transfor macao.pdf, consulted on 29 September 2014.

16 Máximo, L. (2013) 'Escola pública perde alunos com alta da renda no país'. *Valor Econômico*, 23 April 2014, A14.

17 Veloso, F. (2011) 'A Evolução Recente e Propostas para a Melhoria da Educação no Brasil', in *Brasil: a nova agenda social*, Edmar Lisboa Bacha and Simon Schwartzman (eds) Rio de Janeiro: LTC. www.schwartzman.org.br/sitesimon/?page_id=2327&lang=en-us, consulted on 29 September 2014.

18 Campino, A. (2011) 'Gastos Catastróficos, Iniquidade e Proposta de Reformulação do Sistema de Saúde', in *Brasil: a nova agenda social*, Edmar Lisboa Bacha and Simon Schwartzman (eds). Rio de Janeiro: LTC www.schwartzman.org.br/sitesimon/?page_id=2327&lang=en-us, consulted on 29 September 2014.

19 Trata Brasil (2014) 'Baixo avanço do saneamento básico nas maiores cidades brasileiras compromete universalização nos próximos 20 anos', www.tratabrasil.org.br/datafiles/estudos/ranking/release-ranking-2014.pdf, consulted on 29 September 2014.

20 CNI (2012) 'Cidades: Mobilidade, Habitação e Escala. Um Chamado à Ação', www.cni.org.br/portal/data/files/FF808081394933EC013977401A5B486D/CNI%20-%20Cidades%202012_web.pdf, consulted on 29 September 2014, 14.

21 Nussbaum, M. (2011) *Creating Capabilities. The Human Development Approach*, Cambridge, MA, The Belknap Press of Harvard University Press.

22 www.petronoticias.com.br/archives/52986, consulted on 29 September 2014.

23 Fearnside, P. (2006) 'Dams in the Amazon: Belo Monte and Brazil's Hydroelectric Development of the Xingu River Basin', *Environmental Management*, July, *38*(1): 16–27. www.internationalrivers.org/files/attached-files/belo_monte_dec_making_em_01136.pdf, consulted on 2 July 2015.

24 Mathiesen, K. (2014) 'Do dams destroy rivers'? *The Guardian*, 27 August. www.theguardian.com/environment/live/2014/aug/27/do-dams-destroy-rivers, consulted on 29 September 2014.

25 See ipsamazonia.org.br/, consulted on 2 July 2015.
26 IMAZON, IPAM & Amigos da Terra Amazônia Brasileira (2014) *Amazônia e as Eleições 2014: Oportunidades e Desafios para o Desenvolvimento Sustentável.* http://imazon.org.br/publicacoes/amazonia-e-as-eleicoes-2014-oportunidades-e-desafios-para-o-desenvolvimento-sustentavel/ consulted on 2 July 2015.
27 Leslie, J. (2014) 'Large Dams Just Aren't Worth the Cost', *The New York Times Sunday Review.* 22/08. www.nytimes.com/2014/08/24/opinion/sunday/large-dams-just-arent-worth-the-cost.html?smid=tw-share&_r=0, consulted on 29 September 2014.
28 Ansar, A., Flyvbjerg, B., Budzier, A. and Lunn, D. (2014) 'Should We Build More Large Dams? The Actual Costs of Hydropower Megaproject Development', *Energy Policy*, March, 1–14. http://papers.ssrn.com/sol3/papers.cfm?abstract_id=2406852, consulted on 28 September 2014.
29 Pereira, R. (2013) 'Orçado em US$ 16 bilhões, custo da Usina de Belo Monte já supera os US$ 30 bilhões'. *O Estado de São Paulo*, 11 May 2013. http://economia.estadao.com.br/noticias/geral,orcado-em-r-16-bilhoes-custo-da-usina-de-belo-monte-ja-supera-os-r-30-bilhoes,153398e, consulted on 28 September 2014.
30 Abramovay, R. (2014) 'Innovations to Democratize Energy Access Without Boosting Emissions', *Ambiente & Sociedade XVII*(3): 1–18. July/September. http://ricardoabramovay.com/innovations-to-democratize-energy-access-without-boosting-emissions/, consulted on 2 July 2014.
31 Rifkin, J. (2012) *The Third Industrial Revolution. How Lateral Power Is Transforming Energy, the Economy, and the World.* Palgrave/Macmillan. Heck, S. and Rogers, M/ (2014) *Resource Revolution. How to Capture the Biggest Business Opportunity in a Century*, Amazon Publishing.
32 Esposito, A. and Fuchs, P. (2013) 'Desenvolvimento tecnológico e inserção da energia solar no Brasil' *Revista do BNDES*, 40. www.bndes.gov.br/SiteBNDES/export/sites/default/bndes_pt/Galerias/Arquivos/conhecimento/revista/rev4003.pdf, consulted on 29 September 2014.
33 Abramovay, R. (2008) 'Eficiência e Contestação Social no Caminho do Etanol Brasileiro', *Política Externa*, 17(2), september, october, november.
34 Macedo, I.C. (2007) *Sugar Cane's Energy – Twelve Studies on Brazilian sugar cane agribusiness and its sustainability.* São Paulo. UNICA. http://sugarcane.org/resource-library/books/Sugar%20Canes%20Energy%20-%20Full%20book.pdf, consulted on 2 July 2015. Goldemberg, José., Suani Coelho, Plínio Nastari and Osvaldo Lucon (2003) 'Ethanol Learning Curve – The Brazilian Experience'. *Biomass and Bioenergy*. Vol. 26/3:301–304. www.sciencedirect.com/science/article/pii/S0961953403001259, consulted on 2 July 2015.
35 Gonçalves, J., Souza, S. and Ghobril, C. (2007) 'Agropecuária paulista: especialização regional and mudanças na composição de culturas de 1969–1971 a 2002–2006'. Instituto de Economia Agrícola.
36 Bonomi, A., Poço, J. and Trielli, M. (2006) 'Biocombustíveis – A solução brasileira para uma matriz energética e sustentável'. *Revista Brasileira de Engenharia Química*. October, 16–21.
37 EPA (2010) 'EPA Finalizes Regulations for the National Renewable Fuel Standard Program for 2010 and Beyond'. Regulatory Announcement. www.epa.gov/otaq/renewablefuels/420f10007.pdf, last viewed 29 September 2014.

38 Hawken, P., Lovins, A. and Lovins, L.H. (1999) *Natural Capitalism: Creating the Next Industrial*. Boston. Little, Brown and Co. www.natcap.org/images/other/NCchapter2.pdf, last viewed 29 September 2013.

39 Kalmbach, R., Bernhart, W., Kleimann, P. and Hoffmann, M. (2005) 'Automotive landscape 2025. Opportunities and challenges ahead'. Roland Berger Strategy Consultants. www.rolandberger.com/media/pdf/Roland_Berger_Automotive_Landscape_2025_20110228.pdf, consulted on 3 July 2015.

40 KPMG (2014) *KPMG's Global Automotive Executive Survey 2014. Strategies for a fast-evolving Market*, www.kpmg.com/BR/PT/Estudos_Analises/artigosepublicacoes/Documents/Industrial_Markets/GlobalAutomotive survey14A4WebAccessibleFile.pdf, consulted on 3 July 2015.

41 Marli Olmos (2013) 'Excesso de capacidade ameaça planos de montadoras no país'. *Valor Econômico*. 8/10, B4.

42 *Valor Econômico* (2014) 'Incentivo eleva peso do setor automotivo na indústria do país', 06 March.

43 Becker, U., Becker, T. and Gerlach, J. (2012) 'The True Costs of Automobility: External Costs of Cars Overview on existing estimates in EU-27'. Final report, www.greens-efa.eu/fileadmin/dam/Documents/Studies/Costs_of_cars/The_true_costs_of_cars_EN.pdf, last viewed 29 September 2014.

44 Cardoso, T. (2013) 'Trânsito enfrenta situação alarmante', *Valor Econômico*. 24/06, F6.

45 KPMG (2012) *KPMG's Global Automotive Executive Survey 2014. Managing growth while navigating uncharted routes*, www.kpmg.com/GE/en/IssuesAndInsights/ArticlesPublications/Documents/Global-automotive-executive-survey-2012.pdf, consulted on 3 July 2015.

46 Sperling, D. and Gordon, D. (2009) *Two Billion Cars. Driving Toward Sustainability*, Oxford University Press.

47 Moreira, A. (2014) 'Produção global deve crescer4% em 2014 e 2015'. *Valor Econômico* 9/10. www.valor.com.br/empresas/3728002/producao-global-deve-crescer-4-em-2014-e-2015, consulted on 28 October 2014.

48 *McKinsey Quarterly* (2014) 'Bill Ford Charts a Course for the Future', www.mckinsey.com/Insights/Innovation/Bill_Ford_charts_a_course_for_the_future?cid=mckq50-eml-alt-mip-mck-oth-1410, consulted on 28 October 2014.

49 Nepstad, D., McGrath, D., Stickler, C., Alencar, A., Azevedo, A., Swette, B., Bezerra, T., DiGiano, M., Shimada, J., Seroa da Motta, R., Armijo, E., Castello, L., Brando, P., Hansen, M., McGrath-Horn, M., Carvalho, O. and Hess, L. (2014) 'Slowing Amazon deforestation through public policy and interventions in beef and soy supply chains', *Science*, 6/06 Vol. 344, no. 6188, 1118–1123, www.sciencemag.org/content/344/6188/1118, consulted on 3 July 2015.

50 PNUMA, Red Mercosur (2011) *Eficiencia en el uso de los recursos en América Latina: Perspectivas e Implicaciones Económicas*. www.pnuma.org/reeo/, consulted on 3 July 2015.

51 http://gestion.pe/economia/china-destina-77-inversion-directa-region-amazonica-y-peru-representa-1513-2095546?utm_source=gestion&utm_medium=-mailing&utm_campaign=newsletter_2014_04_28, consulted on 3 July 2015.

52 Vaughan, A. (2014) 'Ecuador signs permits for oil drilling in Amazon's Yasuni park', *The Guardian*, 23/05. www.theguardian.com/environment/2014/may/23/ecuador-amazon-yasuni-national-park-oil-drill, consulted on 3 July 2015.

53 www.avina.net/esp/10956/incontext-39/, last viewed 3 July 2015.
54 Imazon *et al.* (2014) op. cit. A Amazônia e as eleições
55 Ibid.
56 www.teebweb.org/, consulted on 3 July 2015.
57 Chiaretti, D. (2014) 'Brasil eleva emissões sem aumentar riqueza, diz Observatório do Clima'. *Valor Econômico*. 20/11, A2.

Chapter 8

1 OECD (2012) *Inclusive green growth: For the future we want*, OECD. UNDESA (2011) *World Economic and Social Survey 2011: The Great Green Technological Transformation*, UNDESA.
2 World Bank (2012) *Inclusive Green Growth – A pathway for sustainable development.*
3 Hoffmann, U. (2011) 'Some Reflections on Climate Change, Green Growth Illusions and Development Space', UNCTAD Discussion Paper No. 205, UNCTAD/OSG/DP/2-11/5.
4 UN General Assembly (2012) *The Future We Want*. Resolution adopted on 27 July 2012. RES/66/288. 11 September.
5 Green jobs meet the conditions of decent work (formal employment that ensures adequate wages, occupational safety and health, social protection, workers rights and the right to organize representative associations) in any economic sectors that: (i) reduce consumption of energy and raw materials; (ii) limit greenhouse gas emissions; (iii) minimize waste and pollution; and (iv) protect and restore ecosystems. Green jobs help reduce environmental impact to levels that are ultimately sustainable. (UNEP/ILO/IOE/ITUC (2008) *Green Jobs: Towards decent work*).
6 ILO (2013) *Sustainable development, decent work and green jobs*, Report V, International Labour Organization (ILO).
7 ILO (2012) *Working towards sustainable development: Opportunities for decent work and social inclusion in a green economy, ILO.*
8 Kirov, V. and van den Berge, J. (2012) 'Green and Decent? Working conditions in the waste sector in Europe and implications for trade union policy', *International Journal of Labour Research* 4(2).
9 Gereffi, G., Humphrey, J. and Sturgeon, T. (2005) 'The governance of global value chains', *Review of International Political Economy* 12(1): 78–104.
10 Barrientos, S., Kothari, U. and Phillips, N. (2013) 'Dynamics of unfree labour in the contemporary global economy', *Journal of Development Studies* 49(8): 1037–41.
11 As derived from the ILO concept of decent work, which refers to jobs that are productive, provide adequate incomes and social protection, respect workers' labour rights and give workers a voice in decisions that affect their lives.
12 ILO (2013) *Green Jobs: Draft guidelines for the statistical definition and measurement of employment in environmental sectors*, General Report prepared for the International Conference of Labour Statisticians (2–11 October), Chapter 4, Department of Statistics.
13 UNEP/ILO/IOE/ITUC, 2008.

14 Chan, C.K. and Lam, M.C. (2012) 'The reality and challenges of green jobs in China: An exploration', *International Journal of Labour Research* 4(2).
15 ILO (2012).
16 Olsen, L. (2012) 'Editorial: What policies for a green economy that works for social progress?', *International Journal of Labour Research* 4(2).
17 ILO (2012).
18 Chan and Lam (2012).
19 Cunniah, D. (2012) 'Foreword', *International Journal of Labour Research* 4(2).
20 Olsen (2012).
21 Do Carmo, M.S. and Puppim, J.A. (2010) 'The semantics of garbage and the organization of the recyclers: Implementation challenges for establishing recycling cooperatives in the city of Rio de Janeiro, Brazil', *Resources, Conservation and Recycling* 54(12): 1261–68.
22 Chan and Lam (2012).
23 Rustico, L. and F. Sperotti (2012) 'Working conditions in "green jobs": Women in the renewable energy sector', *International Journal of Labour Research* 4(2).
24 UNEP/ILO/IOE/ITUC, 2008.
25 European Parliament (2010) *Resolution on developing the job potential of a new sustainable economy*, 7 September.
26 Rustico and Sperotti (2012).
27 Bourahli, A. *et al.* (2011) 'A reciclagem como fator de inclusão socioeconômica dos catadores de lixo do Distrito Federal do Brasil', *Revista Capital Científico* 9(2).
28 Barrientos *et al.* (2013).
29 Crang, M., Hughes, A., Gregson, N., Norris, L. and Ahamed, F. (2013) 'Rethinking governance and value in commodity chains through global recycling networks', *Transactions of the Institute of British Geographers* 38(1): 12–23.
30 IBGE (2011) *Pesquisa Nacional de Saneamento Básico*. IBGE.
31 Müzell, L. (2014) 'Mais do que fim de lixões, desafio é aumento da reciclagem no Brasil', RFI.
32 ABRELPE (2013) *Panorama dos Resíduos Sólidos no Brasil 2013* (www.abrelpe.com.br).
33 CEMPRE (2013) *CEMPRE Review 2013*.
34 Ribeiro, L.C.S. (2010) *O impacto econômico dos materiais recicláveis das cooperativas de catadores no estado do Rio de Janeiro em 2006: uma análise de insumo-produto*. Salvador, UFBA.
35 IPEA (2010) Pesquisa sobre Pagamento de Serviços Ambientais Urbanos para Gestão de Resíduos Sólidos, IPEA.
36 The CBO describes the functions of the occupation of a waste picker in the following way: 'Gathers, selects and sells recyclable materials such as paper, cardboard and glass, as well as metal and non-metal materials and other reusable materials' (Classificação Brasileira de Ocupações (CBO) (2001) 'Código 5192 – Catador de Material Reciclável', Ministério de Trabalho e Emprego).
37 Do Carmo and Puppim de Oliveira (2010).
38 IPEA (2013) 'Situação Social das Catadoras e Catadores de Material Reciclável e Reutilizável no Brasil', IPEA.

39 ILO (2012) *Perfil do Trabalho Decente no Brasil*, ILO Office in Brasilia.
40 Do Carmo and Puppim de Oliveira (2010).
41 Gutberlet, J. (2008) 'Empowering collective recycling initiatives: video documentation and action research with a recycling co-op in Brazil', *Resources, Conservation and Recycling* 52(4): 659–670.
42 IPEA (2013).
43 IBGE (2011).
44 Kirov and van den Berge (2012).
45 IPEA (2011).
46 For more details see Muçouçah, P.S. (2010) 'A política nacional de resíduos sólidos e a geração de empregos verdes', *Revista Bahia Análise & Dados* 20(2/3).
47 In order to distinguish between false and true cooperatives, the waste pickers' organizations are required to provide evidence of collective management and equal distribution of income among members in order to access benefits provided by public policies. It should be mentioned that cases of 'false cooperatives' exist in Brazil, which are merely companies created by an individual (not an association of individuals) with the aim of availing of tax benefits and other cost savings (Soto, M.M.T.(2011) *Análise e formação de redes de cooperativas de catadores de materiais recicláveis no âmbito da economia solidária*. COPPE).
48 Santos, I.J. (2013) 'Determinantes dos rendimentos de catadores de materiais recicláveis no Brasil: uma abordagem a partir dos microdados da amostra do censo IBGE 2010', *Revista Pegada* 14(1).
49 Alencar, M.C.B., Cardoso, C.C.O. and Antunes, M.C. (2009) 'Condições de trabalho e sintomas relacionados à saúde de catadores de materiais recicláveis em Curitiba', *Revista Ter. Ocupação, Universidade de São Paulo* 20(1): 36–42.
50 IPEA (2013).
51 Do Carmo and Puppim de Oliveira (2010).
52 Baranhuk, T.E.S. (2010) *Avaliação da evolução da renda e qualidade de vida dos catadores de materiais recicláveis de Curitiba, após a implantação do projeto Ecocidadão da Prefeitura de Curitiba*. SPEI, Curitiba.
53 Fé, C.F.M. and M.S. Faria (2011) 'Catadores de resíduos recicláveis: autogestão, economia solidária e tecnologias sociais'. In Zanin, M. and Gutierrez, R.F. (Eds), *Cooperativas de catadores: reflexões sobre a prática*. Ed. Clara Luz.
54 Medina, M. (2008) 'The informal recycling sector in development countries', *Gridlines*, Note no. 44 – October.
55 Do Carmo and Puppim de Oliveira (2010).
56 Nidecker, F. (2015) 'Striking Gold – at a Rubbish Dump', *BBC News Magazine*, 21 January.

Chapter 9

1 Bullard, Robert (1990) *Dumping in Dixie: Race, Class, and Environmental Quality*, Westview Press.
2 McCully, P. (1996) *Silenced Rivers: The Ecology and Politics of Large Dams*, Zed Books.
3 Carrere, R. and L. Lohmann (1996) *Pulping The South: Industrial Tree Plantations and the World Paper Economy*, Zed Books.

4 Guha, R. and Martinez-Alier, J. (1997) *Varieties of Environmentalism. Essays North and South*, Oxford.
5 Robbins, P. (2004) *Political Ecology: A Critical Introduction*, Blackwell.
6 Gerber, J.-F. (2011) 'Conflicts over Industrial Tree Plantations in the South: Who, How and Why?' *Global Environmental Change XXI*(1): 165–76.
7 Fischer-Kowalski, 'Society's Metabolism: On the Childhood and Adolescence of a Rising Conceptual Star', 119.
8 Raikes, P., Jensen, M.F. and Ponte, S. (2000) 'Global Commodity Chain Analysis and the French Filière Approach: Comparison and Critique', *Economy and Society* 29(3): 390–417.
9 Fischer-Kowalski, 'Society's Metabolism: On the Childhood and Adolescence of a Rising Conceptual Star'.
10 Hornborg, A. (2009) 'Zero-Sum World: Challenges in Conceptualizing Environmental Load Displacement and Ecologically Unequal Exchange in the World-System', *International Journal of Comparative Sociology* 50(3–4): 237–62.
11 Haberl, H. *et al.* (2007) 'Quantifying and Mapping the Human Appropriation of Net Primary Production in Earth's Terrestrial Ecosystems', *Proceedings of the National Academy of Sciences of the United States of America* 104(31): 12942–47.
12 Singh, S.J., Krausmann F., Gingrich, S., Haberl, H., Erb, K.H., Lanz, P., Martinez-Alier, J. and Temper, L. (2012) 'India's biophysical economy, 1961–2008: Sustainability in a national and global context', *Ecological Economics* 72(60–69).
13 Pérez Manrique, P.L., Brun, J., González-Martínez, A.C., Walter, M., Martínez-Alier, J. (2013) 'The Biophysical Performance of Argentina (1970–2009)', *Journal of Industrial Ecology* 17(4): 590–604.
14 Vallejo, M.C., Pérez-Rincón, M.A., Martinez-Alier, J. (2011) 'Metabolic Profile of the Colombian Economy from 1970 to 2007', *Journal of Industrial Ecology* 15(2): 245–67.
15 González-Martínez, A.C. and Schandl, H. (2008) 'The Biophysical Perspective of a Middle Income Economy: Material Flows in Mexico', *Ecological Economics* 68(1–2): 317–27.
16 West, J. and Schandl, H. (2013) 'Material Use and Material Efficiency in Latin America and the Caribbean', *Ecological Economics* 94: 19–27.
17 Russi, D., González, A.C., Silva-Macher, J.C., Giljum, S., Martinez-Alier, J. and Vallejo, M.C. (2008) 'Material Flows in Latin America: A Comparative Analysis of Chile, Ecuador, Mexico, and Peru, 1980–2000', *Journal of Industrial Ecology* 12(5–6): 704–720.
18 West and Schandl, 'Material', 19.
19 Muradian, R. and Martinez-Alier, J. (2001) 'Trade and the Environment: From a "Southern" Perspective', *Ecological Economics* 36(2): 281–97.
20 Bunker, S. (2007) 'The Poverty of Resource Extraction'. In *Rethinking environmental history: Worldsystem history and global environmental change*, edited by Alf Hornborg *et al.*, Altamira Press.
21 Hornborg, A. (2006) 'Footprints in the Cotton Fields: The Industrial Revolution as Time–Space Appropriation and Environmental Load Displacement', *Ecological Economics* 59(1): 74–81.

22 Hornborg (1998) 'Ecological unequal exchange', 127.
23 Samaniego, P., Vallejo, M.C. and Martinez-Alier, J. (2015) 'Déficit Comercial y Déficit Físico en Sudamérica'. FLACSO, Quito, working paper.
24 Samaniego, 'Déficit'.
25 Singh et al., 'India's'. Martinez-Alier, J., Temper, L. and Demaria, F. (2014) 'Social metabolism and environmental conflicts in India', *Indialogs 1*(1): 51–83.
26 Martinez-Alier, J. and O'Connor, M. (1996) 'Ecological and Economic Distribution Conflicts', in Robert Costanza *et al.*, *Getting Down to Earth: Practical Applications of Ecological Economics*, Island Press.
27 Martinez-Alier, J. (2005) *The Environmentalism of the Poor. A Study of Ecological Conflicts and Valuation*, Oxford U.P. Delhi.
28 Benford, R.D. and Snow, D.A. (2000) 'Framing processes and social movements', *Annual Review of Sociology* 26: 611–639.
29 Martinez-Alier, J. *et al.* (2011) 'Between Science and Activism: Learning and Teaching Ecological Economics with Environmental Justice Organisations', *Local Environment 16*(1): 17–36.
30 Robbins, *Political Ecology*.
31 Kapp, K.W. (1950) *The Social Costs of Private Enterprise*, Harvard U.P.
32 Guha and Martinez-Alier, *Environmentalism*.
33 Agarwal, B. (1992) 'The Gender and Environment Debate: Lessons from India', *Feminist Studies 18*(1).
34 Bandyopadhyay, J. and Shiva, V. (1988) 'Political Economy of Ecology Movements', *Economic and Political Weekly* 23(24): 1223–1232.
35 Temper, L. and Martinez-Alier, J. (2013) 'The god of the mountain and Godavarman. Net Present Value, indigenous territorial rights and sacredness in a bauxite mining conflict in India', *Ecological Economics* 96: 79–87.
36 Padel, F. and Das, S. (2010) *Out of this Earth: East India Adivasis and the Aluminium Cartel*, Orient Black Swan.
37 Pérez-Rincón, M.A. (2014) 'Conflictos Ambientales en Colombia', 253–326, in *Minería en Colombia: Control público, memoria y justicia socio-ecológica, movimientos sociales y posconflicto*, edited by Luis Jorge Garay. Bogota: Contraloría General de la República de Colombia.

Chapter 10

1 Shrivastava, Aseem and Kothari, Ashish (2012) *Churning the Earth: The Making of Global India*, Viking/Penguin Books; for a short accessible summary of the book, see www.kalpavriksh.org/images/CLN/Globalisation%20Brochure.pdf, accessed on 22 June 2015.
2 An early treatment of this concept is in Kothari, A. (2009) 'Radical Ecological Democracy: Escaping India's Globalization Trap', *Development* 52(3): 401–09; subsequent development is in Shrivastava and Kothari, *Churning the Earth*, Kothari, Ashish (2014a) 'India 2100: Towards Radical Ecological Democracy', *Futures* 56: 62–72, and Kothari, Ashish (2014b) 'Radical Ecological Democracy: a Path Forward for India and Beyond', *Development* 57(1): 36–45.
3 Pathak, N. and Gour-Broome, V. (2001) *Tribal Self-Rule and Natural Resource Management: Community Based Conservation at Mendha-Lekha,*

Maharashtra, India, Kalpavriksh, Pune/Delhi and International Institute of Environment and Development.

4 Pathak, N. and Taraporewala, E. (2008) 'Towards self-rule and forest conservation in Mendha-Lekha village, Gadchiroli, India', report of a consultation for a ICCA Consortium and IUCN TILCEPA-TGER project sponsored by GTZ, Kalpavriksh,www.iccaforum.org/images/media/grd/mendha_india_report_icca_grassroots_discussions.pdf, accessed April 2013; Vasundhara and Kalpavriksh (2012) *A National Report on Community Forest Rights under Forest Rights Act: Status and Issues*, Vasundhara and Kalpavriksh in collaboration with Oxfam India.

5 Pathak Broome, N. (2014) 'Communitisation of Public Services in Nagaland – A step towards creating alternative model of delivering public services?', case study for project on 'Alternative Practices and Visions in India: Documentation, Networking, and Advocacy', unpublished report, Kalpavriksh. www.vikalpsangam.org/static/media/uploads/Resources/nagaland_communitisation_neema.pdf, accessed July 2015.

6 Menon, S. (2009) 'Participatory Budgeting. Decade of Education for Sustainable Development', www.desd.org/efc/Participatory%20Budgeting.htm, accessed March 2013.

7 Purohit, J.K. (2010) 'Integrating sectoral and spatial approaches for strengthening planning processes under MGNREGA', unpublished report, Society for Promotion of Wastelands Development.

8 Hasnat, S.N. (2005) 'Arvari Sansad: The farmers' parliament', *LEISA India*, December, www.agriculturesnetwork.org/magazines/global/practice-and-policy/arvari-sansad-the-farmers2019-parliament, accessed April 2013; see also www.tarunbharatsangh.org.

9 Paranjape, S. and Joy, K.J. (Undated), 'The Ozar Water User Societies: Impact of society formation and co-management of surface water and groundwater, Society for Promoting Participative Ecosystem Management (SOPPECOM)', Pune, available at www.soppecom.org/pdf/Ozar%20WUA%20study%20report.pdf, accessed April 2013.

10 Muhlberger, S. (1998) 'Democracy in Ancient India', www.nipissingu.ca/department/history/muhlberger/histdem/indiadem.htm#text20, accessed on 22 June 2015; Roper, B. (2013) *The History of Democracy: A Marxist Interpretation*, Pluto Press; Lang, M. and Mokrani, D. (eds) (2013) *Beyond Development: Alternative visions from Latin America*, Rosa Luxemburg Foundation and Transnational Institute.

11 www.ddsindia.com; www.greenconserve.com/; www.navdanya.org/campaigns/jaiv-panchayat.

12 www.anthra.org.

13 Pathak, N. (ed.) (2009) *Community Conserved Areas in India: A Directory*, Kalpavriksh.

14 www.tarunbharatsangh.org; www.sahjeevan.org/ta_drinking_water.html.

15 www.hunnar.org/iup.htm; www.sahjeevan.org/ta_urban_initiative.html.

16 e.g. see www.janaagraha.org.

17 R. Elango, personal communication, January 2013; Cajka, A. (2014) 'Kuthambakkam', case study for project on 'Alternative Practices and Visions in India: Documentation, Networking, and Advocacy', unpublished report,

Kalpavriksh, www.vikalpsangam.org/static/media/uploads/Resources/kuthumbakkam_1st_july.pdf, accessed July 2015.

18 www.justchangeindia.com.

19 Dhirendra Kumar, MD, Jharcraft, personal communication, February 2013; Kothari, A. (2013a) 'Being the Change', *The Hindu*, 21 April, www.thehindu.com/features/magazine/being-the-change/article4636561.ece, accessed April 2013.

20 Devika (2014) Don't Let the Magic Fade: Thoughts on Kudumbashree's Sixteenth Anniversary, *Kafila*, 16 August, http://kafila.org/2014/08/16/dont-let-the-magic-fade-thoughts-on-kudumbashrees-sixteenth-anniversary/, accessed November 2014; see also www.kudumbashree.org.

21 Bidwai, P. (2009) *An India That Can Say Yes*, Heinrich Boll Foundation; SELCO (undated) *Access to Sustainable Energy Services via Innovative Financing: 7 Case Studies*, SELCO.

22 It is therefore a matter of some concern that the new government that has taken over in India in 2014 is proposing to restrict MGNREGA's scope from being universal to being applicable in only a select number of districts.

23 Avani Mohan Singh, NAPCL Board, pers. comm., 2009; www.timbaktu-organic.org/aboutdharani.html; www.facebook.com/pages/Qasab-Kutch-Craftswomen-Producer-Co-Ltd/120970047978656.

24 www.uea.ac.uk/env/ijccr/index.html, accessed on 22 June 2015; www.uea.ac.uk/env/ijccr/pdfs/IJCCR%20vol%2012%20(2008)%201%20deMeulenaere.pdf.

25 Kalpavriksh and TPCG (2005) *Securing India's Future: Final Technical Report of the National Biodiversity Strategy and Action Plan*, Kalpavriksh, available at www.kalpavriksh.org/index.php/conservation-livelihoods1/72-biodiversity-and-wildlife/national-biodiversity-strategy-action-plan/224-nbsap-final-technical-report.html, accessed April 2013.

26 www.urmul.org; see especially www.urmul.org/?product=beyond-novella-memories-of-change.

27 www.wastepickerscollective.org; www.swachcoop.com; www.hasirudala.in

28 Sharma, M. (2011) *Green and Saffron: Hindu Nationalism and Indian Environmental Politics*, Permanent Black.

29 http://peopleslinguisticsurvey.org/.

30 www.ddsindia.com/www/psaale.htm; www.ddsindia.com/www/Education.htm; www.narmada.org/ALTERNATIVES/jeevanshalas.html; http://adharshilask.tripod.com/aboutadh.html; www.Adivasiacademy.org.in; www.navdanya.org/earth-university; www.bhoomi.org; www.swarajuniversity.org.

31 Gudynas, E. (2011) 'Buen vivir : Today's tomorrow', *Development* 54(4); Lang and Mokrani, *Beyond Development*; Demaria, F., Schneider, F., Sekulova, F. and Martinez-Alier, J. (2013) 'What is degrowth? From an activist slogan to a social movement', *Environmental Values* 22: 191–215; UNEP (2013) *Development strategies of selected Latin American and Caribbean countries and the green economy approach: A comparative analysis*, United Nations Environment Programme

32 Kothari, A. (2013b) 'Development and Ecological Sustainability in India: Possibilities for a Post-2015 Framework', Oxfam India, Delhi, available at: www.oxfamindia.org/sites/default/files/Working%20paper%2016%20-%20Dr.%20Ashish%20Kothari.pdf, accessed March 2013.

33 For more details see Peoples' Sustainability Treaty on Radical Ecological Democracy, http://radicalecologicaldemocracy.wordpress.com/, accessed January 2013.

34 Detailed strategies and actions in the sector of biodiversity awareness and education are provided in Kalpavriksh and TPCG, *Securing India's Future.*

35 Acosta, A. (2013) 'Extractivism and Neoextractivism: Two sides of the same curse', in Lang and Mokrani, *Beyond Development*; Prada, R. (2013) 'Buen Vivir as a Model for State and Economy', in Lang and Mokrani, *Beyond Development.*

36 Kothari, A. (2015) 'Confluence of hope: converging for a better world', *India Together*, 11 March, http://indiatogether.org/vikalp-sangam-champions-of-alternative-sustainable-development-op-ed; see also www.vikalpsangam.org or www.alternativesindia.org.

37 Kapoor, R. (2007) 'Transforming Self and Society: Plural paths to human emancipation', *Futures 39*(5): 475–486.

Chapter 11

1 Nussbaumer, P., Bazilian, M. and Patt, A. (2013) 'A statistical analysis of the link between energy and the Millennium Development Goals', *Climate and Development* 5(3): 101.

2 Singh, R., Wang, X., Mendoza, J.C. and Ackom, E.K. (2014) 'Electricity (in) accessibility to the urban poor in developing countries', *WIREs Energy Environ.*

3 Oldfield, F., Barnosky, A.D., Dearing, J., Fischer-Kowalski, M., McNeill, J., Steffen, W. and Zalasiewicz, J. (2014) 'The Anthropocene review: its significance, implications and the rationale for a new transdisciplinary journal', *The Anthropocene Review* 1(1): 3.

4 Rockström, J., Steffen, W., Noone, K., Persson, Å., Chapin, S.F. *et al.* (2009) 'A Safe operating space for humanity', *Nature 461*: 472.

5 Daly, H. (1998) 'Sustainable Growth: an Impossibility Theorem'. In J. Dryzek and D. Schlosberg, *Debating the Earth: the Environmental Politics Reader 1998* (1–3). Oxford: Oxford University Press.

6 Hallegatte, S., Heal, G., Fay, M. and Treguer, D. (2012) 'From growth to green growth – A framework', Cambridge, MA: National Bureau of Economic Research (NBER) – NBER Working Paper Series 2012, 3.

7 Organisation for Economic Co-operation and Development (2009) 'Declaration on Green Growth', *Adopted at the Meeting of the Council at Ministerial Level.* Organisation for Economic Co-operation and Development, 1.

8 Sun-Jin, Y. and Bluemling, B. (2015) 'Giving Green Teeth to the Tiger? A Critique of Green Growth in South Korea', Chapter 5 of this volume.

9 Huber, P. and Mills, M.P. (2005) *The Bottomless Well: The Twilight of Fuel, The Virtue of Waste, and Why We Will Never Run Out of Energy*, New York: Basic Books.

10 Sherwood, L. (2012) '*U.S. Solar Market Trends 2012*', Latham, New York: Interstate Renewable Energy Council (IREC) 2012; Renewable Energy Policy Network for the 21st Century (REN21) (2014) 'Renewables 2014 – global status report', Renewable Energy Policy Network for the 21st Century, Paris.

11 Energy Information Administration (2013) 'International Energy Outlook 2013 – with projections to 2040', Energy Information Administration, Washington DC.
12 Byrne, J. and Toly, N. (2006) 'Energy as a Social Project: Recovering a Discourse'. In J. Byrne, N. Toly and L. Glover, *Transforming Power: Energy, Environment, and Society in Conflict* (1–34). New Brunswick, NJ: Transaction Publishers.
13 Lovins, A. (1977) *Soft Energy Paths: Towards a Durable Peace*, Harper Colophon Books.
14 Byrne and Toly, *Energy as a Social Project*, 8.
15 Byrne and Toly, *Energy as a Social Project.*
16 Byrne, J. and Yun, S.-J. (1999) 'Efficient Global Warming: Contradictions in Liberal Democratic Responses to Global Environmental Problems', *Bulletin of Science, Technology & Society 19*(6): 493.
17 Leiserowitz, A., Maibach, E., Roser-Renouf, C., Feinberg, G., Marlon, J. and Howe, P. (2013) *'Public Support for Climate and Energy Policies in April 2013'*, Yale Project on Climate Change Communication. New Haven, CT: Yale University and George Mason University.
18 Foster, J.B. (2008) *The Sustainability Mirage: Illusion and Reality in the Coming War on Climate Change*, London, UK: Earthscan.
19 Byrne and Yun, *Efficient Global Warming.*
20 Newell, P. and Paterson, M. (1998) 'A Climate for Business: Global Warming, the State, and Capital', *Review of International Political Economy 5*(4): 679.
21 Mumford, L. (1964) 'Authoritarian and Democratic Technics'. In L. Mumford, *Technology and Culture 5*, 6.
22 Schreuder, Y. (2009) *The Corporate Greenhouse: Climate Change Policy in a Globalizing World*, New York: Zed Books Ltd.
23 Böhmelt, T. (2013) 'Civil Society Lobbying and Countries' Climate Change Policies: A Matching Approach', *Climate Policy 13*(6): 1.
24 Paterson, M. and Stripple, J. (2012) 'Virtuous carbon', *Environmental Politics 21*(4): 569.
25 Byrne and Yun, *Efficient Global Warming.*
26 Rockström, J., Steffen, W., Noone, K., Persson, Ä., Chapin, F.I., *et al. A Safe Operating Space for Humanity.*
27 Hoffmann, U. (2015) 'Can Green Growth Really Work? A Reality Check that Elaborates on the True (Socio-)Economics of Climate Change', Chapter 1 of this volume.
28 Jackson, T. (2011) *Prosperity Without Growth*, London: Routledge.
29 Steinberger, J.K, Krausmann, F., Getzner, M., Schandl, H. and West, J. (2013) 'Development and Dematerialization: An International Study', *PLoS ONE 8*(10), e70385.
30 Peters, G.P., Marland, G., Le Quere, C., Boden, T., Canadell, J.G. and Raupach, M.R. (2012) 'Rapid growth in CO2 emissions after the 2008–2009 global financial crisis', *Nature Clim. Change* 2(2); Friedlingstein, Pierre, *et al.* (2014) 'Persistent growth of CO2 emissions and implications for reaching climate targets', *Nature Geoscience 7*, 709; Hoffmann, U., 'Reality Check'.
31 Bindoff, N., *et al.* (2013) '2013: Detection and Attribution of Climate Change: From Global to Regional'. In Stocker, T., Qin, D., Plattner, G.-K., Tignor, M.,

Allen, S., Boschung, J., Midgley, P. *Climate Change 2013: The Physical Science Basis. Contribution of Working Group I to the Fifth Assessment Report of the Intergovernmental Panel on Climate Change*, Cambridge, UK and New York, NY: Cambridge University Press.

32 Olsson, L., *et al.* (2014) 'Chapter 13. Livelihoods and Poverty' In *Climate Change 2014: Impacts, Adaptation, and Vulnerability. Contribution of Working Group II to the Fifth Assessment Report of the Intergovernmental Panel on Climate Change*, Cambridge, UK and New York, NY: Cambridge University Press.

33 Mumford, 'Authoritarian and Democratic Technics', 8.

34 Steinberger, J.K. and Roberts, J. Timmons (2010) 'From constraint to sufficiency: the decoupling of energy and carbon from human needs, 1975–2005', *Ecological Economics* 70: 425.

35 Byrne, J., Martinez, C. and Ruggero, C. (2009) 'Relocating energy in the social commons: ideas for a sustainable energy utility', *Bulletin of Science, Technology & Society* 29(2): 81.

36 Byrne, J. and Taminiau, J. (2015) 'A review of sustainable energy utility and energy service utility concepts and applications: realizing ecological and social sustainability with a community utility', *WIREs Energy and Environment*.

37 Byrne and Taminiau, 'Sustainable energy utility'.

38 Byrne and Taminiau, 'Sustainable energy utility'.

39 Byrne, M. and Ruggero, 'Energy in the social commons'.

40 Byrne and Taminiau, 'Sustainable energy utility'.

41 Lovins, *Soft Energy Paths*.

42 International Energy Agency (2015) 'Energy technology perspectives – mobilizing innovation to accelerate climate action', OECD Publishing, Paris, 64.

43 Rockefeller Foundation (2012) *United States building energy efficiency – Market sizing and financing models*, The Rockefeller Foundation & Deutsche Bank Group Climate Change Advisors.

44 Granade, H.C., Creyts, J., Derkach, A., Farese, P., Nyquist, S. and Ostrowski, K. (2009) *Unlocking Energy Efficiency in the U.S. Economy*, McKinsey Global Energy and Materials.

45 Crowdfunding is an intriguing example of the effort to democratize finance by expanding conventional financial resource pool inputs of big banks and private investors to a much wider audience. 'Crowdfunding' or 'democratic finance' allows for individuals to become reinvested in the energy decision-making landscape and actively participate in the selection of energy futures by pooling many small investments from a large number of community members. A proposal by the authors to apply the SEU model in conjunction with democratic finance options was awarded by the Massachusetts Institute of Technology (MIT) Climate CoLab competition with a first prize in its category and shared second prize for the contest overall. Taminiau, J., Saul, K., Schweitzer, G., Mohazzam, S. and Byrne, J. (2014) 'Democratic finance: energy of the people, by the people, for the people', Foundation for Renewable Energy and Environment, Policy Note No. 2.

46 Byrne and Taminiau, '*Sustainable energy utility*'.

47 However, a growing body of research suggests that this effect is overblown and the argument is counterproductive to effective change. For instance,

Gillingham *et al.* deem the position a 'distraction' and an illegitimate excuse for inaction (Gillingham, K., Kotchen, M.J., Rapson, D.S. and Wagner, G. (2013) 'Energy Policy: The rebound effect is overplayed', *Nature* 493: 475).

48 Citi, *Energy Efficiency Revenue Bonds.*

49 Byrne and Taminiau, *'Sustainable energy utility'.*

50 International investigation is, among others, documented in a special issue of the *Bulletin of Science, Technology & Society*. This special issue contains articles on SEU investigations in, inter alia, South Korean, Indian and African development contexts. *Bulletin of Science, Technology & Society*. Special issue: Sustainable Energy Utilities: new energy strategy for the new climate. Volume 29, No. 2.

51 Authors' calculation based on the performance record of the Delaware SEU.

52 Schafer, Z.B. (2012) The future of federal energy efficiency finance: Options and opportunities for a federal Sustainable Energy Utility, Analytical Paper for the fulfilment of the degree of Master of Energy and Environmental Policy, University of Delaware.

53 Mumford, 'Authoritarian and Democratic Technics', *8*.

Chapter 12

1 Parker, M., Cheney, G., Fournier, V. and Land, C. (Eds). (2014) *The Routledge Companion to Alternative Organization*, Routledge, 15.

2 Ibid.; Gibson-Graham, J.K. (2002) 'Beyond global vs. local: economic politics outside the binary frame'. *Geographies of power: Placing scale*, 25–60; Gibson-Graham, J.K. (2006) *The End of Capitalism (as We Knew It): A Feminist Critique of Political Economy; with a New Introduction*. University of Minnesota Press; Gibson-Graham, J.K., Cameron, J. and Healy, S. (2013) *Take back the economy: An ethical guide for transforming our communities*, University of Minnesota Press.

3 Parker *et al.*, 15.

4 Parker *et al.*; Gibson-Graham *et al.*, 2013; Böhm, S., Bharucha, Z.P. and Pretty, J. (Eds) (2014) *Ecocultures: Blueprints for Sustainable Communities*. Routledge.

5 Moore, J. (2011) 'The Socio-Ecological Crises of Capitalism'. In *Capitalism and Its Discontents: Conversations with Radical Thinkers in a Time of Tumult* (136–152). Oakland, CA: PM Press.

6 Alexandratos, N. and Bruinsma, J. (2012) 'World agriculture towards 2030/2050: the 2012 revision'. ESA Work. Pap, 3.; Jarosz, Lucy. 'Defining world hunger: Scale and neoliberal ideology in international food security policy discourse'. *Food, Culture & Society 14.1* (2011): 117–139; McMichael, P. (2009) 'A food regime genealogy', *Journal of Peasant Studies 36*(1), 139–169; Patel, R. (2008) *Stuffed and Starved: Markets, Power and the Hidden Battle for the World Food System*. Portobello.

7 Alexandratos, N. and Bruinsma, J. (2012) 'World agriculture'.

8 O'Kane, G. (2012) 'What is the real cost of our food? Implications for the environment, society and public health nutrition', *Public Health Nutrition* 15(02): 268–276.

9 Alexandratos, N. and Bruinsma, J. (2012) 'World agriculture'.

10 Alexandratos, N. and Bruinsma, J. (2012) 'World agriculture'; Moore, J. (2010) 'Cheap food & bad money', *Review: Journal of the Fernand Braudel Center* 33(1): 225–261; Tilman, D., Cassman, K.G., Matson, P.A., Naylor, R. and Polasky, S. 'Agricultural sustainability and intensive production practices', *Nature 418*, no. 6898 (2002).
11 BonAnno, A. and Cavalcanti, J.B. (2012) 'Globalization, food quality and labor: The case of grape production in Northeastern Brazil', *International Journal of Sociology of Agriculture and Food* 19(1): 37–55; Burkitt, I. (1994) 'The shifting concept of the self', *History of the Human Sciences* 7(2): 7–28.
12 Smith, P., Ashmore, M.R., Black, H.I.J., Burgess, P.J., Evans, C.D., Quine, T.A., Thomson, A.M., Hicks, K. and Orr, H.G. (2013) 'REVIEW: the role of ecosystems and their management in regulating climate, and soil, water and air quality', *Journal of Applied Ecology* 50(4): 812–829; IAASTD, 2009. 'Agriculture at a Crossroads. International Assessment of Agricultural Knowledge, Science and Technology for Development (IAASTD)', Global Report. Island Press.
13 Abbots, E.-J. and Coles, B. (2013) 'Horsemeat-gate: The Discursive Production of a Neoliberal Food Scandal', *Food, Culture & Society* 16.4: 535–550.
14 O'Connor, J. (1991) 'On the two contradictions of capitalism', *Capitalism, Nature, Socialism* 1(1): 11–38.8, October. O'Kane, G. (2012) 'What is the real cost of our food? Implications for the environment, society and public health nutrition', *Public Health Nutrition* 15(02).
15 Moore, J. (2011) 'Transcending the metabolic rift: a theory of crises in the capitalist world-ecology', *Journal of Peasant Studies* 38(1): 2
16 Moore, J. (2010) 'Cheap food & bad money'; Moore, J. (2011) 'Transcending the metabolic rift'.
17 Moore, J. (2011) 'Transcending the metabolic rift', 28–30.
18 Moore, J. (2011) 'The Socio-Ecological Crises of Capitalism'.
19 Bittman, M. (2013) 'How to Feed the World', *The New York Times*, [online], 15 October. Available at: http://mobile.nytimes.com/2013/10/15/opinion/how-to-feed-the-world.html [Accessed 5 May 2014].
20 Tappeser, B., Reichenbecher, W. and Teichmann, H. 'Agronomic and Environmental Aspects of the Cultivation of Genetically Modified Herbicide-Resistant Plants'. Available at: www.bfn. de/fileadmin/MDB/documents/service/skript362. pdf [accessed on 6 July 2014]; Deshpande, R.S. and Arora, S. (2010) *Agrarian Crisis and Farmer Suicides*. SAGE; Hebbar, R. (2010) 'Framing the Development Debate: The Case of Farmers' Suicide in India'. In *Agrarian Crisis and Farmers' Suicides*, (Eds R.S. Deshpande and S. Arora), SAGE Publications.
21 Shiva, V. (2000) *Stolen Harvest: The Hijacking of the Global Food Supply*, India Research Press.
22 Altieri, M.A. (2002) 'Agroecology: The Science of Natural Resource Management for Poor Farmers in Marginal Environments', *Agriculture, Ecosystems & Environment* 93: 1–24.
23 Deshpande and Arora, *Agrarian Crisis and Farmer Suicides*; Hebbar, 'Framing the Development Debate'; Revathi, E. and Galab, S. (2010) 'Economic Reforms and Regional Disparities'. In Agrarian Crisis and Farmers' Suicides, (Eds R.S. Deshpande and S. Arora), SAGE Publications; Reddy, T.P. (2004) 'Farmers' Suicides'. *Economic and Political Weekly*, 39, 3958.

24 Vaidyanathan, A. (2010) *Agricultural Growth in India: Role of Technology, Incentives, and Institutions*, Oxford University Press.
25 Shiva, V. (2000) *Stolen Harvest: The Hijacking of the Global Food Supply*, India Research Press.
26 Craig, R.J. and Amernic, J.H. (2004) 'Enron Discourse: The Rhetoric of a Resilient Capitalism', *Critical Perspectives on Accounting 15*: 813–852.
27 Elkington, J. (1994) 'Towards the sustainable corporation: Win–win–win business strategies for sustainable development', *California Management Review 36*(2): 90; Adger, W.N. (2000) 'Social and ecological resilience: are they related?' *Progress in Human Geography* 24(3): 347–364.
28 Mendez, V.E. (2010) 'Agroecology'. In *Encyclopedia of Geography* (Ed. B. Warf), SAGE.
29 Altieri, M.A. (1983) 'The Question of Small Farm Development: Who Teaches Whom? Agriculture', *Ecosystems & Environment*, 9, 401–405; Altieri, M.A. (1993) 'Ethnoscience and Biodiversity: Key Elements in the Design of Sustainable Pest Management Systems for Small Farmers in Developing Countries', *Agriculture, Ecosystems & Environment* 46: 257–272; Altieri, 'Agroecology: The Science of Natural Resource Management'; Mendez, 'Agroecology'.
30 Altieri, M.A. (2008) 'Small Farms as a Planetary Ecological Asset: Five Key Reasons Why We Should Support the Revitalisation of Small Farms in the Global South'. *Third World Network* (TWN); Altieri, M.A. and Trujillo, J. (1987) 'The Agroecology of Corn Production in Tlaxcala, Mexico', *Human Ecology 15*: 189–220; Mendez, Agroecology.
31 Mendez, 'Agroecology'.
32 'Agroecologically efficient agricultural systems for smallholder farmers: contributions to food sovereignty'. *Agronomy for Sustainable Development* 32(1): 1–13.
33 Bernstein, H. (2014) 'Food sovereignty via the "peasant way": a sceptical view', *The Journal of Peasant Studies* 41(6): 1031–1063.
34 Jansen, K. (2014) 'The debate on food sovereignty theory: agrarian capitalism, dispossession and agroecology', *Journal of Peasant Studies* 42(1), 213–232.
35 Fidler, M. (2012) 'Preferring rabbits to revolution: A comparative analysis of Marxist and local food movement critiques of capitalist agriculture', *Intersect: The Stanford Journal of Science, Technology and Society 5*: 14.
36 Boillat, S., Gerber, J.F. and Funes-Monzote, F.R. (2012) 'What economic democracy for degrowth? Some comments on the contribution of socialist models and Cuban agroecology', *Futures* 44(6): 600–607.
37 Jansen, K. (2014) 'The debate on food sovereignty theory'; Harvey, D. (2003) *The New Imperialism*, Oxford: Oxford University Press.
38 Patel, R. (2008) *Stuffed and Starved: Markets, Power and the Hidden Battle for the World Food System*, Portobello.
39 Innis, D.Q. (1997) *Intercropping and the Scientific Basis of Traditional Agriculture*, Intermediate Technology Publications.
40 Lang, C. (2009) 'Forests, Carbon Markets and Hot Air: Why the Carbon Stored in Forests Should Not Be Traded'. In *Upsetting the Offset: The Political Economy of Carbon Markets* (Eds S. Böhm and S. Dabhi), MayFlyBooks; Paterson, M. (2009) 'Resistance Makes Carbon Markets'. In *Upsetting the Offset: The Political Economy of Carbon Markets* (Eds S. Böhm and S.

Dabhi), MayFlyBooks; Checker, M. (2009) 'Double Jeopardy: Pursuing the Path of Carbon Offsets and Human Rights Abuses'. In *Upsetting the Offset: The Political Economy of Carbon Markets* (Eds S. Böhm and S. Dabhi), MayFlyBooks; Dabhi, S. (2009) 'Where Is Climate Justice in India's First Cdm Project?' In *Upsetting the Offset: The Political Economy of Carbon Markets* (Eds S. Böhm and S. Dabhi), MayFlyBooks.

41 Gilbertson, T. (2009) 'How Sustainable Are Small-Scale Biomass Factories? A Case Study from Thailand'. In *Upsetting the Offset: The Political Economy of Carbon Markets* (Eds S. Böhm and S. Dabhi), MayFlyBooks; Mate, N. and Ghosh, S. (2009) 'The Jindal Cdm Projects in Karnataka'. In *Upsetting the Offset: The Political Economy of Carbon Markets* (Eds S. Böhm and S. Dabhi), MayFlyBooks; Carrere, R. (2009) 'Carbon Sink Plantation in Uganda: Evicting People for Making Space for Trees'. In *Upsetting the Offset: The Political Economy of Carbon Markets* (Eds S. Böhm and S. Dabhi), MayFlyBooks; Böhm, S. (2009) 'Clean Conscience Mechanism: A Case from Uruguay'. In *Upsetting the Offset: The Political Economy of Carbon Markets* (Eds S. Böhm and S. Dabhi), London: MayFlyBooks.

42 Sage, C. (2003) 'Social embeddedness and relations of regard', *Journal of Rural Studies 19*(1): 49; Sonnino, R. and Marsden, T. (2006) 'Beyond the divide: rethinking relationships between alternative and conventional food networks in Europe', *Journal of Economic Geography 6*(2): 183.

43 Hinrichs, C.C. (2000) 'Embeddedness and local food systems: notes on two types of direct agricultural market', Journal of Rural Studies, 16(3) 295–303.

44 Marsden, T. and Smith, E. (2005) 'Ecological entrepreneurship: sustainable development in local communities through quality food production and local branding', *Geoforum 36*(4).

45 Lin, B.B. (2011) 'Resilience in agriculture through crop diversification: adaptive management for environmental change', *BioScience 61*(3): 183–193.

46 Hinrichs, C.C. (2000) 'Embeddedness and local food systems', 298.

47 Thompson, C.J. and Coskuner-Balli, G. (2007) 'Enchanting Ethical Consumerism: The case of Community Supported Agriculture', *Journal of Consumer Culture 7*(3); Venn, L., Kneafsey, M., Holloway, L. and Cox, R. (2006) 'Researching European "alternative" food networks: some methodological considerations', *Area 38*(3).

48 Flora, C., Bregendahl, C. and Renting, H. (2012) 'Collaborative community-supported agriculture: balancing community capitals for producers and consumers', *Journal of Sociology of Agriculture 19*(3): 330.

49 DeLind, L. (2002) 'Place, work, and civic agriculture: Common fields for cultivation', *Agriculture and Human Values*: 217–224.

50 Schoneboom, A. and May, J. (2013) 'Working through the allotment. Ephemera', *Theory and Politics in Organization*, *13*(1): 137–150, 146 and 142.

51 Schoneboom, A. and May, J. (2013) 'Working through the allotment'; McClintock, N. (2010) 'Why farm the city? Theorizing urban agriculture through a lens of metabolic rift', *Cambridge Journal of Regions, Economy and Society 3*(2).

52 Wittman, H. (2009) 'Reworking the metabolic rift: La Vía Campesina, agrarian citizenship, and food sovereignty'. *Journal of Peasant Studies 36*(4): 805–826.

53 Harvey, D. (2014) *Seventeen Contradictions and the End of Capitalism*, Oxford University Press, 3.

54 Kleba, J.B. (1994) 'Cooperação agrícola e cooperativismo em assentamengos de reforma agrária'. *Revista da Associação Brasileira de Reforma Agrária* 4(3): 132–139; Borges, J.L. (2010) 'Bases históricas do cooperativismo no MST'. *Revista Fatos & Versões* 2(3): 157–173.
55 Stédile, J.P., Fernandes, B.M. *Brava gente: a trajetória do MST e a luta pela terra no Brasil.* Perseu Abramo.
56 Fernandes, B.M. (1999) 'Contribuições ao estudo do campesinato brasileiro: formação e territorialização do MST (1979–1999)'. PhD Thesis, Universidade de São Paulo, 169.
57 Ribas, A.D. (2002) 'Gestão politico-territorial dos assentamentos no Portal do Paranapanema (SP): uma leitura a partir da COCAMP'. MSc dissertation, Universidade Estadual Paulista. Roe, E. (2013) 'Global carcass balancing: horsemeat and agro-food network', *Radical Philosophy* 9, 2–5. Retrieved from http://eprints.soton.ac.uk/351729/.
58 Rezende, G.C. (1999) 'Programa de Crédito Especial para Reforma Agrária (Procera): institucionalidade, subsídio e eficácia'. IPEA.
59 Bradford, S. and Rocha, J. (2004) *Rompendo a cerca: a história do MST.* Casa Amarela, 136.
60 Guanziroli, C.E. and Basco, C.A. (2010) 'Construction of agrarian policies in Brasil: the case of the National Program to Strengthen Family Farming (PRONAF)'. *Comuniica* 5: 44–63.
61 Harvey, D. (2014) *Seventeen contradictions and the end of capitalism*, 66.
62 Santini, D. (2012) 'Pão de Açúcar anuncia compra de 17 toneladas de arroz do MST'. Posted at 19 June 2012. Available at: http://reporterbrasil.org.br/2012/06/pao-de-acucar-anuncia-compra-de-15-toneladas-de-arroz-do-mst/ (accessed 4 December 2014).
63 Parker, M., Cheney, G., Fournier, V. and Land, C. (Eds). (2014) *The Routledge Companion to Alternative Organization.* Routledge; Williams, C. (2005) *A Commodified World? Mapping the limits of capitalism.* Zed.
64 Gibson-Graham, J.K. (2002) 'Beyond global vs. local: economic politics outside the binary frame'. *Geographies of power: Placing scale*, 25–60; Gibson-Graham, J.K. (2006) *The End of Capitalism (as We Knew It): A Feminist Critique of Political Economy; with a New Introduction.* University of Minnesota Press; Hopkins, R. (2008) *The Transition Handbook: From oil dependency to local resilience.* Green books.
65 Gibson-Graham, J.K. (2008) 'Diverse economies: performative practices for other worlds', *Progress in Human Geography* 32(5): 615.
66 Gibson-Graham, J.K. (2008) 'Diverse economies'.
67 Foster, J.B. (2002) 'Marx's ecology in historical perspective', *International Socialism*, (96); Bittman, M. (2013) 'How to Feed the World'. *The New York Times*, [online], 15 October. Available at: http://mobile.nytimes.com/2013/10/15/opinion/how-to-feed-the-world.html; Böhm, S., Misoczky, M. C. and Moog, S. (2012) 'Greening capitalism? A Marxist critique of carbon markets', *Organization Studies* 33(11): 1617–1638.
68 McMichael, P. (2009) 'A food regime genealogy', 161; Clark, B. and York, R. (2005) 'Carbon metabolism: Global capitalism, climate change, and the biospheric rift', *Theory and Society* 34(4): 391–428; McClintock, N. (2010) 'Why farm the city? Theorizing urban agriculture through a lens of metabolic

rift', *Cambridge Journal of Regions, Economy and Society* 3(2); Wittman, H. (2009) 'Reworking the metabolic rift: La Vía Campesina, agrarian citizenship, and food sovereignty', *Journal of Peasant Studies* 36(4): 805–826.

69 Clark and York (2005), 404; Foster (2002); McClintock (2010), 194.

70 Foster (2002), 2; Clark and York (2005), 399.

71 MST (2015) 'Stédile recommends that militants "prepare their game shoes" because "the game has just begun"', 12 March, www.mstbrazil.org/news/st%C3%A9dile-recommends-militants-prepare-their-game-shoes-because-game-has-just-begun.

72 Perez, J., Allen, P. and Brown, M. (2003) *Community supported agriculture on the central coast: The CSA member experience*; Psarikidou, K. (2015) 'Rethinking innovation through a moral economy lens: The case of alternative agro-food and mobility practices', *Ephemera: Theory & Politics in Organization* 15(1): 87.

73 Blake, M., Mellor, J. and Crane, L. (2010) 'Buying local food: shopping practices, place, and consumption networks in defining food as "local"', *Annals of the Association of American Geographers* 100(2): 409–426.

74 Fraser, N. (2014) 'Behind Marx's hidden abode: For an expanded conception of capitalism', *New Left Review II*, 86: 55–72; see also Böhm, S. and Land, C. (2012) 'The new "hidden abode": reflections on value and labour in the new economy', *The Sociological Review* 60(2): 217–240.

75 Fraser, N. (2014) Behind Marx's hidden abode.

76 Mészáros, I. (2002) *Para Além do Capital*. Boitempo, 711.

77 Paniago, C. (2010) 'Challenges of the control and the autonomous participation of the workers in contemporary capitalismo'. In: 28th International Labour Process Conference Information and Abstracts.

78 Moore, J.W. (2003) 'The Modern World-Systemas environmental history? Ecology and the rise of capitalism', *Theory and Society* 32(3): 307–377; Moore, J. (2010) 'Cheap food & bad money'.

INDEX

Abramovay, Ricardo, 12–13, 150–66
agriculture: agribusiness and alternative food movements, 218, 221, 228, 229, 253–70; carbon emissions, 276 n.47; contradictions with green growth, 68–69, and green jobs, 171; industrial agriculture, 133, 254–57; Ricardo's theory of value, 105; role in capitalism, 48–49, 56–57; *see also* agroecology; food
agroecology, 18–19, 257–59, 264–67
alienation: of finance capital from real economy, 38; inherence to capitalism 15, 70; of labour, 262, 267; of nature, 51, 59
alternatives to capitalism, 16–19, 90, 212–232, 233–252, 253–69
Amazon, the, 69, 151, 156–59, 162–65, 205
Andhra Pradesh, 218, 221, 224, 259
Argentina, 193, 196, 205, 207
Asia, 74, 115–30, 189, 212; *see also* China, Japan, India
Australia, 125

Bellamy Foster, John, 31, 98, 106
biodiversity: and agroecology, 258, 259; conflicts and resistance over, 208, 229; measuring pressure on, 193; and trading in ecosystem services, 62, 63, 146, 164
biofuels: conflicts over, 204; land requirements, 275 n.25; limitations of, 29, 145; sugar cane ethanol in Brazil, 12, 13, 159–61, 165, 174
biomass, 187, 197, 193, 199, 208; *see also* biofuels; deforestation
Bluemling, Bettina, 5, 9, 12, 80–81, 114–30, 131
Blueprint for Survival, 3
Böhm, Steffen et al, 18, 19, 253–69
Bolivia, 192, 205, 226
Brandt Commission, 3
Brazil: agroecology in, 254, 263–65, 267; and false cooperatives, 301 n.47; and green growth, 12–13, 14, 150–65; green jobs in waste recycling, 166–86; and social and environmental movements, 18, 189, 263–65, 279 n.26 (*see also* Landless Workers Movement); social metabolism of, 192, 193, 196
Britain: and coal, 10; and ecosystem services trading, 60; employment and productivity, 101; energy efficiency, 30, 33; 'Green New Deal Group', 5–6; local food movements, 154, 261, 267–68; 'One Million Climate Jobs', 15; textile industry, 47; wealth inequality, 77; wind energy projects, 139
Byrne, John, 2, 17, 233–52

Canada, 80, 192
capitalism: and economic growth, 7, 14–16, 35–36, 84, 90–92, 143; and environment/nature, 4, 6, 10, 19, 32, 34, 36 40–41, 42–57, 90–92, 106, 144, 147–49, 256, 266; and food and agriculture; 254–59; and green growth, 2, 4, 6, 57–71, 82–83, 85, 88, 132, 147–49, 239, 253, 256; and inequality, 77–78 (*see also* inequality); and labour, 15, 44, 106, 107, 147, 268, 269, 286 n.34, 280 n.42; and modernity, 239; regulation of, 38–39, 40; and social relations, 15; and wealth, 84, 96–97; *see also* neoliberalism
carbon taxes, 32, 34, 39, 75, 91, 222
carbon trading, 32, 58, 61, 60–63, 240, 282 n.65; *see also* European Union emissions trading scheme (ETS)
carbon intensity, 2, 11, 24–26, 35, 90-91, 273 n.8
cars, 27, 99, 276 N.41, 159–62, 274 n.19
China, 129, 140, 163, 172, 173, 200, 201
civil society: and alternative communities, 218; effectiveness, 238–39; inclusion in green growth, 115, 117, 118, 122; inclusion in green growth in Republic of Korea, 120–21, 122, 126, 127, 129; inclusion in sustainable development, 5, 116–17, 130; and industrial agriculture, 257; and resistance, 121, 228–29, 232
Clean Development Mechanism (CDM), 260
climate change: and carbon trading, 60, 65, 240; climate change projections, 24, 37, 40, 41; and conflicts, 208, 216; and economic growth, 11, 24, 25, and equality, 23; and green growth, 22–23; and greenhouse gases, 23–24; and green jobs, 170; and renewable energy, 235
climate jobs, *see* green jobs
coal: and Brazil, 165; and Britain, 10; and conflicts, 192, 204, 205; current consumption of, 29, 30; and the EU, 137, 140, 141; and India, 197; and industrialization, 46, 52; Jevon's Paradox, 9–10, 30
Colombia, 190, 193, 196, 197, 207
colonialism: and appropriation of nature, 46, 48, 50, 56–57, 63; and green growth, 62–64, 69; of nature, 106, 144
commodification of nature, 4, 6, 7, 16, 17, 42–71, 85, 146, 203, 240, 262; *see also* carbon trading; ecosystem services, payment for; natural capital
commons: appropriation through capitalism, 4, 43–71, 76; commons-based energy consumption, 17–18, 245–56
community-supported agriculture (CSA), 261, 262, 268
competition, in green growth, 82–83, 85, 87; in green growth in the EU, 132–48; inherence to capitalism, 15, 36, 40, 54, 84, 85, 97
conflict, socio-environmental, 71, 138, 187–210, 226
conservation: and capitalism, 32, 65; and conflicts, 205, 226; energy conservation through SEUs, 17, 245, 246, 251; and green growth, 4, 5, 57–59, 61, 65–67, 75, 146; and social movements in India, 219, 220
consumers: citizens as consumers, 17, 221, 239, 243, 248, 251; consumer action, 133, 239, 267–68
consumption: changing consumption habits, 35, 38, 40; correlation with income increases, 28; correlation with population increases, 25–26; measuring consumption, 9, 192–99; relationship to

production, 99–103, 110, 261–62; and the rebound effect / Jevon's Paradox, 9–10, 27,29, 30–32, 40, 150
cooperatives: in Brazil, 178–86, 263–67, 301 n.47; in India, 219, 221, 260–61; *see also* workers' associations
corporations: agribusiness, 257–66; and capitalism, 239; compromise between corporations and social movements, 18, 19; and EU environmental policy, 137–43; and green growth, 4, 12, 42, 68, 85, 132, 147, 176, 240; power of, 79–80, 82, 136; and SEUs, 142, 233–52
crises: of agrifood system, 254–55; environmental, 1, 14, 54, 86, 111, 266; global economic crisis 2008, 5, 6, 34, 80, 95, 114, 115, 127, 131, 139, 141, 196; and green growth, 42, 62–67, 235; of capitalism, 2, 35, 90, 132, 143–45, 256, 148, 266, 268; in nature-society relations, 10; necessity of, 37, 40; overcoming crises of capitalism, 46, 259, 269; and neoliberalism, 78; and GHG reductions, 241
Cuba, 226

Daly, Herman, 8, 36, 234, n.17
dams: in Brazil (*see* hydropower in Brazil); in India, 215, 223-24; in Republic of Korea (*see* Four Major Rivers project)
decarbonization, 25, 32, 35, 158–59, 241, 245
decent work, 72, 167–71, 174, 299 n.5
decoupling economic growth from environmental degradation, 10–11, 14, 23, 26–27, 32, 90–91, 115, 125, 127, 128, 133, 241–42, 273 n.15; *see also* Jevon's Paradox, rebound effect
deforestation: in Brazil, 12, 13, 151, 157, 162–63, 193; in India, 16; and industrialization, 45–46; and payment for ecosystem services, 60, 66, 69
degrowth, 25, 90–111, 115, 130, 225
Delaware, USA, 17, 247, 249–50, 309, n.51
dematerialization, 8–9, 36, 40, 135, 188, 194, 201, 209–10, 241; *see also* decarbonization; decoupling; Jevon's Paradox; rebound effect;
democracy: civil society vs. consumer democracy, 17, 239; democratic-authoritarian bargain, 239–41, 251; and social movements, 203, 209; and sustainable development, 5
democratization: of the economy, 15, 36, 308 n.45; of energy, 17, 149, 238, 251; of production, 107, 111; *see also* Radical Ecological Democracy
development: alternatives to mainstream development, 202, 212–31; and climate change, 23; measuring, 14; and economic growth, 3, 123, 152–54, 164; and green growth in Republic of Korea, 114–30; and modernity, 233–40; *see also* sustainable development
displacement of communities, 13, 69, 156–57, 197, 215, 257
Domestic Material Consumption, 9, 197-99
Dongria Kondh Adivasis, 16–17, 204, 213–14

ecological economics, 3, 189, 200
Ecological Modernization Theory (EMT), 5, 9, 142, 148, 187, 201, 210
economic development *see* economic growth or development
economic growth: in Brazil, 150, 164, 165; and capitalism, 16, 35–36, 84, 97, 143; environmental

impacts, 1, 7-11, 32, 36, 54, 72–73, 101, 150, 187–88, 197, 201, 209, 241 (*see also* decarbonization, decoupling, dematerialization, rebound effect); fetishization of, 35–36; and green growth, 1, 6, 73, 74, 115, 117, 123, 132, 137, 148, 236; and inequality, 73–78, 81, 84, 150, 197; and social justice/wellbeing, 6–7, 36, 98, 124, 153–55, 164, 201, 236; and sustainable development, 3–4, 115; *see also* degrowth; development; GDP

economics, neoclassical, 90–111

eco-swaraj, *see* Radical Ecological Democracy (RED)

ecosystem services, payment for, 2, 4, 57-71, 76, 146, 281 n.50; *see* also carbon trading; commodification of nature; EU emissions trading scheme (ETS); natural capital

Ecuador, 69, 163, 190, 196, 204, 205, 207, 226

EFA (energy flows accounting), 191–92

EMR (energy/material/resource) efficiency, 31–33

energy: and capitalism, 46–47, 50–54; efficiency, *see* rebound effect; Jevon's paradox; technological innovation; energy requirements for growing population, 25–26; in the EU, 12, 131–49; and GDP, 101; and green growth, 247; and inequity, 233–34; jobs in energy sector, 171–72, measuring energy consumption *see* social metabolism; and modernity, 233–34, 237; production in Brazil, 151, 156–62, 165; SEUs, 17–18, 233–52

energy return on energy input (EROI), 28–30, 138, 192–93

environmental economics, 60, 96

environmental justice, 74, 149 ,188–210

Environmental Kuznets Curve (EKC), 8–10

environmental movements, *see* social and environmental movements

environmentalism of the poor, 8–9, 190, 201–3, 210

EROI, *see* energy return on energy input

ethanol, *see* biofuels

European Union: environmental conflict, 206, 207; environmental/green growth policy, 12, 70, 71, 131–43, 187; financial policy, 80; fuel consumption, 27; green jobs, 173; horsemeat scandal, 255; social metabolism, 193–99, 225, 266, trade unions, 181, wealth, 77

European Union emissions trading scheme (ETS), 32, 58, 63, 139, 276, n.38

externalization: internalization of environmental externalities, 14, 34-35, 61, 67, 70, 73, 84, 135, 196; of nature, 16, 17, 34, 38, 48–52, 54–70

extraction, *see* mining

food: alternatives to capitalist food production, 224, 226, 239, 253–269; and biofuels, 159; and capitalism, 44, 46, 49, 147, 188, 239, 254–59; food crisis, 254–55; food prices and financial markets, 146–47

fossil fuels: and capitalism, 34, 44, 46–47, 59; and climate change, 23, 65; and conflict, 204, 205, 208; EROI of fossil fuels, 138; and EU policy, 141, 143, 148; and the externalization of nature, 65; fossil fuel prices and financial markets, 146; and industry, 148; and social metabolism, 190, 199; and the transport sector, 29; *see also* coal, oil, gas, mining,

Foucault, Michel, 82–84

Four Major Rivers project, Republic of Korea, 119–22, 128
fracking, 80, 138, 140, 193, 204
France, 25, 77, 207
Fraser, Nancy, 71, 268
free market, *see* free trade
free trade: limitations of, 32, 79, 84, 85, 91; and EU climate policy, 141; and green growth, 4, 73, 85

gas (as energy supply), 29, 137, 140, 138, 140, 145, 165, 201–2, 204, 205; *see also* fracking
GDP, critique of, 7, 13–14, 38, 95-103, 123–24, 128, 129; *see also* economic growth
gender, *see* women
genetic engineering, 4, 257
geo-engineering, 1
Germany, 25, 121, 141–42, 160, 207, 277 n.59
Geun-hye Park (President), 12, 128
GHG intensity, 2, 11, 26–27, 32–33, 91, *see also* carbon intensity
globalization, 213, 217–18, 233, 255
global warming, *see* climate change
Greece, 33
Green Gone Wrong, 18
green governmentality, 86–87
Green Growth at a Glance, 117-19
green jobs: 'One Million Climate Jobs', 14; in Republic of Korea, 72, 119–21; and SEUs in the USA, 250; wastepicking in Brazil, 166–86
Green Revolution, 46, 48, 68, 145, 256
gross domestic product, *see* GDP
growth, *see* economic growth

HANPP (human appropriation of net primary production), 191, 193
Harvey, David, 78–79, 146, 264
Haryali agroforestry project, 259-61, 266
HDI, *see* Human Development Index
Hoffman, Ulrich, 1, 11, 15, 22–41, 133–37
human appropriation of net primary production, *see* HANPP
Human Development Index (HDI), 14, 191, 213
hydroelectricity, *see* hydropower in Brazil
hydropower in Brazil, 13, 156–59, 163, 165

ILO, *see* International Labour Organization
India: agroecology in, 254, 259–61, 265–66, 267; environmental and social conflict in, 203–4, 206–208; and environmentalism of the poor, 201–3; and green growth, 129, 187, 209; and renewable energy, 158; social metabolism, 196–201; and social movements, 16, 18, 212–232 (*see also* Dongria Kondh Adivasis; Mendha Lekha)
indigenous peoples, and appropriation of commons, 49, 53, 56, 60, 64, 69, 71; and conflict and resistance, 16, 188, 189, 195, 201–3, 206–8, 213–15
Indonesia, 197
Industrial Revolution, 26, 44, 234, 257
inequality: in Asia, 124; in Brazil, 12, 152; and conflict, 200; and economic growth/wealth, 7, 76–78, 87, 88, 235, 240–41; and energy, 233–34; and food and agriculture, 262; and green growth, 13, 149, 150, 166; in India, 222, and trade, 144
Intergovernmental Panel on Climate Change, 23-24, 92
International Labour Organization (ILO), 120, 166, 129, 170-72, 179, 184

Jackson, Tim, 24–25, 37, 90–94, 100, 111

Japan, 115, 129, 193, 196
Jevon's Paradox, 9–10, 30–31, 188

Kallis, Giorgos, 34, 35
Keynes, John Maynard, 6, 96, 100, 102, 132, 143
Kothari, Ashish, 8, 16, 17, 212-232
Kuznets, Simon, 8, 10, 98, 102
Kyoto Protocol, 63, 216

labour: and capitalist relations, 2, 15, 42–71, 84, 90–111; changes proposed for labour market, 39, 90, 92, 101; and erosion of nature, 31, 36, 40, 105–7, 133, 147, 266, 267; unemployment, 15, 31, 101, 106, 107; *see also* decent work; green jobs; labour unions
labour unions, 13, 15, 80, 107, 134, 135, 151, 169, 181, 203, 229 *see also* workers' associations
Landless Workers Movement (Movimento dos Trabalhadores Sem Terra, or MST), 18, 19, 254, 263–65, 267
Latin America, 153, 156, 158, 187–210, 217, 230, 263; *see also* Argentina, Bolivia, Brazil, Colombia, Ecuador, Peru, Venezuela
Latouche, Serge, 93
Latour, Bruno, 50
Lee Myung-bak (President), 5, 11–12, 80, 82, 114–16, 119, 121, 122, 127–29
Lélé, Sharachchandra, 3
Lohmann, Larry, 2, 16, 42–71

Maharashtra, 16, 213, 217, 219, 221
Mahnkopf, Birgit, 12, 14, 131–49
Malthus, Thomas Robert, 48–49, 105
Martinez-Alier, Joan, 8, 9, 13, 93, 187–210, 212
Marx, Karl: and abstract labour, 49; and capitalism's appropriation of soil and labour, 43, 259, 266; and capitalist logic, 54; and the circular underground ,102; 'hidden abode' of production, 71; relation of growth to capitalism, 84, 143–44; and local food movements, 258; primitive accumulation, 144; and relative surplus value, 61; and Say's Law, 100; and theory of value, 105–8, 111
material flows accounting, *see* MFA
Material Footprint, 9, 272 n.23
Meadway, James, 2, 7, 15, 84, 90–111, 143
Mendha Lekha, 16–17, 213–14, 215;
metabolic rift, 144, 146, 263, 266
Mexico, 80, 193, 195, 200
MFA (material flows accounting), 191–93
Mill, John Stuart, 15, 90, 93, 94, 99–100, 108–10
mining: conflicts, 16, 138, 145, 188–210, 213; and green jobs, 169; and industrial capitalism, 44, 47; levels in Brazil, 163, global levels, 188; levels in India, 188; levels in Latin America, 187; non-extractivism, 69; and recycling, 167; and renewables, 33, 138, 141; rising costs of, 145
Mirowski, Philip, 79, 81, 85
modernity: and energy, 233–42; industrial modernism 2, 7; modern economic thinking, 93, 102, 124; modernization of Asian economies, 128; the modern model / modernization project, 2, 130, 233–242; reflexive modernism, 5
monetary reform, 39, 100, 102, 104, 106, 221–22
Moore, Jason, 44–46, 71, 147, 254, 256, 269
MST *see* Landless Workers' Movement
Muçouçah, Paulo Sergio, 8, 13, 14, 166–86
Mumford, Lewis, 239, 241–43, 250

natural capital, 2, 4, 68, 75, 146; *see also* commodification of nature; ecosystem services
nature-society relations, 2, 6, 10, 17, 42–71, 238, 240, 256
neoliberalism: crisis of post-2000, 5; and economic growth, 78, 84; and the EU, 134; and food 254; and green growth, 65, 76–89, 148; green neoliberalism, 4; and labour, 107; neoliberal governmentality 2; principles of, 228; and the state, 79, 84, 88
new political actors, 65, 75–76, 86, 117
Nigeria, 189–90
nuclear energy: conflicts over, 204–5, 208; and decarbonisation / France, 25; and the EU, 137; in Germany, 141; and market domination, 34 ; in Republic of Korea, 12, 122, 125

Odisha, 16, 200, 205, 213, 219
oil: and capitalism, 59–60; and conflict, 204–5; EROI of oil, 138; and EU climate and energy policy, 138; peak oil, 144–45; prices, 3, 99, 135, 140; *see also* fossil fuels
Organisation for Economic Co-operation and Development (OECD), 3, 126, 235
Our Common Future, 116

Parr, Adrian, 2, 72–89
physical trade balance (PTB), 192, 194, 195
Pickett, Kate, 7
Piketty, Thomas, 76–78, 81, 84, 97
Poland, 139
Polanyi, Karl, 79
political ecology, 189, 190, 200
Polluter Pays Principle, 3
pollution: and biofuels, 13; and conflict, 200, 203, 204, 205; and economic growth, 8–9; and nature trading, 32, 60–71
population: population density and conflict, 187, 188, 193; population increases and food crisis, 254, 257, 258; population levels and resource consumption, 24–26, 40, 91–92, 209
post-2015 sustainable development agenda, 212, 226
Posthuma, Anne, 8, 13, 14, 166–186
poverty reduction: and the environment, 12–13, 25–26, 196–97; energy poverty, 234; in India, 212–13; and green growth, 13, 75, 85, 117–18, 166; in Brazil, 12–13, 152–53
primitive accumulation, 65, 106, 144
private sector, *see* corporations
privatization of nature, *see* commodification of nature; ecosystem services; natural capital
PTB, *see* physical trade balance

Radical Ecological Democracy (RED), 16, 212, 213–31
Rajasthan, 216, 217, 219, 223
rebound effect, 23, 30–32, 150, 247
recycling, 8, 13, 39, 139, 166–86
Republic of Korea, 5, 11–12, 14, 72, 80–81, 114–30, 131, 235
renewable energy: in Brazil, 151; and the EU, 133–42, 135; in Germany 141–42; and green growth, 235; improvements in, 158, 236; jobs in, 72, 171–72; limitations of, 28–30, 137, 138, 142, 274 n.24; 293 n.10, 293 n.13; and market domination, 34, 66, 80, 142, 238; requirements of, 29–30, 34, 242–43; SEUs, 243–50; solar in India, 220, solar in USA, 237; *see also* Jevon's Paradox; rebound effect; technological innovation
resistance *see* social and environmental movements
Ricardo, David, 104–9, 108, 111

Rio+20 (UN Conference on Sustainable Development), 5, 22, 117, 156, 170, 256, 264, 271 n.9
Rio Earth Summit (United Nations Conference on Environment and Development), 3, 116, 117, 123, 128, 170, 189, 290 n.62
Rogers, Heather, 18
Russia, 11, 25, 140, 192

SAMTFMACS cooperative, 18–19, 260-261
São Paulo, 8, 151–53, 161--62, 183, 267
Schumacher, E. F, 93
shale gas, *see* fracking
sharing economy, 38, 39, 277 n.61
Singapore, 115
Smith, Adam, 7, 104
Smith, Neil, 50
social and environmental movements; alternative food movements, 253–69; and breaking with capitalism, 16, 89; in Brazil, 18–19, 189, 263–65, 279 n.26 ; and commodification of nature, 68, 70; and environmentalism of the poor, 201-210; global environmental justice movement, 66, 189–210; in India, 16–17, 213–14; 229, 230, 232; 259–62; and neoliberalism, 87; in Republic of Korea, 121; in the UK, 261–63
social metabolism, 187–210
Solow, Robert, 94
South Africa, 14, 207
steady state economy, 15, 36, 90–111
sufficiency, 15, 23, 38, 127–28, 241, 243
sugar cane ethanol, *see* biofuels
sustainable development: and civil society participation, 114–19, 122–23, 126, 129–30; composition of, 240; distinction from green growth, 4–6, 122, 166; origins, 3–4, 11
Sustainable Energy Utilities (SEUs), 233–52, 308 n.45, 309 n.50
Switzerland, 33

Tamil Nadu, 219, 221, 222
Taminiau, Job, 2, 17, 233–52
technological innovation: in Brazil, 160, 162; in the EU, 137-140; and reducing environmental impact, 31, 34, 36, 40, 91–92, 94–99, 239–40 (*see also* rebound effect); in Republic of Korea, 115, 128; *see also* Jevon's Paradox; rebound effect; renewable energy
temperature, planetary average, 2, 24, 37, 40
trade: alternative economies, 219, 221, 222; and capitalism, 94; and ecologically unequal exchange, 194-197; *see also* free trade
Turkey, 197

UK, *see* Britain
UNFCCC (United Nations Framework Convention on Climate Change), 58, 170, 260, 276 n.44
unions, *see* labour unions
United Nations (UN): Brundtland Commission, 3, 116; and carbon trading, 60; and decent work, 170; and green growth, 11, 22, 164, 169; and sustainable development, 116; perception of nature, 57; Stockholm Declaration on the Environment, 3
United Nations Framework Convention on Climate Change, *see* UNFCCC
United Nations Conference on Environment and Development, *see* Rio Earth Summit
United Nations Conference on Sustainable Development, *see* Rio+20
USA: climate change commitments, 238; energy consumption, 125;

environmental conflict in, 206–7; environmental justice movement, 189; green jobs, 173; local food movements, 258; and shale gas production, 140; small scale renewable energy, 17, 243, 246, 250–52, 258; solar PV growth, 236; and trading in ecosystem services, 58, 60–61,66; wealth inequality, 77; *see also* Delaware
Uttarakhand, 219, 223, 224

Venezuela, 192, 226, 230
Via Campesina, la, 68, 264

Washington Consensus, 6
waste: and conflicts, 187–90, 201–9; and decoupling, 125; and green jobs in Brazil, 8, 13, 15, 166–86, 300 n.36; measuring, 190–92; nuclear, 125, 204
water: and conflicts, 205, 208; decentralization, 217, 219–20, 250; price increases, 146; Republic of Korea's Four Major Rivers project, 80–81, 119, 121; shortages in Brazil, 154, 157; trading in ecosystem services, 58, 60; *see also* dams; hydropower
wealth: and addressing climate change, 92; addressing wealth redistribution, 35–36; 38–39; and capital, 84, 97, 104–5; and carbon emissions, 28; as an indicator of wellbeing, 124; and green growth 2; and inequality, 77–78, 81; and Mill, John Stuart, 109–10; and modernity, 7; source of wealth, 105
Wiedmann et al, 9
Wilkinson, Richard, 7
women: and alternatives to capitalism in India, 218, 222–23, 228; and environmental movements, 200–3; and exploitation through capitalism, 44, 103; gender inequality in India, 213, 215; and green jobs, 173–4; and poverty, 7
workers' associations, 170–85, 217, 223, 299 n.5; *see also* cooperatives; labour unions
World Bank, 62, 68, 75, 82, 129, 153, 277 n.57

Yun, Sun-Jin, 5, 9, 12, 80–81, 114–30, 131